Praise for **LIMITLESS DAILY**

"In a world that constantly tells us we're not enough, Jim Kwik offers a wiser path: grow every day while remembering your worth isn't tied to tomorrow's achievements. **LIMITLESS DAILY** *is a powerful reminder that becoming more and appreciating what already is can coexist beautifully."*

— **BLAKE MYCOSKIE**, founder of TOMS, co-founder of Madefor, and author of *Start Something That Matters*

*"***LIMITLESS DAILY** *reminds us that happiness, resilience, and purpose are not destinations—they're small daily practices. Jim Kwik has created a beautiful companion that helps us nurture our minds, awaken our potential, regain our attention, and live our days with greater intention, connection, joy, and possibility."*

— **GOLDIE HAWN**, Academy Award–winning actress, creator and founder of the MindUP program for mental health and well-being

"Jim Kwik has spent his career teaching people that their potential is far greater than they believe. What I admire most about his work is that he doesn't just inspire people to think differently. He gives them practical ways to act differently every day. That's where real transformation happens: through small, consistent behaviors that compound into extraordinary results."

— **DR. BJ FOGG**, *New York Times* best-selling author of *Tiny Habits* and founder of Behavior Design Lab at Stanford

"Your brain is the organ of your personality, character, and intelligence, and **LIMITLESS DAILY** *gives you simple, science-based practices to optimize it every day. Jim Kwik has created a powerful mental fitness program to help you think better, feel better, and ultimately live better."*

— **DR. DANIEL AMEN**, double board-certified psychiatrist, clinical neuroscientist, founder of Amen Clinics, and 12-time *New York Times* best-selling author

Praise for Jim Kwik and **LIMITLESS**

"There's no genius pill, but Jim gives you the process for unlocking your best brain and brightest future."

— **MARK HYMAN, M.D.**, Head of Strategy and Innovation for the Cleveland Clinic Center for Functional Medicine and 14-time *New York Times* best-selling author

"I'm keenly aware of how important it is to keep your mind and memory sharp. Jim Kwik's tools and techniques in LIMITLESS *are your brain's best friends."*

— **MARIA SHRIVER**, Emmy award–winning journalist, founder of the Women's Alzheimer's Movement, and *New York Times* best-selling author of *I've Been Thinking*

"While I was at GE, Jim Kwik coached our executive team and spoke at many of our company meetings with high reviews. He is a world-class expert at delivering the training and tools that high-impact teams need to elevate their organization."

— **BETH COMSTOCK**, former Chief Marketing Officer and Vice Chair at General Electric and best-selling author of *Imagine It Forward*

"Jim Kwik's LIMITLESS *is a revelation in learning how to learn. You'll discover new possibilities to challenge your mind and live your best life."*

— **RUDOLPH E. TANZI, PH.D.**, Professor of Neurology at Harvard University, director of the Genetics and Aging Research Unit at Massachusetts General Hospital, and *New York Times* best-selling author of *Super Brain*

"As somebody who puts lots of emphasis on exercising the brain and not just the body, I found Jim Kwik's work very empowering. LIMITLESS *will take you to incredible places you never expected."*

— **NOVAK DJOKOVIC**, professional tennis player, winner of 23 Grand Slam singles titles

"I've worked with on-screen superheroes throughout my career, and Jim's ability to level up your learning and life is one of the world's great super-powers."

— **JIM GIANOPULOS**, Chairman and CEO of Paramount Pictures

"Jim Kwik has the ability to expand your mind and shine a light on your inner genius. Like my song 'Unwritten' says—your life is your story. LIMITLESS *will help you write yours with new possibilities."*

— **NATASHA BEDINGFIELD**, Grammy award–nominated singer and songwriter

"Jim Kwik knows how to get the maximum out of me as a human being."

— **WILL SMITH**

LIMITLESS DAILY

ALSO BY JIM KWIK

Limitless

Limitless Expanded Edition

All of the above are available at your local bookstore, or may be ordered by visiting:

Hay House USA: www.hayhouse.com®
Hay House Australia: www.hayhouse.com.au
Hay House UK: www.hayhouse.co.uk
Hay House India: www.hayhouse.co.in

• • •

LIMITLESS DAILY

366 KEYS TO TRAIN YOUR BRAIN, MASTER YOUR MIND & WIN EVERY DAY

JIM KWIK

HAY HOUSE

HAY HOUSE LLC
Carlsbad, California • New York City
London • Sydney • New Delhi

Published in the United Kingdom by:
Hay House UK Ltd, 1st Floor, Crawford Corner,
91–93 Baker Street, London W1U 6QQ
Tel: +44 (0)20 3927 7290; www.hayhouse.co.uk

Cover design: Pete Garceau • Interior design: Bryn Starr Best

A catalogue record for this book is available from the British Library.

Hardcover ISBN: 978-1-4019-7894-5
E-book ISBN: 978-1-4019-7895-2
Audiobook ISBN: 978-1-4019-7896-9

10 9 8 7 6 5 4 3 2 1

The authorized representative in the EU for product safety and compliance is Penguin Random House Ireland, Morrison Chambers, 32 Nassau Street, Dublin D02 YH68, Ireland. https://eu-contact.penguin.ie

Printed and bound by CPI Group (UK) Ltd, Croydon CR0 4YY

FSC www.fsc.org MIX Paper FSC® C013604

To my children.

For as long as I can remember, I've had a simple morning practice.

In addition to reading, I would wake up and write. Sometimes it was gratitude. Sometimes it was what I needed to focus on that day. Sometimes it was just clearing my mind so I could think more clearly.

It was my way of getting my mind right before the world had a chance to get to it.

But something changed the day my daughter was born.

I was sitting there in the hospital, looking at her and then looking at her older brother. And in that quiet moment, I started thinking about their future. About the days when life would feel hard. When they'd feel unsure, overwhelmed, or stuck.

And I had this thought I couldn't shake:

What would I want them to hear from me . . . on a day when they needed it most . . . if I wasn't there?

Not a long lecture. Not a big book. Just a few words. Something simple. Something real. Something they could read in a few minutes . . . and feel a little more clear, a little more confident, a little more capable.

So the next morning, I wrote them a note.

Then I did it again the next day. And the next.

What started in that hospital room became a daily practice. Every morning for a year, I wrote them short messages if I was not there. Things I hoped would guide them when they were older, to ground them, and remind them of who they are, especially on the days they might forget.

And somewhere along the way, I realized: This isn't just something my kids need. It's something all of us need.

Because we don't change our lives from one big insight. We change our lives from the small things we do—consistently. The thoughts we practice. The focus we choose. The actions we take.

That's what *Limitless Daily* is. Not something to read once. Something to return to. Every day. A few minutes to reset your mind, refocus your attention, and remind yourself of what matters.

Because when you win that moment in the morning, you have a much better chance of winning the day.

And when you win enough days . . .

You start to build a life that feels limitless.

A YEAR OF LIMITLESS

366 Days of Mental Conditioning

(Included FREE with your copy of *Limitless Daily*)

Each dated page in this book is built around four powerful forces of transformation:

- **INSPIRATION**—a new possibility.
- **IDEATION**—new perspective.
- **IMPLEMENTATION**—a new behavior.
- **IDENTITY**—a new version of yourself.

But there is a fifth *I*. Intention.

Because insight alone doesn't change your life. Attention does.

What you consistently focus on becomes what you consistently think about. What you consistently think about influences what you consistently do. And what you consistently do becomes who you become.

That's why I've created a companion experience for every reader of *Limitless Daily*.

You've already invested in the book. This is my investment in you.

Every morning for the next 366 days, you'll receive one powerful question based on that day's lesson.

Not a newsletter. Not more content. Not another thing to read. Just one carefully crafted question designed to direct your intention and attention toward the most important idea of that day.

Why? Because your brain is a goal-seeking instrument.

Research in cognitive psychology shows that questions activate the brain's attentional networks and Reticular Activating System (RAS), causing you to notice opportunities, insights, resources, and solutions that were always there—but previously outside your awareness.

The questions you ask determine what your mind searches for.

Change your questions. Change your focus. Change your future.

As the creator of the world's leading speed and smart reading course, Kwik Reading, I know that this Intentional Question practice will also help you:

- Remember more of what you read
- Apply ideas faster
- Make better decisions
- Stay focused on what matters most
- Build lasting habits
- Strengthen your limitless identity

Think of it as having me as your coach in your pocket, prompting your mind daily.

Every day. For an entire year. One lesson. One question.One intentional action. One step closer to your limitless self.

Most people read a book once. This companion helps the book read you.

So it's not about "getting through" another book, it's about this book getting through you.

Are you ready to turn information into implementation? Implementation into integration? And integration into identity?

Join A Year of Limitless. Included at no additional cost with your book purchase.

Scan the QR code or visit: LimitlessDaily.com/companion

The person you become over the next 366 days will largely be determined by what captures your attention each day. One question can change a day. A year's worth of the right questions will change a life.

– JIM KWIK

CONTENTS

INTRODUCTION: You Hold the Key xiii

RESET: The Season of Clearing 1

REWIRE: The Season of Growth 95

RISE: The Season of Power 189

RADIATE: The Season of Impact 283

Limitless Appreciation 377

About the Author 379

INTRODUCTION

You Hold the Key

How did your day start this morning?

If you're like most people, it didn't start with intention. It started with reaction. Not direction, but distraction.

Maybe you woke up, reached for your phone, and within seconds your mind was somewhere else entirely. Scrolling, checking, consuming. Before you had a chance to think your own thoughts first, you were already living inside someone else's agenda. Someone else's news. Someone else's highlight reel. Someone else's demands of you.

And it happened so fast you didn't even notice.

But here's what was really going on in that moment. Your attention, your most valuable asset, was being pointed somewhere for you. Not by you.

Your day immediately became more limited, before you were even fully awake.

If that sounds familiar, good. You're not alone, and you're not weak. This is what the world is designed to do to you right now. We are living in the most accelerated, most distracted, most cognitively demanding moment in human history. A world where your focus is under constant attack, your memory is being outsourced to devices, and the demands on your mind have never been higher. You're expected to learn faster, think clearer, adapt quicker, decide better, and stay sharp in an environment that is specifically built to pull you away from your best self.

And somewhere underneath all of that, quiet questions keep surfacing:

Am I falling behind? Am I still relevant? Is this really as good as it gets?

I hear these questions everywhere I go. In boardrooms and classrooms. From students and CEOs, from parents who feel like they can't keep up, and from professionals who are burning out trying. These aren't small questions, and in the age of artificial intelligence and rapid technological change, they are only getting louder. And it's become increasingly more difficult to find peace, positivity, and progress in a world of never-ending noise.

After more than three decades working with people all over the world, teaching and coaching them to learn anything—any skill or capability—to expand their knowledge and become a desired version of themselves, I can tell you what I've seen over and over again.

Rapid technological change and AI are not your biggest threats. An untrained brain and an undirected mind are.

Many people see the rise of artificial intelligence as a technology story. I see it as a human story.

The future doesn't belong to the people with the best technology. The future belongs to the people who make the best use of it.

Those who can focus when others are distracted. Think when others react. Learn when others stop. Create when others consume. Connect when others isolate. Lead when others follow.

And continue growing when others settle.

In a world filled with artificial intelligence, human intelligence becomes more valuable than ever.

That's why I believe the AI revolution could become the greatest era of human transformation in history. Not because machines will replace us. But because they will challenge us to elevate ourselves.

And that's what this book is about.

Each day in *Limitless Daily* is designed to help you strengthen the abilities that matter most in a rapidly changing world—not just your ability to know more, but your ability to become more.

To think more clearly.

Learn more effectively.

Focus more deeply.

Remember more of what matters.

Make better decisions.

Adapt to change.

Cultivate resilience.

Expand your creativity.

Strengthen your character.

Deepen your relationships.

Clarify your purpose.

And live with greater intention.

In other words, to develop your human intelligence. Because intelligence is not merely the ability to acquire information. It's the ability to use information to improve your life and the lives of others.

The goal of this book is not simply to fill your mind with ideas. The goal is to help you build the mindset, motivation, methods, and daily habits that unlock more of your potential—one day at a time.

Technology will keep evolving. It will process faster, automate more, and reshape entire industries in ways we can barely map right now. But there is something it cannot do. It cannot replace your ability to think originally, to imagine what doesn't yet exist, or to connect ideas across lived experiences. It cannot feel, care, create meaning, or make decisions rooted in something you actually believe in and value deeply.

External technology like AI can amplify and scale. But here is the question that matters most: What does it amplify? What does it scale?

Whatever you bring to it.

Think of it like a Formula 1 race car. The most advanced machine ever built. Breathtaking speed, extraordinary precision. But without a skilled driver, it goes nowhere, or worse, it crashes. Technology is the engine. You are the driver. Your thinking determines the direction. Your questions determine what it produces. Your judgment determines whether it creates value or just more noise.

In the same way a world-class instrument only sounds extraordinary in the hands of someone who has practiced for years, external technology only becomes exceptional when guided by a trained brain and a directed mind. It doesn't make you smarter automatically. It magnifies how you already think. If your thinking is clear and focused, technology like AI becomes something extraordinary. If it's scattered and shallow, it scales that too.

The future won't belong to those who use technology the most. It will belong to those who think the best.

That is your edge and advantage. It's your human intelligence. But not intelligence the way most people think of it.

Intelligence is not your IQ score. It's not your grades. It's not the number of facts or figures you can store in your head.

Be honest. We've all met people who are incredibly smart by those measures, and yet their lives don't quite reflect it. You know what I mean.

The person who can quote every study and every theory but can't seem to follow through on the things they say matter most. The friend who gives the best advice but never takes their own. The family member who knows exactly what to do for a better body or bank account but doesn't believe they deserve it or is too distracted to do it. We've all seen it. And if we're being really honest, we've all been that person at some point. I know I have.

Because knowing is not the same as doing. Doing is not the same as becoming.

This is why I define intelligence differently.

Intelligence is the ability to use your brain and direct your mind to create the life you want.

And here is the best news. Your intelligence is not limited. It's not a number assigned to you from a test you take at age 8 that sets your potential at age 88. Because your brain and mind are not fixed. They're fluid and functional. And they can grow daily.

THE BOY WITH THE BROKEN BRAIN

Helping people use their brain and direct their mind to create the life they want is deeply personal work.

I didn't come to it from a place of strength, but from struggle. Growing up, I never believed I was capable of much more than getting by.

When I was five years old, I suffered a traumatic brain injury. After that, everything that had felt natural and easy became painful and hard. I suffered with debilitating migraines daily. Focusing felt like trying to see through glass that was always slightly fogged. Remembering things, even small things, felt like trying to hold water in cupped hands.

It took me three extra years just to learn how to read like the other children.

Three years.

While other kids moved ahead, I fell quietly behind. I was bullied for being different and terrified of being called on in class. I learned that the safest thing to do was to shrink down and stay invisible. Don't take up space. Don't be seen. Don't ask questions.

One afternoon when I was nine, my invisibility failed me.

I was sitting in class, struggling to follow along while my teacher repeated the lesson again and again to the whole group, but clearly for me specifically. The other kids grew restless. Whispering started. Then laughter. They called me slow, which felt especially brutal because my last name really is Kwik.

My teacher, who I'm sure had good intentions to protect me, silenced the room. She pointed at me in front of everyone and said the two words that I would carry with me for years.

"Leave him alone. That's the boy with the BROKEN BRAIN."

When someone in authority gives you a label, especially when you're young, when you're already afraid, when you're already secretly wondering if something is permanently wrong with you, that label doesn't just describe you. It becomes you. And suddenly the question stops being *How do I learn this?* and becomes *What is wrong with me?*

Do you ever wonder where your own negative self-talk came from? Often an adult's external words become a child's internal words. So every time I was picked last in gym class or received a poor grade, I would remember saying to myself, "It's because of my broken brain." And as you can imagine, my grades suffered along with my confidence and self-worth. You could say that my brain and mind were making me limited daily.

I barely made it through school, but somehow I made it into college. When I got there, I thought "freshman" meant "fresh start." I made myself a promise to make something of myself. If I just pushed even harder, studied longer, hustled past every edge of exhaustion, I could finally prove I was enough.

So I pushed and pushed on the door of success. I pulled and pulled. But the door was locked.

The harder I tried using the same broken methods, the more I came apart. The tuition, the time, the effort, all of it going out with nothing coming back. I remember sitting alone in my dorm room one night, completely hollowed out, thinking: *I'm done. I can't do this.* I was ready to quit. I just didn't know how to tell my friends and family.

Before I could make that call, a friend who knew the pressure I was under invited me to join him to visit his family for the weekend to get some perspective. I didn't want to go, but something inside said I had to, so I said yes.

Little did I know that visit would change my mind, and my life.

The family had a beautiful home in a quiet town, big yard on the water. That evening before dinner my friend's father took me for a walk along the property. He turned to me and asked something so ordinary it almost felt like a test, and you can imagine how I loved tests.

"So, Jim, how's school?"

It was literally the last question I wanted to answer.

But something in me opened. The pressure inside me had been building up for so long, and all of it came out—the failure, shame, and exhaustion. The bone-deep certainty that the broken brain label had been right all along, and I had simply been fooling everyone, including myself.

He listened. Really listened. The way almost no one ever had.

And when I finished, he didn't offer a pep talk. He didn't tell me to try harder. He asked me something no one had ever thought to ask.

"Why are you in school? Not what others want, not what you think you're supposed to say. If anything at all were possible, what would your life look like?"

He ripped out a few pages of a notebook he was carrying, handed it to me along with his pen, and asked me to write it all down.

I hesitated. Writing my dreams felt like setting myself up for one more fall. But I picked up the pen. Without limits, what could I be, do, have, and contribute?

I wrote big dreams. Audacious ones. The kind I had never let myself say out loud because they seemed absurd for someone struggling just to be enough.

When I finished, I started to fold the paper up. But before I could put my new bucket list in my pocket, he reached out and took it from my hands.

Startled, I began to watch and listen as he read *every* dream out loud.

His voice, carrying my words out into the open air. The strangest thing happened. Hearing my own most private hopes spoken by someone else felt real in a way they never had inside my head. They felt like they belonged to someone who might actually deserve them.

Then he did something I have never forgotten.

He held up both hands and extended his two index fingers, holding them about a foot apart in the air between us.

"You are this close," he said, "to everything on that list."

I shook my head. There was no way. Based on my past history, I couldn't achieve that list in 10 lifetimes.

And then, slowly, he brought his two fingers together and placed them gently on either side of my head.

"And this," he said quietly. *"This is the key."*

FROM *LIMITLESS* TO *LIMITLESS DAILY*

Something cracked open in me that evening. A door I had kept shut for years opened just enough for light to get through.

And that light changed everything.

I stopped asking *How can I try harder to learn?* I started asking *How do I learn better?* That one question became the most important shift of my life. I became obsessed, not with pushing more, but with understanding how my brain and mind worked so I could work my brain and mind. I studied everything I could find on memory, focus, mindset, accelerated learning—both ancient techniques and modern neuroscience. And more than all the reading, more than everything else combined, because I was so desperate for a change, I practiced.

Daily.

Slowly, with the quiet power of small things done consistently, things began to shift. I could focus. I could learn. I could remember. But those were almost secondary. The most profound shift was that I stopped seeing myself as broken.

I started seeing myself as capable. My grades improved. Then my confidence. Then my relationships. Then my world. And the dreams on that list, the ones I had been afraid to even whisper, over time I started checking them off. One by one.

My mentor was right. How you train your brain and direct your mind is how you live your life.

For over 34 years, I've dedicated my life to one thing: advancing human intelligence. I've worked with students and CEOs, Olympic athletes and Hollywood stars, Fortune 500 companies and universities. Our online academy has participants in nearly every country in the world. And I've seen countless examples of what happens when someone learns how to learn. When they discover that their brain is not fixed, that it is flexible and trainable and capable of far more than anyone ever told them.

In 2020, I wrote a book called *Limitless: Upgrade Your Brain, Learn Anything Faster, and Unlock Your Exceptional Life*. I wrote it because I kept meeting people who were smart, capable, and working hard, and still not getting where they wanted to go. Not because they lacked information, but because nobody had ever taught them how to actually train their brains and use their minds—to focus, remember, learn faster, and break free from the beliefs that were running them on autopilot.

People all over the world wrote to me about that book. Students, parents, entrepreneurs, teachers, artists. Those messages are among the most meaningful things in my life.

But I kept hearing the same question:

"Jim, but how do I actually live this every day?"

That question is why you're holding this book. Because insight is powerful, but insight without daily practice fades. You can read the most life-changing book in the world, feel completely different on a Tuesday afternoon, and wake up Wednesday morning doing everything exactly the same as before.

Knowledge alone is not power. Applied knowledge is. And when you apply it every day, that's when something actually changes. Consistency compounds, and little by little, a little becomes a lot.

Limitless Daily is the daily practice that *Limitless* was always pointing toward.

It also might be my most personally moving book, because it's inspired by my children. Shortly after the birth of my second child, I began writing daily morning messages to my kids. I've long had a morning journaling routine, but this time I wanted a way to share with them the lessons I've learned in life, almost like a guide that I could give them when they finish school. I didn't want a long book for them, just short and simple insights that they could read in under five minutes.

And that's what *Limitless Daily* is designed around—short, simple insights that you can apply immediately to win your day. Because the more days you win, the more you win at life.

THE LIMITLESS MODEL

Think of your potential like a door.

Limitless is not about being perfect, but about progress.

But where in your life do you feel you are not progressing? In what area of your life do you feel stuck in a box you can't expand or escape? Is it your health, happiness, income, maybe your learning speed?

If you think about that box or cube, it's three-dimensional (3D). So there are three dimensions that contain and limit your progress inside that box, and these are the same three forces that can liberate you.

Most people keep trying to push it open—harder effort, more time, more pressure.

But it doesn't open that way.

It opens with the right key.

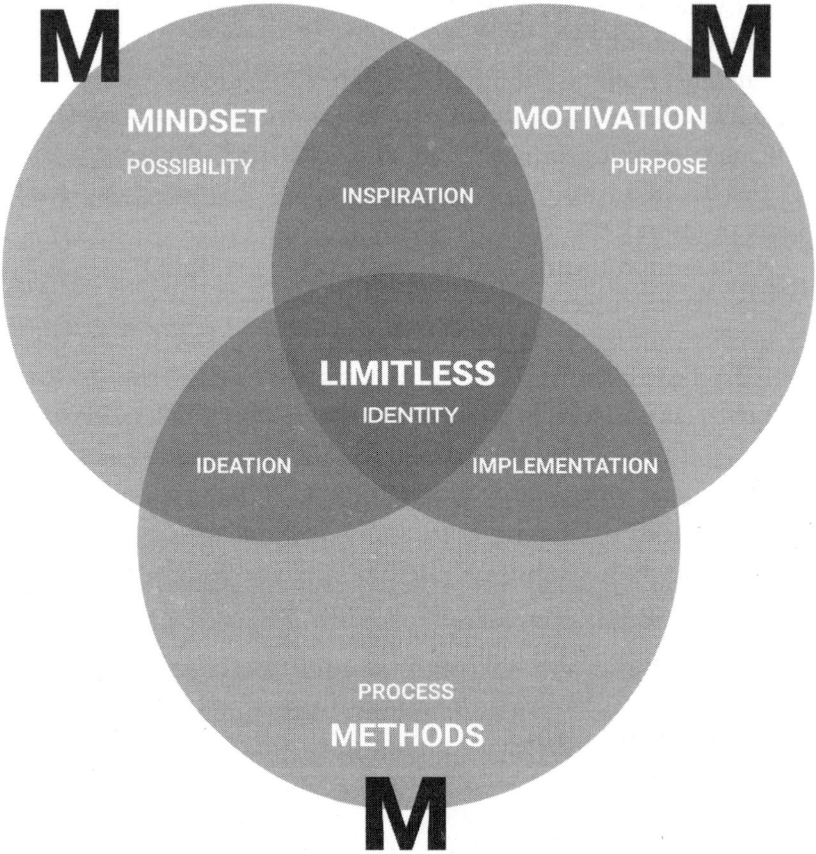

In *Limitless*, I shared the three keys that unlock human potential:

Your **Mindset**—what you believe.

Your **Motivation**—what drives you.

Your **Methods**—what you do.

When these keys turn together, something powerful happens.

Mindset + Motivation creates **Inspiration**—you feel it.

Mindset + Methods creates **Ideation**—you see it.

Motivation + Methods creates **Implementation**—you do it.

But when all three align, you don't just unlock performance. You unlock **Identity**.

Limitless Daily is designed to hand you those keys every single day.

Each page gives you:

Idea to open your mind.

Inspiration to lift your belief.

Implementation action to move you forward.

Identity affirmation to lock in who you're becoming.

Because one key alone won't always open the door. But together, when used consistently, they don't just open it. They change what you believe is possible on the other side.

YOUR BRAIN AND YOUR MIND ARE NOT THE SAME THING

Imagine a river.

The riverbed is your brain.

The flowing water is your mind.

The shape of the riverbed guides where the water flows—just like the structure of your brain influences how you think, feel, and respond. But over time, the water doesn't just follow the path, it reshapes it. With enough repetition, it carves new channels, deepens existing ones, and redirects the current entirely.

The same is true for you. Your brain shapes your mind. And your mind reshapes your brain.

This is neuroplasticity.

Every thought you think.

Every habit you practice.

Every conversation you have.

Every moment you choose to focus, reflect, or learn.

You are reinforcing certain neural pathways and letting others weaken. You are, quite literally, rewiring your brain. Which means your patterns are not permanent. Your limits are not fixed.

The way you think today is shaping the brain you'll use tomorrow.

And the more intentionally you direct your mind, the more powerfully you reshape your brain.

That's where change begins

The distance between where you are and the life you want is not out there somewhere. It's not a better opportunity, a different circumstance, or a luckier break.

It's in here, inside you. It's in how you use your brain and in how you direct your mind.

This is the distinction that changes the way you see yourself.

Your brain is the physical organ inside your skull. About 86 billion neurons firing through electrical and chemical signals at speeds that make the fastest computer look slow. Your brain governs your ability to focus, remember, and learn. Every thought you think, every habit you practice, every action you repeat, you're strengthening a neural pathway. With enough repetition, those pathways become automatic. This is neuroplasticity, your brain's ability to rewire itself based on what you do consistently. Your brain is changing right now, whether you're guiding that change or not.

Your mind is different. Your mind is the meaning you make from what happens to you. The beliefs you carry, the stories you tell yourself, the interpretations that shape your reality. Two people can go through the exact same experience and walk away in completely different places, not because their brains processed the event differently, but because their minds did.

Think of it this way. Your brain is the hardware. Your mind is the software.

Most people spend their whole lives trying to change their results through effort alone, without ever looking at the system running underneath everything. You upgrade your phone when it gets slow. You update your apps. But when was the last time you upgraded what's inside your head? The thing between your ears that runs every other system in your life.

You can't outwork a distracted brain. And you can't outperform a limiting mind.

Real change, the kind that actually sticks, happens when you train your brain and direct your mind at the same time. Because when you repeat a thought, your brain wires it. And when you believe that thought, your mind lives it.

That is what this book is built to do.

HOW THIS WORKS

Imagine your life as a series of doors.

Behind one is the *clarity* you've been looking for. That settled sense of knowing who you are and where you're going.

Behind another is *confidence*, not the kind you perform for other people, just the kind that's actually there when you need it.

Behind another is *focus*, *memory*, and the *ability to learn* whatever you decide to learn, at whatever age, starting now.

Behind another is the *version of you* that you know, somewhere deep and quiet, you are capable of becoming.

Most people spend their lives pushing on these doors. Trying harder and wondering why, no matter how much effort they put in, something won't open. But the doors were never meant to be forced open. They were meant to be unlocked.

And like Dorothy's ruby-red slippers in *The Wizard of Oz*, the key has been with you the whole time. You just needed someone to show you how to use it.

Each daily entry will give you a key to unlock those doors and so many more. Every daily key follows the same pattern. You'll get a powerful insight to shift the way you think. A science-backed explanation grounded in neuroscience or psychology, so you understand not just what to do, but why it actually works in your brain or mind. Because when the why makes sense, the how becomes something you can sustain.

You'll also get a small, immediate action to create real momentum today, not someday. And a Limitless affirmation to anchor who you're becoming and start rewiring your identity from the inside.

Each entry is designed to be read in the morning. So instead of starting your day reaching for your external tech, you can begin by upgrading your internal tech—your brain and your mind. You can certainly read the entry whenever you need it most. But I encourage you to commit to putting this book on your nightstand, and instead of rolling over and grabbing your phone, you reach for this.

There's a reason for this. The most powerful window of time happens as soon as you open your eyes. And what you decide to do in those first few minutes will set the course for your entire day.

Sleep inertia is the transition we go through from the sleep state to the waking one. As you regain consciousness, parts of your brain slowly come online. Your focus comes online, your alertness, your attention, your awareness, your emotional regulation, and your creativity all are waking up.

At this moment, your short-term working memory is least full. During the day, it holds and toggles between three to five items at once. So you're remembering to pick up the kids after school, cook dinner, prepare for a meeting, pay a bill, or work on a project simultaneously. But when you wake, it's like you get a memory reset.

Put these two things together and it means that the window of waking becomes especially potent for attentional priming—guiding your brain toward what to focus on during the day. So what you choose to feed your brain in the first few minutes can disproportionally affect and influence the rest of your day.

Think of it this way: You wouldn't wake up and feed your body five cupcakes and a liter of soda. But that is what you're doing when you roll over and reach for your phone. As you scroll, you're feeding your brain with distraction, despair, social comparison, and fear—and that will disproportionally affect three things:

- **Mood.** What you take in affects your emotions and emotional regulation. Notice how you feel after you watch or read content driven by fear, despair, or anger. You'll likely feel irritable, annoyed, angry, depressed, or sad. Then reverse this and notice how you feel when you take in material that's uplifting, inspiring, motivational, empowering, and joyful.
- **Focus.** The images and material you feed your brain show it what to focus on in the outer world. If you watch two people fighting online, then you're likely to see scenes of conflict play out during the day.

- **Framing.** Everything that happens to you during the day can be an opportunity or a crisis. If you show your brain stressful, fear-based, and anxiety-provoking situations first thing in the morning, then you're more likely to see crisis instead of opportunities.

I know how tempting it is to pick up your phone first thing. So many people do this. But you can change this. Grabbing this book and spending five minutes reading will set you up to win the day. Remember the mantra: Mind Before Media.

Just one key, one unlock, every day. This is how real, lasting change gets made. Because change doesn't come from doing everything all at once. It comes from doing the right things consistently. Especially on the ordinary days, when nothing feels urgent and it would be easy to skip. Those days are not less important. They might be the most important ones.

If you miss a day, don't miss two. Your power has never been in being perfect. It's always been in coming back. Every time you return, you prove to yourself that you're someone who returns. And that proof builds on itself.

The Four Seasons of This Year

Your 366 days will move in a rhythm your brain already understands, the rhythm of seasons. Each one is necessary, each one preparing the ground for what comes next.

First, you *Reset*. You clear the mental clutter. Release the noise, the overwhelm, the patterns of thinking that have been quietly running you without your permission. This season might feel slow, like nothing dramatic is happening. But beneath the surface, everything is being prepared. You can't build something new on ground that hasn't been cleared.

Then, you *Rewire*. New beliefs start to form. New habits take root. Your brain literally changes, building new neural pathways through the science of neuroplasticity. What once felt hard starts to feel more natural. What once seemed impossible starts to feel within reach. Your mind begins to see possibilities it genuinely couldn't see before.

Then, you *Rise.* Action and momentum gather. Confidence builds, not the fragile kind that depends on everything going right, but the kind that comes from keeping promises to yourself, day after day. You show up differently. You trust yourself in a new way. You don't just think differently, you are different.

And, finally, you *Radiate.* What you've built inside starts to show up outside. Your growth touches the people around you, your family, your colleagues, your community. Your creativity expands. Your contribution deepens. You realize that training your mind was never only about your own life. It was always going to affect the people you're around.

At some point, something shifts. You don't go back. Because this isn't a one-time change. It's a new way of operating where you become the master key.

When you make it to the end of your year, keep going. Just as nature's cycles never stop, growing your human intelligence, learning, and becoming limitless is a never-ending journey too.

I wrote this book with dates tied to the seasons in the Northern Hemisphere. But if you live in the Southern Hemisphere, the seasonal names are simply the names of your four phases. The inner journey they describe is universal, even when your sky looks different.

Whatever today is for you, even if it's not January 1, that's your "Day One," so start there. And trust it's where you're meant to begin.

You Don't Have to Do This Alone

One of the things I've learned in over 30 years of teaching is that growth is faster when it's shared.

There's a reason my mentor read my dreams out loud that evening. Because something that lives only inside us can stay small. But when we speak it, share it, bring it out into the world, it becomes real. It finds traction. It finds other people doing the same thing.

You didn't come to this book by accident. Something brought you here. Someone may have given it to you. Or you found it at exactly the right moment. However it happened, here you are. And I want to invite you to pay that forward.

Share what you're learning. Talk about what's changing. When you teach something, you get to learn it twice. And every person you bring into this practice is one more mind being trained, one more life being unlocked, one more ripple going out into a world that needs people who know how to think.

We become limitless in a limited world not by going it alone. We do it together. The more of us who train our minds every day, the more the world changes. That's not just a nice thought. That is the mission.

WHO YOU'LL BE A YEAR FROM NOW

I know you may have tried something like this before. A book you started and set aside a few days or weeks later. A practice you meant to keep and didn't. A version of yourself you could *almost* see and then lost sight of somewhere between a busy week and a hard month.

That's okay to admit. It's honest. And that's what we want, to keep it raw and real.

Here's what I want you to know: Every attempt that didn't stick was you simply gathering information. It was your mind learning what doesn't work and getting closer to what does. You weren't falling behind. You were figuring something out. And the fact that you're here now, with this book in your hands, tells me you haven't given up. You're still looking, and that matters more than you know.

So if part of you is skeptical right now, good. Bring that skepticism with you. You don't need to believe this will work before you begin. You just need to begin.

Before we do, I want you to do something. Close your eyes for a moment after you finish this paragraph and imagine yourself 366 days from now.

You wake up and the first thing you notice is that you didn't reach for your phone. You lie there in the quiet, in your own thoughts, knowing what today is for. Your mind is clear in a way that used to feel like something other people had.

You're not perfect, you're still human, life is still life, but you have a relationship with your own thinking that you didn't have before. You know how to focus when you need to. You know how to let go of what isn't serving you. You know how to learn from what happens to you instead of being buried by it.

The confidence you feel doesn't need to announce itself. It's just there, steady. It's been built from 366 mornings of showing up for yourself, even when it was small, even when no one else saw it.

And the person holding this book right now, the one who maybe isn't completely sure this will work, you'll look back at them with a smile, knowing this was the moment everything changed. You'll know what it took for them to begin. And you'll be glad they did.

That person is not far from you. Not separated from you by talent you don't have or time you can't find or circumstances that need to change first.

They are one year of daily practice away. They are 366 keys away. They are, in the most real sense, already inside you.

• • •

I want to leave you with something else before you turn this page:

A year will pass either way.

Three hundred sixty-six days from right now, that time will have gone. The only question is, who will you be when it does?

Will you be different by design, or by default?

I know which one you're here for. I can tell by the fact that you're still reading.

So let me ask you what my mentor asked me on that evening that changed my life.

If anything were possible, anything at all, what would your life look like a year from now?

Hold that. Feel it. Let it be real right now, not someday. That wanting you feel is your brain and your mind beginning to orient toward something they're capable of. You don't need more time. You don't need more talent. You don't need to become someone else first.

You need to learn to use what you already have. And then practice it, one day at a time, one key at a time, until it stops being something you do and becomes who you are.

You are the greatest project you will ever get to work on. Take time. Make time for it.

There's a more limitless version of yourself patiently waiting, so keep showing up each day until you are introduced.

The keys are in your hands.

They always were.

Let's begin.

—Jim Kwik
World expert in human intelligence,
brain performance, and accelerated learning
New York Times best-selling author of *Limitless*

RESET

The Season of Clearing

(January 1–March 31)

You cannot become limitless with a mind clouded by limits.

In a world drowning you in noise and urgency, distraction and overstimulation have hijacked your nervous system, critical thinking, and creativity. Before you dive into building new habits, new beliefs, new mindsets, and taking new actions, you need to let go of overwhelm, overthinking, anxiety loops, mental clutter, emotional exhaustion, perfectionism, and regret.

This is what Reset is all about.

Winter is a time for stillness, but that doesn't mean nothing is happening. It's simply happening beneath the surface. The next three months are designed to help you release *everything* clouding your mind and overwhelming your brain. These insights will guide you to go within and help you create the space, stillness, and clarity you need to set the direction for the rest of the year.

In the coming pages, you'll learn to:

- Release cognitive clutter
- Calm your nervous system
- Reclaim attention from overstimulation
- Break free from comparison and perfectionism
- Let go of the stories that no longer serve you
- Create space for transformation

Welcome to your season of clarity, calm, and fresh beginnings.

THE POWER OF YET

Sometimes the very skills, knowledge, and habits we long for feel so far away. It can even feel like they're for other people, not us. But those thoughts are simply LIEs (Limited Ideas Entertained) playing on repeat.

The truth is, there's a version of yourself patiently waiting for you to arrive. This future self *has* mastered the skills, gained the knowledge, and built the habits that your present self wants.

To meet this version of you, you show up every day, loving yourself enough to learn and practice the fundamentals, to eliminate distractions that don't serve, and to transform the mindsets that keep you limited.

But first, you have to believe that version of you exists.

What you believe becomes your truth. Your brain will find information in your environment to support your beliefs—whatever they are. This effect is known as confirmation bias. If you believe something is impossible, then it becomes impossible. But when you believe something is possible, it becomes possible too.

Instead of believing you lack something, what if you believed it simply hasn't happened *yet*?

"I can't read and comprehend quickly *yet*."

"I don't know how to concentrate for more than twenty minutes *yet*."

"I don't have the skill to prioritize my to-do list *yet*."

The power of "yet" is the power of possibility. It's the path to your future self, the one who already lives with all the abilities, mindsets, and routines that your present self is working on creating.

If you keep showing up day after day, then one day you will meet this person. That is the power of "yet."

KWIK STEP: Set a timer for three to five minutes and visualize the person you will be 12 months from now. What skills, habits, and routines do they possess? How does it feel to be that version of you?

AFFIRMATION: *"I am willing to do the daily work to meet this version of myself patiently waiting a year from now for me. I am limitless."*

JANUARY 2

DISCONNECT TO RECONNECT

There's a war raging for your attention, and your brain is caught in the crossfire.

Whether it's on social media or over texts and e-mails, what offers us invaluable ways to connect and learn is also driving our brains to distraction. At the center of our digital lives lies dopamine, a neurotransmitter that plays a key role in motivation and learning. It's released in various situations, including when we're exposed to novelty and surprise.

The wonder, the waiting, and the anticipation of finding out what's behind every ping, ding, and ring releases a little dopamine drip, making us feel good and rewarding that behavior. So constantly checking our devices becomes addicting as our brains seek out the new and novel, quick and easy dopamine hits.

This also explains why activities requiring deep concentration, attention, and focus such as writing, studying, creating, even holding meaningful conversations, feel harder than they actually are. Our brains have been trained to crave the quick rewards of distraction rather than the slower, deeper fulfillment that comes with progress over time.

But you weren't born to scroll. You were born to create, to connect, and to contribute.

To do that, you first have to reconnect with the most important person—you. That means taking breaks from your devices, carving out time to focus without distraction, and helping your brain fall in love with the slow, steady, satisfying work that comes from studying, creating, and learning.

When you need to focus, leave your phone in another room; use website blockers; put your phone on "airplane mode" or "do not disturb"; set your status to "away"; switch your setting to grayscale.

Practice not checking your devices for 30 minutes, then increase it to 60, and upwards to an entire day.

Whether it's reading, journaling, connecting with a loved one, exercising, or being still, do one thing at a time with intention, focus, and attention.

Disconnect to reconnect, and your progress becomes sustainable.

KWIK STEP: Find one thing you can do to disconnect to reconnect today. Then do it.

AFFIRMATION: *"I guard my attention, choosing where, to what, and to whom I give it. I am limitless."*

"NAME IT TO TAME IT"

Have you ever noticed how when you go to do something important like apply for a new job, suddenly your inner critic speaks up, "You'll never get it. You're not good enough."

Maybe you've procrastinated on something important, something you know will alter your life, but all you can hear echoing inside your head is, "You're lazy. You'll never do it."

This voice can even pop in after you make a mistake, lashing at you with, "Of course you didn't get that right. You're so stupid."

It's easy to believe these voices, mistaking them for the truth. They constantly run in the background of our days, shaping who we believe we are, what we believe we're capable of doing, and what actions we actually take.

But you are not your inner critic. It's just a part of you, trying its best to protect you from feeling disappointment, embarrassment, fear, failure, or rejection. But left unchecked, the inner critic can prevent you from taking chances, growing, learning, and fully living.

To help quiet that voice, you can use a technique called *"name it to tame it,"* coined by neuroscientist Dr. Dan Siegel. When your inner critic speaks, pause and identify the emotion, matching it to a name like "Procrastination Patty," "Negative Nick," or "Skeptical Stan." By identifying the feeling and giving your inner critic a name, you do two things:

1. **YOU CREATE DISTANCE.** That voice isn't who you are—it's a part of you. Giving it a name helps you to put some space between this part and who you really are.
2. **YOU CALM YOUR BRAIN.** Studies show that when you feel intense emotions like fear and anxiety, the amygdala lights up. But naming your feelings activates the prefrontal cortex, which sends soothing signals to the limbic area—where your amygdala resides—effectively calming and regulating it.

Name your inner critic, and you will begin reclaiming your power.

KWIK STEP: List two to three recurring inner voices and give them names. As you move through your day, try to pay attention to your thoughts, and when an inner critic pops up, name it.

AFFIRMATION: *"I am more than my inner critic. I am limitless."*

JANUARY 4

CALM YOUR THOUGHTS. QUIET YOUR MIND.

When you wear a lot of hats and your to-do lists have their own to-do lists, it can feel challenging to turn down the noise in your head and create peace. Yet that's exactly what your brain needs to be more creative and productive.

Take a few minutes to create a space of peace for yourself today.

Close your eyes. Bring one hand to your heart and the other to the top of your head. Focus your awareness, pulling all your attention to your breathing. Then ask yourself, "What do I want?" and "What do I feel grateful for?"

Open your eyes and notice how you feel.

When your mind constantly spins, your nervous system can get stuck in sympathetic overdrive. This floods your brain with stress hormones like cortisol, adrenaline, and norepinephrine, which can cause you to feel irritable, overwhelmed, distracted, and anxious. Slow breathing activates your vagus nerve, which helps signal your nervous system that it's safe to shift into the parasympathetic state. As this more relaxed state comes online, activity in your prefrontal cortex increases. This helps you stay focused on goals, brings better emotional regulation into the picture, and improves decision-making.

Relaxed moments often produce the best insights and inspiration.

Before starting something challenging or heading into a meeting, pause for a few minutes to close your eyes and breathe deeply, allowing each exhale to slow down your body and mind. Let your nervous system settle. Let peace wash over you. Let your attention, focus, and creativity activate. Then get to work.

Calm your thoughts. Quiet your mind.

KWIK STEP: Take a few minutes before any deep work, important meeting, or when you need to perform at your peak to close your eyes and breathe slowly and deeply.

AFFIRMATION: *"I allow my mind to quiet. I am limitless."*

JANUARY 5

CHANGE IS INEVITABLE. GROWTH IS A CHOICE.

You may think growth and change are hard. But staying stuck somewhere you don't belong? That's much harder.

Because in the quiet moments, you can't escape feelings of self-doubt, anxiety, and fear that arise as you sense—as you *know*—your life is passing you by.

There's a reason why it's hard to make big changes, even though you know they would benefit your life. It's because your brain's primary job is survival, not success.

Your brain is wired to scan for threats and avoid uncertainty. This is the role of the amygdala—the threat detector. Your brain interprets what's known as safe. Growth feels uncomfortable because your brain reads "new" as "dangerous."

The next time you find yourself hesitating, procrastinating, or second-guessing, remind yourself, "That's protection, not a limitation. And I am stepping into something bigger."

Remember, you don't need to have all the answers, but you do need to stay in motion—mentally, emotionally, professionally. Because in a world that's constantly shifting, the real edge isn't your title, degree, or even past experience.

It's the ability to learn your way out of any situation, to train your brain to constantly adapt, to rewire new pathways, and to grow beyond what you thought possible.

And lifelong learners? The people who adopt a growth mindset, believing their abilities and intelligence can continue developing—they're the ones who always stay ahead.

Change is inevitable. Growth is a choice. Choose wisely.

KWIK STEP: Identify where you feel the most resistance, then tell yourself, "This growth isn't unsafe, just unfamiliar." Then identify one small step forward and take it.

AFFIRMATION: *"I am safe to grow, expand, and step into the unknown. I am limitless."*

JANUARY 6

PULL BACK TO SLINGSHOT FORWARD

On the surface, a slingshot doesn't look very powerful. But pull back the string, pause, then let it go, and suddenly the object flies forward, quickly and powerfully.

In a world pushing you to stay online, take in more information, and be accessible to everyone at all times, slowing down and silencing the external world can feel like laziness, or like you're going to fall behind and miss out.

You're not. That's you becoming a slingshot, pulling back and pausing before propelling yourself forward.

Your brain needs stillness to reach peak performance. Studies show creativity and clarity flourish when you allow your mind to rest. Slowing down helps activate the default mode network. It's the area of your brain that becomes active when you daydream. It helps create your sense of self, generate insights, forecast possible future scenarios, engage in creative problem-solving, and integrate memories.

Brain imaging studies also suggest that silence may support neurogenesis—the birth of new neurons—in the hippocampus, a region central to learning and memory.

To train your brain for stillness and silence, start with scheduling five minutes in your calendar each day. During this time, look out a window, take a walk, or meditate. Leave your phone in another room, put it on airplane mode or do not disturb, and mentally sign off from being connected.

Stillness isn't laziness. It isn't procrastination. And you're not missing out or falling behind. By giving your brain a chance to reset and relax, you're giving it the space it needs to work out solutions to problems, to respond to difficult situations from confidence, clarity, and emotional regulation, and to ensure your actions align with your goals.

Stillness is pulling back so you can slingshot forward.

KWIK STEP: Schedule five minutes of silence. Note what you'll do during that time (walk, sit quietly, look out the window and daydream).

AFFIRMATION: *"I seek the silence to restore my mind. I am limitless."*

KEEP THE MOST IMPORTANT THING THE MOST IMPORTANT THING

You're deep into an important project when suddenly your phone dings. You reach for it, thinking you'll just check it quickly. Before you know it, you've fallen down a rabbit hole and 20 minutes have passed.

When this happens, you haven't just lost time, you've lost focus. And with it, the kind of deep concentration needed to produce your best work or show up as your best self.

Research shows every time you switch tasks or get interrupted, it takes your brain on average 23 minutes to return to its previous focused concentration. And the more often you surrender to the temptation of checking every ping and ding, the stronger the habit loop becomes.

You'll never stop all notifications, nor should you. But in a digital world fighting for your focus, you still need to keep it where it matters most. Willpower alone won't work. You need a process.

When you're tempted to check a notification, pause and ask yourself two questions:

- "What's the best use of this moment?"
- "What's the most important thing I can focus on now?"

If either answer is something other than checking, don't. Get comfortable pausing and re-evaluating. Just a few seconds helps disrupt the habit loop. More importantly, it begins retraining your brain to stop operating on autopilot.

Keep the most important thing, the most important thing.

KWIK STEP: When you're tempted to check your phone or any notification, pause and ask, "What's the best use of this moment?" then "What's the most important thing I can focus on now?"

AFFIRMATION: *"My focus is valuable. I keep the most important thing, the most important thing. I am limitless."*

JANUARY 8

DON'T CONFUSE FAMILIAR WITH FACTUAL

We use 100 percent of our brain power, 100 percent of the time.

Brain imaging proves this. It shows that we use nearly every region of our brain. But many people still believe we only use 10 percent. In fact, one international study found that nearly half of all teachers believe this.

Why does this myth survive? Because it's *familiar.* We've heard it repeated so often in school, on podcasts, in books, and in film that we've confused familiar with factual.

This pattern plays out in our thoughts too. You might think, "I'm not a good reader," or "I'm not a fast learner," or "I'm not good enough." And you might come to believe these "truths" because they're repeated so often that your brain builds a shortcut to them. When we see an image, word, or phrase repeatedly, it leads to *cognitive ease.* And the brain likes what's familiar—what's easier to access—treating it as fact. The easier it is for the brain to process information, the more confident you are that it's true.

Yet these thoughts are myths no different than believing intelligence is fixed, that mistakes are failures, or that genius is born rather than built.

To break your negative thought patterns, you must first become aware of them, learn to question them, then put more empowering thoughts in their place. When you catch a thought like "I'm not a good learner," swap it with "I am a great learner" or "I am becoming a great learner."

If you think, "I'm not a good reader," switch it to "I am becoming a great reader" or "I am an excellent reader."

Take "I'm not good enough" and rewrite it to "I am good enough to . . ." or "I am becoming good enough to. . . ."

This is how you teach your brain to stop automatically defaulting to negative thinking, and how you start intentionally creating the thoughts—and life—you want to live.

Just because a thought feels familiar doesn't mean it's true.

KWIK STEP: Identify one negative, repeating thought, switch it, then try to repeat the positive thought to yourself at least once every hour.

AFFIRMATION: *"I intentionally create my thoughts. I am limitless."*

JANUARY 9

SELF-COMPASSION ISN'T WEAKNESS, IT'S STRENGTH

If you want a piano to sound its best, you keep it tuned.

If you want your brain to perform its best—creative, focused, and sharp—you need to keep your brain tuned too. One important way to do this is to practice more self-care.

Self-care for your brain requires more than eating healthy brain foods like blueberries, walnuts, and salmon, getting good sleep, and exercising. It's looking in the mirror after missing a deadline, snapping at someone, or getting an answer wrong, and saying, "This happened, *and* it's okay. I got this next time."

This is self-compassion. Instead of criticizing, it's honoring the person staring at you, recognizing everything they've been through, then choosing to treat yourself with the same loving kindness and compassion you would a good friend. It's recognizing *everyone* has flaws, makes mistakes, and neither defines your worth.

Speaking kindly to yourself reduces amygdala activation and increases activity in the prefrontal cortex, improving emotional regulation. Self-compassion also elevates your self-worth, protects you from comparing yourself to others, and reduces ruminating thoughts, self-consciousness, and procrastination.

You can train yourself to be more self-compassionate. Notice what you say to yourself, and replace it with how you'd speak to a good friend. Remind yourself what you're already doing well, and celebrate your small daily wins. That might mean recognizing that you're clearly communicating, actively listening, or consistently practicing your memory and speed- reading drills.

Self-compassion isn't weakness—it's strength.

KWIK STEP: Think of a recent mistake you made. Then look at yourself in the mirror and say out loud, "That happened, and it's okay."

AFFIRMATION: *"I am compassionate with myself. I am limitless."*

JANUARY 10

CLARITY CREATES MEANING. MEANING GIVES YOUR MIND DIRECTION.

Driving fast doesn't matter if you're headed in the wrong direction.

In today's world, it's easy to mistake busyness for productivity. But doing more means nothing if you don't know what you're doing it for.

You need stillness, a pause, a chance to turn inward and gain clarity to ensure you're headed in the right direction.

Stillness helps create clarity by giving your brain the space it needs to identify priorities, set goals, and integrate what matters. Pausing activates the default mode network, which supports introspection—reflecting on the past, imagining the future, and shaping the story you tell about yourself.

You can enhance your clarity through the power of questions. Your brain won't leave a question unanswered. So ask better questions, and your brain will search for better answers.

Ask yourself, "What matters most to me in my life?" Is it an adventure? Growth? Contribution? Love?

Next, ask yourself, "What matters most to me in every area of my life? My career? Relationships? Health? And the legacy I want to leave?"

Finally, ask yourself, "Are my daily actions aligned with what I say matters?"

Be sure to write your answers by hand. Research shows this activates more areas in the brain and can improve memory, focus, and follow through. It also gives you accountability. You can regularly revisit them to see if you're in alignment.

Remember, the more clarity you have about what truly matters to you, the more your brain can direct your attention and energy toward your goals.

Clarity creates meaning. Meaning gives your mind direction.

KWIK STEP: Ask yourself the questions in this insight and write down your answers.

AFFIRMATION: *"I am clear on what matters most in my life. I am limitless."*

FIND CALM IN THE CHAOS

You can no more stop the sun from rising than you can stop a stressful experience from happening.

The truth is, situations don't always go your way. People say things that may wound you. Working and raising a family is harder than you expected.

Instead of trying to stop these things from happening, what if you could change how your nervous system and brain interpreted them? What if instead of stress and conflict, you could create more calm and centeredness?

That's where meditation comes in. It's long been associated with structural changes to the brain. A study from Harvard and Yale found that long-term meditators showed an increase in thickness in regions associated with attention, sensory processing, and interoception—the nervous system's ability to perceive and interpret internal signals like hunger and heart rate. Neuroimaging from UCLA also suggests that meditators have more gray matter (which handles information processing, cognitive function, and memory) in certain regions, and less age-related atrophy.

To start, sit comfortably and close your eyes. Slow your breathing so your exhalations are longer than your inhalations. Focus on your breath as it moves in and out. When a thought arises, gently say "nope" and return to the breath. This technique helps activate your vagus nerve, triggering your parasympathetic nervous response. Essentially, it tells your brain, "You're safe. Everything is okay. You can rest, recover, and take a break."

Just like getting good sleep, exercising, and eating healthy are daily practices, meditation works best when practiced regularly. Begin by committing a few minutes a day and slowly add time as you go. And you can use this whenever you feel stressed during the day.

Find calm in the chaos, and you'll create a steady foundation to meet whatever comes.

KWIK STEP: Whenever you feel stressed during the day, meditate for two minutes.

AFFIRMATION: *"I find calm in chaos. I am limitless."*

ONE AND DONE TO FIX YOUR FOCUS

True or false? Multitasking is a powerful productivity hack.

If you answered "true," you've been sold one of the biggest myths in modern work.

For years, multitasking was promoted as the ultimate productivity flex. You could do and accomplish more in less time and effort, or so the story went.

Except now we know the truth. It's not helping us. It's decreasing our performance and increasing our stress.

Research done at Stanford found that heavy media multitaskers—people switching between working on a computer, responding to texts, and checking apps—performed significantly worse on tests of working memory, attentional filtering, and task switching. Other studies show switching tasks can cost up to 40 percent of your productive time.

One of today's biggest multitasking villains? Your devices. Every scroll and swipe, every ping and ding, hijacks your attention, focus, and concentration.

If this feels familiar, know it's not your lack of willpower. Your brain has been trained to chase every flicker of stimulation. All the devices and apps you use daily were designed to draw you in. While you can't redesign the tech, what's been trained in your brain can be untrained.

You can relearn how to shift from multitasking to *single-tasking*. Instead of jumping from e-mail to text to apps, stick with one until done. Finish what you start, or move it forward as far as you can, and you help retrain your brain to flex its focus, attention, and concentration muscles.

KWIK STEP: Pick three tasks to accomplish today. Rate each for priority (high, medium, low), and the focus load (light, moderate, deep). Then schedule your hardest, deepest task for the time of day when you're at peak performance.

AFFIRMATION: *"I focus on one task at a time until it's finished, or I've taken it as far as I can today. I am limitless."*

FRESH AIR. FRESH MIND.

When was the last time you listened to a robin sing or waves crash against a rocky shore, and felt your breathing slow?

When was the last time you paused to watch the sky light up in reds, oranges, and yellows as the sun slowly set, and felt your muscles unclench?

When was the last time you stepped outside, felt the cool air hit your face, and noticed as your racing mind began to quiet?

We spend so much of our days inside, sitting under artificial light, feeling scattered, stressed, and strung out. Yet have you ever noticed how stepping outside, even for a few minutes, can leave you feeling refreshed, calmer, and more energized?

There's a real reason for that. Our brains weren't designed for constant multitasking and digital overload. They evolved under conditions very different from modern life—periods of activity followed by quiet stillness, rapid sensory bursts followed by longer stretches of calm.

In our world today, our brain still craves something primal: connection to nature.

In one study from the University of Michigan, researchers found that walking in a natural setting or even viewing images improved working memory and attention by 20 percent. That's a lot.

Here's the key to making this connection work: no music, no scrolling, no texting or talking on the phone. Just you, your breath, and the world around you. Scientists call this *soft fascination*, a term from what's known in psychology as Attention Restoration Theory. Nature gently draws your attention without demanding too much of it, allowing your prefrontal cortex—the command center for focus, decision-making, and planning—a chance to rest and reset.

So step outside. Use all your senses. Be fully present. You're just one gentle walk away from experiencing more calm, more energy, and more focus.

Fresh air. Fresh mind.

KWIK STEP: Spend at least 10 minutes outside. Don't think about your worries or stresses. Focus on being fully present with nature.

AFFIRMATION: *"I am connected to nature, and it restores, soothes, and rejuvenates me. I am limitless."*

JANUARY 14

STRESS IS A SIGNAL

Green light. Yellow light. Red light.

We need traffic signals to know when to move forward, slow down, and stop, especially on busy roads. Otherwise, we'd never make it where we want to go on time. We might even crash.

On the bustling road that is your life, there are traffic signals too, telling you when to go, slow down, and stop. One of them is *stress*—it's your nervous system trying to grab your attention.

Maybe it's telling you to prioritize self-care. Are you regularly exercising? Eating a balanced diet? Getting restorative sleep? Meditating? Incorporating short brain breaks to reset your focus and energy? Research regularly notes these practices help reduce cortisol and lower the brain's stress response.

Maybe it's about setting boundaries. When you say yes to someone, are you really saying no to yourself? Do you need to protect your personal time, energy, focus, and heart to avoid burnout?

Maybe it's telling you to communicate better under pressure, training yourself to pause before responding, especially in difficult conversations. In the pause, your prefrontal cortex can come online rather than your amygdala running the show.

Or maybe it's a call for more mental clarity. We often make things complex, but the brain loves bite-size, manageable steps. This reduces cognitive overload, keeping you proactive.

Perhaps it's reminding you to build support systems. This might mean mentors, colleagues, or peers who understand your pressures, or a life coach or therapist who can offer new tools.

Stress could also be asking you to maintain perspective. When you zoom out, will this matter in a month? A year? Cognitive reappraisal like this reduces emotional intensity and builds resilience.

Don't bottle up your stress. Don't ignore it. And don't judge yourself for it. Work with it. Talk to it. Let it help you see yourself and life more clearly.

KWIK STEP: Sit quietly and take a few deep, slow belly breaths, then ask your stress, "What are you trying to show me?" You can also use this as a journaling exercise or ask someone you trust to pose the question.

AFFIRMATION: *"I use stress as a signal to gain clarity and strength in life. I am limitless."*

JANUARY 15

CUT THE MENTAL CLUTTER

If you're thirsty, you go to the faucet, turn on the tap, and sip from a cup. What you don't do is turn on a fire hose and try to drink.

Yet that's what most of us are doing with information.

It's estimated that every two days we create roughly the same amount of information that was created from the *beginning* of human civilization until 2003.

Like trying to drink from a fire hose, it's nearly impossible to keep up without drowning. From constant texts and social media alerts to endless blogs, podcasts, and newsletters, we're living in a digital deluge.

And it's affecting your brain. When your attention gets pulled in different directions, the prefrontal cortex—the region responsible for decision-making, focus, and emotional regulation—gets overwhelmed. Your attention becomes scattered. You start skimming and rushing. You start switching between tasks more rapidly. And it becomes more difficult to concentrate, do deep work, learn, or stay present in conversations.

Information won't stop being created. That's why you must slow the flood.

Be selective with what you consume. Say no to nonessential newsletters. Put group texts and people on silent. Switch your tablet and phone to airplane mode or do not disturb. Remove social media apps from your phone. Close unnecessary browser tabs.

Do this, and you will help your brain focus, use time more efficiently, and feel more peaceful and relaxed. Cut the mental clutter, and you will free up your mind to think more clearly and remember more vividly.

KWIK STEP: List the top five digital drains in your day, then decide what you can delete, mute, or unsubscribe from.

AFFIRMATION: *"I choose what information to allow into my life. I am limitless."*

JANUARY 16

SELF-CARE ISN'T SELFISH

Imagine when you turn 18, you're given a free vehicle. But there's a catch: It's the only one you'll get for the rest of your life.

If this was true, would you take care of your vehicle? Of course! You'd do everything you could to keep it running smoothly and efficiently—regular oil changes, tire rotations, interior detailing, washing, repairing, refueling.

Now think of your brain.

Your brain is the only brain you get in this life. To harness its full power and potential, you must keep it healthy, and that includes refueling.

Neuroenergetics is the study of how the brain uses energy to function, examining how neurons convert oxygen and glucose into electrical signals. From this science, we understand that every thought, decision, even emotion takes energy, as neurons depend on constant fuel to communicate. If you're struggling to concentrate, your brain feels foggy, your memory blanks, or you're paralyzed making decisions, it might mean your brain is short on energy.

From the best brain foods to physical exercise, quality sleep, stress management, and supplements, you have many tools to improve your brain's energy and enhance its performance.

Self-care isn't selfish. It's the maintenance work essential to ensuring your brain has the energy it needs—and you need—to learn, perform, and live a long, productive, and fruitful life.

KWIK STEP: Start a "self-care kit" for your brain. List at least five healthy brain practices (such as sleep hygiene, eating brain-boosting foods, hydrating, exercising, or setting boundaries) and commit to using at least one today.

AFFIRMATION: *"I care for my brain. It's the only one I have. I am limitless."*

YOU CAN DO ANYTHING, BUT NOT EVERYTHING

Have you ever reached the end of your day and felt so drained, yet you think: *What did I actually accomplish?* You stare at your to-do list, and almost nothing is crossed off.

If you're busy all day but still falling behind, you might be working hard but not smart.

Working smarter has nothing to do with multitasking, because multitasking doesn't exist. Research shows the brain can hold only about four chunks of information at once in its working memory. It also doesn't juggle multiple tasks simultaneously; it switches. But not quickly. It can take up to 20 minutes for you to regain focus and concentration after an interruption.

Working smarter has everything to do with focus. Real productivity comes from prioritizing what matters most and ruthlessly eliminating what doesn't. That's what the most successful people do. They aren't the ones doing the most—they're the ones doing the least but focusing the most. They apply the *Pareto Principle*, which shows that 20 percent of your effort creates about 80 percent of your results.

You can do anything, but not everything. So give yourself permission to *stop* trying to do it all. No one can, and no one does.

Instead, create a "not to do list." Write down every task or responsibility you can off-load, then pick one to outsource, pause, or stop altogether.

By removing tasks from your day, you reduce cognitive overload, decision fatigue, and stress. Plus, you free up valuable mental bandwidth to focus on what catapults you forward.

Focus isn't about doing more. It's about doing what matters most.

KWIK STEP: What's your priority today? What are three steps you can take to keep the focus where it matters most?

AFFIRMATION: *"I am clear on what matters most. I am limitless."*

DON'T SKIP THE WISDOM SILENCE OFFERS

You live in a world that tells you "more is better," so you keep adding. You plug more meetings into your calendar, say yes to more commitments, clients, and projects, and keep posting on social media.

Except the more you add, the more stressed, overwhelmed, and exhausted you're likely to feel. And when you can't keep up, you're left wondering, *What's wrong with me?*

Nothing. *Nothing* is wrong with you.

When you're constantly on the go, your prefrontal cortex becomes taxed, affecting creativity, emotional regulation, decision-making, focus, and rational thought. Your nervous system stays locked in the sympathetic state, flooding your body with stress hormones including adrenaline and cortisol.

The success you long for isn't found in doing more—it's found in slowing down and bringing stillness to your mind.

This allows the parasympathetic nervous system to take over, easing stress hormones and releasing serotonin and endorphins that help restore calm.

Stillness allows your mind to wander, activating the brain's default mode network, which is linked to imagination, reflection, and creative insights. It helps you zoom out from the daily chaos to ask questions that bring more clarity, so you make real progress. Questions like:

- "Why do I feel stuck?"
- "What decisions align with my values?"
- "Which paths are worth my energy, time, and attention?"
- "Am I moving toward what I really want? And if not, what do I need to do?"

Busyness doesn't mean you're progressing any more than moving fast means you're moving forward. Don't skip the wisdom that silence offers.

KWIK STEP: Set a timer for three to five minutes. Place one hand on your heart and one on your head, and breathe slowly while silently repeating, "I am still," for about a minute. When you feel calmer, then ask yourself one question like "Why do I feel stuck?" or "What decisions are worth my energy, attention, and time?" and patiently listen for the first answer that arises.

AFFIRMATION: *"I am still. I am limitless."*

JANUARY 19

YOUR VOICE, YOUR CHOICE

If you understood just how powerful your mind is, you wouldn't think anything you didn't want to be true. You wouldn't think "I'm so forgetful," "I'm so busy," or "I'm always late."

Every time you think thoughts like these, you're training your brain to link them with your identity. In neuroscience, Hebb's law states, "Neurons that fire together wire together." When thoughts or behaviors repeat, the brain strengthens those connections. With enough repetition, the brain creates a "shortcut" (or habit) that makes the thought or behavior easier to run.

Having a negative thought or two will no more ruin your life than eating a donut occasionally will ruin your health. But if you ate one donut 30 times a day, and you did that every day for a month, there's a strong chance you would experience some health consequences.

The goal isn't to stop negative thoughts completely—you can't. The brain has a negativity bias. It's a survival mechanism to help anticipate and predict potential problems. And a little self-criticism can give you a reality check and help motivate you to gain new skills or take new risks.

But there's a big difference between having the occasional thought "I need to read more" and the constant narrative of "I am not that smart," "I have a horrible memory," or "I'll never amount to anything."

Your brain believes what you repeat. You can choose more empowering thoughts, and the more you practice this, the more you rewire those neural pathways, making positive thoughts easier and more automatic for your brain to access in the future. While some thoughts will always run on autopilot, you have the power to rewrite them.

Your voice. Your choice.

KWIK STEP: Take any negative self-talk thoughts and flip them. For instance, "I'm not good enough" becomes "I am good enough" or "I am great."

"I'm not smart enough" transforms into "I am brilliant" or "I am smart."

Before you do anything else, repeat your positive self-talk thoughts five times each. Throughout the day, keep repeating them as often as you can.

AFFIRMATION: *"My voice creates my world. I am limitless."*

A STILL MIND IS A CLEAR MIND

Your mind is like a pond. When it's disturbed, everything appears murky and muddled. But when it's calm, everything becomes clear.

This is the essence of inner stillness. It's the space where clarity is born. And clarity leads to better decision-making, emotional control, time management, self-control, and discipline.

Many people think stillness means doing nothing, sitting quietly, or escaping from the world. It doesn't. Stillness brings *awareness*. It's the art of being fully present, of showing up mindfully in a moment with your mind, body, and spirit aligned.

Practice mindfulness during mundane tasks. Instead of checking your phone while walking from one room to the next, focus on each footstep, what's on the walls, and how your body moves. Notice how it feels to brush one tooth at a time. How the water feels in your mouth when you're drinking. Really listen to the sound of someone's voice when they're talking. Tune in to your senses, using as many as possible.

If a thought arises, it's okay. Rather than linger on it, let it drift by, and bring your attention back to whatever you're doing.

This is how you can begin cultivating clarity, bringing stillness to your mind, and intentionally directing your thoughts instead of allowing them to scatter.

The more you practice, the more your attention circuits strengthen. Your focus will sharpen, and your thoughts will become more organized. This clarity of focus will become a superpower, helping you learn faster, decide smarter, and live more consciously.

The truth is, your external world will likely never be calm. The demands on your time and attention won't cease. So you must be the one who creates calm within.

A still mind is a clear mind.

KWIK STEP: Pick one ordinary routine today and commit to focusing your attention on the act (for example, brushing your teeth, drinking a glass of water, eating a meal, listening to a loved one).

AFFIRMATION: *"I still my mind so I can see clearly. I am limitless."*

JANUARY 21

YOU CAN'T SHAME YOUR WAY TO GREATNESS

When imposter syndrome or burnout strikes, how do you treat yourself?

When you've lost something important like a job, a goal, or your confidence, what do you tell yourself?

When this happens to your friends, you're probably quick to offer kindness, compassion, and encouragement. When it's you, if you're like most people, your first move is self-criticism.

But you need—and deserve—the same grace.

Shame never builds anything remarkable. It simply stops you from moving in any direction. As researcher and author Brené Brown has shown, the pain of shame triggers the body's threat systems, driving you out of your prefrontal cortex, where reason, creativity, and decision-making reside, and into the amygdala, your threat detector, triggering fight, flight, freeze, or fawn.

But practicing self-compassion changes everything. Neuroimaging studies show that neural networks connected to the brain's threat response get reduced when you reassure and speak positively to yourself.

Be kind to yourself, especially on the days when you don't feel your best and everything feels hard. Think about what you'd say to a friend or loved one, then say it to yourself. You deserve the same love, patience, and compassion that you give freely and easily to everyone else.

You can't shame your way to greatness. But you can love yourself to it.

KWIK STEP: Find one small way you can show yourself kindness today.

AFFIRMATION: *"I am willing to love myself to greatness. I am limitless."*

JANUARY 22

STOP FIGHTING FOR YOUR LIMITATIONS AND START FIGHTING FOR YOUR LIMITLESS POWERS

There's an old saying: "The walls have ears." It's a warning to be careful with your words, because you never know who's listening.

In our story, here's the twist: Your brain is always listening to what you say.

And what you say about yourself ultimately becomes a self-fulfilling prophecy, because your beliefs drive your behaviors. So if you say, "I'm a failure," "I can't pay attention," or "I'm too lazy to finish this," then that becomes the program your brain runs, and you unconsciously act in ways that make it come true.

If you believe, "I'm no good at remembering names," your brain will expect to forget. When you meet someone new, your mind will wander, you'll forget to repeat their name during the conversation, and you won't test your memory later. Then when you go to remember their name, you won't be able to. This only confirms the expectation, which reinforces the belief, and the feedback loop continues.

Without realizing it, every time you speak negatively about yourself, you're fighting *for* your limitations. And when you argue for your limitations, you get to keep them.

Swap the limiting programming to a limitless one. "I'm too old to make a change" becomes "I am always capable of changing."

"I'm lazy" can turn to "I take action toward what matters."

Switch "I don't have the resources" to "I have limitless resources."

Make your positive programming your new self-fulfilling prophecy.

Stop fighting for your limitations and start fighting for your limitless powers.

KWIK STEP: Catch one limiting label today and replace it with a limitless belief.

AFFIRMATION: *"I am not my labels. I am limitless."*

JANUARY 23

YOU'RE NOT LAZY. YOU'RE OVERWHELMED.

In all my years working with everyone from elite performers to high school students, I've yet to meet a truly lazy person. Usually, what looks like laziness signals either a brain caught running an outdated, negative self-talk program that has turned inaction into a habit or an overwhelmed nervous system trapped in protection mode.

The faster your to-do list grows beyond your capacity to manage it, the more your brain's alert system—the amygdala—activates the stress response, flooding your body with hormones including cortisol and adrenaline. This shifts your nervous system into the sympathetic fight, flight, freeze, or fawn state.

In this space, activity in your prefrontal cortex decreases. This is the zone of productivity, where creativity, problem-solving, critical thinking, planning, and emotional regulation reside. When it's not fully online, motivation vanishes. Instead of clear and focused thinking, with energy directed toward pursuing goals and productivity, your brain locks into survival mode, constantly on alert, scanning your environment for threats, and directing fuel to keep your body safe.

Your nervous system wasn't designed to stay stuck in this mode 24/7. It was meant to toggle between short bouts of stress (the sympathetic state), and rest, digest, and repair (the parasympathetic state).

So instead of saying "I'm lazy," what if every time you had that thought, you paused and asked your brain, "What do you need?"

If your brain screams at you to "rest," then give yourself permission to do it.

You're not lazy. You're overwhelmed. And that's fixable.

KWIK STEP: Schedule a 10-minute "be unproductive" meeting in your calendar. During this break, focus on deep breathing, meditate, go for a walk, stretch, or let your mind wander. Then notice how you feel after.

AFFIRMATION: *"I give my brain the rest it needs so it can rejuvenate and renew itself. I am limitless."*

JANUARY 24

IF LESS THAN TWO, DO

Too many open tabs will slow down your computer. But close some, and instantly your computer runs faster, more efficiently, and smoothly.

Unfinished tasks during your day act a lot like open windows on your computer, slowing down your brain's cognitive power and making everything feel harder. Every unfinished task adds to your cognitive load: what your brain can reasonably handle at one time. The more cognitively overloaded your brain becomes, the harder it is to solve problems, remember, or think clearly.

When working memory is maxed, the brain also avoids further demands—that's one reason why procrastination appears. It's not laziness causing you to put off important tasks; it's how your brain is managing energy, focus, and emotions. When tasks feel overwhelming and uncertain, the brain leans into procrastination as a strategy to soothe and calm an overloaded system.

One way to reduce cognitive load and avoid procrastination is the *two-minute rule*. If a task will take you two minutes or less, do it immediately.

This prevents small tasks from piling up, reduces mental clutter, and helps you build momentum moving from small wins to the bigger ones.

A word of warning: Don't stop deep work and sustained focus every time an under-two-minute-task, like scheduling an appointment or checking e-mail, pops into your mind. This kind of context switching—jumping from one task to another—can cost you valuable time, energy, and focus. Instead, set aside time once or twice a day to batch the mini-tasks.

Time is the only resource you'll never get back. Learning how to utilize it well isn't just a productivity hack—it's a life skill.

If less than two, do.

KWIK STEP: What is one task that you've put off that would take you less than two minutes to do? Go do it now.

AFFIRMATION: *"My time is valuable. I use it wisely. I am limitless."*

YOUR MIND IS LIKE A PARACHUTE; IT ONLY WORKS WHEN OPEN

The ancient Zen Buddhist "Parable of an Empty Cup" tells a story about a master and his apprentice. The master is pouring tea into a tea cup. Instead of stopping when the tea gets to the rim, he keeps pouring until tea overflows.

The apprentice, expecting his master to stop pouring, just sits there. But the master merely goes on pouring.

Finally, the apprentice speaks up. "Master, the tea is overflowing everywhere."

With those words, the master stops. "I'm glad you see this," says the master. "You must empty the cup first to pour more tea in."

Sometimes as we grow older, our minds become like the tea cup—so full that there's no room for learning.

Research has found that the brain tends to prioritize and interpret new information that supports our existing beliefs, giving less weight to contradictory information. Brain imaging studies have also found that the posterior medial prefrontal cortex—associated with decision-making and memory—becomes more active when exposed to opinions that confirm a belief than opinions that oppose it.

These phenomena are examples of *confirmation bias*—the brain's tendency to give more weight to the known than the unknown.

When you encounter a new idea, information, or any learning opportunity, become a beginner again. Forget what you know so you open your mind. Because your mind is like a parachute; it only works when it's open.

KWIK STEP: When you encounter new information or an idea, practice forgetting what you know, what's not urgent, and any limiting beliefs.

AFFIRMATION: *"My mind is a beginner's mind, ready and eager to learn, expand, and grow. I am limitless."*

JANUARY 26

MOVE YOUR WAY FORWARD

The business plan you keep meaning to write.

The new hire you keep meaning to make.

The online class you see yourself taking.

So many people have dreams like these. They can feel and vividly imagine what their lives would look like if they just took action toward these changes. Yet they can't. It's not the right time. They don't have the right training, skills, or experience. They don't have the right resources, connections, or capital.

What's actually happened is they've become trapped in *analysis paralysis*—overthinking every detail, every outcome, and every "what if . . ." scenario. So the dream ends before it begins.

Underneath this need for perfection is actually fear of making a mistake. Fear of looking bad. Of being criticized, judged, or rejected. When you step toward a new future, you step toward uncertainty. To the brain, this signals danger. The amygdala—the fear and threat detector—activates when it can't predict what happens next.

Analysis paralysis isn't treated with more thinking, more research, or more waiting. *Action* cures it. Just one small, simple step in the direction of your dreams and goals. This is because hardwired into your brain is what's called *the action bias.* The brain prefers action to staying still. Movement brings relief. It triggers more activity in the prefrontal cortex—the part of the brain that plays an important role in planning, goal-directed behavior, and emotional regulation.

Each time you stumble—and you will—you also teach your brain to stop treating uncertainty as a threat. Over time, instead of triggering the brain's fear response, you rewire it through neuroplasticity to treat uncertainty as opportunities for learning, progress, and growth.

Thinking is a superpower, but overthinking is your kryptonite. Don't let your thoughts keep you playing small. Take one small step toward executing that business plan, adding someone to the team, or finishing that class.

You don't think your way forward. You move your way forward.

KWIK STEP: What's one small step you can take to help quiet the noise and move forward?

AFFIRMATION: *"I am someone who moves forward. I am limitless."*

JANUARY 27

SUCCESS HAPPENS FROM THE INSIDE OUT

What do developing a skill, showing up consistently to practice, and starting a business have in common?

They all start inside you.

From putting in for a promotion to leading a team to launching a new product or service, it all begins with you making decisions, analyzing situations, solving problems, imagining futures, planning, and communicating your thoughts.

Except many people aren't aware of what's happening inside themselves. They're caught reacting to life, politics, social media, and how people treat them. They're giving away their power to people, things, and situations outside their control.

Really, what they're giving away is their *attention*. Where attention goes, so goes energy, concentration, creativity, thinking, and motivation, because the brain prioritizes what we focus on.

If you want to transform your life, then that starts by reclaiming and redirecting your attention.

Begin by sitting quietly, or grabbing a journal, and ask yourself: "Where am I giving away my power?"

Then ask, "What is one thing I can do to reclaim my power?"

This process helps you develop *metacognition*—thinking about your thinking. In learning, it's used to self-evaluate memory, problem-solving, and effectiveness. But you can apply metacognition to everything. It's self-knowledge. This process also helps create distance between the stimulus (what's fighting for your attention) and your response.

You can't grow yourself if you don't know yourself.

When you take responsibility for what's happening inside, you stop blaming and complaining about life, and you start owning it. And when you own your life, you have the power to make things better.

If you want the outside to change, focus on changing the inside first.

Success happens from the inside out.

KWIK STEP: Where are you giving your attention away? And what's one thing you can do to reclaim it?

AFFIRMATION: *"I own my attention, directing it where I choose. I am limitless."*

JANUARY 28

YOUR DEVICES ARE TOOLS, NOT YOUR MASTER

When we scroll through life, life scrolls past us.

Our brains evolved to take in and process slower, steadier streams of information—not the constant digital deluge we're drowning in now. Almost daily, our brains are forced to filter flashing notifications, rapid cuts, and constant sounds bombarding our senses.

While it's more than our brain can usually handle, we also can't look away. Novelty commands the brain's attention, and that's what's waiting for us behind every swipe. It's the anticipation of answering the unspoken question, "What's this?" and the dopamine drip that brings with it.

Breaking these dopamine-fueled digital-device loops begins with awareness. Track how often you check your devices during the day. What gets measured gets managed. The iPhone has Screen Time, Android has Digital Wellbeing, and there are free apps too.

You can take this further by tracking how many times you open certain apps, how often you check texts from specific people, or even how long you watch a video on your favorite streamer. Before going to bed, review your list and find ways to reduce or eliminate your footprint by giving yourself a digital detox.

Maybe you could put your devices aside while you eat or when you take a break. Maybe you could plan to go device-free for at least one hour or stop checking them from bed. Could you stop keeping them next to you when studying, working, or meeting with someone? Perhaps you could take a digital-free day on the weekend.

By bringing more intentionality and mindfulness to how and when you check, you punch the Pause button, interrupting the automatic habit, and giving you a chance to reclaim control over your time, energy, and attention.

Your devices are tools, not your master.

KWIK STEP: Track your device usage today, then tonight look for at least three opportunities to cut back tomorrow.

AFFIRMATION: *"I use my devices as tools to explore and expand my life. I am limitless."*

JANUARY 29

COMPARE LESS. SHARE MORE.

If you walk through the woods at night without a light, all you can see is what's directly in front of you.

When you're caught comparing yourself to others—to their successes, sharper thinking, incredible memory, problem-solving, and creativity—that can feel like trying to find your way through a dark forest too.

When your brain feels threatened by social comparisons, its attention narrows. It can fixate on questions like "Why do they have it so easy?" "Why do they always get so lucky?" "Why are they successful and not me?"

These thoughts are what's known as *social comparison bias*. Your brain makes quick decisions and judgments based on where it perceives you stand in relation to others. But that doesn't mean your brain is right. It just means it's operating on a loop.

To break the pattern, turn your focus outward by engaging in acts of kindness and helping others. Researchers have found that acts like cooking dinner for friends or family, doing chores for family members, even paying for someone's coffee in line behind you can lead to increased self-confidence, a greater sense of competence, and feeling socially connected.

When you're connecting with people, the brain releases the neurotransmitters oxytocin and dopamine—chemicals that leave you feeling good. Shifting your attention outward also helps quiet the threat response that social comparison often triggers.

In a limited world, how do we become limitless? We do it together.

Compare less. Share more.

KWIK STEP: Challenge yourself to perform three acts of kindness today, and pay attention to how it feels.

AFFIRMATION: *"I compare myself less and share myself more. I am limitless."*

JANUARY 30

YOU'RE FIVE DECISIONS AWAY FROM UPGRADING YOUR LIFE

Every morning you have a choice to make your life better. A choice to expand your mind and to move yourself in the direction you desire and deserve.

There are a lot of areas in life where it might feel like you don't have this power. But you do.

When you make intentional choices, it can increase what's called *perceived control*—that's your sense of being able to exert control over situations and events.

Research shows that having choice and perceived control helps reduce activation of stress pathways in the brain, lowering fear and stress responses. It also stimulates your brain's reward pathways, releasing dopamine, which helps reinforce intentional behavior and increases the likelihood you'll make more conscious choices in the future.

One way to remind you of your power is to focus on five key areas and commit to making a real choice in each:

1. What do you want to do MORE? This is something that you're already doing that you love.
2. What do you want to do LESS? Is it scrolling on social media, skipping workouts too often, or saying yes too much?
3. What is something you want to START? Something that when you close your eyes, you've always dreamed of doing?
4. What is something you want to STOP? Is it something like smoking or drinking, procrastinating, or keeping your phone attached to you?
5. What is something you want to CONTINUE? What in your life is working?

More. Less. Start. Stop. Continue. These five choices give you clarity with action, which, in turn, gives you the power to alter your brain, body, and life.

KWIK STEP: Take five minutes and respond to each question, then commit to taking the action today.

AFFIRMATION: *"I have the power to transform my life through the choices I make. I am limitless."*

POSITIVE WORDS CREATE POWERFUL MINDS

Imagine your mind is a garden. Every thought, every word you speak aloud or silently is like a seed. What kind of garden do you want to plant?

Do you want one overrun by weeds—negative thoughts and self-talk? Or one flourishing with flowers, blooming with positivity?

Most people default to planting gardens of weeds without wanting to. This isn't bad, necessarily. Fearful thoughts can protect you. Sad ones can signal self-care. And anger can motivate. But over time it can cause the brain to get stuck in survival mode, putting your creativity, critical thinking, and confidence on lockdown.

Positive self-talk does the opposite. It activates brain regions linked to critical thinking, logic, creativity, reward and motivation, emotional regulation and processing, and self-awareness. When you're more positive, you also see more possibilities. Your brain connects ideas, and it's open to learning.

To start shifting into the positive, do a "Mind State Inventory." First, write three negative beliefs or recurring thoughts. Then replace each by writing a positive, empowering belief.

Try framing the new belief in the third person: "I always mess up" can become "[Your name] uses mistakes as lessons." Research from the University of Michigan has found this can improve emotional regulation and self-control.

Thoughts happen automatically, but you also have power over what seeds you plant in your mind's garden. Plant positive words, and you'll create a powerful mind.

KWIK STEP: Take a "Mind State Inventory," writing three negative thoughts, then reframing them positively. Repeat them during the day and/or write them on Post-It notes to stick around your house.

AFFIRMATION: *"I use positive words to create a powerful mind. I am limitless."*

THE ART OF SUCCESS IS THE ART OF ATTENTION

What if you could add 100 days to your year?

Imagine what you could accomplish, who you could *become*, with that extra time. Three more months. No more lying awake wondering where the day went or worrying life is passing you by. Instead, you fall asleep feeling content and fulfilled from working on your writing, a martial art, foreign language, or computer code.

The average person checks their devices 85 times a day—about once every 10 to 12 minutes during their waking hours. Over time, this can quickly add up to more than 100 days lost to digital distraction.

Reclaiming those days isn't wishful thinking. But you need to understand you're not lacking time, you're lacking attention—the foundation of memory, focus, and peak mental performance.

Fortunately, attention is a skill you can train. Here's how: think FOCUS.

F — FREE TIME SCHEDULING. The brain isn't meant to run nonstop, so schedule "white space" for rest and recovery. This activates the Default Mode Network, a system connected to creativity, insight, and self-reflection.

O — ORGANIZED. Clutter increases cognitive load, drains working memory, and activates the amygdala—the brain's stress center—making focus harder.

C — CONSCIOUSNESS. Bring awareness to your digital habits. Social media is designed around dopamine-driven reward loops, making frequent checking more addictive. Ask yourself: "Is this serving me or stealing my focus?"

U — UNPLUG. Regularly disconnect by putting devices on "airplane mode" or "do not disturb," or leave them in another room when you need to focus.

S — SET BOUNDARIES. Practice opening your e-mail twice a day, or set time limits for scrolling on social media. This protects your prefrontal cortex from the energy drain that comes with task switching.

If you can't direct your attention, you can't direct your life. The art of success is the art of attention.

KWIK STEP: Apply FOCUS to your life today, writing down what you'll do for each step.

AFFIRMATION: *"I protect my attention, directing it where I consciously choose. I am limitless."*

FEBRUARY 2

BREAKTHROUGHS ARE BORN IN STILLNESS

When the harsh winter snows arrive, when the trees are barren, and the ground is frozen, it's easy to believe nothing is happening. That everything has died and gone still.

But underneath the snow and ice, amid the darker days, seeds grow, roots dig deeper, and trees and plants rest, readying themselves for spring, the season of growth and renewal.

This is what stillness does for us too. It's when we're still that we heal, integrate what we've learned, and open ourselves to new innovations and creative ideas.

But in today's digitally distracted world, we have to train our brains to welcome this. We've become addicted to the drip of dopamine from the busyness, the noise, and the flashes. The stillness that our brains once craved—and still need—now feels uncomfortable and threatening.

This comes at a cost. Studies show that constant stimulation weakens our focus, dampens our creativity, reduces our productivity, and increases feelings of stress and anxiety.

Don't fear the stillness. Lean in to it. Use it. Breakthroughs are born in stillness.

KWIK STEP: For five minutes, sit in stillness. No phone. No music. No computer. No meditating. Just silence and doing nothing.

AFFIRMATION: *"I welcome stillness, allowing breakthroughs to be born. I am limitless."*

FEBRUARY 3

LEARN TO OPERATE YOUR SUPERCOMPUTER

If someone showed you a giant supercomputer and commanded you to "make it work," the first thing you'd probably ask is, "Where are the instructions?"

You'd want to know how to use it, or you might break it, and you definitely wouldn't get its best performance. No one would expect you to use a supercomputer without first teaching you how.

Your brain operates like a supercomputer. Except no one has taught you *how* to use it. You never got the manual.

This is why you can walk into a room, meet someone, and within 30 seconds, have their name vanish from your memory. It's why you might draw a blank while giving a presentation, read a page and retain nothing, or feel like everyone in the meeting is processing information faster than you.

Most people believe they need to just accept that their brain "is as good as it's going to get or that "it isn't what it used to be." But these are LIEs (limited ideas entertained).

Your brain power isn't capped and it isn't fixed. In just a few minutes of strategic practice every day, you can improve anything—reading, languages, learning. It's all available to you, no matter your age. No matter your education. No matter your past.

One strategy is to practice *active recall.* When you finish a chapter, complete a lesson, or come out of a meeting, write down or say aloud everything you remember. Then go back to the source—reread the chapter, listen to the meeting recording—and note how much you recalled.

Your brain isn't flawed or broken. It's ready and able to be used. You simply have to learn how. Learn to operate your supercomputer, and you can learn anything.

KWIK STEP: Practice active recall by reviewing today's entry, closing the book, and writing or saying aloud what you remember. Then return to the material and note your accuracy.

AFFIRMATION: *"I am learning how to run the supercomputer that is my brain. I am limitless."*

FEBRUARY 4

BREATHE TO BALANCE

We can survive about three weeks without food, three days without water, but only a few minutes without air.

Breathing is one of the few functions that's both automatic and consciously controllable. And working with your breath has never been more needed. Your brain isn't meant to go fast all the time. Yet that's what the modern world pushes many of us to do.

Pushing nonstop can trap your nervous system into a state of sympathetic dominance: fight, flight, freeze, or fawn. This state evolved for short bursts, not as your baseline. When stress becomes chronic, your body and brain get flooded with stress hormones including cortisol and adrenaline. This can increase inflammation, disrupt the immune system and healing, impair sleep, and reduce cognitive function—including decision-making, focus, and emotional regulation.

You can counter this response with controlled breathing, which helps stimulate the vagus nerve, signaling safety to the brain and shifting you toward the parasympathetic state—rest, digest, and repair. When stress spikes, try the 4x4x4x4 practice:

1. Inhale deeply for four seconds.
2. Hold for four seconds.
3. Exhale for four seconds.
4. Hold for four seconds.

You can place one hand over your heart, and one over your abdomen or your head too. If a count of four feels too easy, increase to five or six. Repeat this two or three times, or more if you like.

The world will never stop spinning, but you don't have to spin inside. With each deep, slow breath, you train your brain to stay peaceful under pressure and confident in chaos. Breathe to balance.

KWIK STEP: Use the 4x4x4x4 deep breathing practice at least three times today, or whenever you feel stress spiking.

AFFIRMATION: *"I use my breath to bring balance to my mind and body. I am limitless."*

REACH. REST. REPEAT.

How do you profit in life?

That doesn't mean making money. It can, but it doesn't have to. Whatever profit you want in life—whether that's expansion in your business or career, thriving relationships, or flourishing health—then you must take care of your brain.

It controls *everything*. Just like your devices, your brain needs regular software updates. New knowledge. New capabilities. New habits. New experiences. New ways of thinking, feeling, and being in the world.

To continually update your brain, think: *Reach. Rest. Repeat.*

Reach: Growth doesn't happen without challenge; it happens when you stretch past your comfort zone. Just not too much. Author Steven Kotler described the 4 percent rule in his book *The Rise of Superman*. To reach peak performance, we want to challenge ourselves about 4 percent past our current abilities, meaning not too much and not too little. That will keep your brain learning and growing instead of stagnating or becoming overwhelmed.

Rest: After you stretch, you need to stabilize to hold the progress you've made in place. Here, rest is the best. This isn't optional. Your brain and nervous system need it. Sleep, relaxation, daydreaming, walking, being outside—it's in the pause that your brain repairs and restores itself, clearing away debris, strengthening neural connections, integrating memories, and learning.

Repeat: Once you've rested, you reach again, then you rest again. Then reach and rest, reach and rest, reach and rest in a never-ending cycle.

Reach. Rest. Repeat. This is how you not only grow your brain, but you create a profitable life.

KWIK STEP: What is one thing that you want to apply the Reach > Rest > Repeat formula to today? In your calendar, schedule time to reach and time to rest.

AFFIRMATION: *"I reach. I rest. I repeat. And so I become. I am limitless."*

COMPOSE YOUR BELIEFS

Kids fear the dark because they can't see in it. Their minds create wild stories of monsters and goblins creeping from the closet and lurking beneath the bed. But give them a light, and their fears start to fade.

Right now, your mind is likely creating monsters too, only they're in the form of limiting beliefs and thoughts like "I'm broken." "My brain can't do this." "There must be something wrong with me."

Feelings are not facts, and beliefs are not truths. They're simply repeated thoughts. If you repeat a thought often enough, it can bias the brain toward flagging it as true. This is how we're wired: According to False Tagging Theory, our brains default to accepting ideas as truth until the prefrontal cortex "tags" them as false.

That's where your power lies—in your ability to consciously interrogate the repeating, automatic thoughts that have turned into beliefs.

For example, when you notice a thought like "I can't learn this," follow it with "Is this absolutely true?"

Often, it's not that you can't learn, it's that you need something to make learning easier. That could be more effective methods and techniques. It could be that you need more energy, so you need to focus on improving your sleep quality, eating more brain-friendly foods, hydrating, or exercising. It could be you need to reduce distractions, change when you're learning, or shape your environment to enhance studying and work.

Every day, you have a chance to make your life a little bit better and your brain a little bit brighter, all because you can make a new choice.

Your life is the sum total of all the choices you've already made. And your beliefs can either be imposed on you or composed by you. You get to decide.

KWIK STEP: Identify one false thought and ask, "Is this absolutely true?" Then ask, "What do I need to gain or do to change this belief?"

AFFIRMATION: *"I am potential in progress. I am limitless."*

FEBRUARY 7

LIFE BEGINS WITH A CRACK

Great things always begin from the inside.

Take an egg. If it's broken by an outside force, life ends. But if the egg is broken by an inside force, life begins.

In this world, external forces will try to break you. From deadline pressures to demanding bosses and clients, to the dizzying and distracting onslaught of information, to people wanting more and more of your time, energy, and attention. It's easy for your brain to become cognitively overloaded, plagued by decision fatigue, and constantly stressed.

And while you'll never stop these pressures from outside you, you have greatness within. What's inside of you is so much stronger than any outside force.

Let your life begin with an inside crack, by breaking through whatever limitation is keeping you from realizing your greatness.

Maybe that's a limiting mindset like low confidence and a lack of belief in yourself, your capabilities, what you deserve, or even what you think is possible for your life.

Maybe it's limited motivation—you can't find the drive, purpose, or energy to move, so you feel stuck.

Maybe it's limited methods, so you need to upgrade your skills or process through learning and consistent practice.

Whatever is stopping you, find it and break it. Because the minute you do, your brain will break through its self-imposed limits, and a new life will begin.

Life begins with a crack.

KWIK STEP: Take a minute to consider which limitation is holding you back. What is one thing you can do today to start breaking through the limitation? Visualize yourself taking this action, then do it.

AFFIRMATION: *"I break through inside limitations so I can create the life I desire and deserve. I am limitless."*

FEBRUARY 8

YOUR POWER TO PRODUCE LIES IN THE PAUSE

Farmers understand that their fields can't constantly produce.

They need to rest them, allowing the land to lie fallow, sometimes planting cover crops to protect the soil and add nutrients. It's only in this quiet season that the land can rest, replenish, and restore itself, so it can once again nourish new growth.

Just as land needs a pause, your brain does too.

This is something high performers understand. They aren't the ones who never stop. They're the ones who know when to break for recovery. Research shows that regular micro-breaks (less than 10 minutes) can improve well-being, focus, and performance, while longer recovery periods can help lower the risk of burnout.

When your brain rests, your *default mode network* also activates. This region of the brain helps generate creative ideas, plays a role in introspection and self-reflection, assists in processing emotions and episodic memory, and empathy.

Rest and recovery don't just mean sleep. They're about refueling with activities that don't require your brain to exert a lot of energy or effort. Think of activities that allow your mind to wander and relax—gardening, cooking, listening to music while staring out the window, and walking in nature.

The key isn't to push harder—it's to recover smarter. This means scheduling regular brain breaks during the day just like you would other essential meetings. It means setting clear boundaries with colleagues and loved ones around your availability. And it means reframing rest as a productivity strategy.

You can't outperform burnout, exhaustion, or being mentally overwhelmed, just as a farmer can't grow crops from a soil that's nutrient and mineral depleted.

Your power to produce lies in the pause.

KWIK STEP: Today, schedule three 15-minute breaks during the day, and in the evening, give yourself at least one hour to relax—no learning, no working, no doing—just being.

AFFIRMATION: *"My power to produce lies in the pause, so I pause to give my brain the rest it needs and deserves. I am limitless."*

FAILURE IS AN EVENT; IDENTITY IS A CHOICE

Sometimes the only thing holding you back isn't a real barrier. It's the invisible one your mind has created.

You were not born procrastinating, doubting yourself, or playing small. Those are patterns your mind picked up along the way through experiences, conditioning, and other people's opinions and expectations of you. Those limiting beliefs and behaviors became survival strategies—protective habits your mind built to keep you "safe" and avoid perceived threats.

The empowering truth is: If it was learned, it can be unlearned.

All of life is all about learning, unlearning, and relearning. That's what neuroplasticity teaches us—that our brain is capable of changing, strengthening, or reorganizing new neural pathways at any age.

Too often people confuse what they've done with who they are. "I failed. Therefore, I am a failure." So they don't even attempt changing, because they don't believe they can.

But failure is an event, not an identity. Identity is a choice—one you get to make.

Those thoughts and behaviors are not who you are; they are things you've done. And the moment you separate the two, you create space to choose differently.

Self-limiting behaviors and beliefs don't have to define you. They can remind you that you're ready for the next level. Growing your human intelligence and becoming limitless starts with recognizing those mental walls, then choosing to step beyond them.

Failure is an event. Identity is your choice.

KWIK STEP: Identify one invisible limit you are ready to release.

AFFIRMATION: *"I am in charge of my identity. I am limitless."*

FEBRUARY 10

LEARNING TO LEARN IS A SKILL THAT SCALES

As we race deeper into the millennium of the mind, where technology, AI, and information change so rapidly, how can we ensure we're not left behind?

According to Demis Hassabis, CEO of Google's DeepMind, it's learning how to learn. He reasons it's the only way we'll keep pace with the shifting landscape and even have an advantage over it.

Most of us never learned how to learn. Schools train us to memorize facts and figures. They don't teach us the strategies and tools to learn.

Fortunately, this skill has nothing to do with your age, background, financial status, or what you already know. You can learn how to learn, starting now.

This begins with understanding working memory—the limited bandwidth you have to consciously hold information at once. Think of your working memory like mental Post-It notes, of which most people can hold about three to five.

So learning depends on chunking information—breaking it down into smaller bits of information. This makes it more likely you'll remember. Instead of memorizing a seven-digit number, break it into three sets. When reading, look for the headings in the text and focus on learning what's in one paragraph at a time under each.

Your brain is like a pattern-seeking machine. It wants to make patterns and connections between information. Chunking acts like a cheat sheet for your brain, helping it form and recognize patterns faster.

Learning to learn is a skill that scales.

Master it, and instead of feeling overwhelmed by the onslaught of change, you'll gain the confidence to continually adapt, pivot, and keep scaling too.

KWIK STEP: Find one piece of information you can chunk to learn today.

AFFIRMATION: *"I am learning how to learn. I am limitless."*

BOREDOM ISN'T THE ENEMY

When was the last time you felt truly bored?

In our world of endless scrolling and streaming, silence can feel like unnecessary torture. So the second we sense boredom rising, we rush to fill it. That's partly due to our brains being hooked on the steady dopamine drips we receive every time we respond to the prompting of our devices.

But what if the key to unlocking more creativity, better problem-solving, and increased productivity was actually in allowing ourselves to get bored?

Studies show that mildly boring activities can result in increased creativity. Boredom can also lead you to exploring the big—and often uncomfortable—questions about life, its meaning, and your sense of fulfillment, happiness, and purpose.

When the brain isn't focused on a specific task, networks connected to creativity, focus, and planning activate. One of those is the default mode network, which helps in replaying past moments and simulating future possibilities. Another is the executive control network, which steps in to organize and refine ideas that arise.

When you find yourself in a seemingly dull moment like standing in line, waiting for coffee to finish brewing, or walking from one room to the next, instead of reaching for a distraction, practice embracing the moment. Be fully present. You can even let your mind wander. It's in this space that surprising connections, new possibilities, and unexpected insights can arise.

Boredom isn't the enemy. It's the moment before something extraordinary breaks through.

KWIK STEP: Pick a time today when you'll allow yourself to get bored for 5 to 15 minutes. For example, on a walk, while making dinner, commuting, or standing in line at a store, don't listen to a podcast, talk on the phone, or scroll on a device.

AFFIRMATION: *"I am willing to allow myself to feel bored. I am limitless."*

FEBRUARY 12

SINGLE-TASK YOUR WAY TO SUCCESS

Do you ever feel mentally fatigued, like you're thinking too slowly, or your brain goes blank? Or maybe it's more like brain fog and your thoughts seem jumbled, cluttered, and scattered.

Have you ever wondered if maybe this is because you're asking your brain to do too much at once?

For decades, we were told multitasking was the secret to productivity, efficiency, and peak performance. Except it's a myth. Your brain cannot run two demanding cognitive processes in parallel.

What feels like multitasking is actually *task switching*. When you're focused on a specific cognitive task, certain networks in your prefrontal cortex light up. To switch, your brain has to shut down one circuit and activate another. This process requires glucose—your brain's primary fuel—which also requires a lot of energy.

Multitasking also costs you something even more valuable: time. Research from the University of California shows it can take up to 23 minutes to fully refocus after an interruption.

So instead of multitasking, think, *single-tasking.*

When you give one task your full attention, you strengthen your attention networks, train your working memory, and improve performance and output quality.

Single tasking is the way to success.

KWIK STEP: Make a list of the three highest-priority tasks you're facing. Start one and stick with it until it's complete or you can't go further.

AFFIRMATION: *"I focus on doing one task at a time, and that one thing moves me forward. I am limitless."*

FEBRUARY 13

SAY NO TO GOOD SO YOU CAN SAY YES TO GREAT

Warren Buffett says the difference between most people and the really successful is that the really successful say no to almost everything.

For many of us, saying no is hard, while yes feels automatic. We want to help others, be useful, and make people happy. That's partly because the brain pulls us toward social connection. Research using fMRIs shows that social approval—being liked and having a good reputation—activates the brain's reward circuitry. It feels good, so we seek more of it.

So saying no feels threatening. It risks our social acceptance and can activate the amygdala, the brain's threat detector, prompting that knee-jerk "yes."

Yet every "yes" comes with a cost. Not only does it become a "no" to something else, often something that truly matters to us, but it drains mental resources. The prefrontal cortex plays a critical role in working memory, creativity, focus, problem-solving, and emotional regulation. This region is prone to *cognitive overload*, where the demands placed on the brain exceed its capacity. This can lead to poor decisions, procrastination, brain fog, distraction, forgetting information, and feeling overwhelmed and stressed.

That's why borders and boundaries around what you say yes or no to matter. They protect your energy, your brain's superpowers, and your goals.

Saying no is an act of honor—toward your brain, your priorities, and your values. Be okay with saying no to good so you can say yes to great.

KWIK STEP: Say no to one thing today that doesn't serve your values or priorities.

AFFIRMATION: *"I say no with confidence so I can say yes to what really matters. I am limitless."*

FEBRUARY 14

LOVE EXPANDS WHEN EXPRESSED

When people talk about wanting to improve their memory, they often want to remember facts, figures, and formulas. And without question, this is a super skill that serves us well.

But more importantly, when you improve your memory, you get to remember your life. Not just the big milestones but the small moments with your loved ones, like your kids climbing into bed Sunday morning, laughing while washing dishes with your spouse, or lingering over coffee with a friend.

Like motivation, energy, and focus, love can be more than a feeling—it can be an act. You don't have love; you *do* love.

Think of the most important relationship in your life. Maybe that's your spouse or partner, a friend, child, parent, or sibling. Or maybe it's your relationship with yourself.

Now, express your love to that person.

This doesn't have to be a grand gesture. It can be simply saying, "I feel so grateful for you because ___________" or "Thank you for being ___________."

It could be saying, "I love you for who you are."

It could be actively listening when they're telling you a story or surprising them with their favorite drink if they're stressed. It could be acting affectionately, giving them a short hug or holding their hand.

Just as small daily actions lead to big changes in your life, small acts of daily love change your relationships. They signal to your nervous system it's safe to relax. Research links supportive, affectionate relationships with increased oxytocin, lower blood pressure, and more resilience to stress.

Show up as a loving force. Act loving to the loved ones around you and the person in the mirror in front of you. Love expands when expressed.

KWIK STEP: Write a short love note expressing your appreciation to someone, or to yourself.

AFFIRMATION: *"I give and receive love openly. I am limitless."*

FEBRUARY 15

YOUR CHOICES CREATE YOUR LIFE

Do I stay or do I go?

At some point, we all know when something needs changing. Yet we often resist releasing what we've created, whether that's a career, company, client, relationship, habit, or behavior.

Sometimes the *sunk cost fallacy* is operating. That's a cognitive bias whereby the brain leans toward continuing a behavior, relationship, or commitment because of the resources—time, money, attention—we've already invested in it.

And sometimes it's because we register letting go as loss. It's been shown that the brain experiences the pain of loss more intensely than the pleasure of potential gain. Some losses, particularly social ones like rejection or grief, can activate similar brain regions as those involved in physical pain.

But that doesn't make staying right. Sometimes what's best for our learning and life is leaving. If you find yourself struggling with this, then ask:

- What might I be afraid to lose?
- Why am I afraid of this?

Then begin visualizing your future, asking yourself:

- What do I stand to gain by letting go?
- What would my 90-year-old self tell me to do?
- A year from now, how will I feel if I keep doing what I've always done?

Reflective questions like this help you interrupt the automatic fear response that sunk cost fallacy and loss aversion often trigger. They also reawaken the power of possibility, reminding you that your life—whether you stay or go—is created by *your* choices.

You may not control all the circumstances around you, but you do control your choices. And your choices create your life.

KWIK STEP: Think of something you're struggling to release, then ask yourself reflective questions. You can do this in meditation, journaling, or talking with a trusted friend.

AFFIRMATION: *"I control my choices, and so I control my life. I am limitless."*

FEBRUARY 16

BACK TO BIRDSONG

We live in a noisy world.

The constant hum of appliances, the dings of devices, and traffic along the roads can make it easy to forget that our brain wasn't designed to function amid the constant racket.

For thousands of years, the score to human existence was water, birdsong, and wind. Somewhere in the recesses of our minds, our nervous system still carries the imprint of those soundscapes, and our brains respond positively when exposed to our ancient roots.

Listening to bird song, running water, rainfall, wind, or other nature-based sounds has been shown to quiet the mind, lift moods, and sharpen focus. One study found that after participants listened to nature sounds, they felt calmer, more relaxed and comfortable, and their moods improved.

This is because regions of the brain connected to stress and relaxation change when nature sounds are present. Listening to these sounds can increase parasympathetic activity (rest, digest, and recover) while decreasing sympathetic activity (fight, flight, or freeze).

In research using fMRI, when people listened to the sounds of nature versus the sounds of a city, brain regions linked to stress and rumination showed reduced activity, while networks involved in attention and working memory had stronger functional connectivity.

So the next time you need to study, do deep work, concentrate, or are feeling overwhelmed and overloaded, go back to birdsong. Let the water, wind, and call of the wild help steady your breath and restore your mind.

KWIK STEP: Listen to nature sounds for 10 to 15 minutes. Step outside if that's available to you, or just put it on in the background while at home or the office, and notice how it makes you feel.

AFFIRMATION: *"I am restored by listening to nature. I am limitless."*

PROTECT YOUR ATTENTION

You'd never leave your front door wide open at home. Anything could wander in, filling your rooms with chaos, noise, and unruly strangers.

Yet that's exactly what happens when you leave your brain unprotected.

Every ring, ding, and ping on your phone or device is something at your brain's front door, demanding to come in. And if you let them inside, then they will hijack your scarcest, most precious resource: your attention.

When you constantly give your attention to incoming texts, social media alerts, or in-box messages, it means you're ignoring something else. And if that something is someone you're talking to, a meeting, or work you need to do, then it can hurt your credibility, productivity, efficiency, and performance. Distractions can also cause cognitive overload and fatigue, overwhelming the prefrontal cortex, where decisions and focus reside.

That's why it's important to install a *mental screen door.* At least once per quarter, do a thorough "unsubscribe" from newsletters and "unfollow" audit on social media. Sign off from all your accounts rather than staying logged in. And remove apps from your phone's home screen or from the device entirely.

Intentional actions like this allow you to consciously choose what information gets in and when. By saying no to constant digital distractions, you're saying yes to deep thinking, creativity, problem-solving, and connection.

Just as your front door protects your home, you need to protect your attention. It's just as valuable.

KWIK STEP: Identify one *mental screen door* you can use during your day today.

AFFIRMATION: *"I protect my attention. It is one of my greatest assets. I am limitless."*

FEBRUARY 18

FIND THE SPACE BETWEEN YOUR THOUGHTS

Modern life has come to feel like a circus, and we're the performers. We're spinning plates faster and faster, terrified that if we pause even for a few minutes, everything will crash.

Deep down, we know the unrelenting pace is unsustainable, but our brains have learned to link busyness and constant motion with safety and security.

Yet slowing down is what a scattered, overwhelmed brain needs. This is what meditation does. It helps the brain shift from chronic threat mode and back into a state of clarity, calm, and self-regulation.

Neuroimaging studies have found that a regular meditation practice is associated with increased gray matter density in regions involved in self-awareness, cognitive control, and emotional regulation.

One widely used meditation practice is Transcendental Meditation (TM). Research suggests TM practitioners experience increased activity in regions associated with executive function and attention, and reduced activity in regions connected to reactivity and fear.

Regular practice has also been linked with more mental clarity, lower stress, less depression and fatigue, and increased resilience to stressors.

In TM, you repeat a word or phrase, also known as a mantra, allowing the mind to settle into a state described as "restful alertness." The goal isn't to stop your thoughts, which you can't do any more than you can stop your heart from beating. It's to notice your thoughts, give them space, let them leave, and return to the mantra.

As you do, you begin to sense the gap between stimulus and response, and within this gap there exist infinite possibilities to choose differently and from a different state. Not from fear or terror, but from peace and clarity.

Find the space between your thoughts.

KWIK STEP: For at least five minutes this morning and evening, practice TM or another mantra meditation.

AFFIRMATION: *"I am safe to pause and slow down. I am limitless."*

FEBRUARY 19

YOU MAKE MISTAKES; MISTAKES DON'T MAKE YOU

No matter our age, we all make mistakes.

Maybe you've said something at the wrong time that hurt someone's feelings. Maybe you've fumbled in a meeting, messed up a presentation, or lost a client.

With it can come this sinking feeling in your stomach, even a sense of shame. You might keep replaying the scenario over and over in your mind as you think about what you should have, could have, and would have said differently.

What's happening is that your brain is trying to protect you. Your amygdala has interpreted the experience as a threat, flooding your body with stress hormones to get your attention. Except the threat is emotional, not physical.

As the saying goes, "To err is human, to forgive divine." In those moments, no one needs forgiveness more than you. No one is perfect. No one knows everything. And no one gets it right all the time.

In fact, mistakes are good—they show you're trying. The truth is, you will make more mistakes when you stray from the comfortable path and stretch yourself in new directions.

So what if you stopped fearing mistakes and just went for it without worrying about looking silly, messing up, or getting it "wrong"? Imagine how much lighter you'd feel, how much more motivated to act, how much more confident you'd be when you fell, and how much stronger you'd be when you stood?

What if you welcomed mistakes—placing each under your feet to use as stepping stones to rise to the next level?

Because that's what mistakes are. They help your brain create and strengthen new pathways. When you make a mistake, you activate your anterior cingulate cortex, detecting errors and signaling your brain to adjust.

When it comes to mistakes, be *smart* enough to recognize them, *secure* enough to admit them, and *strong* enough to fix them.

You make mistakes, but mistakes don't make you.

KWIK STEP: Think of one mistake you made this past week. What did you learn from it?

AFFIRMATION: *"It's okay to make mistakes. I am limitless."*

FEBRUARY 20

THE ONLY LIMIT IS THE ONE YOU SET

In 1954, Olympic runner Roger Bannister set a goal to be the first person to run a sub-four-minute mile.

Physiologists told the 25-year-old Oxford medical student it was impossible and too dangerous to try. Bannister was also coming off a heartbreaking defeat at the Olympics in Helsinki, where he was expected to win the 1500-meter race. Instead, he failed to medal at all, finishing fourth.

Despite his naysayers, Bannister achieved his goal, becoming the first person to run a mile in 3 minutes and 59.4 seconds.

But what makes his story more interesting is that the following month, Australian runner John Landy bested Bannister's time, and within three years, another 15 runners broke the record too.

During this time, there were no incredible advances in shoe technology, training, or even nutrition that could have given these runners an edge.

What changed was the *belief.*

Bannister rewrote his brain's internal rulebook. In neuroscience, researchers have found that the brain regulates our performance to keep the body safe. This is known as the Central Governor Model. If the brain interprets an effort to be dangerous, it will automatically reduce the body's output—limiting speed, strength, endurance, even energy.

By proving it was possible and safe to run a mile in under four minutes, Bannister changed the threshold for others from a threat to an attainable goal.

Maybe you have a goal your brain interprets as unsafe, so it limits your performance. But the minute you show your brain that the goal is safe and achievable, it begins to reorganize itself from a cautious gatekeeper into an active coach.

Remove the limit, and your brain will work to make the impossible possible. The only limit is the one you set.

KWIK STEP: Think of a goal you want to achieve. What belief is stopping you? Is it too risky? Too hard? Too late in life? Now, close your eyes and visualize yourself succeeding anyway. Notice how it feels in your body, and quietly say to yourself, "This is safe. This is possible."

AFFIRMATION: *"The only limits in my life are the ones I set. I choose to be limitless. I am limitless."*

FEBRUARY 21

START MESSY

George Lucas said he rewrote the original *Star Wars* script four times, and even then, the movie turned out different from his script.

The first version of anything is messy—it should be.

Still, many of us don't want to start messy. We wait for the right time, the right skill, or the right people to start at all. We call it perfection, ambition, even having high standards, but often lurking underneath is fear—fear of making a mistake, fear of getting it wrong, fear of messing up.

But that rough draft, that nervous pitch to investors, that early idea for a new business that's hard to explain, it's all part of the process of learning, creating, and becoming. You will make mistakes. You will get some things wrong. You will stumble and stutter in fits and falls, only to keep standing and stepping forward again and again.

Instead of fearing the falls, what if you gave yourself grace? What if you said, "It's okay. This fall is a sign I'm learning, growing, and advancing toward my goals. I'll do better next time."

The truth is, each falter has the power to spark a chain of adaptations in the brain, helping it to detect errors, learn, and rewire your neural connections. A study from the University of Iowa found that the brain can identify a self-caused mistake in about one second, and remains active for another two to three more as learning begins.

Your brain needs those misses and mistakes for learning, growing, and adapting, and for building competence, confidence, and courage. So start messy. You can make it better later—because you will.

KWIK STEP: What is one small thing you've put off because you're waiting for the "right" time? Go do it today, and celebrate any messes or misses. Tell yourself, "I'm on my way to making it better," and notice how this feels.

AFFIRMATION: *"I start messy and always make it better as I go. I am limitless."*

WITH GREAT RESPONSIBILITY COMES GREAT POWER

"With great power comes great responsibility."

When iconic comic book writer Stan Lee penned these words for Spider-Man, he struck a timeless truth about us that still resonates. It's the idea that when we're granted power, we're also given a responsibility to use it.

But the inverse is true too.

The moment you start taking responsibility for your actions, choices, and habits is the moment you have the power to direct your life.

When you own your thoughts, emotions, decisions, and actions, you develop what psychologists call *internal locus of control*—the belief you can influence outcomes in your life. Studies find that people with strong internal locus of control experience more life and job satisfaction, more positive emotions and fewer negative ones, and they score higher in every psychological well-being measure.

Every time you decide to sign up for a course, open a book, ask a mentor for advice, practice a speech, or tuck into bed at 9:30 P.M., you're also increasing your *self-efficacy*. It's the belief and confidence in your ability to succeed. Research shows that high self-efficacy fuels motivation, persistence, better performance, and more resilience in stressful events.

Every small intentional act also teaches your brain, "I follow through. I am consistent." It might seem small, but over time, this will alter your brain's perception of who you are and your identity.

You will always face unexpected moments, sudden transitions, and experiences that you never planned for and didn't want.

Still, you are more powerful than you realize. Your strength comes from your ability to take responsibility for what you *can* control. That's your thoughts. Your emotions. Your decisions. Your actions.

With great responsibility comes great power.

KWIK STEP: Where in life have you given away your power by blaming someone or life, or waiting for the perfect moment? Find one small act of responsibility you can take to reclaim it today.

AFFIRMATION: *"I control my thoughts, emotions, decisions, and actions. Every act of responsibility multiplies my power. I am limitless."*

YOU'RE WIRED FOR CONNECTION

Just as neurons that fire together wire together, the people you spend time with wire into you too.

Science calls this idea *social contagion*. When you're around other people, their emotions, behaviors, even their stress can become yours (and vice versa).

So sometimes the uncomfortable feelings—say, unworthiness—aren't even yours. They're coming from the people surrounding you who harbor those feelings themselves, or from people around you who treat you badly.

Escaping negative influence isn't always easy, especially when it comes from a partner, your parents, or close friends. I'm not talking about generational trauma, which can get unconsciously passed on through families—that's a bigger and much different conversation. I'm talking about what you can control, like how you can remove or reduce the energy vampires in your life, while increasing the nourishing relationships that revive you.

Not only will this just feel good, but it's good for your body and mind. In the longest study of happiness and longevity in history, Harvard researchers tracked people for 80 years. They found that the biggest predictor for who thrived and who was happiest in older age wasn't diet or exercise. It wasn't even sleep or wealth.

It was *relationships*.

Not just romantic relationships, but connections with close friends and in community with others. When you're surrounded by the right people, it boosts oxytocin and dopamine, reduces stress, strengthens resilience, improves memory, and simply leaves you happier and healthier.

When you can, choose your people wisely. Your brain is wired for connection.

KWIK STEP: Think of one person in your life, past or present, who leaves you feeling happier and lighter. Notice how your body feels when you think of them. As a bonus, reach out to them. Send them a quick text or e-mail, and consider finding time to connect, whether that's a call or in person.

AFFIRMATION: *"I surround myself with people who uplift, support, and leave me feeling lighter and happier. I am limitless."*

FEBRUARY 24

LIVE LIFE ON YOUR OWN TIMELINE

Imagine logging on to your favorite social media site. As you scroll, you see the worst parts of people's day—kids melting down, bosses yelling, flubs during presentations, or people procrastinating.

But you never see this. No one posts the raw and real parts of their lives. Instead you're left with watching people's highlight reels. And it's a quick leap from the polished images to thoughts like What's wrong with me? Why is my life messed up? Why am I so behind?

Without realizing it, you judge your worth, your value, even your life's journey based on lives crafted for the screen.

Some of this is your brain's natural activity; it's wired to make unconscious social comparisons, looking down and up the social ladder to evaluate your skills, intelligence, and likelihood of reaching a goal. In theory, this can help you with learning, motivation, and decision-making.

But social media distorts the evaluation. The brain sees only people who appear more successful—though they aren't necessarily. Studies show that when people repeatedly engage in upward social comparisons on social media—especially during passive scrolling—it can decrease self-esteem and well-being, lead to feelings of inadequacy and less satisfaction, and cause us to see ourselves in a worse light.

No one's life is perfect, stress-free, worry-free, or carefree. Everyone is at a different stage in their life's journey. Don't compare your chapter 4 to someone's chapter 21.

In fact, don't compare yourself to anyone but your best self. And become so busy growing that you have no time for self-judgment.

Live life on your own timeline.

KWIK STEP: When you use social media today, notice your thoughts and feelings. If they turn negative, pause, name them, then sign off and do something uplifting.

AFFIRMATION: *"I live life on my own timeline. I am limitless."*

NO ONE IS BORN SMARTER. THEY JUST TRAINED SMARTER.

Imagine a genie suddenly appeared who could grant you the ability to master one subject or skill for the rest of your life.

What would you wish for? Why?

How about wishing for the ability to learn anything? That's like wishing for infinite wishes, because if you master the art of learning how to learn, then you become your own genie.

Your brain wants to learn, grow, and adapt. It's designed to do this. It's called neuroplasticity. Your brain creates and deepens new neural pathways, and clears away the ones it doesn't need.

Knowing how to learn means you can apply that toward anything you're interested in or need—from marketing to Mandarin, music, management, even martial arts.

Every single thing in your life gets easier and more enjoyable the better you are at learning. Progress builds confidence. Confidence builds competence. And that confidence-competence loop keeps working in your favor.

Better learners become better thinkers. Better thinkers become better creators. Better creators become better doers.

Learn how to learn, and you give yourself the ability to learn anything. No one is born smarter than you. They just trained smarter.

Kwik Step. Teaching is one of the quickest ways to learn. Think of someone who could benefit from today's message. In your own words, how would you teach that person what you just learned?

AFFIRMATION: *"I train my brain to learn. I am limitless."*

FEBRUARY 26

YOUR IDENTITY CREATES YOUR LIFE

Your life doesn't reflect your intentions as much as it reflects your identity.

Every habit, decision, and standard you accept is filtered through who you believe you are. Your reticular activating system (RAS) filters what you see, hear, and notice based on your identity.

If you believe "I am the kind of person who forgets names," then your RAS will unconsciously find instances that reinforce this belief.

But your RAS is neutral. So if you believe you're someone who always capitalizes on opportunities, then it will identify opportunities for you to capitalize on.

Change your identity, and you change what your brain will notice, remember, and motivate you to act on.

You don't get what you want. You get what you believe you are.

KWIK STEP: Write "I am the kind of person who . . ." and complete the sentence with one trait you want to cultivate. Then identify one action you can take today to prove and reinforce who you are becoming.

AFFIRMATION: *"I am the creator of my identity. I act in alignment with who I choose to be. I am limitless."*

FEBRUARY 27

NATURE IS YOUR BRAIN'S RESET BUTTON

Have you ever noticed how you can spend just 10 to 15 minutes in nature and return feeling renewed? It's like you can breathe again. Your energy has returned. Your head feels clearer and less muddled, and your creativity has exploded.

This isn't your imagination—nature really is influencing your brain.

Studies show spending time outdoors, especially in forests, reduces stress, improves focus, concentration, and memory. Another study found that people who spent time outdoors daily had a greater volume of gray matter in their right dorsolateral prefrontal cortex—a region involved in executive control, working memory, and decision-making. Gray matter is where much of the brain's information processing—thinking, learning, and memory—take place.

One explanation for nature's restorative power comes from *Attention Restoration Theory*, which proposes that modern life overloads our *directed attention*—the conscious focus on a task managed by the prefrontal cortex. Constant decision-making, multitasking, and digital distractions can lead to cognitive overload and mental fatigue.

But when you're in nature, your brain uses *soft fascination*—a relaxed focus where your senses gently roam. You notice everything around you, from birds chirping to the shape of a leaf and the feel of the path beneath your feet. Nothing demands intense concentration, so the prefrontal cortex gets a chance to rest.

This is why even brief moments in green space—or gazing out a window—can leave you feeling clearer, calmer, and more peaceful.

Nature may seem like an afterthought in our modern world, but to your brain it's a Reset button—one always within reach.

KWIK STEP: Spend at least 10 minutes outside today without texting, checking your phone, or listening to anything. Just be in your body and notice how it feels.

AFFIRMATION: *"I restore my brain by being in nature. I am limitless."*

FEBRUARY 28

DESIGN YOUR DIGITAL DISTRACTION

Have you ever noticed how, the moment you swear off sweets, suddenly you want them all the time? It's like the only thing you can think about.

This is known as the *ironic process effect*—coined by Harvard psychology professor Daniel Wegner, PhD, in his famous "white bear" study. When he asked participants not to think of a white bear, they thought of it at least once per minute. Wegner's research found that when you're trying to suppress a thought, one part of your mind avoids it, while another "checks in" to ensure it's gone. Ironically, this pulls the thought into your consciousness.

Our digital world works the same way. Telling yourself to "just stop checking" your social media feeds, texts, and e-mails works about as well as "just stop eating sweets." What you try to suppress still arises.

So instead of banishing distractions, what if you designed them?

Give yourself permission to let your mind wander down whatever digital rabbit hole it wants. But with perimeters. Schedule 10 to 15 minutes to scroll. When time's up, you're done. This is how you can stay in the seat of power. You get to give your brain the break it needs without it being lost in the digital universe.

Don't let the digital world dictate your day. You design your digital distraction.

KWIK STEP: Set a timer for 15 minutes, then let your brain be distracted in whatever way it wants. When time's up, stop.

AFFIRMATION: *"I design my distractions. They serve me, not the other way around. I am limitless."*

FEBRUARY 29

SHOW YOURSELF YOU CARE

If you love someone, you show it—not only with words, but with actions.

You make them dinner, run errands, and listen to their struggles. You ask questions. You protect. You encourage them to say 'no' when they're drained.

Every day, in so many ways, you do micro-acts that show you care.

Now, here's a tough question: Do you do any of these things for yourself? Do you show yourself the same level of care and love? And how often?

We often put others first, not because we don't want to care for ourselves. It's just that, sometimes, deep down, we doubt we're deserving of the same care.

We are. *You* are.

One of the strongest ways to prove you care for yourself is moving your body. It not only improves your physical health, but it's also good for your mental and emotional health. Exercising regularly releases dopamine, serotonin, and endorphins, and BDNF (brain-derived neurotrophic factor), which can elevate your mood and improve self-esteem.

Even small amounts of exercise—like 10 to 15 minutes—daily can do this.

Just as you show the people you love that you care, show yourself. You are equally deserving and worthy of it.

KWIK STEP: Choose one micro-act of care to give to yourself today, then do it before the day ends.

AFFIRMATION: *"I treat myself with the same love and care that I give to those closest to me. I am limitless."*

BUSY DOESN'T MEAN PRODUCTIVE

We live in a culture that tells you "more is better." That you have to do more, have more, and be more to be happy and fulfilled.

This is a lie.

It's this mindset that has led a lot of us to become very busy—with work, side gigs, families, volunteering, exercising, and the hundreds of other ways we can spend our time.

But being busy for the sake of being busy is a lot like running on a treadmill. Sure, you can log many miles, but you go nowhere fast. Similarly, you might do a lot during the day, but that doesn't mean you're making progress or are productive. In fact, you're probably less productive.

Staying on the go and feeling overworked is also likely keeping your nervous system in a stress state, which can disrupt cognitive performance and reduce your sense of well-being.

Instead of saying yes to filling your calendar in the pursuit of staying busy, say no to more of your daily to-dos.

For instance, instead of keeping your e-mail open all day, can you check it three times—in the morning, midday, and an hour before you wrap?

Are there any meetings or commitments you could eliminate?

Is there anything you could automate, say, grocery shopping?

Getting clear on what *not to do* will give you clarity on what matters to your ultimate goals. Remember, your brain likes goals and will direct your attention toward achieving them.

Real productivity means making steady progress toward what's important. Being busy doesn't mean being productive.

KWIK STEP: Create a "not-to-do list" today and stick to it.

AFFIRMATION: *"I release the tasks, obligations, and responsibilities that no longer serve me so that I make space for the ones that do. I am limitless."*

MARCH 2

FROM "I CAN'T" TO "I CAN'T *YET*"

We tend to think in black and white.

We have a good memory or we don't. We are fast learners or we're not. We can concentrate or we can't.

But the brain isn't black or white. Although the brain is an organ, when it comes to learning, it's more like our muscles. The more we use it, the stronger it becomes.

You don't have a bad memory. You're not bad at remembering names, finishing what you start, achieving your goals, focusing, or anything you think negatively about yourself.

You simply haven't done it . . . *yet.*

In that one small word lies extraordinary power. When you add the word *yet* to any negative sentence, it removes feelings of shame, failure, and struggle—universal themes many of us grapple with.

"Yet" helps to unlock what noted Stanford psychologist Carol Dweck calls a *growth mindset.* Dweck's research has uncovered that students who believe intelligence is malleable ("I can learn with effort") routinely outperform those with a *fixed mindset,* who believe intelligence can't change.

Her research went deeper, finding that students experienced more confidence and persistence toward learning and solving problems when they used "yet" or "not yet."

So the next time you think, "I can't," "I don't," or "I'm not," remind yourself: Struggle is a part of the journey. Your brain has an almost infinite potential for learning and thinking. Just as you need to challenge your muscles to grow stronger, you need to challenge your brain. Keep telling yourself:

"I don't have a great memory . . . yet."

"I'm not a fast learner. . . yet."

"I can't focus . . . yet."

One word reframes struggle, unlocks learning, and persistence, and reminds you of a simple truth: Your brain is growing, changing, and *becoming.*

KWIK STEP: Identify one to three negative statements you make about yourself, say them aloud, and add "yet" at the end. Then pause and notice how you feel. Throughout the day, try noticing when these thoughts arise, adding "yet" each time.

AFFIRMATION: *"I am not behind. I am becoming. I am limitless."*

MARCH 3

START BEFORE YOU'RE READY

Whatever you're waiting to start—an exercise program, a business, a difficult conversation with your partner, or a class—there's no such thing as the perfect time, perfect plan, or perfect moment.

Best-selling author Stephen King says, "The scariest moment is always just before you start." He's right, and also, it's what will give your brain the most relief.

When you're caught ruminating and overanalyzing, it creates more discomfort and stress for the brain. It's also energetically expensive.

Perfection isn't where growth happens—action is. Action shifts the brain from analysis to goal-oriented focus. It's like taking your foot off the brake while going downhill. The brain revs into forward motion, releasing dopamine as a signal of progress toward completion.

This is why people often think, Why didn't I do this sooner? after finally acting on something they've thought about a long time.

Just as there's no perfect time to act, no action you take will be perfect. You'll make mistakes. You'll get messy. But guess what? You'll learn too. That's what life is about.

Along the way, you'll also feel courage, joy, and pride. Not because you're doing things right all the time, but because you're doing things that matter and that make your life and time meaningful.

You probably don't need more information, more advice, or more analysis. You have what you need to take the next step, so let this be your invitation to launch today.

Start before you're ready.

KWIK STEP: What's one thing you've felt scared to start because you didn't want to mess up? Think of one small action you could take today to begin.

AFFIRMATION: *"I start before I'm ready. I am limitless."*

FAILURE IS FEEDBACK

Most people feel terrified of failing.

They believe they'll lose everything, that they themselves are worthless, that they'll look bad, be rejected or humiliated, lose opportunities, or have wasted time and money. With thoughts like these, it's no wonder failure feels like something to be avoided at all costs.

But the most successful people in the world see it differently. To them, there is no such thing as failure, only *feedback*. It's just data, showing them what worked and what didn't, so they can reassess, refine, and improve.

From a neuroscience perspective, failure is essential for the brain—that's how it learns. Every moment, your brain is predicting what's about to happen in your environment and how you should respond through actions, thoughts, or emotions.

When the outcome doesn't match the prediction, your brain generates what's called a *prediction error*—that's the gap between what you expected and what actually happened. When the outcome is better than expected, it's called a *positive prediction error*. When it's worse, it's a *negative prediction error*.

Seen in this light, failures are merely negative prediction errors—information your brain can use to learn, grow, and adapt.

So failure isn't something to avoid; it's valuable feedback to welcome and embrace.

KWIK STEP: At the end of the day today, write down one to three "failures" and what you learned from them. Then celebrate yourself for having learned them.

AFFIRMATION: *"I see failure as valuable feedback, helping me to grow and move closer to my goal. I am limitless."*

GIVE YOUR BRAIN ITS MEDS

When your body feels worn out, you rest.

You make sure to get plenty of sleep, hydrate, trim back your calendar, and maybe even pop extra vitamins, supplements, or other meds. This is taking care of your body.

Just as sometimes your body needs medicine, sometimes your brain needs help to heal too. So when you feel mentally exhausted, give it the MEDS it needs:

Meditation. Living in a digital-first world means your brain gets bombarded with constant information and inputs that increase stress and make it hard to focus. Meditation is one way to silence the noise and distraction.

Exercise. Research consistently finds that our brain performs better when we regularly move our body. Even just a 15-minute walk outdoors can boost memory and attention.

Diet. It's no secret that the foods we feed our brain matter. Avocados, blueberries, broccoli, eggs, green leafy vegetables, salmon, turmeric, and walnuts are just some of the best brain foods you can eat.

Sleep. It may not seem like it, but sleep is where a lot of magic happens. From your brain processing and recording memories and integrating emotions from the day's events to it literally "flushing" metabolic waste and toxins. That's the stuff left behind from all the work your brain did during the day, thinking, remembering, problem-solving, creating, even moving.

Meditation. Exercise. Diet. Sleep. Give your brain these "medicines" consistently, and you will help it to heal and build cognitive resiliency.

KWIK STEP: Pick one of the four medicines and prioritize giving it to your brain today.

AFFIRMATION: *"I give my brain the 'meds' it needs to stay cognitively healthy and resilient. I am limitless."*

MARCH 6

YOUR ATTENTION IS YOUR LIFE

Just as you can't ignore a crying baby, it feels impossible to ignore your phone when it lights up. But this comes with a cost.

While cell phones have offered us incredible opportunities to connect, share information, and access knowledge, there's a dark side. Research suggests that merely having your phone near you can distract you enough that it diminishes your attention and performance, especially on tasks requiring greater focus and cognitive demands.

Memory and learning begin with attention, and what you focus on determines what gets encoded. What you focus on strengthens as your attention rewires your brain through *synaptic plasticity*—the strength of connections based on increasing or decreasing activity.

So think: "I want to starve distractions and feed my focus."

There are many ways to do this, like putting your devices on "do not disturb" or leaving them in another room. You can use app blockers to stop notifications. If you're worried about missing an important call, then set your phone to only allow emergencies or calls from specific people. You can place a "please do not disturb" sign on your door.

These are all ways you can start clawing back your attention, intentionally redirecting it. The goal is to start freeing up your attention so your brain can better sink into deep focus, creativity, problem-solving, and learning.

Your attention is your life—treat it as such.

KWIK STEP: Protect one hour of focused work today using one or more focus tools.

AFFIRMATION: *"I am in control of where my attention and focus go. I am limitless."*

MARCH 7

JEALOUSY IS YOUR FUTURE CALLING YOUR ATTENTION

Imagine your co-worker lands a big promotion, a raise, or public praise from your boss. What's your first reaction?

If you felt a stab of jealousy, it's okay. It doesn't mean you're a bad teammate or have failed some invisible test of character.

Jealousy isn't something to suppress or beat yourself up for feeling. It's something to decode.

All emotion is data. The more intense the emotion, the more your brain is signaling something is important. When you feel jealous, it often points to a desire you haven't acknowledged or something you haven't attained yet.

Instead of shrinking from feelings of jealousy or ignoring them, let the emotion guide you. Ask yourself questions like:

1. "What is it that I deeply want?"
2. "What is this feeling of jealousy trying to show or tell me about my life?"
3. "What decision or action must I take so I can release this feeling?"

If you can allow it, jealousy can guide you toward your most precious dreams and desires—the ones you may have blocked yourself from acknowledging because they matter to you so much.

Jealousy is your future calling your attention.

KWIK STEP: Think of someone who recently triggered feelings of jealousy, and ask yourself, "What does this feeling reveal about what I truly want?" Next, consider one small, aligned action you can take today to move you forward.

AFFIRMATION: *"I am guided by my emotions. I am limitless."*

MARCH 8

YOUR BRAIN NEEDS REST TO FUNCTION ITS BEST

Your brain needs rest.

This isn't a revolutionary idea, yet knowing something in your head and believing it in your heart aren't always the same. Especially since we live in a world that glorifies hustling and where being constantly busy and productive can feel like a badge of honor.

So how do you take time off without feeling guilty, without FOMO, and without thinking that you're sacrificing progress?

You start by reminding yourself that rest isn't a luxury—it's a necessity.

Studies show that when overworked people experience changes in regions of the brain connected to executive function and emotional regulation.

Your brain evolved to toggle on *and* off from moments of intense focus and concentration to periods of rest and relaxation. By giving your brain regular breaks, it helps prevent burnout, reduces mental fatigue, improves concentration, enhances problem-solving and creativity, *and* boosts productivity.

But recovery won't happen unless you intentionally prioritize it. Try scheduling rest in your calendar just like a doctor's appointment, lunch with an investor, or a team meeting. This helps you mentally prepare for downtime while recognizing its priority.

Aim for five to six hours in a 24-hour period. In one of the largest studies on rest in the world, researchers found that participants who got five to six hours of rest—not sleep but time doing activities that restored them—within 24 hours reported the highest well-being.

In that same study, the top three activities participants reported as being the most impactful and rejuvenating included: reading, being in nature, and spending time with themselves. But this is about what restores you. Maybe for you it's cooking, painting, listening to music, taking a bath, playing with your kids or pets, visiting with friends, even watching TV.

When you give your brain a rest, it will function its best.

KWIK STEP: Schedule at least 30 to 60 minutes of rest in your calendar today, and identify what restorative activity (or activities) you plan to do.

AFFIRMATION: *"I rest my brain so it functions at its best. I am limitless."*

LEARNING HAPPENS IN STAGES

Flying an airplane. Baking macaroons. Juggling. Playing chess. Speed reading. Dancing salsa.

These activities share something in common: Each has skills we must learn first to perform them well.

For the brain to master any skill, it moves through the *Four Stages of Competence*:

1. **UNCONSCIOUSLY INCOMPETENT:** You don't know a skill exists, and you can't do it.
2. **CONSCIOUSLY INCOMPETENT:** You're now aware of it, but you still don't have it.
3. **CONSCIOUSLY COMPETENT:** You know the skill exists, and you can do it, but it takes more focus because you're still learning.
4. **UNCONSCIOUSLY COMPETENT:** Finally, your brain has mastered it. You don't have to think about doing it; it's automatic like tying your shoe laces or driving a car.

When you understand the cycle your brain loops through when mastering a skill, it allows you to plot where you are today so you can tailor your learning.

It also helps you stop expecting perfection. No one expects fourth graders to do calculus, or someone to walk onto a dance floor and immediately know all the steps to the salsa. So practice meeting yourself where you are in your own growth.

Learning isn't one and done; it happens in stages. The key is consistency.

Keep learning. Keep practicing. Keep improving. Day by day.

Learning isn't about one and done; it's about consistency.

KWIK STEP: Consider a skill you are mastering, or want to master. What stage of competence do you fall into? And do you need to make any adjustments in your learning journey? Are you expecting too much of yourself? Or not enough?

AFFIRMATION: *"I am consistent with my learning. I am limitless."*

MARCH 10

YOUR BRAIN NEVER RETIRES

If you've ever thought, *It's too late for me,* or *As I age, my brain won't stay sharp,* these words are for you: Those are worries, not prophecies.

It's normal to want your brain to stay sharp, capable, and confident as you get older. And while your shoe size, height, and biological age are outside of your control, your brain's performance isn't.

Yes, about one-third of it is influenced by genetics, and, yes, aging will cause some natural brain changes. But about *two-thirds* of your brain's capabilities are determined through your daily lifestyle, choices, and habits.

Isn't that extraordinary? Isn't that empowering?

Even more extraordinary, your brain is adaptable. It can reorganize itself, form new connections, prune away old pathways you no longer need, and strengthen the ones you do. This happens until your last breath. It's neuroplasticity in action. That's your brain's lifelong ability to rewire itself through experience, attention, and intention.

How encouraging is this?

You can reshape your brain through diet, adding more brain-friendly foods like blueberries, salmon, and walnuts. You can change it through movement and exercise, which releases BDNF (brain-derived neurotrophic factor), helping neurons grow stronger and more resilient and supporting learning and memory.

You can change it through breathwork and meditation, which calms the nervous system, activates the parasympathetic rest-and-digest state, and delivers more oxygen and increases blood flow to the brain.

And you can rewire your brain through novel, challenging activities like playing an instrument or chess, table tennis, or a board game; reading; learning a new language; traveling; or dancing.

You're never too old to change, to build new habits, or to improve your brain's performance. So the question isn't "Can I change?" It's "Am I choosing to rewire my brain today?"

Your brain never retires. So keep giving it reasons to grow.

KWIK STEP: What is one activity, at the edge of your limitations, that you can do today?

AFFIRMATION: *"My brain never retires.*
I give it reasons to keep growing. I am limitless."

MARCH 11

DO LESS, GAIN MORE

"I'm so busy."

Does that sound familiar?

For many of us, it's become a default response when we're asked, "How are you?"

It's not that we're lying or faking it. We are busy. We're caught in tasks, commitments, and projects with never-ending to-do lists that grow weekly.

There's just one catch. We might be busy, but that doesn't mean we're productive. It doesn't mean we're making real progress toward what matters.

There are habits, commitments, responsibilities, even people who are likely eating up your limited time, attention, focus, creativity, and problem-solving.

And it will keep happening until you can let go of the belief that the more you do, the more productive you are.

It's actually the opposite. By doing less, you'll gain more.

KWIK STEP: Consider what you have to do today and find one to two things that you can eliminate that aren't helping you make progress on what's important. Next, commit to using that time for something that matters.

AFFIRMATION: *"I choose to let go of the tasks, people, and commitments that don't move me forward, so that I can free up time for those things that will. I am limitless."*

MARCH 12

CHOOSE PEOPLE WHO CHEER YOUR CHANGE

Here's a tough truth: Not everyone is rooting for your growth.

Some friends and family might feel uncomfortable when you start changing. Maybe they're not ready to face their own habits. Maybe they're afraid of losing you because you're growing. Maybe your progress challenges their comfort zone. Maybe they're simply afraid for you.

Whatever the reason, it can feel confusing, even hurtful, when the people you love don't understand your growth and don't appear supportive. Honor your emotions, and know it doesn't mean your path is wrong.

What it means is that you might have to set more boundaries. This isn't putting up walls. It's being clear and direct about how important your learning journey is and asking for their backing. You might say, "I'm committed to taking this online class three times a week. It's important to me, and I'd really appreciate your support."

If they're not on board, that's okay. You don't need to cut them out, but you don't have to hide your light to make them comfortable.

You can also consider leaning in to relationships that nourish, support, and lift you up.

The brain has what's called mirror neurons that help us empathize with the emotions, and mimic the behaviors, of the people around us. Your brain will mirror whomever you're around. So if you want growth, look for the people who are growing.

Find communities you can join—online or in person. Or create your own circle of people who are growing and giving. Surround yourself with people who reflect the version of yourself you're working to become.

The right circle of people won't just witness your victories—they'll magnify them. Choose people who cheer your change, and you'll rise higher.

KWIK STEP: Pick one person in your life whose support for your growth has felt uncertain. Close your eyes and visualize yourself calmly and confidently telling them why it matters to you, and how you'd appreciate their support. Notice how it feels speaking your truth. If it feels right, consider having a real conversation with them.

AFFIRMATION: *"I am allowed to grow. I am limitless."*

MARCH 13

THE WORLD CONSTANTLY EVOLVES—YOU SHOULD TOO

In a world that will always evolve, always change, and always grow, your human intelligence must too.

So what do you want to grow? Your business? Brand? Bank account? A relationship? Career? Parenting? A hobby? A skill?

Whatever it is, your brain must grow first, and that happens through learning.

By challenging your brain to learn something new, you strengthen the synaptic connections—the communication channels—between neurons. In some regions of the brain, particularly the hippocampus, learning even stimulates the growth of new neurons through a process called *neurogenesis*. This is how brain cells become stronger, more adaptable, and more resilient.

One way to turn constant learning into a habit is to create a "to-learn list."

We all have "to-do lists" that guide what needs doing throughout our days. A "to-learn list" guides how our brain grows. This isn't about becoming a master overnight, but making consistent, steady progress toward it.

Instead of thinking you can learn a foreign language in a week, what if you learned one new word a day? Or how about practicing a new hobby like watercolor painting, writing, or making jewelry? Or maybe it's improving a professional skill such as networking, public speaking, or communicating more effectively.

Commit to learning every day. The world constantly evolves, and you should too.

KWIK STEP: Create your "to-learn list," including as many topics, hobbies, skills, or habits that you want to learn, and pick one to start today.

AFFIRMATION: *"I constantly evolve by learning something new every day. I am limitless."*

MARCH 14

SWIPE SMARTER

When we're easily distracted, exhausted, and struggle to focus, we often blame stress or burnout. But what if the real culprit was hiding in our hands?

In a study of 467 people, researchers had participants block all Internet access on their phones for two weeks. Participants still could call and text. They just cut passive screen time. No apps. No scrolling. No web browsing.

In just 14 days, without major lifestyle changes, participants showed improvements in sustained attention equivalent to reversing *10 years* of age-related decline. And more than 90 percent improved in at least one cognitive area—mental health, well-being, or focus.

Just two weeks. That's all it took for people to reclaim their brain and performance.

You're not exhausted because scrolling is hard. It's that your brain is hooked on the novelty and anticipation of what it will find when it checks your phone. Every time you pick it up, you activate your dopamine system. That's why scrolling can feel good. But the more you do it, the more desensitized the dopamine receptors become.

Now, your brain needs more time on your phone and more scrolling to feel that same pleasure. This helps explain why scrolling starts to feel hollow, and why you keep checking even when you're not enjoying it. Your brain is hooked on the quick dopamine hit. This is known as *dopamine desensitization.*

But you can recalibrate your reward system, beginning with a "Dopamine Detox." Don't pick up your phone for the first 30 minutes of the day. Stop browsing after work hours. Reduce the number of social media posts you make daily. Take "no scroll" weekends. Don't check your phone for one hour, working your way up to a full 24 hours. And practice replacing passive scrolling with active rest—walks, reading, doing a puzzle, or journaling.

You don't need to quit your phone. Just use it more intentionally. Swipe smarter.

KWIK STEP: What's one Dopamine Detox habit you can practice today?

AFFIRMATION: *"I choose when I swipe and where to put my attention. I am limitless."*

MARCH 15

MAKE GRATITUDE AN ATTITUDE

Many of us go through our days focused on what we believe we lack—the money, the house, the car, the vacations, the bodies, the lives—that others seem to have.

This isn't your fault. Your brain is wired for social comparisons, often making them automatic. Neuroscientists believe this helps the brain make more efficient decisions and judgments, saving cognitive resources. Yet such comparisons can also come with downsides. Frequent social comparisons correlate with low self-esteem and depression, unhappiness, and feelings of guilt and envy.

One way to shift this unconscious thinking is through gratitude. According to the Mayo Clinic, gratitude can decrease symptoms of depression, anxiety, chronic pain, and disease risk, while improving sleep, mood, and immunity. And in a study from the University of California, researchers found that participants who engaged in writing long-form gratitude letters to a specific person showed more positive emotions and boosted their well-being.

Being grateful for your life now isn't about settling or giving up on your goals. It's about teaching your brain to stop waiting to reach some far-off goal before you're allowed to feel happy, satisfied, and content.

Gratitude rewires your brain for presence, for appreciation of the now and all that you have.

Make gratitude an attitude.

KWIK STEP: Write three things you are grateful for now.

AFFIRMATION: *"I focus on what is working in my life. I am limitless."*

MARCH 16

CLEAR YOUR MENTAL CACHE

When a browser tab on your computer can't close, your work stops. Screens freeze, notifications pop up, and the device becomes unusable until you open Task Manager and force-close what's unresponsive.

In the supercomputer that is your brain, windows can get stuck too—in the form of looping thoughts.

After difficult conversations, stressful situations, or failures, your brain keeps replaying the moment and creating "I should have . . ." scenarios.

It's the type of thinking that keeps you up at night and pulls you from being fully present at work or with your family. When a thought isn't responding, it's not just a distraction, it amplifies stress and destroys productivity.

Just as your computer won't work until you address that tab that's not responding, your brain can't move on until you acknowledge what happened. Instead of pushing down or avoiding your thoughts and feelings, try journaling about them.

Take 5 to 10 minutes and write down everything you feel and think. No filtering. No judgment. No shame or guilt. Just pure expression and release.

Putting thoughts and feelings into words creates clarity, perspective, and emotional mastery. Neuroimaging studies show that naming emotions decreases activity in the amygdala—the fear center—and increases activity in the prefrontal cortex—the emotional regulation and decision-making core.

Leadership, growth, and creativity begin with emotional mastery.

When you feel overwhelmed or upset about a situation, don't suppress it—process it. That's how you clear your mental cache.

KWIK STEP: Set a timer for 5 to 10 minutes and reflect on a situation that your brain keeps replaying. Write down all your thoughts and emotions, unfiltered, then notice how you feel when the time is up.

AFFIRMATION: *"I choose to close the open loops in my mind. I am limitless."*

MARCH 17

STOP BELIEVING EVERYTHING YOU THINK

Most people have about 6,000 thoughts per day—about 2 million a year. And roughly 80 percent of them are the same thoughts on repeat.

But what really matters is this: You are not your thoughts.

Let's dig a little deeper. Your thoughts aren't even facts. They're patterns of electrical and chemical activity firing through your brain's networks. And your brain doesn't label thoughts as "good" or "bad," "positive" or "negative" at first. They're just neutral.

Once a thought appears, then different parts of the brain get involved, such as the amygdala, which assesses the emotional significance—is it scary? Exciting? The insular cortex also jumps in to help focus your attention to how the emotion feels in your body.

After the emotional tagging, other areas in the brain, including the prefrontal cortex, integrate the information to assign meaning.

At no point does your brain stop to evaluate whether these thoughts and meanings hurt or harm you, or if they move you closer to your goals.

That's where you come in. The more you consciously challenge and reframe negative thought patterns, the more you train your brain to seek, build, and strengthen new thought patterns that are empowering, uplifting, and limitless.

Stop believing everything you think. Start training your thoughts to create new possibilities.

KWIK STEP: Choose one empowering thought and repeat it to yourself 10 times, with feeling.

AFFIRMATION: *"I create new thoughts and patterns that serve me. I am limitless."*

MARCH 18

WALK YOUR WAY TO A BRIGHTER BRAIN

When we hear the word *exercise*, we often imagine working out for at least an hour, sweating profusely in the gym, and pushing our bodies to their limit.

If we miss a workout, it's easy to spiral into a self-loathing pattern, thinking we're lazy and undisciplined and we'll never get in shape.

But exercise doesn't have to look this way, and your brain doesn't need perfection. It needs movement and consistency. Activity increases neurochemicals including dopamine, serotonin, and endorphins that support memory, mood, and learning.

Start gently by walking, then gradually increase the intensity and duration. Research continues to show the numerous cognitive benefits from it, like supporting increased connectivity and activity between brain regions including the default mode network (critical for introspection), working memory, and the salience network (involved in filtering our attention and focus).

Walking is also associated with increased creativity and executive functioning—planning, focusing, and regulating emotions.

Want to enhance the benefits of walking? Head outside. Researchers found that a 15-minute walk outdoors improved attention and memory even more than a walk indoors.

Exercise doesn't have to feel like a burden. Nor do you have to max out to get results. Set the intention to walk more. You can park farther away from where you're going, walk while on a call, take a 10-minute walk after meals, or choose the stairs.

Walk your way to a brighter brain.

KWIK STEP: Find at least two opportunities to incorporate more walking into your day today.

AFFIRMATION: *"I walk my way to a brighter brain. I am limitless."*

MARCH 19

YOUR BRAIN IS NOT FIXED LIKE YOUR SHOE SIZE

When we think of genius, we often think of someone with a high IQ. Someone who was born "naturally" smart.

But genius isn't how smart you are—it's how you are smart.

Some people are effortless speakers, dazzling audiences with their words and energy. Others have a talent for intense focus, deep work, and creativity. Others have a natural way with people. The list goes on.

While genetics play some role in our strengths, most talents, traits, and skills are trainable. Your brain can change. It's flexible, adaptable, and capable of growing in skills, knowledge, and intelligence.

This comes from neuroplasticity. Your brain can rewire itself after a brain injury. And it can form new neural connections and pathways throughout your life, allowing you to develop new skills and capabilities.

Regardless of age and stage, through practice, consistency, and repetition, you can improve more than you realize.

If you want to learn creative writing or how to analyze issues, you can.

If you want to become a better leader, parent, or teacher, you can do that too.

If you want to improve your health, relationships, and finances, it's all within reach.

The only limit is . . . you. Don't underestimate your own capabilities, power, and potential. Don't stop before you start. And don't hold yourself back.

You are capable of so much. Your brain is not fixed like your shoe size.

KWIK STEP: Write down a skill or capability that you think you lack. Then write, "I haven't mastered _______ yet." Find one small action to take that demonstrates you're learning and growing.

AFFIRMATION: *"I can change my brain for the better. I am limitless."*

MARCH 20

DO WHAT MAKES YOU COME ALIVE

How does life make you feel?

If you answered, "stressed and burned out," then you're like most people. A recent survey from the American Psychological Association found that 57 percent of workers experienced negative impacts from work-related stress. Another study on students in higher education showed that 73.2 percent of them were moderately to highly stressed, with almost a third reporting burnout.

When you feel stretched to your limit, it's common to believe it's because you're doing too much. But what if you're not burned out because you're doing too much?

What if you're burned out because you're doing too little of what makes you come alive?

In a culture that overvalues productivity and worships busyness, rest and activities that restore our brain, body, and soul can feel "wrong." We think we don't have the time, it won't make a difference, or we feel guilty and ashamed for needing a break.

Yet that's exactly how our brain replenishes.

When you're intensely focused on achieving external goals, your *task positive network* gets activated. Energy intensive regions in the brain, including the prefrontal cortex and parietal cortex, work to help you sustain focus, concentration, problem-solving, and motivation. But too much time spent with these networks "on" can lead to mental fatigue, decision fatigue, and less cognitive flexibility.

Incorporate activities that give your brain a break. Maybe that's dancing, cooking, going to a comedy club, being in nature, reading, or crafting. Whatever you do, do it without guilt, without fear, and without self-criticism.

Do what makes you come alive to reset and replenish your brain.

KWIK STEP: Pick one activity that makes you feel alive and schedule it in your calendar today.

AFFIRMATION: *"I make time to do the things that light me up. I am limitless."*

MARCH 21

ATTENTION BY INTENTION

When a child wants your attention, they often act out. They shout, throw things, and tug on your sleeve. They make it so you can't concentrate on anything else but them.

Know what else does that today?

Technology.

Every time you pick up your phone or power up your computer, endless messages, ads, and updates bombard your brain. These flashy, noisy, distraction traps appear almost everywhere, triggering dopamine drips with the promise of novelty and the anticipation of rewards.

Digital environments are designed to grab your attention faster than your brain can defend against them. And it's taking its toll. Some studies suggest that on average, we can only stay focused on a single screen for about 47 seconds.

As your attention gets more scattered, your ability to learn becomes slower, your ability to recall information gets weaker, and your goals get pushed farther beyond reach.

So what can you do? You can practice intentionally directing your intention. Try blocking the first 30 minutes of your day for reflection, planning, and movement. No phone, e-mail, or scrolling.

You can turn off all notifications on your devices, then set a timer, take your most important task for the day, and do focused work on it for a prescribed period of time to minimize task switching.

You can set "check-ins" during the day. Carve out 10 to 15 minutes in the morning, midday, and at the end of your day to open and respond to e-mails, texts, and messages. This helps retrain your attention toward deep focus rather than the flicker of stimulation.

You can use a "digital sunset" at night. Turn off your devices, put them on silent, and stop checking them 60 to 90 minutes before you go to bed.

Focus isn't about shutting out the world but about intentionally choosing where your attention goes, minute by minute. Attention by intention paves a path to progress.

KWIK STEP: Choose one action you can take to protect your attention, directing it intentionally today.

AFFIRMATION: *"I intentionally direct my attention. I am limitless."*

RESENTMENT BLOCKS GROWTH

For years, I resented the teacher who called me "the boy with the broken brain."

What I didn't realize was that for all the years I spent holding on to the anger and bitterness of her label, my brain held on too.

Feeling resentment is holding on to a past we can't change. This emotion arises when we've been wronged by someone, taken advantage of, or mistreated. While those feelings are real, they also impose a heavy tax on our brain. Resentment drains everything: our focus, concentration, energy, productivity, and creativity.

It can often cause chronic stress too, which can shrink our hippocampus, impairing our memory and learning and slowing all our mental processes.

Letting go of resentment and forgiving those who hurt you is one of the most challenging actions you can take. It's also the most liberating.

Forgiveness doesn't mean condoning or excusing what was done to you. It's about freeing yourself from a burden that's slowly and silently draining you.

When you can release resentment, even just a little at a time, it frees up cognitive energy that you can redirect toward more productive pursuits.

Forgiveness isn't weak. It's strategic. And it isn't about the other person. It's about you, your brain, your performance, and your life because resentment blocks growth.

KWIK STEP: Think of someone who's causing you to feel resentment, anger, or hurt. Take a few minutes to write down everything you want to say to them and how they still make you feel today. Then destroy what you wrote—tear up the paper or trash the file—while repeating, "I am willing to release any resentment I am carrying."

AFFIRMATION: *"I release any resentment holding me back so I can move forward freely. I am limitless."*

MARCH 23

LAUGHTER FUELS THE BRAIN

When was the last time you really laughed? Like a deep-belly, almost-crying type of laughter?

It's easy to take our lives seriously. There's a lot we have to do, people depending on us, and tight schedules.

Yet what if you chose to laugh during the moments you usually feel frustrated, annoyed, or angry?

Just think about how often your day "gets ruined" by spilling coffee beans on the ground or knocking over a glass of water. Now imagine what it would be like to laugh during those times. How much lighter would you feel? Couldn't this change your energy, your attitude, even your entire day?

We've long heard that "laughter is medicine." To the brain, it truly is. Laughing lowers stress and cortisol levels. It releases endorphins that can help reduce pain, serotonin to boost happiness, and dopamine, which gives you that sense of pleasure and reward. When you laugh, it also strengthens learning, motivation, and memory.

Just as you can train your brain to improve memory, focus, and creativity, you can train it to access laughter more easily. Like any habit, with repetition the neural pathways grow deeper, showing the brain where to go next time.

So cancel your subscriptions to drama and negativity—and renew the ones that bring you joy, laughter, and growth. Make time to read jokes. Watch funny videos. And look for opportunities to laugh more.

Laughter truly is fuel for the brain.

KWIK STEP: Take five minutes to watch, read, or listen to something funny. Then look for chances to laugh more as you go through your day.

AFFIRMATION: *"I laugh in life. I am limitless."*

MARCH 24

THE WORLD MOVES FAST; YOU DON'T HAVE TO

What do I have to do next?

How would my life be different if I changed careers, left my relationship, or moved?

Why did John say that to me in the meeting? I wish I had responded differently.

Just as our outer world has gotten louder, so has our inner world. It's the constant chatter coming from our minds telling us we have to do more, go faster, make bigger changes, and never slow down if we want to get ahead.

While taking action in the direction of your goals and learning is crucial to removing the constraints around what's possible for your life, your worth is not defined by how busy you are, how full your calendar is, or how many tasks you can accomplish in a day.

If you keep going at a pace that's too fast for you, you run the real risk of cognitive overload, decision fatigue, and trapping your nervous system in fight, flight, freeze, or fawn.

Instead of "go, go, go," what if you adopted "go, rest, go?"

In the middle of the busiest part of your day or when you start feeling overwhelmed, take a break. Close your eyes and repeat a calming mantra to yourself. Visualize yourself breathing out stress and anxiety. Practice taking slow, steady, deep breaths in through your nose and out through your mouth. Get up and walk around for a few minutes, or go outside and get some fresh air.

Studies show short breaks help the brain learn faster. Even a five-minute pause while working on a complex task can improve concentration and attention, increase energy, and reduce fatigue.

By taking short breaks to quiet your mind, you increase activity in your prefrontal cortex. This helps you to make more rational decisions, engages your critical thinking, and brings deeper emotional regulation online.

The world moves fast; you don't have to.

KWIK STEP: Practice quieting your mind for two to five minutes right now. Close your eyes, and breathe deeply, noticing whatever thoughts pass without judging, responding, or avoiding.

AFFIRMATION: *"I sit in stillness, and there I find my wisdom. I am limitless."*

MARCH 25

FORGE NEW PATHWAYS TO POSSIBILITY

The first time you walk through a forest, it feels unfamiliar, confusing, and uncomfortable. But walk the same path for 20 years, and step by step, day by day, it would become so well worn that you would easily find your way. That's because the more often you walk those trails, the clearer and faster those pathways become.

Every time you learn something new and keep practicing it, your brain forges fresh neural pathways too, leaving a trail to follow just like in a forest, and it strengthens those pathways when neurons fire together repeatedly.

What's most empowering is that this never stops. Even as you age, your brain is capable of not only creating new neural pathways through neuroplasticity, but some regions can even generate new cells. This is known as adult neurogenesis; it mostly occurs in the hippocampus, your memory and learning hub.

This means there's a world that exists beyond what you can currently understand, imagine, or anticipate. Your brain is constantly updating its internal map, so every new skill, every failed attempt, every spark of curiosity redraws the edges of what you believe you can do.

So find something—a skill or subject—that excites you, and do it. Maybe it's learning a new language, a new dance, an instrument, or a magic trick. The "what" doesn't matter. Neuroplasticity and adult neurogenesis are activated by novelty, attention, emotion, and repetition.

Learn. Stumble. Then keep learning. And most of all, have fun.

This is how you keep growing your brain and forging new pathways to possibility.

KWIK STEP: What is one skill or subject that excites you? How can you find a way to incorporate it into your day today?

AFFIRMATION: *"I create new pathways of possibility in my brain every day. I am limitless."*

MARCH 26

"NO" ISN'T PUNISHMENT; IT'S PROTECTION

Most of us instinctively say yes when we should probably say no.

Whether it's taking on an extra project at work, a client request, attending an event, or volunteering at our child's school, we raise our hands.

But very quickly, this leads to lengthy and sometimes insurmountable to-do lists that leave us cognitively overloaded (when we've exceeded our memory capacity), wracked by decision fatigue (when we've had to make too many decisions in a day), and mentally and physically exhausted.

The world's top performers do things differently, though. Instead of the knee-jerk "yes," it's more like an immediate "no."

They are very selective and strategic about what they say yes to. They understand the power of intention and focus, and the very real risk that comes with giving too much of themselves in too many directions.

They're exceptional at creating boundaries around what matters most, especially their commitments. It's a powerful way for them to consciously direct their time, energy, and focus, so they create momentum without burnout.

Instead of fearing saying no and worrying about what others might think of you, or that you're letting them down, be strategic. Only say yes if it moves you forward, feels exciting, and is aligned with your goals.

If it doesn't, say no.

"No" isn't punishment; it's protection of you and your brain.

KWIK STEP: Audit your activities and commitments. Prioritize them based on the tasks that consume the most energy but yield the least results. Then commit to saying no by taking one of these out completely (if you can), or, at least, dialing it back.

AFFIRMATION: *"I protect my time and energy by saying no to what doesn't matter in my life, so I can say yes to what does. I am limitless."*

MARCH 27

FORGET WHAT YOU KNOW

One of the greatest barriers to learning isn't what you *don't* know—it's what you *do* know,

The moment you think you know something, you close your mind to curiosity. And when it comes to learning, curiosity is more important than certainty.

Curiosity activates dopaminergic circuits, releasing the neurotransmitter dopamine, which is linked to pleasure and motivation. Studies show that curiosity actually increases activity in your brain's reward centers, fueling motivation and enhancing learning.

Plus, when you're curious, your hippocampus—the brain's memory center—also gets activated. Research has found that people remember more information when they learn in a curious state.

So while thinking you know something closes your mind, curiosity blows it open.

How do you unlearn something? Take things you do automatically and change them up. If you brush your teeth with your right hand, switch to your left. If you take the same road to a store, take a different path. If you hold a book with both hands, use a finger or pen as a tracer. If you face forward walking up a hill, turn around and walk backward (safely). If you slip on your sneakers, untie your laces each time. Actions like these make your brain work harder. It has to learn again, so memory, focus, even creativity get enhanced.

The most successful people are incredibly fast not only at learning new techniques but at unlearning old ones.

If you want to know more, try forgetting what you already do.

KWIK STEP: Choose a task you do without thinking (brushing your teeth, making coffee or tea, tying your shoes) and do it differently today.

AFFIRMATION: *"I am a lifelong learner. I constantly seek, embrace, and find joy in every opportunity to learn. I am limitless."*

MARCH 28

REWILD YOUR BRAIN

The human brain wasn't built for a world of constant motion, glowing screens, and the pings, dings, and rings of 24/7 notifications. Every day, it's forced to filter more information at a faster pace than at any time in human history.

No wonder we're exhausted as soon as we wake, we walk into rooms and forget why we're there, or we struggle to focus for more than 10 minutes without checking our phones. Technology has brought incredible benefits, but it has also created a mental apocalypse filled with digital distraction, digital deluge, even digital dementia that has left us overstimulated, anxious, and overwhelmed.

While you can't opt out of the digital age, you can help your brain thrive in it. One secret is something your brain remembers deeply: the natural world.

Science is now revealing how it helps unlock the brain's superpowers. *Attention Restoration Theory* shows how natural environments improve working memory, attention, problem-solving, and mood. *Stress Recovery Theory* finds that viewing nature, compared to urban environments, can accelerate stress recovery, lowering blood pressure, heart rate, and cortisol levels.

While the longer you can spend immersed in nature, the better, small micro-doses like working near a window, adding potted plants to a room, or listening to nature sounds still help. Even viewing a nature scene for 40 seconds can improve attention and reduce errors.

These may sound like small details, but not to your brain. By reuniting it with the natural kingdom, you help calm the cognitive chaos—restoring clarity, connection, and creativity where it belongs.

Rewild your brain.

KWIK STEP: Choose one way to immerse yourself in nature and do it today.

AFFIRMATION: *"I am connected to nature. Every fresh breath restores my mind, resets my brain, and recharges me. I am limitless."*

LOVE YOUR BRAIN

Everyone longs to improve something about themselves.

Whether it's reading or comprehension, memory or recall, confidence or creativity, we're all working to be better.

But there's a difference between wanting to improve and *hating* something about ourselves that motivates us to change.

When we're overly critical about ourselves or some capability of ours, the repetitive negative thoughts can trigger the brain to interpret the environment as dangerous.

This activates the amygdala, which detects threats in the environment, and engages the hypothalamic-pituitary-adrenal (HPA) axis. This releases stress hormones including cortisol and norepinephrine to keep the body alert and ready to respond to dangers.

When stress becomes chronic, the brain struggles to adapt to changing situations—known as cognitive flexibility—by keeping the amygdala more active, and the prefrontal cortex less. This makes decision-making, cognition, memory, emotional regulation, and concentration harder.

So what if instead of self-hate, you fell in love with your brain for how extraordinary it is?

Like the fact that it can keep learning until the day you die. It has about 86 billion neurons, each one forming up to 10,000 synaptic connections. There are more connections in your brain than the Milky Way has stars.

Or the fact that it cleans itself, its glymphatic system flushing out toxins while you sleep.

Or that it's capable of forming and reorganizing new neural connections in response to learning, injury, and experiences—that's neuroplasticity.

No matter your age, background, or finances, your brain is capable of so much more than you realize. It can learn. It can change. It can grow in just about any direction you choose to take it.

There's nothing wrong with your brain. So love it. It just needs an upgrade.

KWIK STEP: Make a list of 5 to 10 things your brain did in the last 24 hours. Sit with each and feel how extraordinary each one was.

AFFIRMATION: *"My brain is amazing. I am limitless."*

MARCH 30

ATTENTION IS CURRENCY

We live in the attention economy. You *pay* attention—making withdrawals from your limited mental bank account—with every choice you make.

Imagine you woke up tomorrow and had to hand over your credit card for everything currently costing you attention. Before checking your e-mail, doomscrolling, responding to every text, or mindlessly surfing the web . . . every action would come with a cost.

Then how much would you want to spend on the things that gave you little to no return? How much could you save this way, and then invest in the people, projects, and experiences that truly matter?

Wealth management in all its forms begins with mind management. Your prefrontal cortex is like your brain's executive manager. It handles goal setting, self-control, emotional regulation, and decision-making. But the digital world is designed to hijack this system through dopamine-driven reward loops that get triggered every time you check, scroll, or surf.

The most valuable math you can learn is how to calculate the cost of your attention.

The secret to creating the life you dream of is simple, but not easy. Stop feeding the one you don't want, and start intentionally feeding the one you do.

Attention is your currency. Spend yours on the life you're trying to build.

KWIK STEP: Using pen and paper, make one mark every time you check your phone, e-mail, or social media today. Note the time of day, and ask, "How valuable was this? Did it move me toward something that matters?" Tonight, review your notes and choose one way to protect more of your attention tomorrow.

AFFIRMATION: *"I give my attention to what matters. I am limitless."*

MARCH 31

SELF-SABOTAGE IS IDENTITY CONFLICT

Everything we achieve in life—learning, reading, memory, even success—comes back to our identities.

It comes back to who we *believe* we are and who we *believe* we can become. This is what drives our behaviors and creates our habits.

You can learn all the best tools and strategies to upgrade your learning, memory, reading speed, leadership, or any other skill, but if you don't believe you're capable of these things, you will unconsciously sabotage yourself.

You'll forget to practice, find reasons to procrastinate, or feel too exhausted to do it. Very quickly, you will fall back into old, predictable patterns of behavior. That's because when your actions don't match your identity, your brain pulls you back to what feels "normal," even if it's unhealthy and not aligned with who you want to become.

The next time something feels "too hard" and you want to skip, procrastinate, or stop. . . pause. Hard isn't a red flag, signaling you to stop. Hard means "go." It's a sign you're doing something that matters, and hard things are usually connected to who you're becoming.

If it feels hard right now, you're probably in the middle of building something worth finishing.

Remember, self-sabotage is identity conflict. It's the friction between who you are today and who you are becoming. But when you upgrade your identity, your behavior follows.

KWIK STEP: Act like your future self in making one decision today.

AFFIRMATION: *"I am aligned with the person I am becoming. I am limitless."*

REWIRE

The Season of Growth

(April 1–June 30)

Reset, the season of clearing, created space and stillness. Now it's time to rewire your operating system. Over the next three months, you will build the habits, beliefs, and systems to thrive in an ever-changing, always-evolving world.

These months mirror spring, the season of planting and nurturing the seeds of expansion. This season will help you to:

- Build habits, routines, and behaviors that stick
- Strengthen memory, reading, and learning methods
- Upgrade limiting beliefs and master internal self-talk
- Develop consistency and confidence through small wins
- Train your focus and attention

Welcome to the season of rebuilding your brain's operating code.

APRIL 1

THERE'S NO MAGIC PILL FOR WHAT YOU WANT; BUT THERE IS A MAGIC PROCESS

We live under hypnosis, walking through life as if in a trance, believing we're not smart enough, sharp enough, or skilled enough.

So we don't go after what we want. We don't persevere when things get tough. And we don't have the conversations or take the chances that could change our lives.

Becoming limitless, creating the life you desire and deserve, requires that you break whatever trance you're under. Here's how to start:

What is it you *really* want?

Is it to create, write, or express yourself without second-guessing?

Is it to remember what you're reading or what you wanted to say in a meeting?

Is it to focus without jumping from to-dos or getting distracted?

To end the trance, you must end the belief that what you want—creativity, memory, focus—are traits outside of you that you're either born with or lacking.

To do this, take nouns and turn them into verbs.

You don't have creativity—you *do* creativity.

You don't have a good memory—you *do* memory.

You don't have focus—you *do* focus.

Then you link small behaviors with the verbs. If you want to do creativity, schedule 10 minutes outside, letting your mind wander. If you want to do focus, leave your phone in another room.

The brain learns identity from actions. Every time you *do* these things, you're teaching your brain, *"This is who I am."*

There's no magic pill for what you want, but there is a magic process.

KWIK STEP: Choose one noun you want to turn into a verb (e.g., curiosity, courage, confidence). What are three actions you can take to *do* this?

AFFIRMATION: *"I am capable of becoming who I choose to be. I am limitless."*

APRIL 2

BEFORE THE DAY LEADS YOU, YOU MUST LEAD YOUR MIND

Leadership is about more than managing others. It begins with leading yourself, and that starts the moment you wake up.

Most people begin their day reacting. They pick up their phones, check their e-mail or social media feeds, and instantly they respond to the thoughts, demands, and emotions of others. But the first hour of your day acts like a neurological warmup. This is when your brain is most susceptible to programming. Whatever you do, say, or think now will shape the rest of your day.

Creating a morning ritual allows you to set your day's direction. Start by reflecting on your current routine. Does it support or hurt your brain? Next, fine-tune your morning by adding elements like these:

Remember your dreams. As soon as you wake, recall your dreams or write them in a dream journal. This can support memory recall and creativity.

Make your bed. Make it look great, and you'll take that excellence into other activities.

Hydrate. Drink a glass of water. Even mild dehydration can impair focus, reaction time, memory, and mood.

Exercise. Morning movement, especially aerobic exercise, can benefit blood pressure and sleep. Aim for 30 minutes, but do what works like jumping jacks, push-ups, burpees, or core work to get blood and oxygen flowing.

Brush your teeth with the opposite hand and without checking your phone. Novelty sharpens attention and supports neuroplasticity.

End your shower on cold. This can increase alertness, possibly reduce inflammation, and boost mental resilience. Start with 10 seconds and build up.

Journal. Fast-forward to the end of your day and complete the sentence: "It was amazing because. . . ." Write three personal and three professional wins.

Read. Choose something inspiring to set your mindset for the day.

Meditate or breathe. This helps calm your nervous system and focus your energy.

Get sunlight. Natural light within the first hour helps align your circadian rhythm, regulating stress hormones and improving sleep.

Before the day leads you, you must lead your mind.

KWIK STEP: Identify at least three brain-enhancing morning habits you can use to create your morning ritual.

AFFIRMATION: *"My morning ritual helps me win the day. I am limitless."*

APRIL 3

LEARN TO DISCERN

Every book you read, podcast you listen to, and expert you follow comes from you making a choice.

With only so many hours in a day, you must decide how to invest your time and what gets your focus and attention. This is more than what you're doing. It's about what you're consuming.

The longer something has lasted, the longer it's likely to last. This is the Lindy Effect. It's why classics like Homer's *Odyssey,* Shakespeare's *Romeo and Juliet,* or Dale Carnegie's *How to Win Friends and Influence People* remain popular picks. A book in print for decades has earned a different kind of trust than a social media post that went viral last week.

When you're choosing what to read, what content to invest in, or what knowledge to acquire, don't just chase the latest trend or most recent release. Give weight to material that has survived, that has stood time's test and still remains powerful and potent.

Old wisdom is rarely wrong. Learn to discern the latest from the greatest.

KWIK STEP: Take an inventory of all the content you're consuming based on when it was created. Then swap one thing for something that has had more staying power.

AFFIRMATION: *"I discern what knowledge and information to consume to allow my mind and brain to expand. I am limitless."*

APRIL 4

DON'T FALL IN LOVE WITH SUCCESS; FALL IN LOVE WITH THE HABITS THAT LEAD TO IT

The world's greatest athletes mentally rehearse their routines before performing.

They don't just visualize standing on the podium with a gold medal around their neck or lifting a national trophy into the air.

They visualize the movements.

They see themselves jumping into the air and shooting a three-pointer. They see pulling their arm back and flashing forward as they use their forehand to smash the tennis ball over the net. They picture bending their knees, distributing their weight over their feet on their skis as they zip and turn, zip and turn down the mountain, hitting gate after gate in their alpine race.

Maybe your goal isn't to win an Olympic medal or a national championship. But whatever you dream about achieving—becoming a quicker learner or reader, a better speaker, or a more effective leader—it's the movements you make, and the habits you form around them, that will get you there.

Visualizing a movement activates many of the same neural pathways as actual movement. So don't just visualize the result, the treasure waiting at the end of the road. Imagine what you have to do to get there. In a study out of UCLA, students who visualized good study habits improved their grades more than students who only visualized getting the better grades.

By rehearsing the right habits, you're training your reticular activating system—your brain's filter—on what to prioritize too. So you'll start noticing people, opportunities, and ideas that can help support you as you move closer to your goal.

Don't fall in love with success; fall in love with the habits that lead to it.

KWIK STEP: Close your eyes and take a deep breath, then visualize one goal for today. Imagine in detail what it looks like when you reach the goal. Next, visualize the habits or behaviors you must execute to log the win using the same amount of detail.

AFFIRMATION: *"I focus on the habits that will make my goals real. I am limitless."*

STOP SOMETHING TO START SOMETHING NEW

It's easy to focus on what you want to add to your life, like the new habits you want to build and the new actions you want to take.

Except your brain can't endlessly stack new routines on top of the old. That can quickly lead to cognitive overload.

You first need to *stop* something to *start* something new.

The brain operates much of your daily life on habit loops—the automatic patterns stored in the basal ganglia, the region in charge of repetition and routine. These habits help your brain conserve energy by automating processes and allowing it to direct more resources to other regions, such as the prefrontal cortex, that require more complex thinking.

The more you do something, the more ingrained the neural pathway becomes, and your brain doesn't want to let go of the habit loop. That's why you need to deactivate that habit loop by simultaneously replacing it with another. Otherwise, your brain will revert to the old loop.

Habit substitution is the process of replacing one habit with another. As you engage the new habit, the neural pathways for the old one begin to fade. As they grow weaker, your brain prunes them, until one day the old habit is gone and the new one has replaced it.

So if you want to stop watching television for 15 minutes at night, replace that habit loop with 15 minutes of meditating, journaling, or reading. If you want to stop drinking alcohol with dinner, replace it with a healthier, yet still tasty, drink. If you want to stop scrolling on your phone when you wake up, replace it with writing down your dreams or visualizing what has to happen that day to make it amazing.

Stop something to start something new.

KWIK STEP: Think of something you want to start, then ask, "What needs to stop first?" Take one action today toward making this happen.

AFFIRMATION: *"I stop what no longer works to make space for what will. I am limitless."*

APRIL 6

DON'T FIGHT THE FIDGET

How do kids today defeat distraction and annihilate anxiety?

They use fidget toys. By keeping their hands busy moving, they divert excess physical energy, calm their nervous system, and increase their focus.

What works for kids also works for adults. A study from UC Davis found that adults who fidgeted with their arms or legs, or by using a fidget toy such as a stress ball, did better on cognitive tasks that demanded attention.

So next time you have to listen closely and remember what you hear, fidget. You can use a fidget toy, or repeatedly move your hand or fingers, shake a leg, or tap your foot. You can also try doodling. Studies show drawing while you listen activates more brain regions including the medial prefrontal cortex, which is associated with long-term memory processing.

The next time someone talks, and you need to listen carefully, don't fight the fidget. Use it.

KWIK STEP: At least once today, fidget while someone is talking. Then practice recalling key moments of the conversation once it's done and notice if your memory improved.

AFFIRMATION: *"I release any excess energy and anxiety that stops me from focusing and remembering what matters. I am limitless."*

APRIL 7

CREATE. CONSUME. CLEAR.

A campfire has a rhythm.

When it's first lit, it burns bright, hot, and intense. As the fire consumes the logs, the flames get lower, they darken, and their intensity wanes. Unless the fire gets stoked with new fuel, the flames will eventually die out.

Your brain performs to a similar rhythm. There are times during the day when it burns brightly, when creativity, problem-solving, and other cognitively demanding tasks seem easier. Then there are times when the flame dims and needs refueling.

To work with the natural rhythm of your brain, think about structuring your day into three categories: *Create. Consume. Clear.*

1. **CREATE**. This is when your brain experiences peak energy, performance, and cognition, so it's ideal for deep work, producing, creating, designing, problem-solving, and innovating—any demanding cognitive tasks.
2. **CONSUME**. This period is when you want to absorb information—listening to podcasts, reading books, and researching.
3. **CLEAR**. Your brain needs mental resets, opportunities to rest and rejuvenate like journaling, talking to a loved one, meditating, taking a bath, doing yoga, or writing a gratitude list.

As you think about your day, consider when your brain experiences peak energy, alertness, and performance. For some, that's in the morning. For others, it's midday or the evening. Remember, like everything else, this isn't about being perfect, and sometimes, you don't have full control over your schedule.

But understanding your brain's natural fire, knowing when to let it burn brightly, when to stoke it, and when to rest, can help boost performance, productivity, and lower stress.

Create when your mind is brightest.

Consume when your mind is open.

Clear when your mind is tired.

KWIK STEP: Today, see if you can structure your tasks and responsibilities into these three categories.

AFFIRMATION: *"I work with the natural rhythm of my brain, creating, consuming, and clearing at the ideal time. I am limitless."*

APRIL 8

ALL LEARNING IS STATE DEPENDENT

Why can we hear a few notes to a song, take a bite of a single meal, or smell a fragrance and immediately it's like we've fallen into the past?

Because memory isn't just stored in the brain—it's shaped by emotion.

In intense emotional states, your amygdala (known partly for emotional processing) signals the hippocampus (known partly for memory and learning) to encode the details of the moment. At the same time, chemicals like dopamine and norepinephrine get released to sharpen your focus and attention, which helps to tag the memory as important. This is why you can quickly recall the most emotional times, good or bad.

This process also fuels learning. If you're bored in a moment, you're likely to forget what you've seen or heard in it. But if you're in a state of excitement, curiosity, or joy, you're more likely to remember.

Whether you want to pay better attention at a meeting, remember what your kids tell you, or develop a new habit, the golden formula to use is:

Information x Emotion = Unforgettable

And you don't have to wait for a powerful emotion to strike. You have the ability to create your state—curiosity, joy, playfulness—instantly. Here's how.

Before you need to remember or learn something, take a few minutes to visualize in vivid detail what it feels like to achieve your greatest "win." Be in your body and really feel it. What do you hear? Smell? See? Sense? Where are you? Who's with you?

You can also think back to a moment when you felt happy or proud. You can get up and dance, jump around, laugh, or think of something silly. Anything that gives you a strong emotional feeling will shift your state. Now you're ready to learn, work, and tackle whatever lies before you.

Learning is state dependent, and the power to change your state lies within you.

KWIK STEP: Before starting an important task today, find one action you can take to shift your emotional state.

AFFIRMATION: *"When I shift my state, I upgrade my brain. I am limitless."*

APRIL 9

MEMORIES AND MEANING ARE MADE IN DREAMS

More than three thousand years ago, the ancient Egyptians believed dreams had the power to heal the mind and body. So strong was this belief, they trained "dream interpreters," who used special dream books—the most famous, the Egyptian Dream Book—to help understand what dreams meant.

Fast forward to today, and we might not look to dream journals for omens or divine guidance, but modern neuroscience has proven the Egyptians had uncovered a truth: *Our dreams matter.*

While you sleep, your brain cycles through four stages. The first and second are the lightest. The third is deep, restorative sleep, and the fourth, REM (Rapid Eye Movement), is marked by surges of increased brain activity. While dreaming can happen in any stage, REM dreams are the most vivid and powerful.

That's because they help your brain consolidate memories, process emotions (especially the supercharged moments of the day), and learn. Upon waking, studies show that your memory, emotional regulation, social skills, and creativity all improve with REM dreaming.

While the Egyptians used dream journals to divine meaning, you can use them as an exercise to improve your memory.

As soon as you wake, write down your dreams. It might be difficult to remember them in detail at first, but the more you do it, the better you'll get at recalling the who, what, where, when, and why. This will carry over into other areas of your life too, enhancing your memory of other moments.

Besides improving your memory, you'll open yourself to a secondary benefit when you record your dreams: self-awareness. Dreams are the realm of your unconscious. The act of writing them down takes the unconscious and makes it conscious, allowing you—if you so choose—to begin exploring the meaning behind them, the symbolism, and what your brain was attempting to make sense of, and why.

Perhaps the Egyptians weren't so far from the truth, after all.

KWIK STEP: Tonight when you go to sleep, place a pen and paper (or a journal) next to your bed. As soon as you wake, grab your paper and write down your dreams, then reflect on them.

AFFIRMATION: *"I have the ability to remember my dreams effortlessly and with ease. I am limitless."*

APRIL 10

MOVEMENT MULTIPLES LEARNING

Imagine a world where every time you moved your body, your brain grew stronger. A world where walking, dancing, or even a simple hand gesture could unlock new levels of memory, focus, and creativity.

This isn't a fantasy. It's neuroscience.

For decades, we've been told a story, one that says learning happens only when we sit still, remain quiet, and listen carefully. But modern research tells something very different.

Movement helps the brain think faster, focus deeper, and retain longer.

When your body moves, your brain lights up in ways that it doesn't while you sit. Physical motion activates the region in your brain called the cerebellum. It's largely known as the center of movement, controlling all your motor skills.

But scientists have found it also plays an important role in cognitive learning, emotional regulation, and working memory.

Research shows that *active learning*, such as using hand gestures to emphasize ideas, taking notes by hand, or pacing while explaining a concept aloud, makes memories stronger.

Your body becomes part of the learning process, and these physical cues act as anchors, which your brain links to the material. Later, when you recall the gesture or the movement, your brain can more easily and quickly retrieve the information.

Don't just think; move. Movement multiplies learning.

KWIK STEP: When you need to engage your brain today, pair it with movement—making hand gestures, writing notes by hand, pacing while in a meeting (if you can). Then try recalling what you learned a few hours later and notice the difference.

AFFIRMATION: *"I move my body to multiply my learning. I am limitless."*

APRIL 11

MAKE THE ATTAINABLE SUSTAINABLE

Let's pretend you need to get past a sleeping guard dog. The last thing you'd do is sprint. Fast, dramatic movement like that would certainly wake the animal, and you'd never make it. But moving slowly and deliberately, tiptoeing past, you'd reach the other side unnoticed.

Progress works the same way.

There's a science and art to building anything, whether it's a body, relationship, skill, business, or career. Success rarely comes from sprinting, from attempting massive change immediately. It comes from the tiny, consistent steps forward.

Understanding your brain explains why.

Your brain is wired to protect you. Big, rapid changes usually trigger the danger detector—the amygdala—sending your nervous system into fight, flight, or freeze. This releases and floods your system with stress hormones including adrenaline and cortisol, increasing feelings of anxiety, overwhelm, and tension. Sometimes, this reaction is so intense it stops you before you even begin.

Simultaneously, the prefrontal cortex goes offline as the brain prioritizes safety over long-term planning, decision-making, learning, memory consolidation, and self-control.

Small steps help you slip past your inner guard dog. They keep the nervous system calm, leaving executive functions online. Tiny wins also release dopamine, reinforcing behaviors that build new neural pathways that strengthen over time. Do this enough, and eventually you can train your brain to see growth as safety, change as possibility, and action as rewarding.

Yes, sometimes, massive action is necessary—starting the business, launching the new program, going back to school. Even then those leaps start with small beginnings—choosing a name for the business or program, or deciding what you'll study and where.

Have big goals. Be ambitious. Desire deep, profound, massive change. Just remember, your brain prefers the opposite—at first. So take small steps to make the attainable sustainable.

KWIK STEP: What's one ridiculously small step you can take toward a goal today?

AFFIRMATION: *"I take small steps, which makes my change sustainable. I am limitless."*

APRIL 12

WHAT THE BRAIN REHEARSES, THE BRAIN REMEMBERS

Most people don't remember what they had for breakfast two weeks ago, let alone naming 15 amazing things that happened to them this year.

What they do remember are the dragons that defeated them—the deal that got away, the fight with their spouse, or the test they didn't ace.

This is partly due to the brain's *negativity bias*, a tendency for the brain to encode more deeply the memory of mistakes, failures, and slip-ups. It's an ancient survival mechanism held over from our days of being the hunter or the hunted. A mistake then was literally life or death.

Today, most mistakes aren't threatening our survival. The downside is that we can learn to *fear* mistakes, while believing that's all we are—our mistakes. Slowly, this can erode our self-confidence and self-esteem.

While we want to learn from the dragons that defeat us, we also want to acknowledge the ones we slay every day.

Before going to sleep each night, write a short note to yourself, naming one to three victories—big or small. "I read for 20 minutes." "I went to the gym." "I admitted I was wrong." "I had a great conversation with my kid."

Recalling positive moments has been shown to help build self-confidence and self-esteem. These memories help manage your stress and improve moods by activating reward networks. And if you reframe a negative memory into a positive one like finding the lesson in a mistake, it becomes a training exercise for your brain.

By acknowledging what you accomplished, you keep your brain motivated and focused on what matters—learning and making progress toward your goals. You also solidify your identity as someone who's always growing, always learning, always moving forward no matter the fears, mistakes, or costs.

What the brain rehearses, the brain remembers.

KWIK STEP: Before you go to sleep tonight, write three wins from today.

AFFIRMATION: *"I choose to remember my daily victories, so my brain remembers my worth. I am limitless."*

APRIL 13

YOU CAN'T STEER A PARKED CAR

Imagine you're sitting behind the wheel of your dream car. You've started the engine, set the destination in your GPS, and queued your favorite playlist. You're ready to go, so you turn the wheel and . . . nothing happens.

You're not moving, because the car is still in Park.

When you're gripped by perfectionism and procrastination, it's a lot like trying to steer a parked car. No matter how hard you try, no matter if you have the vision, resources, and goals set, you can't seem to move.

Fortunately, your brain doesn't need a perfect plan. It just needs movement—any movement, no matter how small—to create the motivation and momentum necessary to overcome perfectionism and procrastination.

One small step is literally all it takes for the brain to want to take the next. That's because of something called the Zeigarnik effect. In 1927, the psychologist Bluma Zeigarnik discovered that unfinished tasks create a tension in the brain that nudges us to finish them. As research suggests, whenever something goes unfulfilled, our thoughts will drift more toward what needs completing than what's been completed.

Modern researchers have also found that we get hits of dopamine—the "feel good" neurotransmitter—not only when we achieve our goals, but anytime we make progress in their direction.

That's why starting small is so powerful. One small action—writing a single sentence, walking for five minutes, making one phone call—shifts your brain into Drive, and it'll want to keep going.

KWIK STEP: Think about something you've put off. Make a list of the steps it involves, then focus on the first small one—a mini-action that you can take today—and do it.

AFFIRMATION: *"I direct the course of my life. I take one step at a time, and I trust that I will end up exactly where I belong. I am limitless."*

APRIL 14

THE POWER OF REMEMBERING

Long ago and far away, a nine-year-old child once played.

They weren't thinking about their long-term goals or five-year plans. They weren't focused on how to improve their lives, achieve success, or even how to realize their dreams. They were simply being—curious, creative, and joyful in the present.

Then that nine-year-old grew up. That nine-year-old was you.

A lot has happened between then and now. But if you could time-travel into the past to sit cross-legged on the floor beside your younger self, what would you want to tell them?

What would you want them to know about their journey ahead? About the trials, challenges, and adversities they'll face?

About the courage and inner strength they'll uncover? About the love they'll experience and the superpowers they'll unlock?

This imagined conversation between your past and present self is more than a fun exercise. It's a neural simulation that engages the same emotional and cognitive circuits that activate during a genuine conversation.

And when practiced with self-compassion, talking with your past self can help soften the negative self-judgments and inner talk that you might have carried about yourself and your life for years. That's because it allows your brain to give new emotional meaning to your past experiences. It takes the old stories of "I can't," "I'm too late," or "If only the past were different" and rewrites them with curiosity, trust, and confidence.

Just as your future self is patiently waiting for you, your nine-year-old self waits too—to remind you how far you've come, how much you've achieved, and how much is still possible.

That's the power in remembering.

KWIK STEP: Imagine sitting cross-legged next to your nine-year-old self and talking to them about the road ahead. Visualize or write down everything that you'd want to tell them, including the obstacles and challenges, how you overcame them, the wins, and what advice you'd give them about what's to come.

AFFIRMATION: *"I see, honor, and welcome every version of myself, including my past. I am limitless."*

APRIL 15

DESIGN YOUR DESTINY

In the 1980s, the Saturday morning cartoon *GI Joe: A Real American Hero* always ended with teaching kids what they should do if they were in danger. The last line became a popular catchphrase: "Now you know. And knowing is half the battle."

Knowledge *alone* isn't power. If it were, then none of us would eat foods we know we shouldn't. We wouldn't stay up late scrolling on our phones. And we wouldn't live in a constant state of stress, never giving our brain a break.

GI Joe's "half the battle" is closer to the truth. Power doesn't come from knowing alone. It comes from application, from pairing knowledge *with* action.

If you pause and get really still for a moment, you'll probably recognize there is something you deeply want to start. Not something you're already doing, but something new and exciting that you know will improve your brain, your body, and your life.

Maybe it's one more workout a week. Maybe it's a 15-minute walk in the morning. Maybe it's keeping a journal on your nightstand to record your dreams. Maybe it's going to the grocery store and buying blueberries to throw into a smoothie, or meditating for five minutes a day.

To change your brain, your body, and your life, you must first change your choices. What you know is half the battle. Now pair it with action. That's how you design your destiny.

KWIK STEP: Identify one new behavior, habit, or routine that you want to start, and act on it today.

AFFIRMATION: *"I design my destiny. I am limitless."*

TRAIN YOUR BRAIN TO READ

A study by the National Endowment for the Arts found that almost half of adults—46.5 percent—didn't read a single book in a year.

It's not because we don't care about learning or improving ourselves. It's that modern life pulls us in so many distractions. Between being burned out by work demands, overwhelmed by family commitments, and overloaded from digital deluge and distractions, it often feels like our brains can't concentrate for more than 30 seconds.

Sitting and focusing for 10 to 20 minutes can feel like trying to run a marathon without having the stamina, muscle strength, or mental preparation to go the distance.

And for many of us, reading can also feel stressful. We worry we're too slow, that we can't understand or won't remember what we just read.

While we may feel there's something wrong with us, neuroscience shows us something different—our brains simply haven't been trained to read. But you can change that.

One of the most powerful reading tools is something your teachers probably would have scolded you for using: your finger.

Your eyes are attracted to motion—it's a basic survival mechanism built into your system. For your ancestors, if a bush moved, they had to pay attention to it. Either it was lunch, or they could be lunch.

Today, emerging research shows that using a visual pacer like your finger, pen, or the keyboard mouse helps improve your focus—helps your eyes better track the movement—which can translate into improving your reading speed, comprehension, and memory.

So forget what your teachers told you. Use your finger to guide your eyes, and you'll train your brain's ability to read.

KWIK STEP: Pick up an easy, light book and mark the line where you start. Next, time yourself for two minutes reading at your normal speed. Then count the lines you just read. Then count the number of words per line, say an average of 10, and multiply that by the number of lines you read. Finally, divide this number by two to give you roughly the number of words per minute.

Now do this exercise again, but use your finger or a pen as a pointer. Calculate your words per minute and see if it's different. Notice how it felt too.

AFFIRMATION: *"I train my brain to read. I am limitless."*

APRIL 17

FILTER, THEN FOCUS

There was a time when the biggest highs and crashes we had to worry about came from sugar. Today, our challenge is dopamine—the neurotransmitter that teaches the brain what to notice and repeat.

Our digital world has unknowingly trained many people to seek quick hits of stimulation. Every notification we check and every feed we refresh engages the reward-learning circuitry. It's not the content hooking us—it's the novelty and anticipation of what we're about to find that triggers dopamine.

Just as a steady diet of soda and sweets leaves the body starving for nutrients, a diet of constant digital cues leaves our brain overstimulated and easily distracted. With each ping, ding, and ring we instantly check, we train our brain to need another quick hit. This can make slower, more meaningful sources of pleasure, such as reading, studying, or being in nature, feel boring.

But your brain can be retrained.

Instead of responding to every digital cue, what if you designated "tech free" rooms in your home? Or set aside 30 to 60 minutes daily, or a day on the weekend, when you don't check devices? Or maybe you don't take them to bed, or avoid using them on breaks, while you're eating, or when outside.

At the same time, you can add healthy dopamine-supporting activities like getting morning sunlight, performing random acts of kindness, listening to unfamiliar music, exercising, studying, even exposing your body to cold. These activities trigger steady dopamine releases that improve your focus, emotional resilience, and motivation.

As you reduce the digital dopamine hits and rebuild the rewarding real-life habits, your brain adapts. Don't let technology control you—you control it. Filter, then focus.

KWIK STEP: Pick one digital detox and one healthy dopamine-supporting activity, and use both today.

AFFIRMATION: *"I control my technology, so I control my focus. I am limitless."*

YOU'RE ONE SMALL STEP AWAY FROM MASSIVE CHANGE

In Olympic competitions like downhill skiing, swimming, or sprinting, the difference between a gold medal around someone's neck or a silver comes down to mere seconds, sometimes a fraction of one. One second, sometimes a fraction of a second, can dramatically change someone's life.

That holds true in other parts of life too. Those who succeed often have put in just a small amount more effort. They've had just a little more discipline. They've done a little more practice. A little more training, learning, or serving. And that little bit more brings incredible rewards.

What area in your life could you put just a little more effort into? Could it be in your relationships, health, physical training? Perhaps it's building a new skill or upgrading a capability?

Just one more rep, one more minute of reading, one more lap around the track, one more run-through of your presentation, one more written page, or one more moment being fully present with someone.

Every time you challenge yourself like this, the brain's reward system strengthens its sense of value in the outcome. This is known as the IKEA effect, a cognitive bias that researchers discovered when they observed that people who built objects for themselves (like assembly-required IKEA furniture) tended to value those pieces more highly than the same objects built by someone else.

When you invest in building skills and capabilities, it creates a sense of ownership, accomplishment, and pride. When you put in a little more effort, your brain's dopamine system reinforces that effort, rewarding you with motivation and helping wire new neural pathways, making it easier for you to take one more small step the next time.

There is a genius inside of you, and to unleash it, your brain needs challenges. They don't have to be monumental—just small steps—but they can lead to massive change.

KWIK STEP: Pick an area of your life that you want to change, and take a small step toward it today.

AFFIRMATION: *"I am only one small step away from changing my life forever. I am limitless."*

APRIL 19

PRIME YOUR BRAIN TO PERFORM

When night turns to day, the sun doesn't pop into the sky immediately; it rises gradually. The same thing happens in the evening when the light slowly fades. These are transitions, and they aren't negotiable. They are a law of nature.

Your brain functions under laws of transitions too. It doesn't just snap into peak performance, focus, or creativity like flipping a switch. It transitions, using circadian and ultradian rhythms to help regulate the rise and fall of your energy, alertness, and attention.

This is where your "brain warm-up" comes in. By creating a regular routine, you help the brain transition to "go time."

Your routine could be reading something inspiring or thought provoking for a few minutes before diving into work or studying.

It could be free writing in a journal, allowing whatever thoughts, feelings, and ideas to come up and out.

It could be meditating for five minutes, slowing your breath, and bringing your awareness into the present moment.

It could be spending five minutes doing cross-crawls, marching in place, jumping jacks, stretches, or other light physical movements.

It could be reviewing your purpose of the work or study you're about to start, asking yourself, "Why does this matter? What's the end goal?"

It could be visualizing what it will look and feel like after you've completed the task.

The best "brain warm-up" is the one that helps your brain begin. Try one from the list above. Combine a few. Make up your own.

Just prime your brain to perform.

KWIK STEP: What's one "brain warm-up" you can practice today?

AFFIRMATION: *"I am priming my brain to perform. I am limitless."*

APRIL 20

PRACTICE BECOMES PERMANENT

Psychologist Wendy Wood discovered that we automatically repeat about 43 percent of what we do every day while we're thinking about something else. That's nearly half of our life lived out of habit, without conscious choice.

What if you could change that? What if every thought you think, every word you speak, and every action you take could be not just a habit, but a practice?

That's how your brain works. Repetition can carve new pathways (that's neuroplasticity) and strengthen existing ones in your brain, making it easier and faster for the brain to access the next time.

Every time you reach for an apple instead of a cookie, you train for healthier choices. Every time you feel stressed, and you pause to give yourself compassion and grace, you train to access calmer responses. And every time you choose a meaningful project over turning on your favorite show, you train your brain for deep work.

This is how you create a habit loop—the more you repeat something, the more automatic it becomes.

Your goal isn't perfection. Your brain doesn't need that. It thrives on learning and progress. So every thought, feeling, and behavior becomes the practice, until one day, you don't even notice what you're doing.

Because what you practice does more than shape your habits—it shapes you. What you practice becomes permanent.

KWIK STEP: Write the top three things you want to practice today, whether they're thoughts, feelings, or actions. Then commit to practicing them throughout the day.

AFFIRMATION: *"What I practice becomes permanent, so I intentionally choose my thoughts, actions, and feelings. I am limitless."*

APRIL 21

YOUR POWER EXISTS HERE

The present is all we have.

We know this universal truth, yet why is it so hard to stay in the now?

You might be talking with a loved one, but mentally replaying a conversation with your boss, employee, or client from earlier. You could be working on a report when your mind shifts to errands you need to run later, or thoughts of *why haven't I started that business yet?*

These aren't character flaws. They're how the brain works. It acts like a pendulum, swinging between past memories and possible futures. At the brain's most basic level, its chief goal is keeping your body alive. To do that, it constantly predicts the future based on information from the past and sensory data from the present.

While the brain is simply doing its job, the downside is the swinging pendulum can lead to anxiety, fear, depression, rumination, and analysis paralysis. That's partly because the brain has a negativity bias. It pays more attention to negative experiences than positive ones. There's also interpretation bias: When an experience is ambiguous or uncertain, the brain tends to gauge it negatively.

Training ourselves to notice when the brain wanders, then returning it to the present, can help regulate the brain's fear response, anxiety, and other negative emotions. This is where mindfulness comes in.

Mindfulness is more than meditation, although that's one useful tool for training presence. Mindfulness simply brings our attention to the moment. It's associated with increased activity in networks supporting attention and emotional regulation, including the anterior cingulate cortex and the prefrontal cortex.

A useful mindfulness technique is the 5-4-3-2-1 method. Count five things you can see, four you can touch, three you can hear, two you can smell, and one you can taste. This helps ground your brain in the now.

The only place your power truly exists is here—making this moment mean everything.

KWIK STEP: Practice the 5-4-3-2-1 method right now, then use it throughout the day as many times as you can remember to help bring you into the present.

AFFIRMATION: *"I live in the now. I am limitless."*

APRIL 22

THE THOUGHTS YOU PLANT GROW INTO THE LIFE YOU LIVE

If you want a flower garden, you can't just wish for it or complain you don't have it. You need to go buy the seeds you want—not weeds, but plants that will one day become beautiful. Then you plant them, water them, and continue nurturing them as they grow.

When it comes to growth, upgrading your brain, and changing your habits, your thoughts are the seeds of the life you create.

The hard, yet honest, truth is you can make excuses, or you can make progress, but you can't make both.

When you focus your thoughts on complaints—on what isn't going right or isn't going your way—it hijacks your attention. It signals what's important to your reticular activating system, so you keep finding more instances of what isn't right.

This is how you get stuck in negative thought patterns, habits, and behavior loops that steal your energy, focus, and time.

Constant complaining and wishing also creates a pattern called *learned helplessness*—the sense that you can't control anything in life. So you don't take risks, learn new skills, set goals, or advance toward them.

But like planting a garden, you choose the seeds to plant in your mind.

Don't wish for something; work for it. Don't say what matters; show it. Don't complain; focus on what you can do to change.

Accept responsibility for your thoughts and emotions. Be accountable to your commitments and actions. Learn from your mistakes.

The thoughts you plant grow into the life you live.

KWIK STEP: Think of one repeating wish or complaint that's been looping. What's one new thought, emotion, or action you can take to change it?

AFFIRMATION: *"I intentionally choose my thoughts to create the life I want. I am limitless."*

APRIL 23

CHANGE YOUR BRAIN, CHANGE YOUR LIFE

Madam C. J. Walker is widely considered America's first self-made female millionaire. An incredible feat for a woman born to sharecroppers in 1867. For most of her life, she faced poverty, illness, and discrimination before launching a line of hair products that transformed her life and thousands of others. She went on to employ 40,000 African Americans and contributed financially to numerous philanthropic organizations.

This wasn't a case of overnight success or luck. It came from Madam Walker's persistence, constant reinvention, and a belief that she could change her life.

You have the same power to change your life—and that starts with changing your brain. To make fast, lasting change, use "The 3 Cs."

1. **CONSISTENCY.** To break old habits, you have to be consistent with new ones—each repetition strengthens new neural pathways. Whether it takes 21 or 120 days, stick with it.
2. **CHANGE.** In today's world of swiftly evolving technology, change isn't something that's nice to have, it's a necessity. You must constantly learn and upgrade your skills and capabilities, change your thoughts, and build new habits.
3. **CHALLENGE.** Transformation requires challenge. The caterpillar can't become the butterfly unless it pushes its way out of the cocoon. It's the struggle that builds the butterfly's strength to fly.

Similarly, your brain can't grow unless you challenge it. This is known as *desirable difficulty*; it's doing tasks that require more effort. At first, it feels harder, but over time, it gets easier as your brain learns, adapts, and grows.

Consistency. Change. Challenge. This is how you change your brain to change your life. Change your life, and you could change the world.

KWIK STEP: Choose one habit, thought pattern, or capability you want to change. Begin by taking three slow breaths, then visualize yourself performing it. If you can, act it out. Finally, when you feel like stopping, hold the visualization or action a little longer.

AFFIRMATION: *"As I change my brain, I change my life. I am limitless."*

APRIL 24

TAKE THE INVISIBLE AND MAKE IT VISIBLE

What do athletes, visionaries, and entrepreneurs share?

They turn their visions into realities.

We're all capable of this, but most people fail for one reason: Their visions stay stuck in their heads. They think about their goals, and that's as far as they get. While thoughts can change the brain, change accelerates when we pair our thoughts with action, emotion, and visualization.

Instead of simply thinking about your goals, write them, feel them, see them.

Studies consistently show that people who write down specific goal plans, especially when paired with actions, are more likely to follow through. When you write something, you're telling your brain, "This matters."

Then pair your goal with a daily action you can measure. If your goal is "lose 20 pounds," combine that with "walk 10,000 steps, eat protein with every meal, and cut sugar." These are known as lag and lead measures. A lag measure is an outcome you can't fully control. A lead measure is a daily action you can control that makes the outcome more attainable.

You want to feel your goals, because your brain is wired to hold on to what's emotional much more than what's just logical and rational. Emotion plus information becomes long-term memory. So as you write your goals down, feel in your body what it's like to have reached them.

You also want to see your goals, because that activates the brain's reticular activating system—what your conscious mind notices. If you write and post them somewhere you'll see them, like on the bathroom mirror or your phone's lock screen, your brain gets the regular reminder to pay attention. So you become more likely to notice information, people, and opportunities that can support your vision.

Write your goal. Feel it. See it. That's how you take the invisible and make it visible.

KWIK STEP: Write down three specific goals, including a lag and lead for each, for the next three months. Feel each one, then place them where you'll see them daily.

AFFIRMATION: *"I take the invisible and make it visible. I am limitless."*

APRIL 25

BREAK THE BAD, BUILD THE BETTER

Breaking bad habits has very little to do with your willpower.

If you're struggling, wondering why you can't stop something, understand it's because your brain is resisting.

The brain builds habit loops using a four-step process: Cue > Craving > Response > Reward.

Habits gets stored in the basal ganglia, a brain area that helps automate behavior. Then when a cue hits—like a time of day, a specific person, a feeling like boredom, or seeing an object—the brain goes, "I know what to do," and kicks in the craving for the habitual response or reward.

That's why your habits feel automatic, happening without much conscious thought, because they are.

This means you can't simply stop a habit. You have to replace it with another. One way to help the brain build a different habit loop is to link a new behavior with something you're already doing consistently.

Let's say every afternoon around 3 P.M., your energy crashes and brain fog rolls in, and that's when you reach for something sweet. Use the time and feeling as your cue to stand, move your body, drink a glass of water, and eat blueberries.

If you want to stop doomscrolling first thing in the morning, leave your phone in the living room the night before. As soon as you open your eyes, write down your dreams in a journal. Visualize what will make the day feel like a victory. Then make your bed, hydrate, and take a walk outside, all before you pick up your phone.

When you *neurostack*—combining multiple brain-boosting habits—onto existing routines, it helps your brain follow a predictable path. Over time, that new loop becomes automatic, just like the old one. Only now, it's working for you.

Break the bad, build the better.

KWIK STEP: What is one habit you want to break? And what new habits will you neurostack today and when?

AFFIRMATION: *"I am capable of building the habits I choose that support my goals. I am limitless."*

APRIL 26

WHAT YOU REINFORCE, YOU REWARD

Are you tired of forgetting where you put your keys, where you parked the car, or blanking on someone's name—again?

Every day can feel like a fight to focus, remember, and pay attention. These aren't just things we do. They're habits we can build and support.

Instead of focusing on forgetting where you put your keys or parked the car or what that person's name is, try reinforcing all the times you get it right by celebrating your victories. That's how you build the habit of remembering, paying attention, and focusing.

The three critical moments to celebrate your victory are:

1. When you remember to remember
2. When you're in the process of doing the act
3. When you've completed it

Say you want to journal. When you remember to do it, celebrate with self-praise. "Yes, I remembered," or "I'm awesome." Then while you're journaling, celebrate again, "I'm great," or "I'm incredible." Finally, when you've finished journaling, congratulate yourself with "I'm limitless," or "wow, I'm epic."

We're good at beating ourselves up for our mistakes, or what we think we've done wrong. Celebrating helps change that by triggering the molecule of motivation—dopamine—that lights up your brain's reward centers, encouraging more of the behavior.

You can use this strategy for anything—remembering where you put your keys or parked your car, learning a new language, exercising, any habit you want to build.

Remember, what you reinforce, you reward.

KWIK STEP: Celebrate yourself right now. Pick a habit, take the action, and celebrate those three moments of victory.

AFFIRMATION: *"What I reinforce, I reward. I intentionally choose the habits I want to grow. I am limitless."*

APRIL 27

BRIGHT BEGINNINGS BUILD A BRIGHTER BRAIN

Your brain doesn't wake up just because your alarm clock goes off.

It relies on signals from your environment that tell it when to release specific chemicals to control the sleep-wake cycle. This is known as your circadian rhythm—it's your body's 24-hour internal clock, regulating when you feel alert and tired.

One of the most powerful signals comes from sunlight, especially in the morning. Just natural light hitting your eyes the way your ancestors experienced it for hundreds of thousands of years. Although our mornings now begin with alarms, the brain is still wired to rise with the sun and rest and sleep in the dark.

When you step outside in the first 30 to 60 minutes of waking, the sunlight hits your eyes, activating your internal master clock. This triggers the release of cortisol, which fuels energy, alertness, and focus. It also helps regulate serotonin, which improves your mood. At the same time, morning sunlight suppresses melatonin, your sleep hormone, so you stop feeling drowsy or foggy.

Every morning, practice stepping outside, even if it's cloudy, hazy, or rainy. This is one way you can give your brain what it needs to wake up and truly shine.

Bright beginnings build a brighter brain.

KWIK STEP: Go outside for 5 to 10 minutes within the first hour of waking today and tomorrow.

AFFIRMATION: *"I align my life with my brain and body's natural rhythm. I am limitless."*

APRIL 28

TO ACTIVATE YOUR BRAIN, FIRST ACTIVATE YOUR BODY

Picture a child learning to walk.

You don't see them reading a manual, sitting in a classroom, or listening to a lecture. No, they learn by moving. They stand up, wobble, fall. Stand up, wobble, fall.

They cycle through this loop again and again; each time, the neurons in their brain strengthen their motor control, balance, coordination, and timing. Through repetition, their brain encodes those movements, and their recall grows faster, until the moment when walking becomes automatic.

Kids don't just learn this way with walking—this learning process happens with everything. They touch, explore, sense, and move through the world, and as they do, their brains constantly learn.

Learning isn't passive, still, and motionless, as we've been taught. It's active, alive, and an embodied experience. This is the idea behind what's called *embodied learning.* Studies show that learning performance often improves when mental and physical activities get paired.

When you move, your brain releases neurochemicals including dopamine, serotonin, and norepinephrine. This helps improve focus, motivation, and regulates your moods.

This doesn't mean running a marathon either. Go for a 15-minute walk before studying, working, or an important meeting. Take notes by hand or doodle. Pace the room while learning or on a call. Gesture with your hands. Stand on one leg.

Think of movement as your brain's natural "on switch." So if you want to activate your brain, first activate your body.

KWIK STEP: Pick a movement and incorporate it into your workflow today—before a meeting, during a work or study session, or when you're stuck on a problem. Notice how you feel during and after.

AFFIRMATION: *"I activate my brain by activating my body. I am limitless."*

OPTIMIZE YOUR BRAIN'S POTENTIAL BY OPTIMIZING YOUR EVENING

Imagine you just woke up after a bad night's sleep. How do you feel? Heavy? Exhausted? Foggy? Already behind?

When you sleep, your brain organizes itself and consolidates short-term memories into long-term ones. It also undergoes a "deep clean," flushing metabolic waste between neurons. Buildup of this waste is associated with a higher risk of neurodegenerative diseases like Alzheimer's.

To improve your sleep, create an evening ritual that helps your nervous system shift into the parasympathetic state—your rest, digest, and repair mode.

MAKE IT DARKER AND COLDER. Darkness and cooler temperatures support melatonin release.

CREATE A "NO DEVICE ZONE." Keep your bedroom for sleep only, and leave the screens out.

GET WARM. A sauna or hot shower raises, then drops your core temperature, promoting relaxation, reducing stress, and releasing melatonin.

READ FICTION. Light reading reduces cognitive overload and supports relaxation.

STOP CAFFEINE AFTER 12 P.M. Caffeine has a half-life of roughly five to six hours. Stopping early gives your brain more time to clear it.

SLOW YOUR HEART RATE. Trade intense workouts with practices that stimulate the vagus nerve, such as meditation, yin yoga, or yoga nidra.

TALK ABOUT YOUR DAY. Tell a loved one what happened, what went well, and what you're grateful for. This strengthens your episodic memory and builds connection.

JOURNAL. Spend five minutes reflecting on the day, what you learned, and what you're looking forward to tomorrow.

KEEP IT CONSISTENT. Your brain loves a routine. Wake up and go to sleep at the same time every day, even on the weekends.

Optimize your brain's potential by optimizing your evening.

KWIK STEP: What are at least three habits you can add to your evening ritual? Start tonight.

AFFIRMATION: *"I use my evenings to effortlessly and enjoyably rest my brain. I am limitless."*

APRIL 30

PRACTICE TURNS THE NOVICE INTO THE MASTER

To create a new trail in the forest, you have to walk the path day after day. The first steps are always the most awkward and difficult, and it can feel like nothing is changing. Yet with each repeated step, it wears away the grass until eventually a path forms. Walking in the woods then becomes easy.

Whatever you want to master—a new skill, habit, or mindset—it comes through repetition. That's not repeating tasks mindlessly. It's *deliberate practice.* Here's how it works:

1. Break a new skill into small steps.
2. Set specific goals for each.
3. Focus on slightly challenging yourself.
4. Get immediate feedback.
5. Assess and adjust.
6. Repeat.

When your practice is intentional, your brain moves from passive exposure to active engagement. This strengthens memory encoding and accelerates how quickly your brain learns and adapts. Each repetition wraps your neural circuits in myelin, a coating around the fibers connecting your neurons that makes signals travel faster and more reliably.

Every time you practice this loop, it's as if you're creating a pathway in your brain that gets deeper, stronger, and more easily traversed the next time.

This is how you make real progress. Practice turns the novice into the master.

KWIK STEP: Choose one small skill or habit to practice (such as speaking up in a meeting, remembering names, learning five words in a new language). Repeat this loop once a day for five days.

AFFIRMATION: *"I am consistent with my practice. I am limitless."*

BREAK FOR BRILLIANCE

Your brain wasn't built to go 24 /7 without rest. Yet, in today's "always-on-the-go" world, we seem to think it needs to. How else can we respond to the constant barrage of texts, e-mails, phone calls, and obligations at work and home?

Hours stuck behind our screens only make it worse. Cognitive science tells us that after about 25 to 30 minutes—roughly the span of a sitcom—our concentration and focus dips, hurting our learning, memory, performance, and productivity.

To counteract this modern life challenge, try giving your brain 5-minute breaks after 25 to 30 minutes of concentrated study or work. This will help recharge and rejuvenate your brain, keeping it sharp, engaged, and ready to learn.

Taking regular breaks helps to create what are called primacy effects and recency effects.

Primacy effects mean you tend to remember more information at the beginning.

Recency effects mean you remember at the end.

So if I give you a list of 30 words, you're more likely to remember the first 5—that's primacy—and the last 5—that's recency. The ones in the middle, you're more apt to forget.

By giving yourself regular brain breaks every 25 to 30 minutes, you create more primacy and recency effects—more "beginnings" and "ends" to retain information. In the long run, you'll boost your memory, learning, productivity, and engagement.

Break for brilliance.

KWIK STEP: Today, take at least one to three 5-minute brain breaks. After 25 to 30 minutes of concentrated focus, pause and do three things (in no particular order) for a quick recharge:

Take a few deep, slow belly breaths to calm your nervous system.

Drink one glass of water to hydrate.

Stand and move—march in place, do jumping jacks, pushups, or burpees—to get blood and oxygen flowing.

AFFIRMATION: *"I honor my brain by giving it the breaks it needs to learn, remember, create, and thrive. I am limitless."*

MAY 2

AUTOMATE TO ELEVATE

When small choices feel hard—like what to eat, what to wear, or even what toothpaste to buy—you've done nothing wrong. It's a sign of decision fatigue.

Your prefrontal cortex, which is like your brain's headquarters where planning, attention, and impulse control largely reside, can get tired as the day drags on. With each decision it makes, it uses up glucose—energy—that fuels your brain's various functions.

The more choices you make throughout the day, the harder each one becomes for a brain that's run low on resources. That's one reason why it can feel easier to order takeout or binge-watch your favorite show after a long, stressful day than to cook a healthier meal or go for a run.

To reduce decision fatigue, you'll see many high performers automate the simple decisions, like what to wear. Steve Jobs was known for always wearing a black turtleneck with jeans and sneakers. Barack Obama only wears blue or gray suits. Tony Hsieh, founder of Zappos, would only wear his company's T-shirts. By making one decision about what to wear, you free up mental space and cognitive power for the brain to focus on the more meaningful and demanding tasks.

You'll never eliminate all decisions, so aim for automating as many small ones as you can. That could be doing meal prep on a Sunday so you eat the same foods all week. Maybe it's simplifying your wardrobe like Jobs or Hsieh, automating your morning routine, or buying the same brand of a product so you aren't deciding every time you shop.

This is how you save energy, allowing your brain to direct resources toward what will make the biggest difference in your life—toward creativity, innovation, and decision-making. Automate to elevate.

KWIK STEP: What is one part of your day that you could automate? Pick one, then commit to doing it today.

AFFIRMATION: *"I save my energy for what matters the most. I am limitless."*

MAY 3

FORGET TIME MANAGEMENT; THINK *PRIORITY* MANAGEMENT

Imagine waking up every morning and finding $86,400 dollars in your bank account. It's yours to spend, but only until midnight, when whatever's left disappears.

There's only one rule: You must spend that money to buy every second of your day—86,400 to be exact. So every time you scroll on your phone, take a call, have a conversation or meeting, or even work out, you pay for it.

If every second has a cost, how would that change what you say yes or no to?

Your time and attention are finite, so are you spending them on what truly matters, on what gives you maximum rewards?

You'll always have responsibilities and obligations that only you can meet. But what about the ones you can delegate or find ways to streamline? Become great at priority management by freeing yourself from low-value activities so you can give more of your valuable time, energy, and attention to the high-impact ones.

It's not about *time* management; it's about *priority* management.

KWIK STEP: Make a list of all your responsibilities and commitments for the day, and identify one to three low-value activities you can cut or delegate. Then do it and notice how your energy, focus, and attention change.

AFFIRMATION: *"My time, energy, and attention are precious. I only give them to high-impact work and people. I am limitless."*

PROGRESS THAT'S HONORED GETS REMEMBERED

It's great to focus on what you need to do to move your goals forward. It's also important to pause and look back at what you've done so far.

It's easy to minimize your successes or small wins. But these matter, perhaps more than the big ones. They are the daily signs you are changing, evolving, and growing. When you stay consistent, day after day, eventually you can look back and see how far you've come.

The person staring at you in the mirror isn't the same person who gazed back at you six months ago. That version of you, whether it's 6 months or 12 months ago, 6 years or 25 years, has been through so much, and they deserve to be acknowledged and honored.

You can tell yourself, "I'm proud of you for sticking with this," or "way to show your strength on _________," or "you were so courageous when you ________."

Celebrating small wins releases dopamine that signals to the brain "this was positive; remember it, and repeat it." This makes celebrating the actions and effort that led to the positive outcome a teaching moment.

It also helps boost your self-confidence and competence. fMRI studies have found that self-affirmations increase activity in the brain's regions connected to self-processing and valuation, linking motivation with behavior.

So go celebrate your successes. Celebrate your small wins. Celebrate your progress.

Progress that's honored gets remembered. And what your brain remembers, it's more likely to repeat.

KWIK STEP: Tonight, write three wins from the day you feel proud of and repeat to yourself, "I am proud of you for ______________."

AFFIRMATION: *"I am proud of my progress. I am limitless."*

MAY 5

PEOPLE REMEMBER PEOPLE WHO REMEMBER THEM

Have you been at the grocery store, in a coffee shop, or at an event, and someone approaches you, smiling? You recognize them, but their name escapes you. What makes it worse? They have the audacity to remember yours.

Moments like this aren't just embarrassing. They erode your self-confidence.

Now imagine walking into a room, meeting 10 new people, leaving, and saying goodbye to everyone by name. Who will they remember when they leave? *You*. Because you made them feel seen and appreciated—and deep down, that's all anyone wants.

That's what makes remembering names a standout skill—one you can improve with practice. To confidently remember names, be SUAVE.

S — SAY. When you meet someone, say their name. Repeating it lets you hear it twice, once from the person, and once from yourself, boosting recall. If their name is Rosita, say "Rosita, it's nice to meet you."

U — USE. During the conversation, use—not abuse—their name, dropping it a few times. "That's really interesting, Shaun." Rehearsal like this helps encode long-term memory.

A — ASK. What's everyone's favorite subject? Themselves. Ask questions about hobbies, interests, or what's lighting them up. If they have a unique name, ask where it's from, what it means, or how to spell it.

V — VISUALIZE. Pair the name with a vivid image. This is called *dual coding*—the brain uses different systems for processing information. If you meet Matt, picture a welcome mat. For David, imagine David and Goliath. With Mary, visualize a wedding dress.

E — END. Use their name at the end of every conversation. "It was nice to meet you, Evelyn."

SUAVE works with people in person or online, while listening to a podcast, or even watching someone get introduced onstage. If you can't use every step, even using two can improve recall.

This way, you won't just remember more people, they'll remember you. Because people remember people who remember them.

KWIK STEP: Practice SUAVE when you meet someone, listen to a podcast with a guest, or need to remember important information today.

AFFIRMATION: *"I am capable of training my memory to better remember names. I am limitless."*

LEADERS ARE READERS

It's estimated the average person reads about one to two books a year.

The average CEO? Roughly four to six books a month. That equates to about a book a week.

Wouldn't you say that's an advantage—almost an unfair one? Well, what if *you* had that advantage?

You can. The reason most people aren't reading a book a week is because they haven't put that time into their day. It doesn't take as long as you might fear, either.

Take the average person who reads about 200 words a minute. The average book length is about 64,000 words, so divide the speed into the length, and it would take you about 320 minutes from front to back. Now, divide that by seven days a week, and it would take you about 45 minutes a day to finish. That's less than a television show.

Now, if you boosted your reading speed to 400 words a minute, you could read for 22 minutes a day, and still finish a book a week (or more if you still read for 45 minutes a day). Grow your speed to 600 words per minute, and you'd only need 15 minutes.

Reading only one book a week means you're downloading 52 new ideas, new skills, new capabilities, and new understandings into your brain every year. (Even if it takes you two weeks to finish a book, that's still 26!)

Wouldn't this unlock new opportunities for growth in your business, health, career, and relationships? Absolutely, and it's all attainable.

Here's how to think of reading: Schedule it the same way you do a workout, an important meeting, or dinner out.

Start where you are, and add 10 minutes more per week. You could break it up too, reading for half the time in the morning, and half at night. Whatever you do, just schedule it. You deserve an unfair advantage too.

Leaders are readers, and you're a leader.

KWIK STEP: Make a list of the books you want to read in the next 90 days. What can change in your life when you finish reading them? What is one change you can make to support creating a habit of reading?

AFFIRMATION: *"Leaders are readers, and I am a reader. I am limitless."*

MAY 7

AS YOUR BODY MOVES, YOUR BRAIN GROOVES

Just like humans, plants need essential nutrients to grow strong, vibrant, and healthy. They take in sunlight via photosynthesis, carbon dioxide from the air, and nutrients—largely nitrogen, phosphorus, and potassium—from the soil.

But sometimes the soil loses its nutrients, and when this happens, we can use special fertilizer to boost growth.

Just as fertilizer can transform a struggling plant into one that's vibrant, strong, and resilient, movement can improve your learning and memory.

Movement is like neuro-gardening. It creates brain-derived neurotrophic factors (BDNF), which act like fertilizer for your brain. BDNF is a type of neurotrophin—proteins that help neurons to grow, become more resilient, and form new connections. BDNF also stimulates the growth of new brain cells, particularly in the hippocampus—the center for memory and learning.

As if that wasn't enough, when you move, increased BDNF can improve your mood and help protect against chronic diseases. Studies show that low BDNF levels have been linked to depression, anxiety, and neurodegenerative diseases such as Alzheimer's.

By moving your body, you gain much more than physical benefits. You gain a healthier, happier, and more resilient brain.

As your body moves, your brain grooves.

KWIK STEP: Challenge yourself to move for 15 to 45 minutes today. Pick whatever makes you feel good—walking, running, biking, dancing, anything.

AFFIRMATION: *"I move my body to accelerate my learning, improve my memory, and lead me to a happier and healthier life. I am limitless."*

MAY 8

BE CLEAR ABOUT THE RESULT BUT OBSESSED WITH THE HABITS

A man once dreamed of writing a book. He visualized it in meditation, feeling the weight of the bound pages in his hands. He saw reviews pour in and felt the excitement of interviews with major media.

There was only one problem: He never wrote consistently. Something always got in the way. He kept telling himself he would do it "tomorrow," but tomorrow never arrived, and neither did the book.

Beginning with the end goal in mind can motivate you, but achieving it requires doing the work—the writing, the studying, the practicing. Not occasionally, consistently. That means turning the practice into a habit.

Behavioral psychologist BJ Fogg and author James Clear have shown that habits stick best when they're tied to identity. And identity change takes time, so start small with these three steps:

1. **CREATE AN IDENTITY-BASED AFFIRMATION PAIRED WITH A HABIT.** Instead of "I need to read for 15 minutes daily," say, "I *am* a reader who reads for 15 minutes daily." Rather than "I have to work on my book," try "I *am* a writer who writes 500 words a day." This can lower stress, improve performance, and activate reward-related regions in your brain.
2. **VISUALIZE YOURSELF PERFORMING THE HABIT.** When we visualize an action, the brain activates the same neural circuits as physically practiced. A study from the University of Chicago showed athletes who only visualized shooting free throws improved by almost as much as athletes who practiced—only 1 percentage point difference.
3. **ACT.** Action locks identity into place. Every repetition strengthens neural pathways until the habit becomes as automatic as brushing your teeth.

You can't force habits to stick—they stick when they become a natural part of who you are. Set ambitious targets. Visualize them in detail. And be clear on the result, but then obsess over the habits that make them real.

KWIK STEP: What is one habit you've struggled to make stick? Use these three steps to get started.

AFFIRMATION: *"I am clear about the results I want to achieve, and I obsess over the habits I'm building to get there. I am limitless."*

MAY 9

YOU DON'T HAVE A FOCUS PROBLEM; YOU HAVE A FILTERING PROBLEM

In 2015, a Microsoft report went viral after claiming the average human attention span had fallen to eight seconds—shorter than that of a goldfish. It turns out, Microsoft was wrong about the numbers but right about the trend.

Our attention span is shrinking.

For more than two decades, University of California–Irvine professor and psychologist Dr. Gloria Mark has studied humans and our interaction with technology. Her research found that in 2004, we stayed on our screens, on average, about two-and-a-half minutes. By 2012, this had decreased to 75 seconds. Today, we average about 47 seconds.

Our digital world bombards us with a constant stream of rings, pings, and dings, pulling our attention toward them, when usually we really need to focus on something more important.

Digital distraction isn't going away, it's only getting worse, making focus one of the most valuable superpowers you can develop. While you can't stop the world from ringing, pinging, and dinging, you do have agency over your brain. You're not a victim.

You're the pilot of your life—and your brain—not a passenger.

To regain focus, practice strengthening your brain's "spam filter"—your reticular activating system. Since it acts like a gatekeeper, deciding what information for you to consciously focus on and what's best ignored, be clear about the most important thing you must do every day.

Do this, and it's like giving instructions to your RAS about what to help you focus on and what to forget.

Every morning, decide what matters most for your day and complete it entirely or get to a comfortable stopping place before moving to the next item.

Remember, you don't have a focus problem. You have a filtering problem.

KWIK STEP: Write down the most important thing you have to do today, professionally and personally. How can you protect that?

AFFIRMATION: *"I focus on what matters. Everything else fades into the background. I am limitless."*

A CONFUSED MIND WON'T ACT

Does it ever feel like you can see the finish line, but your feet are stuck at the start?

Many of us face this challenge every day. We have lofty goals like building multimillion-dollar businesses, finding our soulmate, or getting healthy, yet we have no idea where or how to start.

We often default to blaming a lack of motivation. But that's usually not the problem.

Even when you have strong motivation—a solid "why"—if your goal is too ambitious, too intimidating, or too confusing, you won't move forward.

When a goal feels too vague, or overwhelmingly big, the amygdala can perceive that as uncertainty and danger, triggering a stress or fear response. This suppresses activity in the prefrontal cortex, which is responsible for planning and decision-making. So instead of act-ing, your brain responds with procrastination or avoidance.

To short-circuit this response and initiate action, the path needs to be both clear for your brain and attainable.

Instead of saying you'll read for 45 minutes a day, say you'll read one sentence. Because who stops at one sentence? No one. You'll keep going. With each small simple step, your brain releases dopamine, reinforcing the behavior and making it easier for you to read one more sentence, gaining the victory, then another, and another, and another. That's how you go from not reading to reading 5 minutes, 10, 15, then 20 and so on.

Do this with everything. Instead of saying you're going to work out for 45 minutes, say "I'll put on my running shoes," or "I'll work out for 10 minutes." If you need to study or do deep work, start with five minutes.

A confused mind won't act, but a clear one surely will.

KWIK STEP: What is one small simple step you can take toward a goal that has felt too big, too confusing, or that you've procrastinated and avoided? Do it today.

AFFIRMATION: *"I am clear on the next small simple step I must take toward my goal. I am limitless."*

MAY 11

BE BORING

Go to bed early.

Rise as soon as you wake.

Get sunlight.

Exercise.

Rest.

Eat healthy.

Avoid alcohol.

Learn.

Read.

Connect with positive people.

Say “no” more.

These aren’t just productivity hacks. They’re ways to help your brain function at its best.

Without realizing it, most people chase the easy dopamine rewards from things like scrolling on social media, snacking on sugar, or clicking on content. It all gives us a quick dopamine rush.

But each scroll, snack, and click unknowingly locks us into a cheap dopamine-fueled cycle that slowly erodes our attention, focus, concentration, and motivation. Plus, these fast dopamine spikes with no effort reduce our brain’s sensitivity to reward, making meaningful effort, deep work, and complete presence in the moment feel harder. This is known as dopamine desensitization.

When we say no to one scroll, one snack, or one click, we begin rewiring our brain away from the easy dopamine hits to reorient it toward the challenging yet meaningful work that moves us toward our goals. Over time, we train our brain to respond to progress, effort, and completion—delayed rewards—not quick hits.

If your growth habits make you seem “boring,” take it as a compliment. You’re doing what most people aren’t. Early mornings, healthy meals, exercise, and reading are the foundation of a sharp mind and a long life. Be boring.

> **KWIK STEP:** What’s one growth habit that you’re excelling in? Celebrate that. Then pick one growth habit you want to work on. What is one small thing you can do today?

AFFIRMATION: *“I embrace being boring. I am limitless.”*

MAY 12

BUILD YOUR MEMORY LIKE A MUSCLE

The two most costly words in life are: "I forgot."

"I forgot that meeting."

"I forgot what I was going to say."

"I forgot to do it."

Lapses in memory cost us more than time. They threaten our credibility and can hurt our most important relationships. Nobody chooses to forget, yet it's happening more than ever.

Why? Because we've become reliant on technology to act as our external memory drive—holding phone numbers, addresses, directions, and schedules. This is known as *cognitive offloading.*

In some instances, cognitive offloading helps improve performance. We shouldn't max our brain space to memorize 500 phone numbers. But we're losing some of our mental muscle every time we reach for a device or AI to do our thinking for us. We're losing some of our ability to remember more than a few snippets of conversation, to recall the name of a potential new client, to focus on what needs getting done, and to make decisions.

Fortunately, your brain acts more like a muscle than like an organ, so you can train your brain to remember more. The more you flex your memory, the stronger it becomes.

Instead of outsourcing everything to your devices, practice building your internal memory drive by taking notes by hand in meetings and quizzing yourself after about who said what. Or learn three important phone numbers by heart, or pick a new word a day and learn its definition. These aren't simply parlor tricks. You're retraining your brain to pay attention, focus on important details, and to remember more.

This is how you stay ahead in a world where technology such as AI is rapidly progressing.

Build your memory and your thinking like a muscle.

KWIK STEP: Pick three to five important phone numbers (those of your spouse, kids, best friend, or boss) and learn them by heart. Practice recalling them until they're automatic.

AFFIRMATION: *"I build my memory and thinking like I do my muscles. I am limitless."*

MAY 13

REWIRE TO RISE

You know that moment when you're excited about starting a new habit or routine, such as journaling, exercising, or reading. We've all been there. At first, it's thrilling and fun, and we feel proud about starting something new. And then life gets busy, our kids get sick, an aging parent needs help, or work takes off, so the journal stays closed, the gym gets skipped, and the book remains on the shelf.

Before long, we fall back into our old habits, only to be left thinking, *I failed. I guess this is just who I am.*

Except that's not true and it's not failure. It's an outdated program your brain is running that has pulled you back into the past.

When we can get quiet and real with ourselves, we can see one reason change feels so hard, although we want it, is that deep inside we don't believe it's possible. But change is possible, and we can rewrite the program our brain runs.

To change a habit or routine, try pairing the new action with empowering self-talk. This will give the supercomputer that is your brain a different program to run, one that says, "Change is possible. I can do it."

Every time you go for water instead of soda, reading instead of scrolling, or walking instead of streaming, tell your brain, "See? I can change. I can learn. I can adapt. I can rewire my brain. I am the pilot of my mind, not the passenger."

You can do it. Neuroplasticity is your proof. Science has shown the brain is capable of strengthening and forming new neural pathways every time you practice a new thought or behavior.

So you *can* change. You *can* change your habits. You *can* learn anything.

Every time you try again, and you tell yourself, "I can do this. I am a learner. I am capable of change," you move one step closer to the person you're becoming.

Rewire to rise.

KWIK STEP: Pick one habit that you've struggled to change. Today, perform the new action and pair it with empowering self-talk to rewire your beliefs: "See, I can learn. I can change. I can do . . ."

AFFIRMATION: *"I can change anything in my life. I am limitless."*

DESIGN BEATS DISCIPLINE

Do you choose to stream your favorite show or spend 30 minutes mastering a new skill?

Do you reach for an apple or cake?

Do you stay focused on the important project or check your e-mail every 15 minutes?

We tend to think these choices come down to willpower—the ability to control our actions, emotions, and urges.

But even the world's top performers don't succeed because of superhuman self-control. Instead, they've built systems that bypass the temptation entirely, making the right choice the easy one.

Self-control relies heavily on the prefrontal cortex, the part of the brain responsible for planning and decision-making. This region is also susceptible to cognitive overload, decision-fatigue, and even stress, which can lead to mental and emotional exhaustion, impulsive behaviors, and poor judgment.

That's why systems work. They run automatically, not dependent on how well your brain is operating that day.

Public commitment works because social pressure creates accountability.

Financial commitments work because you have skin in the game.

Time boxing—assigning a fixed amount of time—works because deadlines eliminate negotiation.

Cutting access to your phone or apps works because temptation never enters the equation.

What I just described are known as *forcing functions*—intentional constraints that corner you into growth by removing retreat options.

Reaching your goals isn't about having extraordinary willpower—it's about architecture. Design your environment, your tools, and your defaults, and your brain won't have to wrestle with the right choice—it'll make it automatically.

In the end, design beats discipline.

KWIK STEP: Pick one commitment device and use it today to help you work toward your goal.

AFFIRMATION: *"I design systems that support my brain's limitless potential. I am limitless."*

WAKE UP YOUR BRAIN

Athletes always warm up before competing.

It's a way to slowly raise their body temperature, reduce the risk of injury, get into flow, and prepare their muscles to reach peak performance. Its importance is so universally understood and accepted that it's used in every sport and competition—pro and otherwise. That's because it works.

This isn't just true for sports—it's true for learning too.

Your brain and body constantly communicate. Every movement sends signals to your brain that shapes how you think, focus, and remember. Research into what's called *embodied cognition* shows that the more you involve your body during learning, the stronger and more durable your neural connections become.

Just as an athlete warms up with light movements, you can warm up your brain before deep work. Try stretching, a short walk, or light physical activity. Studies show that even brief bouts of movement increase blood flow and oxygen to the brain, release neurochemicals including dopamine and norepinephrine, and prime your nervous system for focus, motivation, alertness, creativity, and critical thinking.

So don't just hit the Go button on your brain—wake it up first.

KWIK STEP: Pick a simple movement like stretching, marching in place with arm raises, or a cross-body exercise (alternating touching your left elbow to right knee, or toe touches) and do it before using your brain today.

AFFIRMATION: *"I wake up my brain to improve its performance. I am limitless."*

MAY 16

CHANGE PROCEDURE OR CHANGE PERCEPTION

If only they changed, everything would be better.

We often think that if only someone else—our spouse, our co-worker, even our children—spoke more kindly to us, clearly communicated their needs, or stopped reaching for their phone while we were talking, we wouldn't fight so much.

It's frustrating when we're in a challenging situation with someone else and it feels like there's nothing we can do to change it. But that's not true. While we can't change other people, we still have agency.

We can change our actions or change our mindset.

If you're constantly battling with your boss, you can change how you communicate. This might mean softening your tone, or it might mean being more assertive. You can use "I" statements, use plainer language, or otherwise adapt to how they receive information.

If you can't change your actions, then change your perspective. Reframe the situation so it doesn't bother you. When they don't listen, maybe they're not being disrespectful, they're just overwhelmed. When they misinterpret what you've said, maybe it's an opportunity for you to use more direct language.

If you don't change your actions or your mindset, your brain gets caught in cognitive dissonance. This is the psychological tension between seeing what's happening and believing it should be different. The longer you spend in this gap, the more bitter, frustrated, angry, and exhausted you can become.

This isn't punishment—it's your brain pushing you to resolve the conflict. It wants harmony, stability, something no one outside of you can give. Only you can give that to your brain.

When you feel frustrated by someone or a situation ask, "What action can I change? What mindset can I rethink?"

Don't stay stuck in an untenable situation. It won't change until you change. Change your procedure, or change your perception.

KWIK STEP: Think of one situation that's caused you tension. What is one action you can take, or one mindset change you can make, today?

AFFIRMATION: *"I am willing to change my actions and my mindsets to change my situation. I am limitless."*

MAY 17

MAKE A HABIT OF TRUSTING YOURSELF

You're in a meeting and your boss calls on you unexpectedly. How do you feel?

You're at a networking event and you don't know a single person. What's your first thought?

You need to make a social media post to market your business. How do you respond?

There are countless situations during the day that can trigger that sinking dread, the tiny whispers of self-doubt, insecurity, and fear that we'll "get it wrong." That no one will like us, buy from us, or take us seriously.

The most successful people aren't the ones who never feel afraid, anxious, or insecure. They're the ones who never let those thoughts stop them.

They act anyway.

What if, the moment fear or self-doubt struck, you followed it by telling yourself, "It's okay. I don't have to know everything right now, and I'll still figure it out. I'll find a way to grow through this. I am resourceful. I am strong. I am capable. And no matter what happens, I'll be okay."

Research shows cognitive reappraisal like this—reframing negative experiences positively—can increase resilience, while optimism can protect against anxiety. Studies also suggest that positive self-affirmations can restore self-competence and activate brain regions connected to self-reflection, values, and goal-directed behavior.

With repetition, you can reshape neural pathways, strengthening connections associated with self-worth, confidence, and emotional regulation. Eventually, positive self-talk, optimism, and self-confidence become your brain's default instead of self-doubt.

Your thoughts don't just happen—they grow from your habits. Audit your thoughts, change how you speak to—and about—yourself, and you'll build the habit of self-confidence.

You can make a habit of doubting yourself or a habit of trusting yourself.

KWIK STEP: What's an area in which you're doubting yourself today? Write down any negative thoughts, then rewrite them as a more positive, supportive response. Use this throughout the day.

AFFIRMATION: *"I make the habit of trusting myself. I am limitless."*

MAY 18

SLEEP BETTER. THINK LONGER.

A kitchen floor needs washing regularly. Otherwise layers of grime, dust, and dirt build up. It's a natural byproduct of feet and paws walking across the floor, food scraps falling on it, and liquids spilling on it.

Floors need cleaning, and so does your brain.

During the day, cognitive functions leave behind metabolic waste that builds up between neurons. When you sleep, the glymphatic system acts as chief cleaner; it sends fluid through the brain, washing away waste including beta-amyloid plaques, which researchers believe may play a role in the development of Alzheimer's and other neurodegenerative diseases as levels increase.

Yet many of us struggle to get consistent restorative sleep. That's where building healthy sleep habits can make a difference.

By controlling your environment and building an evening routine, you can create the right triggers to help your mind and body relax into sleep mode.

1. **TEMPERATURE.** Aim for between 60 and 68 degrees Fahrenheit.
2. **GENTLE YOGA OR MEDITATION.** Practices that help activate the parasympathetic nervous system signal it's safe to relax.
3. **JOURNAL CARES AWAY.** Releasing your worries and fears helps free working memory and reduce cognitive overload.
4. **ORGANIZE TOMORROW.** Make a list of everything needing your attention.
5. **MAKE YOUR BEDROOM A SANCTUARY.** Don't work, watch television, or use your phone.
6. **TRADE SCREENS FOR PAGES.** Blue light from devices stimulates the brain into alertness. Reading paper books helps reduce stress and calms the mind.
7. **BLACKOUT CURTAINS OR WEAR AN EYE MASK.** Darkness triggers melatonin, a hormone that signals the brain it's time to rest and sleep.

Sleep better. Think longer.

KWIK STEP: Choose one sleep habit you want to add to your evening routine, and start it tonight.

AFFIRMATION: *"I prioritize my sleep to think better. I am limitless."*

THERE'S NO GOOD OR BAD MEMORY—ONLY UNTRAINED OR TRAINED

A puppy isn't born knowing how to walk on leash, sit, or give you their paw. You have to train them.

When it comes to training your memory, it's much the same.

Studies suggest most people can improve their working memory and recall through cognitive training and mnemonic techniques. Many studies also indicate that our memory capacity far exceeds what we think.

If you've ever lost your train of thought, misplaced something, or forgotten what you just read, then know this can all change. And it starts with setting the intention.

When you consciously set an intention, your brain encodes it like a goal. This activates your prefrontal cortex, helping to sharpen your focus and attention and directing your actions toward achieving it.

To train your memory, think: *Decide it. Define it. Do it.*

1. **DECIDE IT.** Be clear in your mind what exactly it is you want—recalling your partner's words, information from a meeting, your thoughts, or where you placed something.
2. **DEFINE IT.** Why does having a better memory matter? How will it improve your life?
3. **DO IT.** What methods or actions will you use daily? Visualization? Rhymes? Chunking information?

These three steps align your head, heart, and hands. Because everything worth achieving first starts in your head, moves to your heart, and finally to your hands. So imagine your intention in your mind, feel why it matters in your heart, and act with your hands. Do this every day.

A great memory doesn't just happen; it's created. There's no such thing as a good or bad memory, just untrained or trained.

KWIK STEP: Apply the three steps—Decide, Define, Do—in some aspect of your life.

AFFIRMATION: *"I train my memory with intention, emotion, and daily action. I am limitless."*

IF YOU'RE PERSISTENT, YOU CAN ACHIEVE IT. IF YOU'RE CONSISTENT, YOU GET TO KEEP IT.

You don't run a marathon without training.

Even on the mornings when you don't feel like getting out of bed, you still go for a run. The only way across the finish line is lacing up your shoes, walking out the door, and running a little longer, a little harder, a little farther every day.

The more you do this, the easier running gets. You're not only physically faster and stronger, you're mentally transformed. There's no negotiating. No forcing yourself like you used to. Now you run because you've built the habit.

Through repetition, the behavior has moved into your basal ganglia, where habits get encoded. It's also who you are—you are a runner—and so running is what you do.

Willpower can help you push through short-term temptation. But willpower relies heavily on your prefrontal cortex, a very energy-dependent region of the brain. When you make too many decisions, when you're cognitively overloaded and short on energy, the brain shifts into energy conservation mode, and self-control collapses.

Shoot for consistency instead. Regular, deliberate, intentional practice daily is what leads to small, incremental improvements.

Little by little, a little becomes a lot, as you also become someone new. That's not only how you win the day, but how you win at transformation.

Persistence demands willpower. Consistency rewires the brain. If you're persistent, you can achieve it. If you're consistent, you get to keep it.

KWIK STEP: Find one small simple step you can take today toward your goals. Then anchor the action to the identity you're building by filling in the following: "I am someone who __________" (e.g., "moves my body daily," "writes when it's hard," "reads nightly," or "learns one new word daily").

AFFIRMATION: *"I take consistent action toward my goals. I am limitless."*

MAY 21

YOU'RE RIGHT ON TIME

There's a common belief that only the young can change, learn, and find success. That once we hit a certain age, we're done.

In fact, there is no age limit. No cap on when you can start a business, change careers, go back school, or pursue your passion.

Stan Lee created *Spider-Man* and the *X-Men* in his 40s.

Sam Walton founded Walmart at 44.

Ariana Huffington started *The Huffington Post* at 55.

Instead of thinking of all the reasons *why* "it's too late" or you're "too old," flip it.

Tell yourself, "I'm right on time. I'm exactly where I need to be. And I'm exactly the person I need to be to [fill in the blank]."

Statements like these are a form of *cognitive reappraisal*. When you think negatively, like "it's too late," it activates your amygdala, the fear center. This can trigger stress and anxiety, making it harder to start and sustain actions in new directions.

Cognitive reappraisals reverse this. They tamp down the amygdala so the prefrontal cortex can take over, helping you to make clearer decisions, better regulate your emotions, and find more innovative solutions to challenges.In this state, anything is possible.

It's never too late to dream into reality the future you desire. You're right on time.

KWIK STEP: Out loud, repeat the following statement three times, then sit quietly for two to five minutes noticing how you feel and any thoughts that arise.

"I'm right on time. I'm exactly where I need to be. And I'm exactly the person I need to be to [fill in the blank]."

AFFIRMATION: *"I'm right on time. I am limitless."*

TAKE A WISH AND TURN IT INTO A WILL

If you want something you've never had, you've got to do something you've never done.

One of the best things you can do is to stop saying, "I wish this would change" or "I hope this will change." Wishing and hoping aren't strategies.

Instead, tell yourself, "I *will* change this."

The secret to making this work lies in neurogenesis and neuroplasticity. Neurogenesis is your brain's ability to make new neurons, primarily in the hippocampus, the center of learning and memory. Neuroplasticity is the brain's ability to rewire itself, forming new connections between those neurons.

One key driver to stimulate neurogenesis and neuroplasticity is novelty. When you expose your brain to new thoughts, new behaviors, new knowledge, new movements, and new skills, it directly activates the dopamine system, improving your mood, enhancing motivation, and boosting memory, attention, and focus.

To make real change real, turn learning into a daily habit. One of the simplest ways to do this is what I call the "Three Tries Approach":

1. **TRY ONCE:** to overcome the fear of the unknown. Whether it's salsa dancing, climbing, or taking a cold shower, this first time tells your brain, "This is safe. I am safe."
2. **TRY TWICE:** to start building the neural pathways for skill. Repetition strengthens connections.
3. **TRY THRICE:** to decide if you like, love, or hate it. You only have so much time in this life. Make it count by learning and building skills that interest you, move you toward personal and professional goals, and make you feel alive.

This is just a guidepost. You might need to try something three times to get over the fear or six times to decide if you like it. Just stick with it.

Every time you learn, your brain grows, and you close the gap between a wish and your will. Take a wish and turn it into a will.

KWIK STEP: First, identify a wish and turn it into a will. For example, "I wish I could speak Japanese" > "I will speak Japanese." Then commit to using the "Three Tries Approach" by implementing one small step you can take today. For instance, look up one Japanese word and learn it.

AFFIRMATION: *"I take 'I wish' and turn it into 'I will.' I am limitless."*

MAY 23

BE A DEEP LEARNER

Most people treat their brains like filing cabinets. Information is input, stored, and retrieved when needed.

But your brain doesn't archive facts. It remembers thought. The deeper you think, the stronger the memory. This principle, backed by decades of neuroscience research, explains why some information sticks while most slides away. It's called *higher-order thinking,* and it's the difference between learning and actually knowing.

Your thinking happens in tiers. The bottom is recognition and memorization. You see information and repeat it back. This is where most learning stops. But in the top tiers lie analysis, evaluation, and creation.

When you analyze, you break concepts into parts and examine how they relate. When you evaluate, you make judgments based on criteria. And when you create, you synthesize information into something new. These processes force your brain to work harder, build more neural pathways, and form stronger memories.

To practice higher-order thinking, build concept maps. Research demonstrates that concept mapping helps organize and synthesize relevant material leading to deeper understanding and learning.

Your brain wasn't designed to remember abstract data. It evolved to remember images, locations, and stories. When you translate dry information into rich mental pictures, you engage multiple cognitive processes simultaneously. Analysis of the original information. Evaluation of which details matter most, and creative transformation into imagery.

Take a blank page. Write your main concept in the center. Then branch out to related ideas. Draw connections between them. Add examples under each topic. Use colors, symbols, and anything that makes the relationship visual.

With higher-order thinking, you swap shallow memorization for deeper learning.

KWIK STEP: Pick a subject and create a concept map.

AFFIRMATION: *"I am a deep learner. I am limitless."*

DON'T JUST FEED YOUR BRAIN—FUEL IT

We spend a lot of time thinking about how we can take better care of our bodies.

We exercise, stretch, eat clean, sleep, rest, meditate, manage stress, socialize, and search for meaning, all in the quest to feel better, live longer, and have more energy.

But what about our brain?

It's one of the most precious gifts we've been given. It's what allows us to learn, love, think, create, and even experience joy.

Just as you can feed your body anything, you can feed your brain anything too. So what if you paused to ask, "Is this good for my brain?" before deciding?

Is watching this show good for my brain?

Is eating this food?

Is spending time with this person?

Is saying yes to this new opportunity?

Is this workout?

It's not that you have to be perfect. The goal is progress. The more you stack healthy habits and intentional decisions, the better your brain can perform—meaning you get a sharper memory, flexible thinking, more energy and creativity, better decision-making and emotional regulation, and deeper concentration and focus.

Quality sleep, whole foods, exercise, spending time with positive people—these aren't just "healthy habits." They fuel your brain's performance, and by extension, your life.

With every choice, you strengthen or weaken connections between neurons through a process called *synaptic plasticity*. This is how new habits get formed and old ones broken. And your choices also help create new neurons—known as *neurogenesis*—which helps with learning, memory, and emotional regulation.

So don't just feed your brain—fuel it to create the life you want to live.

KWIK STEP: Today, when you face any choice, ask, "Is this good for my brain?" when faced with choices, then act accordingly.

AFFIRMATION: *"I fuel my brain's performance through the choices I make during my day. I am limitless."*

MAY 25

MOVE YOUR BODY. CHANGE YOUR BRAIN.

Our brain controls our body, right?

For years, that's the story we were told. It meant that if we just had more willpower, if we were more committed and disciplined, we could improve *anything*—thinking, decision-making, confidence, stress levels, diet, sleep, even health.

How well has that worked for most people? It hasn't. Even when it does work, it's tough to sustain.

If you've struggled with making change, you may think your lack of willpower is at fault. Instead, consider your brain-body connection, which isn't a one-way street with the brain dictating everything. It's a two-way approach with the body capable of influencing the brain too.

Researchers have found the mind-body connection is built into the brain. When you perform specific actions, it activates sensory and motor circuits that drive changes that can help improve memory, focus, decision-making, and mental clarity.

A simple strategy begins with things you do daily. Former Duke University professor and neurobiologist Dr. Lawrence Katz introduced the concept of neurobics. He suggested that practicing daily activities using multiple senses engages sensory and motor circuits in novel ways, which can help improve attention and learning.

Katz's recommendations included reading a computer monitor upside down, listening to music while smelling something fragrant, and brushing or eating with your nondominant hand.

If you're not already doing this, try it. It'll feel awkward at first—as it should. Your brain hasn't memorized the motor pattern yet, so it must fire new neurons and form new pathways. This is neuroplasticity at work.

You don't need hours of brain training to start boosting mental performance. Simple actions can lead to powerful changes. Move your body. Change your brain.

KWIK STEP: What is one daily task you can do practice with your nondominant hand?

AFFIRMATION: *"I move my body to change my brain. I am limitless."*

MINE YOUR DREAMS FOR GOLD

The Terminator was born from it. So was the idea for Google, Frankenstein, the sewing machine, and the periodic table of elements.

I'm talking about *dreams*.

You spend your waking hours learning, making decisions, problem-solving, and focusing. So when sleep finally arrives, your body may rest, but your brain actually begins one of its most active phases.

During REM sleep, your brain processes what happened during the day. It archives memories, regulates emotions, and seeks creative solutions to problems that you faced during the day—problems you may not realize you had.

Some of this activity gets integrated and expressed in the form of dreams, which most people forget when they wake up.

But what if you could remember them?

Instead of reaching for your phone as soon as you wake, reach for your DREAMS. Here's how:

DECIDE. The night before, consciously set the intention that you're going to recall your dreams when you wake up.

RECORD. Keep a dream journal by your bed and record your dream before doing anything else.

EYES. When you first wake up, keep your eyes shut for a minute or two and focus on the details of your dream.

AFFIRM. When you crawl into bed and the light is out, say aloud or silently, "I will remember my dreams."

MANAGE. Prioritize restorative sleep, using the right habits to help you enter REM sleep.

SHARE. Tell someone about your dreams. This will help improve your recall and ability to remember future details.

Even during sleep, your brain is working for you. So work with it by practicing and improving your dream recall, and you just might mine them for gold.

KWIK STEP: Tonight, before you go to sleep, plan to use the DREAMS process. Tomorrow morning, record your dreams as soon as you wake up.

AFFIRMATION: *"I remember my dreams to mine them for gold. I am limitless."*

MAY 27

BUILD MOMENTUM, NOT MOTIVATION

In physics, it's said that an object at rest tends to stay at rest, but an object in motion tends to stay in motion.

Just as an object needs momentum to stay in motion, so do you. If you want to move forward in life, to move beyond feeling stuck and stagnant, to become an unstoppable force where you don't "bounce back" from setbacks but jump forward and create velocity, you need to become *mass in motion.*

Momentum equals mass times velocity.

Remember, limitless isn't about being perfect. It's about advancing and progressing beyond what you currently believe is possible. And you advance through momentum, by keeping the speed and motion going.

How do you keep momentum? You take one small step in the direction of your goals, then you repeat it again tomorrow, then the next day and the next and the next.

Motivation comes after action. Dopamine gets released in anticipation, not just in completion. Action creates momentum. And momentum compounds.

The goal isn't intensity. It's consistency. Build momentum, not motivation.

KWIK STEP: Take the smallest step toward your goal today. Do it again tomorrow, and the next day, and the next.

AFFIRMATION: *"I am building unstoppable momentum. I am limitless."*

MAY 28

STOP MANAGING TIME AND START MANAGING YOUR MIND

If your brain were a runner, it would be built for sprints—not marathons.

Yet most people push their brain to stay focused, alert, and at peak performance for hours at a time.

While some professions truly demand this kind of sustained, intense focus, for most of us it becomes a race that leaves us mentally fatigued, overloaded, distracted, and struggling to deliver high-caliber work.

Instead of forcing your brain to study or work for four or more hours, leverage the Pomodoro Technique. It's simple. You work in 20- to 25-minute intervals followed with a 5-minute brain break. You get up, stretch, move your body, drink water, maybe walk outside, meditate, or let your mind wander. After three or four rounds of this, you take a longer break, 15 or 20 minutes.

This cycle mirrors how the brain naturally operates, oscillating between periods of intense focus and periods of recovery. Working in cycles like this gives your brain structure, clarifies goals, and helps to combat your brain's natural tendency to wander. By closing your work windows, you give your brain a constraint, which creates a sense of urgency, helping improve motivation.

These brain breaks keep you feeling fresh, help you avoid burnout, protect your attention, and allow your performance and productivity to peak.

The goal isn't to log more work hours. It's to make the hours you work count more.

It's to stop managing your time and start managing your mind.

KWIK STEP: What's one task you can try using at least one Pomodoro on today?

AFFIRMATION: *"I manage my mind to manage my time. I am limitless."*

MAY 29

READING IS TO THE MIND WHAT EXERCISE IS TO THE BODY

We exercise to build strong hearts.

We lift heavy objects to build strong muscles.

And we read to build strong brains.

Numerous studies prove this point. Researchers from the Max Planck Institute for Human Cognitive and Brain Sciences used fMRIs to show that reading changes the brain through neuroplasticity. It creates new connections between different regions involved in attention, sensory processing, and motor control, networks crucial to helping the brain imagine, predict, and understand our experience of the world.

In another study from Emory, researchers also used fMRIs to determine that after participants read a novel, regions of the brain crucial for memory, attention, emotional processing, and understanding lit up and remained active for days.

Reading boosts our empathy, reduces stress and symptoms of depression, and can even help us live longer. A 12-year study from Yale found that after controlling for other factors, such as education and health, book readers experienced a 20 percent reduction in risk of mortality over the 12 years of follow-up after the study compared to non-book readers.

If you're looking for one of the best brain workouts around, pick up a book—any book—and read. Reading is to the mind what exercise is to the body.

KWIK STEP: Pick a favorite book and read for at least 15 minutes today.

AFFIRMATION: *"I read to build a strong brain. I am limitless."*

MAY 30

CLARITY LIVES IN A CALM MIND

When do your best ideas strike? How do you feel when you make good decisions?

It's likely not happening when you feel frantic, stressed, and pulled in so many directions that you can barely think straight.

Clarity, creativity, and wise decision-making are born from a calm mind, one that feels safe and peaceful.

When you're constantly in motion, mentally or physically, your nervous system locks into survival mode. Your amygdala takes control, flooding your body with stress hormones that keep you hypervigilant, scanning for threats and dangers that often don't exist.

If you stay in this state for too long, it can lead to chronic stress. Researchers at Yale have found that prolonged stress can reduce gray matter in critical regions of the brain including the prefrontal cortex, which helps regulate emotion, decision-making, and self-control.

Our world isn't designed for peace—it's engineered for speed. It's built to capture and keep your attention.

You have to unplug. *You* have to slow down. *You* have to let your brain rest.

Practice designing your day to include regular breaks to restore a sense of calm to your mind. Take at least 60 seconds before sending an e-mail, joining a call, or working on a big project to breathe slowly in and out through your nose. With each exhale, visualize whatever worries, stress, and negativity leaving your body. With each inhale, imagine calm, creativity, and clarity entering.

The more you practice this, the more you rewire your brain to return to a calm, centered, and peaceful state on demand. This is how you can ensure you're ready for anything during the day.

Clarity doesn't live in speed. Clarity lives in a calm mind.

KWIK STEP: Take 60 seconds to close your eyes and practice slow, deep breathing while visualizing stress leaving your body and clarity and peace entering. Today, commit to using this practice at least three times.

AFFIRMATION: *"I am willing to allow my mind to be calm and clear. I am limitless."*

TRAIN YOUR FOCUS LIKE A MUSCLE

There's a reason why basketball great Steph Curry takes thousands of jump shots in practice. He's training his body and brain, so when the game is on the line and the buzzer is counting down, he doesn't think about nailing the shot, he just does it.

Focus works much the same way. It's your ability to direct your attention, and it's just as trainable as a jump shot.

The trick is to practice when you don't need it, so when you do, your brain knows exactly how to perform.

So instead of scrolling on your phone while brushing your teeth, practice focusing on hitting each tooth. When you're washing dishes, focus on how the warm water feels on your hands. When you're waiting in line, instead of reaching for your phone, just stand there and use all your senses to take in what's happening around you.

By training your focus, you're strengthening what's called your *attentional control*—your brain's ability to focus on relevant information and what matters while ignoring distractions.

Then when you really need to focus, like when you're meeting an intense work deadline, in a conversation with a potential new client, or handling a challenge with your kids, it'll happen. Train your focus like a muscle.

KWIK STEP: Identify three instances when you can train your focus and commit to practice them.

AFFIRMATION: *"I train my focus like I train a muscle. I am limitless."*

YOU DON'T RISE TO THE OCCASION. YOU FALL TO THE LEVEL OF YOUR TRAINING.

Firefighters train for months, sometimes years, before responding to a call. They have live-fire drills, simulated rescues, and practice sessions coordinating as a team under the pressure of heat, smoke, noise, and fatigue.

They're not the only high-stakes professionals who operate like this. Surgeons, ER doctors, search-and-rescue squads, special forces, professional athletes, pilots—they all train under intense pressure.

This is known as *stress inoculation training*—a process where controlled exposures to stress train the brain to remain calm, focused, and adaptive when it matters. Research shows training like this helps increase cognitive resilience under pressure.

Training in difficult situations helps people make rational, clear decisions. It helps their brains reinterpret stress too. It's no longer a signal to panic, but a signal to focus, engage, and perform. And it allows muscle memory to take over instead of fear.

While you may not be in a high-stakes situation, you can use this technique to help your brain level up by making your training environment more difficult.

Learn with distractions. Don't use your noise canceling headphones. Don't tidy your desk. If you have to write, don't give yourself 45 minutes to finish—do it in 20. If you're filming and posting a video to social media, do one take and upload it.

This isn't a practice to use all the time, just occasionally. Train your brain in difficult environments, and performance becomes easy.

You don't rise to the occasion. You fall to the level of your training.

KWIK STEP: Find one task that you can make 10 percent more difficult today.

AFFIRMATION: *"I rise to the level of my training. And I train high. I am limitless."*

MEMORY ISN'T ABOUT TALENT; IT'S ABOUT TECHNIQUE

"My memory is terrible."

"I have such a bad memory."

"I can never remember anything."

Statements like these might feel true, but they're LIES—limited ideas entertained. Memory is trainable. While genetics predetermines some ability, studies show that focus, attention, motivation, and effective methods make memory a skill you can improve.

No matter your age, background, or education level, you can strengthen your ability to remember names, numbers, speeches, client facts, and what matters most in life.

To boost your power, remember the mother of memory principles: MOM.

MOTIVATION. If I showed you a bag with $1 million in it and told you it was yours if you remembered the name of the next person you met, would you remember? Probably.

Not because you became a memory expert suddenly, but because you had motivation. When you're clear on what matters, your brain registers it as a goal, prioritizing attention, self-control, and long-term planning to attain it.

So before you need to remember something, ask yourself, "Why do I want to remember this?" Is it to make friends? Close a sale? Lead your team more effectively? Parent better?

Remember, reasons reap results.

OBSERVATION. When we forget, we blame retention, when the real issue is *attention*. The art of memory is the art of attention. Often, you don't hear someone's name or understand what you just read because your focus is elsewhere.

Don't plan what you'll say next. Don't scan the room. Don't let your mind wander to tomorrow. Be present and observe.

METHOD. What tools are you using? Do you say someone's name when you meet them? Do you repeat it in conversation? Do you create memory palaces—the method of loci—by placing vivid images into familiar locations?

Remembering names, dates, details, and what matters most isn't about talent. It's about technique.

KWIK STEP: Practice MOM today and notice which element of the acronym needs more practice.

AFFIRMATION: *"I build my memory through training. I am limitless."*

JUNE 3

ENERGY IS CONTAGIOUS; PROTECT YOURS

Have you ever walked away from a conversation feeling like you needed a nap—or so energized that anything felt possible?

There are two types of people in this world. Some are like "batteries included." Being with them lifts you up. They're warm and inviting. They listen attentively and ask thoughtful questions. They're grounded and focused, optimistic, and positive. After spending time with them, you feel better about yourself and life. Your mind is clearer, your heart more open, and you feel seen, heard, accepted, and understood.

Then there are those who are like "batteries not included." They drain your energy without you realizing it. Around them, you may share less or feel impatient, withdrawn, or defensive. There's often more complaining and focusing on what's "wrong." You leave feeling a heaviness in your chest, a deep exhaustion in your body, and a fogginess clouding your mind. There's a reason for this.

Your nervous system is wired to connect, empathize, and pick up on the emotions and physiological cues of the people you're around—a process known as *emotional contagion*. Over time, even their habits and attitudes can impact you through what's called *social contagion*.

That's why it's important to seek out the "batteries included" people. If you don't have many in your life today, that's okay. Try joining communities, online or in person. Sign up for an activity that interests you—a book club, painting, martial arts, pottery.

And set guardrails around who you spend time with. You can always say no to the "batteries not included" people or set time limits. When you are with them, be clear about your priorities and how you want their support. When you notice your energy dipping, take slow, calming breaths to help steady your nervous system.

Your energy matters. It fuels your creativity, clarity, learning, relationships, even your memory. Remember, energy is contagious. Protect yours.

KWIK STEP: Identify one "batteries included" person and one "batteries not included" person you know. Send the "batteries included" person a quick message thanking them for being in your life. Then choose one guardrail you can put up for the "batteries not included" person.

AFFIRMATION: *"I protect my energy. I am limitless."*

JUNE 4

DRINK TO THINK

Flowers wilt when they don't get enough water. But give them a drink, and they spring to life—stalks rise, petals unfurl, colors pop, and the entire plant seems to glow.

Your brain is no different.

Made up of 73 percent water, it needs water to stay sharp, alert, and clear. Studies show that even mild dehydration—just 1 to 2 percent fluid loss—can cause memory, thinking, and reaction speeds to slow down. It can even raise the risk of fatigue, irritability, and anxiety.

While you want to stay hydrated all day, the most potent time is after waking. During the night, the body can become mildly dehydrated from natural and normal processes happening while you sleep, such as sweating and breathing.

If you're sleeping six hours or less, then it's even more important to drink a glass of water first thing in the morning. Research suggests you're nearly 60 percent more likely to be dehydrated than someone sleeping seven to eight hours regularly.

So if you want to boost memory, thinking, reaction speeds, and clear "fogginess" and grogginess, then don't go for coffee or tea first—go for water. If you don't like drinking plain water, you can add a pinch of salt and a squeeze of fresh lemon juice or apple cider vinegar. You can also drink it warm.

Remember, drink to think.

KWIK STEP: Before fueling your body with caffeine or breakfast today, go for 8 to 12 ounces of water.

AFFIRMATION: *"I nourish my brain with water, bringing me clarity, energy, and focus. I am limitless."*

FIRST YOU CREATE YOUR HABITS, THEN YOUR HABITS CREATE YOU

What's the first thing you do when you wake? What's your morning routine? How do you move through your day? And at night, how do you unwind?

Whether you're reaching for your phone or a dream journal, a book or a TV remote, a glass of water or cup of coffee, your habits shape everything in your life—your health, happiness, focus, relationships, work, even your limitless potential.

If you're like most people, there are probably some habits you'd like to change. Deep down, do you believe you can?

This belief matters. What you tell your brain you're capable of doing, being, and becoming is how your brain builds your identity.

Lasting habits often come from focusing on identity. When your habits align with who you believe yourself to be, you strengthen your self-control and make the behaviors feel natural.

One way to close the gap between new habits and identity is to speak to yourself in the third person. It may sound strange, but it creates a deep emotional connection, and it creates distance between self-doubts and judgments. Research from the University of Michigan shows that self-distancing—talking to yourself using your name or "you"—can help regulate emotions and reduce stress.

So every time you choose water over soda, say, "I'm doing this because I care about you."

Every time you read at night, say, "I read to support your well-being and success."

When you put your phone in another room while working, say, "I help you focus, because your attention matters."

These small moments of intention train your brain how to see you, what goals to prioritize, and how to support you. The more you do this, the more your brain changes through neuroplasticity, forming and strengthening new neural connections that support your goals.

Identity is what transforms behavior into life, and your life into your lifestyle. First you create your habits, then your habits create you.

KWIK STEP: Pick one habit you're working to change, do it, and pair it with talking to your future self, explaining why the new habit matters.

AFFIRMATION: *"I intentionally create my habits. I am limitless."*

JUNE 6

BRILLIANCE ISN'T BORN; IT'S BUILT BETWEEN THE HEMISPHERES

What was the secret to Albert Einstein's intelligence?

For decades researchers have tried answering that question by analyzing high-resolution images of his brain. One clue may rest in his corpus callosum (CC), which researchers say was thicker than average.

This part of the brain is like a communication highway connecting the left and right hemispheres, allowing information to travel back and forth. While both sides are involved in most tasks, creativity, logic, and even motor skills depend on how efficiently different regions communicate.

Einstein's brilliance wasn't just that he was smart—it was that he blended logic and rational thinking *with* creativity and imagination.

You can support your own brain's communication highway using mental warmups that engage both sides. Before studying, doing deep work, or starting any task demanding focus and problem-solving, pick one of the following exercises and perform it for at least 30 to 60 seconds.

- **CROSS-BODY OR BILATERAL MOVEMENTS.** While standing, touch one hand or elbow to the opposite knee, alternating sides, or march in place lifting the opposite knee and elbow together.
- **DRAW THE INFINITY SYMBOL.** With your nondominant hand, draw a sideways figure eight, about shoulder height, moving from shoulder to shoulder, and following it with your eyes.
- **PUMP THE HEART.** Activities that raise your heart rate increase white matter—the brain's communication fibers—in the CC and elsewhere in the brain.

Neuroimaging studies show sustained physical activity and bilateral motor training like these exercises can be associated with measurable changes in the CC, especially when practiced over time. In the short-term, these movements can improve attention, mental flexibility, and increase blood flow to the brain.

Brilliance isn't born; it's built between the hemispheres.

KWIK STEP: Pick one activity and practice using it before any task that needs focus, or as a brain break while studying or working. Pay attention to how you feel while working.

AFFIRMATION: *"I build my brain's brilliance. I am limitless."*

JUNE 7

MAKING MEMORIES IS EASY AS PIE

More than 2,000 years ago, our ancestors couldn't set meeting reminders on phones, or hit Record during important conversations. Yet remembering names, dates, and critical information still mattered.

Enter the *method of loci*, also known as a memory palace. Ancient Greeks, and later Romans, were widely known to use this mnemonic practice in which you mentally store information in familiar places. It's as easy as *PIE.*

PLACE. We remember things when they're stored in a specific place. Stand up and pick 10 body parts. For each, say it aloud, touch it, and visualize it. The more senses you engage, the deeper the memory becomes.

1. Top of your head
2. Nose
3. Mouth
4. Ears
5. Throat
6. Shoulders
7. Collarbone
8. Fingers
9. Belly button
10. Seat of your pants

IMAGINATION. The brain prioritizes images over words. Take information and create vivid, emotional, funny, or silly pictures to make it memorable.

ENTWINE. Combine place and imagination to create an association between them. To remember the top 10 brain foods, connect each to a body part. Avocados—guacamole as **hair** conditioner. Blueberries—shooting from your **nose.** Broccoli—stuck in your **teeth**. Olive oil—cleaning your **ears** with it. Eggs—stuck in your **throat**. Green leafy vegetables—kale and spinach as **shoulder** pads. Salmon—a salmon **necklace**. Turmeric—your **fingers** coated in golden powder. Walnuts—springing from your **belly button**. Dark chocolate—**sitting** in chocolatey mud.

Are these silly? Yes, by design. Emotion activates the amygdala, which tags information as valuable and signals the hippocampus to prioritize the memory.

You can create memory palaces for anything—names, groceries, meetings, even ideas that strike while showering.

Our ancestors understood the brain is an image-making, story-loving machine. It doesn't cling to boring repetition. Map vivid images to familiar places, and you'll make memories as easy as pie.

KWIK STEP: Practice PIE with important information, facts, or dates. Then test yourself three times during the day.

AFFIRMATION: *"I build my memory through practice. I am limitless."*

JUNE 8

ONE PERCENT BETTER MEANS EVERYTHING

Best-selling author James Clear did the math and found that if you do just *one percent* better each day, it compounds to 37-fold growth in a year.

Most people hear "one percent better" and think it's too small to make a difference. So they shoot for 10X growth immediately, wanting an overnight transformation. They set goals like reading 50 pages daily, running for 30 minutes, or writing for one hour every morning.

But if you haven't built the habit of reading nightly, running regularly, or writing daily, then the brain interprets those goals as too overwhelming. When the distance between where you are and where you want to be is too great, the brain registers that as a threat, shifting into protection mode. That's why you might find yourself avoiding or procrastinating and feeling unmotivated. And one year later, you might find yourself in the exact same place you are now.

But when you aim to get one percent better every day, you set a very attainable goal. It's nonthreatening to the brain. As you repeat the small actions, you activate neuroplasticity—the brain's ability to rewire itself.

Instead of 50 pages a night, you aim for 10. Instead of running for 30 minutes, you run for 5. Instead of writing for an hour, you write for 15 minutes. Each small win—and even the anticipation of it—releases dopamine that helps fuel your motivation to do it again next time.

Keep thinking big, but focus on the easiest, simplest step that gets you one percent better every day. While it may sound like next to nothing, it means everything for your brain.

KWIK STEP: Focus on something you want to improve, and pick one small step you can commit to doing today to get one percent better.

AFFIRMATION: *"By getting one percent better every day, my brain transforms. I am limitless."*

PLAN YOUR POWER BY THE HOUR

Have you ever noticed how some hours you feel more alert, are more focused, and have better ideas, while others, you drag?

That's because your brain runs on a clock. Not the one on your wall. A biological one that determines when you think clearly, when mental fog hits, and when sleep feels natural.

Humans don't share a universal clock. We have distinct *chronotypes* that control our natural sleep and wake times, when our brain experiences peak energy, performance, and alertness, and when rest can restore.

When we go against our chronotype, we can experience what researchers call *social jetlag,* which is similar to what we can get from traveling across different time zones. Studies have found social jetlag to be associated with fatigue, sleepiness, or difficulty concentrating.

Dr. Michael Breus, a double-boarded clinical psychologist and clinical sleep specialist and author of *The Power of When,* identifies four main chronotypes:

LIONS wake around 5 to 5:30 A.M., experience peak energy between 8 A.M. and noon, and naturally go to bed before 10 P.M.

BEARS rise between 6:30 to 7:30 A.M., find their best work happens between 10 A.M.to 2 P.M., and are in bed by 11 P.M.

WOLVES wake between 8:30 to 9:30 A.M., experience peak energy around 12 to 4 P.M., sometimes with a second burst between 7 to 9 P.M., and go to sleep after midnight.

DOLPHINS are light sleepers with irregular patterns, who tend to be insomniacs, and who usually experience their peak between 10 A.M. and 2 P.M.

While you may not completely control your schedule, you can try and protect your peak hours, preserving those for the most cognitively demanding work or meetings.

Fighting your chronotype only wastes energy. Working with it can unlock productivity and performance you may never have realized you possessed.

Plan your power by the hour.

KWIK STEP: First, identify your chronotype by asking yourself, "When would I naturally wake up without an alarm or obligations?" Then find is one thing you can do today to protect your peak energy time.

AFFIRMATION: *"I protect my most powerful hours. I am limitless."*

WHAT STANDS OUT GETS REMEMBERED

Picture yourself watching a dozen horses grazing in a field. Most are brown with some white spots, except for one white stallion.

The next day, someone asks you to describe one horse. Which one do you think you'll remember?

If you guessed the white one, you're describing the cognitive bias known as the Von Restorff Effect (also known as the Isolation Effect). Your brain pays attention to what's odd, making it easier for you to remember.

If you're studying, mark a key concept differently; maybe highlight it in red. When you present, make the point you want remembered look different from everything around it—maybe bracket it in a symbol.

What stands out gets remembered.

KWIK STEP: Highlight one word on this page or from something you're reading right now. Then quiz yourself about what it was before you go to bed tonight.

AFFIRMATION: *"I have an exceptional memory. I am limitless."*

JUNE 11

MIX IT UP TO LOCK IT IN

If you want to learn and actually remember something, cramming never works.

Your brain learns best through spaced repetition. Instead of practicing or studying one topic for an hour, pick three similar ones and switch between them. If you're studying physiology, spend 20 minutes on the cardiovascular system, then move to the nervous system, and finish with the endocrine system. Or practice for 10 minutes on a subject before moving to the next. At the 30-minute mark, loop back to the original and repeat.

This technique is known as *interleaving*. A study from UCLA showed it helped students improve their memory and ability to solve problems. Compared to cramming, students who used interleaving improved their median test scores by as much as 125 percent.

There's just one catch. Your brain will work harder and struggle more, making your practice sessions feel more challenging. But it's this very challenge that forces your brain to encode, retain, and recall the information, and that's what accelerates your learning.

To build real memory, forget cramming. Mix it up to lock it in.

KWIK STEP: Pick one topic and practice interleaving today.

AFFIRMATION: *"I build my memory by mixing up my practice to lock it in. I am limitless."*

JUNE 12

REHEARSE WHO YOU'RE BECOMING

In the early 1980s, Harvard psychologist Dr. Ellen Langer took two groups of men in their 70s and 80s and sent them to live in a monastery for one week.

Their instructions: One group was to reminisce about the 1950s. The other group was to pretend the year was actually 1959 and act as if they were their younger selves. To make this easier, Dr. Langer transformed the monastery into a time capsule. Black-and-white television shows played from the 1950s. The men listened to music from that period, and read issues of Time magazine published that decade. Covers were placed over mirrors so they couldn't see their reflections.

After just seven days, Dr. Langer noted dramatic changes. The men in both groups, who had all undergone tests before entering, saw improvements in their hearing, eyesight, memory, posture, grip strength, and flexibility. But the men who pretended they were 20 years younger saw greater gains.

What happened? They acted "as if." They moved, spoke, even thought differently. They used the power of imagination to change their reality.

Vivid imagination activates overlapping neural circuits related to our perception. Meaning to the brain, it almost mirrors real life.

This means you can use your imagination to create and strengthen new habits, build new skills, and become the version of yourself you long to be.

Schedule imagination time. Block 10 to 15 minutes to vividly imagine yourself reading and remembering, communicating clearly, speaking a foreign language fluently, or focusing intently on a project.

Call in as many senses as you can. Literally "act as if" you already had this capability. Ask, "How would I move, feel, act, and behave if I had ___________?" Then do it. Change your posture, tone of voice, facial expressions, and emotions. The neural pathways you'll activate will make accessing these behaviors easier in real life.

Rehearse who you're becoming, and eventually you become who you want.

KWIK STEP: Schedule imagination time today. Pick one trait you want to develop and visualize and "act as if. . . ."

AFFIRMATION: *"I use the power of my imagination to shape who I'm becoming. I am limitless."*

FAILURE IS NOT THE OPPOSITE OF SUCCESS; IT'S THE FUEL

Watch a baby try walking, and you'll see them fall hundreds of times. Never once do we say, "They're failing." We say, "They're *learning* to walk."

When babies fall, it teaches the cerebellum—the seat of motor learning in the brain—how to fine-tune muscle control, balance, coordination, and strength. Eventually walking becomes natural and unconscious.

The same idea holds true for everything in life. Failure and making mistakes are how your brain learns on its way to success.

In a study out of the University of Iowa, researchers discovered the brain can differentiate between outcomes from a mistake—or error—we made versus something that was out of our control. When the outcome was from something we did, then the brain learns from that error so it's not repeated in the future.

It's just that you've been so conditioned to fear making mistakes, failing, and "falling" that you live in a constant state of stress and tension, desperately trying to keep all of the balls in the air without realizing that it's limiting your performance, creativity, and joy.

Mistakes and failure are not the opposite of success. They're the fuel.

KWIK STEP: Grab a soft ball or a rolled-up sock, toss it into the air a few times, and then let it fall. Notice how nothing "bad" happens. There are no cracks in the floor, holes in the wall, or harm to you at all.

Do this a few times. As the ball hits the ground, tell yourself, "There is no such thing as perfect. I learn by making mistakes, and so I welcome the mistakes. They mean I am growing, learning, and becoming limitless."

AFFIRMATION: *"I welcome mistakes.*
Mistakes help me to learn, grow, and become limitless.
I am limitless."

JUNE 14

PUT YOUR TRUST IN YOUR OWN WINGS

Watch a robin singing from a tree, and you'll notice how calm and confident it looks. It's not because the bird has complete confidence in the tree branch it's sitting on. It's because the bird trusts its own wings and voice.

Like the bird, our sense of security doesn't come from outside of us. We don't find it in someone or some experience. We find it within, from learning to trust in our capacity to grow, adapt, and learn.

One way we can build trust in ourselves is through experience. Every time you practice a skill or follow through on a promise you've made to yourself, your brain rewires itself through *experience-dependent plasticity.* So each time you practice learning a new language, playing an instrument, or controlling your temper, the pathways in your brain become stronger and more efficient.

And you're literally teaching your brain that "I'm someone who follows through. I'm someone who practices. I'm someone who learns. I can count on myself." Over time, you will strengthen those channels of trust in your brain.

But it all starts with curiosity about who you are, your strengths, talents, weaknesses, the skills you have, and the ones you want to cultivate. Then it takes courage to be yourself and to keep showing up when times get tough and stressful—as they will.

Every time you keep going, you teach your nervous system to recover faster and remain balanced no matter what's happening in the world.

It doesn't even matter if the branch you're sitting on cracks. You have built trust in yourself, in your abilities, skills, and knowledge, and in your own voice. And that is what ensures you'll always fly.

Put your trust in your own wings.

KWIK STEP: Recall something you've done in the past week when you did what you said you would. It can be something small, like making an appointment, sending an e-mail, even reading this page. Visualize yourself having performed this action and then repeat, "I can count on me."

AFFIRMATION: *"I place my trust where it belongs, in myself. I am limitless."*

BUILD STRUCTURE WITH FLEXIBILITY

It's hard to learn, lead, or do your best work when you're exhausted. And there's nothing worse than waking up after getting seven to eight hours of sleep and still feeling tired.

Your brain uses 20 percent of your body's energy every day, and unpredictability and decision-making are some of the most draining demands.

To protect your energy, create structure *with* flexibility.

Your brain is a creature of habit. It thrives on routines. The prefrontal cortex, which handles decision-making and complex thinking, uses less energy when actions are automatic.

Structure gives your brain predictability. It acts like a road map, showing the brain where to go, so it doesn't have to direct resources into making a decision. This is why you can feel calmer and less overwhelmed when you have a plan.

Without one, your brain must constantly process uncertainty—this uses energy and can contribute to decision fatigue. That's when the brain gets bombarded by having to make too many choices. It can also contribute to cognitive overload, when the brain must process more information than it has capacity for.

Creating a brain routine around a few anchors—in the morning or evening—reduces unpredictability, allowing your brain to save energy for more cognitively demanding tasks.

In the morning, maybe that's making your bed, drinking a glass of water, and going outside for 10 minutes.

In the evening, it could be gratitude journaling, reading for 20 minutes, and sharing the highlights of your day with a loved one.

Don't become rigid with these anchors. Life is unpredictable. On busy days, if you can't use them all, use one. It'll still help calm the brain, allowing it to direct energy where it matters most.

Build structure with flexibility, and your routine will help rejuvenate your brain, not restrict it.

KWIK STEP: Assess your morning and evening routines. What works well and what needs changing?

AFFIRMATION: *"I build structure with flexibility to support my brain. I am limitless."*

JUNE 16

TRADE YOUR KNOWING FOR GROWING

Thousands of years ago, your value in society was likely measured by your brute strength. Today, it's your *brain strength*.

In the 21st century, the ultimate competitive advantage, the key to your success, lies in your ability to rapidly increase your human intelligence, turning your knowledge into action. And how do you do this?

Through learning.

If you can learn *how* to learn, you can learn *anything*. Focus. Memory. Faster reading. Sharper thinking. Better problem-solving. Leadership. Parenting. Languages. Martial arts. Painting. Marketing. Money management. Effective communication. Public speaking. Whatever you dream of achieving, your brain can learn.

But sometimes, to learn effectively, we need to let go of the *cognitive biases* that get in our way.

Cognitive biases are mental shortcuts the brain uses for quick decision-making, and psychologists estimate there are more than 180. While we do want quick cognition and decision-making, cognitive biases are actually errors in thinking that affect how we perceive, remember, and interpret information.

Some of the biases that interfere with learning include:

- **ANCHORING BIAS:** We give more weight to the first piece of information we learned.
- **CONFIRMATION BIAS:** We prioritize information that aligns with our beliefs rather than those that challenge us.
- **THE DUNNING-KRUGER EFFECT:** We overestimate our competence, thinking we're smarter or more capable than our knowledge or skill bears out.

The goal isn't to eliminate every cognitive bias—that's impossible. Your brain will keep making shortcuts, but you can become more aware of them.

Simply knowing they exist does a lot to lessen their impact on your ability to learn. Studies show mindfulness—and knowing you're susceptible to cognitive biases—help to lessen their influence.

So be willing to trade your knowing for growing.

KWIK STEP: When you encounter a new idea or information today, notice if there's resistance. If there is, ask, "Am I resisting because it's wrong or because it's new?"

AFFIRMATION: *"I trade my knowing for growing. I am limitless."*

JUNE 17

PRACTICE IS POWER

Your brain is a limitless learning machine.

Anything you want to master—focus, creativity, decision-making, problem-solving, memory, listening—your brain can. But it takes practice—not the mindless type where you "just check a box," but intentional practice where you give your full attention, curiosity, effort, and enthusiasm to what you're doing.

By attaching strong emotions to your practice session, you're engaging the emotional centers of your brain, including the amygdala. This helps reinforce what you're learning by signaling "this matters"—a process that activates motivational and reward circuits to keep you engaged.

Your amygdala is also interacting with the hippocampus—the memory center of your brain—to "tag" the practice session as important. This strengthens how the experience gets encoded and retained, making it easier for your brain to retrieve and apply the skill on demand.

This is how you create new skill circuits in your brain for anything.

In about four to eight weeks of consistent, focused practice, the skill can become available to you. That's because the pathways in your brain have formed and strengthened, making the skill feel almost as natural as tying your shoelaces or riding a bike.

So practice is more than doing a task—it's a power you can wield. Practice is power.

KWIK STEP: Pick something that you're working on improving and add a feeling like curiosity, playfulness, or excitement. Then practice the skill and notice how you feel during and after your session.

AFFIRMATION: *"Practice is my power. I am limitless."*

JUNE 18

FICTION IS TRAINING GROUND FOR THE FUTURE

Whether drawn on cave walls, passed down orally, acted on stages, written on scrolls, printed on pages, or flashed onto screens, humans have told stories since the dawn of time.

It's one of our most ancient practices and arts and, it turns out, one of the brain's original learning tools.

Read a gripping mystery, fantasy, or romance, and you're not just escaping your life. Your brain is learning how to be *you*.

Reading emotionally engaging stories transports you into the characters and world. You see life through their perspective. You reflect on their choices, agreeing and disagreeing with them. You predict where the story will go and what will happen. You empathize. You work to understand character motives.

All the while, your brain is learning how to connect with people, how to respond in difficult situations, and how to empathize and understand other people's challenges. And this changes how you move through the world, how you make decisions, what you prioritize, and how you connect, build relationships, and interact with people.

Research backs this up. It's shown that reading emotionally charged fiction can improve your social cognitive abilities including empathy, interpreting social cues, and inferring what others are thinking and feeling.

fMRI studies also reveal that emotionally engaging stories activate numerous regions, including those involved with language, emotion, predictive processing, and the default mode network, which is associated with self-reflection, remembering the past, and envisioning the future.

By reading fiction, you're also enhancing your creativity and imagination.

In a world increasingly shaped by technology and artificial intelligence, where people feel lonely, disconnected, and misunderstood, one the greatest superpowers you can have is the ability to connect, build trust, and collaborate with others.

Fiction is your training ground for the future.

KWIK STEP: Read at least five pages of a novel or short fictional story today.

AFFIRMATION: *"I read to create my future. I am limitless."*

JUNE 19

YOU ARE ENOUGH

You were taught to believe a lie.

Entire industries like marketing and advertising have made you believe that you are not enough.

And so you have built your life trying to "fix" this. You've chased down goals, filled your days to bursting, and worked hard to improve your performance. All the while, you've believed that if you just do more, try harder, and get better at something, then you'll finally be enough and have enough to be worthy, successful, and deserving of the life you want.

"Enough" isn't something you earn or have to prove. It doesn't happen when you develop a new skill, reach a particular goal, or attain a certain level of success.

It's something you already *are*.

"I am enough."

When you keep repeating this phrase, not only will your brain start believing it—your brain will *change*. Research into positive affirmations shows that phrases like "I am enough" help to reshape thought patterns, foster creativity, and strengthen problem-solving, while contributing to emotional regulation and overall happiness at the same time.

Should you stop growing, setting goals, or developing new skills? No. That's a part of life—one of the most exciting and rewarding.

When you realize you are enough, you grow from wholeness, from a sense of inner peace, security, and self-trust rather than from fear, comparison, and self-doubt.

You are enough. Believe it.

KWIK STEP: Sit comfortably on the ground or in a chair with both feet on the floor. For three to five minutes, breathe deeply in and out, quietly repeating, "I am enough." Notice what you feel in your body, and what, if any thoughts or images come up. Whatever arises, imagine it flowing out of you with your exhales.

AFFIRMATION: *"I am enough. I am limitless."*

JUNE 20

GENIUS LEAVES CLUES

The most successful people are smarter than most people in just one way: They know themselves so well that they design their lives for success.

They set up rituals and routines that align with how they're most productive. They know their goals and values so clearly that saying no is about protecting what matters. And they use environmental signals to train their brain to easily drop into deep focus and flow.

Genius is about more than IQ. It's about pattern recognition. And the most important patterns to recognize are the ones inside you.

Whatever change you want to make—building a new habit, reshaping a belief, or reaching a new level of learning—run it through what I call the "Five *W*s and *H* Genius Framework."

WHY? These are your values—the reason you want to make a change.

WHO? This is your identity—who you believe you are.

WHAT? These are the behaviors and habits that help optimize your brain's performance. It's reading, having a "not-to-do list," exercising, eating healthy, sleeping, and spending time with positive people.

WHERE AND WHEN? This is your environment and timing. It's knowing when you do your best work or studying. For some people that's early in the morning; for others, in the evening. It's also creating environments that support focus, like having good lighting and reducing distractions.

HOW? These are the capabilities or skills you have or need to develop.

When you create change, start by picking one level. Maybe the most exciting, or the one generating the most resistance. That's a hint that treasure lies beneath effort. Over time, address every level. That's how change sticks.

Genius leaves clues. Find and decipher the ones inside you.

KWIK STEP: Think of a change you want. What level in the framework do you need to focus on? And what's one thing you can do today to improve it?

AFFIRMATION: *"I am willing to look within to know myself. I am limitless."*

SUBTRACT TO MULTIPLY

Do you ever wonder why you feel mentally exhausted, burned out, or unable to focus?

Could it be that you're saying yes to too many things?

When you overcommit, it's like having too many windows open on your computer. Even if you minimize them, they still drain your brain's working memory, energy, and focus.

Your brain hates unfinished tasks. When it's interrupted from completing something, it remembers what's left undone. This is why you can be doing something else, yet you keep thinking about what you still need to do.

Your brain's working memory has a limited bandwidth. When too many commitments compete for it, then it can lead to overload, which can cause fatigue and burnout, and make focus, creativity, and problem-solving difficult.

In truth, you probably need to say no more than you think. This one small word can free your brain to perform at its best and create space to say yes to what truly matters.

To achieve this, try filtering through "heck yes" or "heck no."

Your brain thrives on simplicity. Instead of closely analyzing every key point, you're simplifying the decision-making, allowing your brain to make faster and more efficient decisions.

So if somebody asks, "Want to grab dinner tonight?" and if it isn't a full-on "heck yes," then maybe you should say, "Heck no." If someone asks you to take on more work at the office, if it isn't a "heck yes" then tell them no. If someone asks you to sign onto a new project or client, and it isn't a "heck yes," then tell them no.

Your life is not defined by how many things you're doing, but whether you're doing the *right* things.

Say "no" more and "yes" less. By subtracting from your life, you're multiplying your productivity and impact.

KWIK STEP: Think of a commitment or responsibility that's been weighing on you and ask: "Is this a 'heck yes' or a 'heck no'?" If it's a no, then get rid of it.

AFFIRMATION: *"I subtract what doesn't add value in my life to make space for what does. I am limitless."*

CURIOSITY EXPANDS YOUR HUMAN POTENTIAL

What's the first thing a young child does when they find a puddle of mud?

They jump into it. They squat down, sink their hands deep into it, pull it up, drop it from above, slather it on their arms. If you're not paying attention, they'll probably try eating it too. They're not doing this to be difficult. They're doing it to learn.

They're touching, tasting, smelling everything they possibly can get their hands on. Kids are constantly asking questions like "What's this? Why is that? How come?" This is because it's how the brain learns.

Curiosity activates and releases dopamine that helps you to focus and encode information better. When you're curious, your brain becomes more alert, receptive, and engaged.

To train your mind to stay engaged, ask better questions, and keep learning in a fast-changing world, get *CURIOUS.*

CHALLENGE assumptions,
UNCOVER new perspectives,
READ outside your expertise,
INQUIRE deeply,
OBSERVE intentionally,
UPDATE your knowledge, and
STAY open-minded.

The moment you stop asking questions, you stop wondering, and the moment you stop being curious is often the moment your growth stalls.

Curiosity expands your human potential. Stay curious.

KWIK STEP: Ask one question about something today.

AFFIRMATION: *"I am curious, open, and constantly learning. I am limitless."*

JUNE 23

YOU BECOME YOUR STANDARDS

Consistency is not about never slipping.

It's about how quickly you get back on track. Missing one day of practice, a workout, or a subpar performance is normal. Work happens. Family happens. Life happens. Missing two days is when the brain starts wiring a new pattern.

High performers don't rely on motivation, they rely on their standards.

One of the most powerful standards you can adopt is this: "I may miss one day, but I do not miss two."

This isn't about beating yourself up, it's about self-compassion, about kindness toward yourself. Self-compassion says that it's okay to make mistakes or even poor decisions. Self-compassion doesn't excuse what happened but empowers you to keep making progress the next day.

When you stop beating yourself up and start recommitting to your growth and goals, your brain learns something important: You are someone who shows up for yourself again and again. You may fall, but you always rise.

Every time you get back on track, you strengthen the identity of someone who keeps promises to themselves.

We get what we tolerate in life. That goes for how others treat us and also how we treat ourselves. You become your standards. Be willing to raise yours, and you'll raise your life.

KWIK STEP: What is one area of your life where you're tolerating something in your own behavior that you probably shouldn't? What is the minimum standard you'll accept? Set it today.

AFFIRMATION: *"I raise my standards to raise my life. I am limitless."*

DON'T IMPLY IT, APPLY IT

Time is the only thing that's equal for everyone.

Not everyone has equal income, equal connections, or equal education. But we all have the same amount of time in a day.

How are you spending yours?

Remember it's not simply time management. It's *priority* management. It's keeping the most important thing that leads to becoming limitless and changing your life for the better.

So what's the most important thing today?

Is it starting or growing your business? Enjoying a deeper connection with your partner or children? Improving your health or fitness? Accelerating your learning and human intelligence?

There is no right or wrong answer, only what's right or wrong for you.

Getting clear on what matters most is like handing instructions to your prefrontal cortex, your brain's executive control center. It evaluates goals, then directs planning, decision-making, and self-control (among other things) to help you attain them. But it can't plan what it doesn't know exists.

First, you need clarity, but then you need to implement—to purposely use whatever knowledge, skills, capabilities, and ideas you've developed in pursuit of your goals.

Your calendar is one of your most valuable tools. If you're not scheduling time, then how will you apply what you've learned?

You don't want to go through a year generating ideas and gaining knowledge without acting on anything. That's ultimately how your life changes.

Don't imply it. Apply it.

KWIK STEP: What is one thing that you've been putting off that needs more application? Schedule it today.

AFFIRMATION: *"I don't say it. I show it with my actions. I am limitless."*

YOU'RE NEVER TOO OLD

So many of us dream of learning or doing something new, yet we never start because one thought stops us: *I'm too old.*

We tell ourselves we've missed our chance or it's too late.

These thoughts feel persuasive, and to the brain, they can be completely convincing. *Identity foreclosure* is when we commit so fully to one version of ourselves that we unconsciously close off other possibilities. It's as if our brain can't imagine us being or doing anything else.

So we don't. We stop learning, growing, dreaming, and becoming.

Except studies show age is no barrier to learning and growing. Research on neuroplasticity shows that the brain is capable of creating new neural connections well into our 60s, 70s and beyond through lifestyle changes including exercising, eating a healthy diet, and challenging your brain. With consistency and challenge, it rewires itself to adapt and grow.

Your birthdate isn't what's stopping you. It's the outdated mental file you're running in the supercomputer of your brain—one that says beginning again means you'll fail, look foolish, or prove that change is impossible.

But files can be rewritten and beliefs reprogrammed. Change the belief, and you change what's possible.

Tell your brain you *can* learn anything at any age, and you will. It will start reorganizing itself and reorienting your goals to execute the new operating code.

You're never too old to learn a new language, play an instrument, start a business, paint, write, dance, sing, travel, or try something new.

You're never too old to grow.

KWIK STEP: Identify one thing you've always dreamed of learning or doing, but you haven't because you've felt too old, that it passed you by, or you missed your chance. Now find one small action you can take today to bring you closer to this and do it.

AFFIRMATION: *"I am never too old to learn, grow, and adapt. I am limitless."*

THE TREASURES YOU SEEK ARE HIDDEN IN YOUR HABITS

It's estimated that up to 95 percent of brain activity happens unconsciously, otherwise known as habits.

Think of habits as mental shortcuts built by your brain to conserve energy. Every time you repeat a habit, it strengthens the neural pathway, making the grooves deeper. That's why, once habits form, the brain resists changing them—it's harder and uses more energy.

The good news is you can use the same brain system that locks in bad habits to rewire better ones.

Here's one way to stop the old unconscious loops and begin building new ones:

1. **IDENTIFY YOUR CUE.** Notice what triggers the habit. Is it stress, boredom, a certain person, place, time of day? The more specific the cue, the better.
2. **DISRUPT THE CRAVING.** If the craving is reaching for something sugary after feeling tired around 3 P.M., change the pattern. Get up and splash cold water on your face, or don't keep sugary snacks around.
3. **OFFER A BETTER RESPONSE.** Swap the unwanted behavior with a healthier alternative that satisfies that same craving, like choosing a cup of blueberries instead of candy. The goal is to break the automatic link between craving and behavior.
4. **REWARD IMMEDIATELY.** Your brain needs a clear signal that the new habit is worth repeating. So create a daily list of goals and include the new habit, do it, then cross it off. Physically checking off the goal gives you a small dopamine hit, making the new habit feel rewarding—which it is.

If you want a new result in life, you must do a new behavior. Do this often enough, and you'll eventually create a new habit that leads to a new life and a new you.

Because the treasures you seek in life and learning are hidden in your habits.

KWIK STEP: Identify one limitless habit you want to create. Write down the old four-step habit loop and the new one you'll use to replace it. Then practice it today.

AFFIRMATION: *"I easily create new habits. I am limitless."*

RISE UP. WIND DOWN.

Many ancient civilizations believed the world was governed by four elements found in nature. These same elements were also thought to live inside humans. Many physicians, including Hippocrates, called them the "four humours" and believed illnesses arose when they were out of balance.

Air meant inspiration, intelligence, and intention. Fire represented energy, transformation, and personal power. Earth symbolized grounding, stability, and inner resources. Water stood for flexibility, emotion, intuition, and reflection.

While medicine has long since abandoned the humours, the problem the ancients were trying to solve still exists. That's how to bring balance to the body and mind in a world that constantly pulls us out of balance. You can use the four elements to build simple morning and evening routines that help regulate your nervous system, circadian rhythm, and stress response.

AIR
- Breathwork with deep, slow inhales and exhales (morning and evening)
- Meditation (morning and evening)

FIRE
- Sunlight (morning)
- Exercise to elevate heart rate (morning)
- Sauna (evening)
- Blue-light blocking glasses (evening)
- Sit by a fire (evening)

EARTH
(for morning or evening)
- Walk in nature
- Sit on a rock
- Go barefoot outside on sand or grass
- Spend time with family, loved ones, and friends

WATER
- Drink a glass of water (morning)
- Take a cold shower (morning)
- Take a warm bath or shower (evening)

You want your morning rituals to activate the sympathetic nervous system, shifting your brain into alertness, focus, and action. Design your evening routine to help shift into the parasympathetic state, allowing your body and mind to recover and rest. Have fun. Be playful. Rise up. Wind down.

KWIK STEP: Incorporate at least two of the elements into your morning and evening routines today.

AFFIRMATION: *"I design my day and evening to rise up and wind down. I am limitless."*

JUNE 28

SUCCESS ISN'T ABOUT WHAT YOU FEEL; IT'S ABOUT WHAT YOU DO

Most people quit when things get hard.

But transformation happens by showing up even when you don't feel like it.

The secret to lasting change isn't motivation. It's mastering habit formation. That way, when it's hard, you don't have to fight your feelings. You can feel exhausted or angry and still do the work, because you've built the habit of showing up.

This is where constant feedback loops matter.

Break all your goals into manageable steps, and design progress measures to give you instant feedback. If your goal is to save more money, set a weekly target and check in on a specific day. If your goal is to read one book a week, set a daily target, and track progress nightly.

This isn't about being perfect. You will miss days. You will feel tempted to quit. But make your progress easier to track, and your progress becomes easier to make.

Remember, success isn't about what you feel; it's what you do.

KWIK STEP: What is one small, instant feedback loop you can create and track daily or weekly?

AFFIRMATION: *"Success is about what I do. I am limitless."*

JUNE 29

YOU'RE THE AUTHOR OF YOUR LIFE

All great stories have a villain.

The X-Men battled Magneto. Batman dueled with the Joker. Luke Skywalker fought Darth Vader. Every hero must confront and defeat an enemy to reach their goal.

In the story of your life, who is your villain? What stands between you and what you want and deserve to experience?

Are you feeling stuck in your learning or career? Do you lack energy or purpose? Are you wracked by negative self-talk? Are you feeling unhappy or burned out? Is there a relationship missing or troubling you? Are you trapped in perfectionism or procrastination?

Right now, your future is unwritten. Not only are you the hero of your journey—you're its author. This is known as *narrative identity.* It's the story your brain uses to make sense of who you are and what you believe is possible.

This is empowering because it means you get to write the script for your future.

You're not your past. You're not what happened yesterday, last week, or last year. Neuroplasticity shows your brain can reorganize itself, making new connections through repeated thoughts, behaviors, and experiences. You simply need to give it a new script.

So take pen and paper, and write your next chapter.

What do you want? What's the reward waiting for you?

Who must you become to reach it?

Who or what is the villain in your way?

What do you need to defeat this villain? What skills, capabilities, knowledge, allies or mentors, energy?

Now, close your eyes and visualize yourself winning. Use all your senses. When you visualize, your brain rehearses success as if it were real. And when you engage in intentional thoughts, you train your brain to notice what matters, bringing opportunities and ideas into greater focus.

Be the hero of your story. And remember, you're also its author.

KWIK STEP: Write the next chapter for your life, then close your eyes and visualize it.

AFFIRMATION: *"I write my story with purpose and power. I am limitless."*

JUNE 30

READING IS ABOUT RETENTION

Think back to when you were in school. What was your memory class like?

Okay, that was a trick question. There are no classes on memory.

If you've ever felt frustrated with reading, ever gotten to the end of a page only to forget what was written, this is one reason. Not being able to remember what you read isn't your fault.

And it's not a reading problem. It's a retention problem—one that you can correct. In the end, you want to focus, understand, and retain information. That's how you eventually implement it.

Here's a three-part method to remember more of what you read.

1. **SCAN FOR A ROADMAP.** Preview what you're about to read by scanning for headlines and bolded text. You could even read a summary or ask AI to give you an overview. This gives your brain a framework, also known as *schema formation*. It's a cognitive process where the brain starts organizing information, so when you read, the brain says, "I know where this goes."
2. **ASK QUESTIONS.** Questions are the answers. As you're reading, ask, "Why is this important? How can I use this? How does this relate to what I already know?" This engages the brain in thinking and comprehension in a deeper way.
3. **TEACH IT.** Learning is not a spectator sport. How do you make it active? By teaching what you learned within 24 hours. This forces the brain to simplify and summarize information in your own words, which helps improve memory. The technique is known as the *protégé effect*. Studies show people make significant gains in learning when they teach the material.

Reading isn't about consumption. It's about retention. That's how you go from "I read it" to "I live it."

KWIK STEP: Use the three-part framework with something you have to read or learn today. If there's nothing, then take one step and use it (e.g., teach this entry to someone).

AFFIRMATION: *"I train my brain to retain. I am limitless."*

RISE

The Season of Power

(July 1–September 30)

Your human potential expands when you have the courage to use it—when you put it into practice, get feedback, and adjust.

Just as the summer season represents peak power, growth, and energy, so do the next three months. This is your time to rise, to step into your power, expand your confidence, and elevate your performance.

Over the next 90 days, you'll learn to:

- Regulate your emotions
- Step into courage
- Activate your purpose
- Build resilience
- Overcome challenges and setbacks
- Master motivation

These months are about living fully, living boldly, and living intentionally.

Welcome to the season where you rise into your true power, purpose, and potential.

JULY 1

PASSION SERVES YOU; PURPOSE SERVES OTHERS

Your passion is not your purpose.

Passion lights you up. It's what you want to do again that's worth pursuing, learning, and improving.

Purpose is how you use your passions to light up other people.

Your purpose isn't being a yoga instructor; it's guiding people to connect and feel strong in their bodies. It's not being a financial planner; it's helping people to unlock freedom. It's not being a teacher; it's giving people knowledge to transform their lives.

You don't need to discover your purpose first. You need to notice what moves you. This starts with curiosity and adding novelty to your life. Your brain pays attention to what's new. It likes new activities, ideas, and learning.

So use curiosity to direct you to things that seem interesting or simply new, then pay attention to what lights you up—that's your passion.

Then ask yourself, "How can I use this to help move other people?" That's your purpose.

Passion serves you. Purpose serves others.

KWIK STEP: What's something you're passionate about, and how can you use it to serve others?

AFFIRMATION: *"I use my purpose to serve others. I am limitless."*

JULY 2

YOUR FUTURE LIES ON THE OTHER SIDE OF CHALLENGES

There's a point in Joseph Campbell's *The Hero's Journey* where the hero faces obstacles and challenges. It's called "The Road of Trials." There's no skipping or fast-forwarding through this. Every hero and heroine must face trials and tribulations on their quest.

Guess what? You're going to face your own road of trials too.

Whatever goal you're working to achieve, there will be obstacles. Maybe it's a stray comment someone made that you can't stop thinking about. Maybe it's lack of sleep because you have a newborn at home. Maybe it'll come in the form of feeling stuck on a problem, or a client who suddenly terminates a contract.

Whatever challenges you face, they may cause you to doubt your abilities, second-guess your decisions, and question whether it's worth continuing the journey toward your goals in the first place.

The only way out of this situation is through it.

Having a clear vision can help sustain and propel you through difficult times. Why did you set out on this quest to begin with? What's waiting for you at the end? What's pulling at you, making this all worthwhile?

To visualize the end goal, imagine your future in five categories:

- **IDENTITY.** Who will you become as a person? More trustworthy? More compassionate?
- **SKILLS.** What skills or capabilities will you develop? A better memory? Faster reading and comprehension? Improved sales or marketing strategies? A better leader? Public speaker? Thinker?
- **EMOTIONS.** How will you feel? Confident? Happy? Fulfilled?
- **BODY.** How will you physically feel? Energized? Engaged? Focused? Stronger?
- **LIFE.** How will this change your relationships, finances, and health?

Get specific. This is the reason you're investing your time into learning, improving, and growing. This is your future calling.

KWIK STEP: Set a timer for at least five minutes, and mentally time travel into the future, envisioning what's waiting at the end of this journey.

AFFIRMATION: *"I persevere through this challenge.*
My future lies on the other side. I am limitless."

JULY 3

TURN OBLIGATIONS INTO OPPORTUNITIES

One of the simplest ways to get more done with less stress and more energy can be summed up in three words:

"I get to."

How often do you go through the day, catching yourself saying, "I've got to write this report," or "I've got to pick up the kids," or "I've got to learn," or "I've got to take this call"? Thoughts like these feel heavy, hard, and exhausting.

But when you change "I got to" to "I get to," the cognitive shift makes a task stop feeling like a burden and more like an opportunity. You're using what's known as the *framing effect* to your advantage. This cognitive bias explains how the brain can make different choices and judgments based on how information gets presented. Marketers use this principle often. It's why items cost $49.99, not $50.

When you shift to "I get to," it changes your brain's appraisal of the situation. The task in front of you feels like a choice, which boosts your sense of autonomy, and with it, motivation and energy.

Instead of saying, "I've got to write this report," practice reframing it as "I *get* to share my ideas."

"I *get* to pick up the kids."

"I *get* to learn and read."

"I *get* to take this call."

Replacing "I have to" with "I get to" turns what feels like pressure into purpose, and obligations into opportunities.

KWIK STEP: What is one thing you've got to do today that you can reframe as something you get to do?

AFFIRMATION: *"I turn my obligations into opportunities. I am limitless."*

JULY 4

YOUR ONCE AND FUTURE SELF

Let's pretend I have a time machine.

One night, I stop outside your home and offer you a chance to travel back and talk to your younger self. There, you can pass along any advice, give them any encouragement, and share any guidance to help them through the coming years. Would you take it?

Or reverse it. If you could go forward through time and gain wisdom, support, and knowledge from your future self about what to do, what to think, or who to be today, would you take it?

I'm 99.9 percent sure you would. Who wouldn't take an opportunity to deliver or receive messages that could reshape the course of their life?

While a literal machine doesn't exist, your brain already gives you the power to travel through time and reap its benefits. *Mental time travel*, as it's called, includes episodic memory (vividly re-experiencing the past), and episodic future thinking (imagining or simulating future events).

It turns out, the brain uses overlapping networks when recalling the past and envisioning the future, making both experiences feel real. One of those is the default mode network, which plays numerous roles, including helping to process memory, regulate emotions, and develop your sense of self, especially when daydreaming or imagining.

By imagining the past and future, you can activate these same pathways to help guide your choices and change the direction of your life.

So have the courage and curiosity to remember your once and future self.

KWIK STEP: Spend at least five minutes mentally traveling into your past and future.

1. Imagine traveling into the past and asking, "What advice do I want to give my younger self? What do they need to hear?"
2. Then imagine projecting yourself into the future to speak to the you of today, and asking, "What would my future self tell me right now? What do I need to hear today?"

AFFIRMATION: *"I am connected to my past and future selves, and so I make my time here count. I am limitless."*

JULY 5

STEAL COGNITIVE REPS WHENEVER YOU CAN

Your habits determine your future capabilities, built through consistent, daily practice to improve and master a skill. But mastery takes time, something most of us don't have enough of. If mastery depends on physical practice alone, then most of us will never get in enough reps to reach our potential.

Fortunately, physical practice isn't the only option. Mental rehearsal works too.

World-class athletes, surgeons, musicians, and elite military forces all visualize themselves performing under pressure. This accelerates the brain's ability to learn, remember, and perform. As research shows, visualizing physical movements activates many of the same motor and sensory circuits as the action itself.

It turns out, the brain treats physical and mental practice similarly. In a University of Chicago study, researchers tested how well people could improve their free-throw percentage. For six weeks, one group practiced on the court daily, while another only visualized shooting. The group that practiced in real life saw a 24 percent increase. The group visualizing improved by 23 percent, just 1 percentage point less.

Mental rehearsal strengthens neural pathways by reinforcing the correct firing patterns, which accelerates learning and boosts self-confidence.

You can mentally rehearse anytime. Before falling asleep or when you wake, visualize yourself in the first person giving a calm and confident presentation, remembering what you're studying, or assertively answering questions during an interview. Mentally rehearse while brewing your morning coffee, showering, or walking outside.

Steal your reps wherever you can—physically or mentally.

KWIK STEP: Identify one skill you're working to improve, then mentally rehearse for five minutes.

AFFIRMATION: *"I rehearse my success under pressure so I master my skills and improve my performance. I am limitless."*

JULY 6

DO WHAT'S EASY, AND LIFE IS HARD. DO WHAT'S HARD, AND LIFE GETS EASIER.

When we want to build physical strength, no trainer recommends lying on the couch. Muscles grow when challenged—when exposed to mild strain for short durations, like from lifting, sprinting, or sparring—and then allowed to rest.

It's in recovery that tiny muscle fibers knit themselves together, slightly stronger, so the next time they face that same stressor, they're capable of withstanding the pressure. This is the biological process known as *hormesis*. And it also happens in your brain.

Learning a language, an instrument, a dance step, or even chess challenges your neural pathways. That effort forces neurons to fire in new patterns as different circuitry and synaptic connections form.

With repetition and rest, these connections grow stronger. Over time, what felt hard becomes easy. But this growth doesn't come from choosing the comfortable path. You must challenge your brain with healthy stress, strain, and recovery, then repeat.

If you find yourself procrastinating, maybe even feeling afraid of a challenge, ask yourself: "Will the rewards outweigh my effort?"

If yes, act now. Even tiny movements release dopamine, motivating you to repeat the behavior. Intelligent, consistent action, especially when you're scared or don't feel like it, cures most everything, including fear.

If that doesn't work, ask: "What will I lose by not acting?" The brain is wired to avoid loss more than to pursue gain—a cognitive bias called *loss aversion*. Make fear work for you instead of trapping you.

If that fails, then consider whether that action is something you want. If it's not, let it go. This will free up space in your working memory for things that will move your life forward.

When you only do what's easy, life is hard. But do what's hard—even scary—and life becomes easier.

KWIK STEP: What is one thing you've avoided or are scared to do? Ask yourself: "Will the rewards outweigh my effort?" If yes, act. If you still feel stuck, ask: "What will I lose by not acting?"

AFFIRMATION: *"I do what's hard, and that makes my life easier. I am limitless."*

JULY 7

DON'T WAIT FOR MOTIVATION; CREATE IT

There's an ancient Chinese story of a farmer who saw a rabbit run into a stump and die. Thinking he'd get an easy meal, day after day the farmer sat by that same stump waiting for another rabbit to appear. Except it never did. Instead, the farmer's crops died, and he was left with nothing to eat..

Just like the farmer, sometimes we wait endlessly for motivation to appear, only it never arrives.

How many goals have you stopped making progress toward because you're waiting like the farmer to feel motivated?

Motivation isn't something you wake up with or wait for. It's not even something you have; it's something you do. You act, and then motivation appears.

The formula for doing motivation whenever you need it is simple:

$$\textit{Motivation} = \textit{Purpose} \times \textit{Energy} \times S^3$$

PURPOSE is *why* you do something. You can be passionate about history, but your purpose is teaching people about it. You can be passionate about health, but your purpose is coaching people to live longer, healthier lives.

ENERGY is literally about powering your brain and body. Without energy, you can't perform at your peak. So prioritizing restorative sleep, hydrating, exercising, and meditating will power your actions.

S^3 (SMALL SIMPLE STEPS) is the action that makes motivation appear. Big goals can overwhelm the brain, paralyzing you from acting. But chunking big tasks into small, manageable actions makes it that much easier to achieve. Remember, inch by inch, it's a cinch. Yard by yard, it's hard.

Wait for motivation to arise, and you'll be disappointed like the farmer waiting for the next rabbit. But do motivation, and you reclaim your power, agency, and potential.

Don't wait for motivation; create it.

KWIK STEP: Take five minutes to work out your motivation formula. Write your purpose, one energy boost, and three small simple steps you can take today to charge your motivation.

AFFIRMATION: *"I create my motivation by knowing my purpose, prioritizing my energy, and taking simple small steps. I am limitless."*

JULY 8

SELF-DOUBT IS A CLUE, NOT A CURSE

You're about to take on something that matters—a new project, a tough presentation, even helping your kid with homework—when it happens. That quiet yet persistent voice in your head whispers: *I can't do this. I'm not good enough.*

That sinking sense of self-doubt can often feel like a curse. But what if it's actually a clue?

Psychologists consider self-doubt to be part of your brain's metacognitive abilities. Metacognition is a process where you ask self-reflective questions to raise awareness and understanding about yourself. Self-doubt is a metacognition about your own capabilities.

So when self-doubt arises, it could be a sign you might need to prepare more, ask for help, or upgrade a skill.

Or maybe you need more confidence. One of the fastest ways to build that is practice. This is known as the *confidence-competence loop*. The more you practice, the more competent you become, which increases your confidence, driving you to practice more, and the cycle continues.

So the next time self-doubt strikes, don't despair. Get curious. Ask, "What are you trying to tell me? Do I need to prepare more? Ask for help? Gain more confidence? Practice more?"

Your abilities aren't fixed. You can change them, and simply embracing a growth mindset—that your abilities, talent, even intelligence can evolve—can lessen the negative impacts of self-doubt.

Self-doubt isn't a curse; it's a clue.

KWIK STEP: Identify an area where you're experiencing self-doubt, then ask, "What is this doubt trying to tell me?"

AFFIRMATION: *"I welcome self-doubt as a clue guiding me to grow, expand, and become limitless. I am limitless."*

JULY 9

DIFFICULT TIMES CAN DISTRACT, DIMINISH, OR DEVELOP YOU

In 2020, nearly 97 percent of California's Big Basin Redwoods State Park burned.

It was home to trees more than 300 feet tall, more than 50 feet wide, and some more than 2,000 years old. Experts assumed the forest had perished.

Within five months, the trees proved everyone wrong. Drawing on buds dormant for centuries and energy reserves stockpiled decades earlier, bright-green shoots emerged at the base of charred trunks. Life sprang from the ruins, bringing rebirth and hope once again.

We too face devastating moments—experiences that can leave us questioning how, even *if*, life can get better. Yet just as the ancient redwoods have endured by drawing on hidden reserves, you can too.

Neuroplasticity and neurogenesis prove that your skills, habits, even beliefs are not lost. Your brain can generate new connections, neural pathways, even cells.

When difficult times strike, it's not just about bouncing back—it's about bouncing forward. Research shows that we have the ability to use adversity, setbacks, and challenges to lead to greater strength, deeper insight, and more meaning.

You can begin this process with curiosity and cognitive reappraisal: intentionally shifting how you think about and interpret a situation.

Consider a setback you're facing now. How can you reframe it as an opportunity? What is it teaching you? What skills or strengths are you developing? What has it shown you about yourself?

If your mind is blank, think about a past struggle you overcame. What did you learn? What skills did you develop? Who did you become?

Like the redwoods, you can't stop the fires from springing up in your life. But on the quest to reveal and realize your potential, difficult times can either distract you, diminish you, or develop you.

KWIK STEP: Consider a past or current setback. Write what you've learned from it, how you've grown, and what you've gained.

AFFIRMATION: *"I use difficult times to develop myself. I am limitless."*

YOUR PHYSIOLOGY AFFECTS YOUR PSYCHOLOGY

Try this: Like Santa Claus, laugh so it shakes your whole body: "Ho! Ho! Ho!"

Now, imagine you're walking down the street and you see an old friend. You grin and wave while saying, "Hi! It's so good to see you."

Next, stand and march in place, or do cross-crawls, jumping jacks, or air squats. Just move your body to slightly elevate your heart rate (safely).

How did you feel after each movement? Did your mood shift? Did your energy change? If you're unsure, try it again.

We think we need to change how we feel before we can act. That we need to feel motivated before we can work on a big project, inspired before we write, or excited before we study. When those emotions don't come, it leaves us stuck, procrastinating, and doubting ourselves, as if there's something wrong with us.

Sometimes emotions do arrive first. But usually we have to change our inner state first. We do that through action. Movement has the power to shift how we feel and think. It alters our hormonal expression, releasing endorphins, dopamine, serotonin, and noradrenaline—chemicals involved in pain relief, motivation, mood regulation, alertness, and attention.

When you move your body, it also helps regulate cortisol levels, reducing stress. And it increases the release of growth factors that support neuroplasticity and your brain's ability to learn, grow, and adapt.

Change your posture or move your body, and you get immediate boosts to confidence, mood, focus, attention, even reaction time.

The next time you have to give a big presentation, ask for a raise, or perform at your peak, move your body first. Take up more space. Be seen. Even if it feels awkward, go. Do. Become.

Your physiology affects your psychology.

KWIK STEP: Before doing something important today—giving a presentation, working on a project, having an important conversation—move your body to change your state. Pick something you can do for two minutes, like cross-crawls, marching in place, intentionally smiling, or laughing, and do it. Notice how you feel during and after.

AFFIRMATION: *"I use movement to change my inner state to the one I choose. I am limitless."*

CLEAR DECISION. DECISIVE ACTION.

High performers like athletes, entrepreneurs, and military leaders train themselves to make smart decisions quickly. Not recklessly. Not impulsively. But efficiently.

What stops most people from doing this? The need for certainty. It's something the brain actually craves—it's an ancient survival instinct.

But high performers know certainty is just the brain seeking patterns. When it faces one it doesn't recognize, fear takes over. Instead of giving in, high performers train their minds to face uncertainty without letting the amygdala trigger a stress response. They stay calm and centered so the rational part of their brain remains in charge.

One way you can learn to do the same is by using the *40/70 Rule,* attributed to the late US Secretary of State and four-star general Colin Powell. It helps you avoid acting rashly or hesitating too long.

If you act with less than 40 percent of the facts, you're guessing. If you wait for more than 70 percent, you're overthinking and risk missing your window.

You can apply this to any decision whether it's applying for a job, submitting a proposal for client work, or signing up for a new course. If you have 40 to 70 percent of the information, go for it.

You'll never know exactly how something will turn out. The only thing you can expect is the unexpected. But every action gives you feedback. You act, learn, adjust, and move forward again. This is the cycle until, eventually, decision-making stops feeling so scary—it becomes automatic.

The faster you learn how to make clear decisions and take decisive action, the faster you'll unlock new possibilities.

KWIK STEP: Pick a decision that has weighed on you, and write down what you know about it and what you don't. If you're 40 to 70 percent informed, decide and act.

AFFIRMATION: *"I make calm, centered, and clear decisions, and then I act. I am limitless."*

JULY 12

YOUR BRAIN RUNS ON ENERGY

Imagine waking up and springing out of bed after your alarm clock goes off, filled with energy. No yawning. No need to chug coffee or psych yourself up. You're ready to go.

For most people, this is a fantasy. They wake up dragging themselves from bed, feeling an ache in their chest and wondering how they'll get through the day.

If this sounds familiar, it's not that you're broken, lazy, or unmotivated. You're exhausted, and your brain is trying to protect you.

When energy is low, the brain shifts resources from energy-hungry regions like the prefrontal cortex, so there's less fuel for willpower, planning, decision-making, and emotional regulation.

The brain shifts into a survival state, prioritizing conservation. Leaving you to feel like you're on autopilot, overwhelmed, irritable, hypervigilant, foggy, or numb.

There are things you can do to help increase your energy and improve how you manage it during the day. Do regular "Personal Energy Audits" to assess what's charging and draining you.

- **SLEEP.** Are you getting enough?
- **DIET.** Are you eating foods that fuel you?
- **EXERCISE.** Are you moving your body to release endorphins and help neurons grow, adapt, learn, and recover from stress?
- **REST.** Are you doing activities that restore you?
- **PEOPLE.** Do the people around you lift you up or drag you down?
- **DEVICES.** Is constant scrolling stealing your energy?
- **EMOTIONS.** Are you cycling through repetitive thoughts or worries?
- **THOUGHTS.** Do you have empowering thoughts?

Just as there's a process for memory and learning, there's a process for generating energy. Your brain runs on energy. Go make it. Y

KWIK STEP: What is one area of your Personal Energy Audit that you want to improve? And what can you do today to achieve that?

AFFIRMATION: *"I create my own energy. I am limitless."*

JULY 13

ACTION BEATS INERTIA

You learn to read one word at a time.

You build your memory starting with just one name.

You create a business by helping one person first.

You lead your team by effectively communicating one sentence at a time.

Everything big starts small.

Every day, millions of people change their lives and make progress toward their goals. And every day, millions more stay exactly where they are.

The only difference? The people who transformed took small actions. Micro actions. Not tomorrow. Not someday in the future. Not "when the time is right." And not after thinking about it more.

They took the actions that were right in front of them. And they did it again and again, day after day.

Taking the small, simple step is one way to overcome the cognitive bias known as *temporal discounting*—the tendency to undervalue future rewards. Research suggests this is one reason why some people procrastinate.

When you feel stuck, when you feel something important is out of reach, stop looking far off into the distance, and look at what's right in front of you. Take the action you can now.

Action beats inertia every single time.

KWIK STEP: What is one area in your life where you feel like you're procrastinating or putting something off? Think of one small action you can take right now, and do it.

AFFIRMATION: *"I act now. I am limitless."*

MORE MAKES MOMENTUM

Steve Jobs was known to practice Zen meditation, something he adopted after dropping out of college. Even as Apple grew into one of the largest companies in the world, and the demands on Jobs grew with it, he continued a regular practice up until his death. He used it as a tool to reduce stress, gain clarity, and train his brain.

The idea of regular practice isn't just about meditation; it could be, but it doesn't have to be. It's about doing *more* of the habits that already support your brain.

Maybe it's eating more brain-boosting foods, like avocados for healthy fats, blueberries for antioxidants, and wild-caught salmon for omega-3s.

Maybe it's journaling a bit longer or more frequently to strengthen memory and emotional clarity. It could even be walking or exercising 10 minutes longer every day, or adding one more workout to your weekly schedule to help release more BDNF (brain-derived neurotrophic factor).

Or maybe you're like Jobs and meditate for 10 minutes daily. What if you bumped that to 15, or added a second daily session, or one more during the week?

If you're unsure what you should do more of, then use the 80/20 principle. It's the idea that about 20 percent of what you do gives you 80 percent of your results.

Get clear on what's generating the most return for you, whether that's energy, focus, clarity, stress management, or joy. Then do just a little bit more.

More makes momentum.

KWIK STEP: Identify one thing in your life that you want to do more of and do it today.

AFFIRMATION: *"I am committed to doing more of what supports my brain becoming limitless. I am limitless."*

ACT HOW YOU WANT TO BE

What do Beyoncé, David Bowie, and Kobe Bryant have in common?

They each built alter egos—Sasha Fierce, Ziggy Stardust, and Black Mamba—to improve their performance and unlock specific strengths within themselves whenever they need it.

Why go to the trouble? Because identity drives behavior. Identity-Based Motivation shows that our identities are dynamically constructed and our actions are determined based on the context of a situation, and our brain's interpretation of how difficult a task, goal, or even life itself is.

So when you choose a role to deal with a life experience, your brain calls up the actions and attitudes necessary to fit the role. Your brain is activating an identity.

If you want to become someone different—someone who's more confident, more charismatic, more focused, or a better learner—act as if. This isn't about faking who you are. It's about helping retrain your brain, through neuroplasticity, to wire in new behaviors and a different identity.

The more you "act as if," the more those circuits strengthen, and then the behavior comes faster and easier next time.

Identity isn't a label, and it isn't fixed. Repetition writes your identity. If you want a different one, act as if you already are, so you become.

Act how you want to be.

KWIK STEP: Think of an aspect of your life that you want to improve. Now who do you see as having mastered it? Visualize yourself becoming that person and using that particular skill or behavior.

AFFIRMATION: *"I am becoming the person who [insert your specific behavior]. I am limitless."*

FEED WHAT WORKS

Maybe you have a cat or dog. For it to live and thrive, you must feed it, give it water and affection, play with it, and make sure it has exercise. This is caring for your animal. What you don't do is just keep bringing home new animals while ignoring the one you already have.

But when it comes to our habits and routines, we tend to do exactly that.

The brain is partly to blame. It's wired to respond to novelty. In the face of something new, your brain releases neurotransmitters, including norepinephrine to sharpen attention and dopamine to heighten motivation. These molecules help trigger your brain's reward system, making the new feel good and exciting. This keeps you hunting for the next new thing.

Plus, humans tend to have what's known as *additive bias*. We problem solve by adding new solutions, even when taking away the ones that aren't working would be more beneficial.

It's true, sometimes we need the new. Yet other times, the real value comes from continuing what already works.

Maybe you already have great sleep or exercise regularly. Maybe you're already learning a new word in a foreign language every day, reading for 20 minutes, scheduling 10 minutes for daydreaming, or putting away devices at dinner.

Don't simply add new things to your life. There's an underrated power in just noticing what works and consciously choosing to keep feeding it. That might mean continuing to invest your time, energy, and attention in it at the same level, or it could mean investing a little more, like learning two words a day, reading for 30 minutes, scheduling 15 minutes for daydreaming, or doing a 24-hour digital detox on the weekend.

Feed what works.

KWIK STEP: Identify one thing that is giving you the results you want, do it today, and keep going.

AFFIRMATION: *"I protect the things I already do that work and add value to my life. I am limitless."*

APPLAUSE LEADS TO ASCENT

We break large projects into smaller chunks. We make one slide for a presentation at a time. We write one chapter at a time. And we study one section of material at a time.

Chunking like this helps make progress easier to attain and sustain. It reduces cognitive overload and overwhelm.

This idea works for celebrating our small victories too.

Every time you tell yourself, "Great job!" or "You were outstanding" or "You're doing excellent work," you're signaling to the brain, "Keep going." Praise releases dopamine as a reward. Rewarding actions tell the brain to repeat what earned the praise.

You also don't complete tasks in a vacuum. Your brain recognizes when you move closer to completing a goal or open loop. By recognizing how far you've come, you show the brain "Look, we're getting there."

If these motivations aren't enough, then consider how praise helps reduce the brain's stress response. Thoughts like "I'm getting there, way to go" counteract more damaging stories like "There's so much to do," "I'm behind," or "I'm failing."

Celebrate your victories, because that applause will lead to your ascent.

KWIK STEP: Think of three recent victories, even small ones, that you're proud of. Praise yourself for your progress.

AFFIRMATION: *"I applaud my ascent. I am limitless."*

JULY 18

STAY TRUE TO YOU

It's so easy to look at someone and think they have it all—the career or job, the money, the looks, the body, the family.

In response, we overthink and judge ourselves. We constantly compare our lives to the movie trailers of others. But sometimes the grass is only greener on the other side because of the filter we're using.

We're always told, "Don't compare yourself to others." Except that's exactly what the brain evolved to do. It has a cognitive bias toward social comparison. It's one way the brain assesses our safety, status, and belonging.

But there's a real emotional and cognitive cost to constant comparison. It can trigger rumination, burnout, perfectionism, procrastination, depression, and fear of negative feedback. It can even increase feelings of envy, guilt, and regret.

Just as you break unhealthy habits by replacing them with healthier ones, you can give your brain a different target for comparison.

And that target is you. Compare yourself to who you were yesterday, or the best version of you that you're in the process of becoming.

You "win" at this game of life by taking consistent effort every day in the direction of your goals. Not by comparing yourself to others.

Comparing yourself to others doesn't just steal your joy; it robs those around you of experiencing tthe rare gift of *you*, the true self who has something unique to share with this world.

Your brain grows through progress and consistent action, not comparison. Stay true to you.

KWIK STEP: Think back to one year ago. What's one way you've grown or improved since then? Write down your answer, then pause and allow your brain to feel the progress.

AFFIRMATION: *"I am my true self. I am limitless."*

JULY 19

EMOTIONS ARE A CALL TO ACTION

Don't get angry with the kids.

Don't feel disappointed you didn't land the promotion.

Stop feeling anxious about your board meeting.

You've probably heard success comes from controlling your emotions, especially the negative. For most of us, that's tough. It can leave us feeling ashamed, guilty, and judgmental when we "fail."

The truth is that emotions aren't obstacles to overcome. Emotions are signposts.

They help us understand how we perceive people and situations. They give us vital information to make better decisions and take actions more aligned with our goals and who we want to be.

Emotion is the energy of motion. The key isn't bypassing the negative or rushing toward the positive. It's becoming aware—listening, acknowledging, and accepting the emotion, then deciding if it needs shifting.

One powerful practice that supports awareness is labeling. An fMRI study from UCLA found that labeling negative emotional experiences reduces activity in the amygdala—the threat detector—while increasing activity in the prefrontal cortex. This helps restore logical thinking, improves problem-solving and decision-making, and grants you better emotional regulation.

When you're overwhelmed, at your wit's end, or about to burst, pause. Take three slow, deep breaths. Focus on the emotion. Name it out loud. "I'm feeling angry," or "this is sadness." Then ask, "What are you trying to tell me?"

Sometimes, anger signals a need to slow down, set boundaries, limit social media, or move your body. Sadness could be a need to connect with others, make a big change, or do something playful and fun.

Emotions are a call to action—they're signals for you to explore, not a finish line.

KWIK STEP: When you feel an intense emotion today, pause, take a few deep, slow breaths, label it, then ask what it's trying to tell you.

AFFIRMATION: *"I accept all my emotions without judgment, and I navigate them with self-compassion and intention. I am limitless."*

JULY 20

FACE IT UNTIL YOU MAKE IT

You've probably heard the old saying "fake it until you make it."

It sounds catchy and clever. And it's been repeated so often that it feels like a fact. It even seems logical. If we want to be confident, then why not just pretend?

But there's a snag: It doesn't always work. Studies show that when we feel we're being inauthentic—pretending to be someone we're not—it raises stress, strains working memory, and can hurt our brain's ability to process information and make decisions.

The key to happiness starts with having the curiosity to know yourself—to know your strengths and your limitations. Then it's having the courage to not just find yourself, but face yourself. To be yourself in the moment, accepting your strengths and limitations. So it's not fake it until you make it. It's *face it* until you make it.

You face the limitation. You face the challenge. And you face the person in the mirror. In doing so, you don't fake confidence; you build it. Confidence in yourself and your abilities can come through the experience of doing hard things.

Over time, those hard things stop feeling hard. They even become fun, and eventually your brain will crave them.

Happiness doesn't come from avoiding struggle. It comes from facing struggle. Face it until you make it, and you will succeed.

KWIK STEP: Write a challenge or limitation that you're currently facing, then close your eyes and visualize yourself taking one small action that you normally avoid. The next time this situation appears, whether that's today, tomorrow, or in the future, take the small action, then praise yourself for doing it.

AFFIRMATION: *"My confidence comes from doing. I will face every challenge until I make it. I am limitless."*

JULY 21

YOUR DESTINATION DETERMINES YOUR DIRECTION

Imagine it's one year from now. What would it take for you to feel you're living a successful life? Not just a busy life, but a meaningful, fulfilling one?

This is more than a rhetorical question. If your brain is your GPS, knowing where you want to go is preloading the destination. It becomes a goal that recruits your brain's attention networks. This is why you notice those synchronicities—the seemingly random social media post, the unexpected encounter with someone, or the perfectly timed e-mail that can help close the gap between where you are and where you're going.

Clear goals also activate the prefrontal cortex—the part of your brain responsible for focus, planning, and self-control. This is how your vision turns into action, and how you separate distractions and busywork from what's actually worthy of your time, attention, and energy.

The more vividly you can visualize where you want to be, who you want to be, and the details of the life you want to live, the more you're engaging in what's called episodic future thinking. The brain uses vivid imagination to plan and prioritize what comes next.

This practice also activates many of the same neural networks as if you were actually experiencing something. It becomes mental rehearsal, another way for your brain to engage in neuroplasticity—building new neural pathways that become habits later.

So where do you want to be in a year?

What would make your life meaningful and successful?

What would make you feel happy and proud?

It's not just about how much effort you put in, but where you focus that effort. Your destination determines your direction.

KWIK STEP: Spend five minutes vividly visualizing what success in a year means to you. See, feel, and step into who you'll become, what your life looks like, and what it feels like, activating as many senses as you can.

AFFIRMATION: *"I know my destination. My direction is clear. I am limitless."*

JULY 22

EVERY EFFORT COUNTS

Some days, you're filled with energy. Other days, you're running on empty.

On the low-energy days, it's easy to beat yourself up for not "doing enough." Yet effort isn't measured against someone else's capacity. It's measured against yours. And not your potential—your actual.

If you only have 40 percent in your tank, and you give that 40 percent, guess what?

You gave 100 percent of what you had.

To your brain, what matters most isn't how much you give. It's that you keep showing up. It's that consistency that rewires your brain for resilience.

When a task requires effort, focus, or self-control, it activates the anterior cingulate cortex (ACC)—the region that monitors effort. Every time you choose to show up, no matter what you have in the tank, your ACC strengthens its communication with your prefrontal cortex—the region involved with motivation, planning, and goals.

So the more you show up, over time, the easier it becomes. Yes, the task still requires effort, but it won't feel so hard to you, and you won't feel the internal resistance or red flags to stop. That's because you've trained your brain to "just do it."

Plus, the more effort something requires, the more your brain will give it a higher worth. Psychologists call this the effort paradox. While effort feels costly in the moment, the brain registers it as more valuable.

So whatever you have in the tank, whether that's 25, 58, or 95 percent, give it. Every effort counts.

KWIK STEP: Estimate how much energy you have in your tank today on a scale of 1 to 100. Then at the end of the day, take a few minutes and reflect on whether you gave it your all. If you did, celebrate yourself. If you didn't, then what is one thing you can do tomorrow to improve?

AFFIRMATION: *"I give my all. Every effort counts. I am limitless."*

JULY 23

FEAR UNBOXED, POTENTIAL UNLOCKED

In Austrian physicist Erwin Schrödinger's famous thought experiment, a cat in a box was alive and dead. He said that both possibilities existed until someone opened the box.

Sometimes we can feel like Schrödinger's cat—stuck in a box where the potential to stay the same or grow in limitless directions lives simultaneously.

But unlike Schrödinger's cat, which had to wait for someone else to open its box, we have the power to break free of ours. The key is understanding what built the walls of whatever box we're living in, and that was *fear.*

When you feel fear, the amygdala, the brain's danger-sensing system, sends signals that activate the sympathetic nervous system, shifting your body and brain into fight, flight, freeze, or fawn. In this state, hormones such as cortisol and norepinephrine flood the body, preparing your muscles for quick movement (think running or punching).

Activity in the prefrontal cortex also decreases, making problem-solving, creativity, emotional regulation, and critical thinking more difficult. So when you feel stuck, it's a sign your brain actually *is* stuck. Yet you have the power to change this. One of the best ways is what I call the "Try Three Times" approach:

1. **GET OVER IT.** Take one small action that scares you. This teaches your brain that you survived. Psychologists call this *exposure therapy,* where you introduce what you fear in small doses safely.
2. **GET GOOD AT IT.** Identify how you can upgrade the skill or ability. Take an online course, read a book, or learn from someone who has mastered what you fear.
3. **SEE IF YOU ENJOY IT (OR NOT).** After steps one and two, ask yourself, "Do I like this?" You may be surprised.

What stops many of us from pursuing a relationship, career, or any dream is often fear—of failing, of what others think, of not meeting expectations. These fears, although they feel real, only keep you trapped.

Imagine what your life could look like, feel like, be like, once you break free.

KWIK STEP: Write one fear that's holding you back today, and outline how you'll apply the Try Three Times method to it.

AFFIRMATION: *"Fear no longer controls me. I control fear. I am limitless."*

DECISIONS ARE INCISIONS

Do you know the feeling when a big choice looms and you just freeze?

The "what if's" race through your mind as future after future passes by. You know you need to decide—in your business, your career, your home, your relationship—yet you don't.

It's not because you can't see the options. It's because choosing one means *losing* the others.

The word *decide* comes from the Latin word *decidere*, meaning "to cut off." You make a choice, and it cuts you off from other futures, from other possibilities. And your brain then interprets this as a loss. It's wired to give more weight to those than gains, a cognitive bias known as *loss aversion*. That's why you might avoid or procrastinate making a decision—it feels safer keeping options open than cutting off others.

When you feel paralyzed with making a big decision, know there's nothing wrong with you. It's how your brain works. The amygdala lights up, flagging uncertainty as a threat. Simultaneously, the prefrontal cortex attempts to find the perfect choice, the risk-free path that won't lead to a feeling of loss.

Except there isn't a perfect choice or a risk-free path—and accepting this is what actually moves you forward. First you get clear on what matters most—your values, your purpose, your why—then you move. Clarity and action calm the brain.

Make a decision and you cut off other possibilities. Yet with each intentional choice, your life also opens to new possibilities, ones you never imagined.

Life changes through your choices. It doesn't happen from staying in your mind or standing stuck at a mental fork. It comes from moving, from making one decision at a time.

Decisions are incisions.

KWIK STEP: Close your eyes and take three deep breaths. Identify a decision that has kept you stuck—either something big like a job change, a relationship, or a move, or something smaller. Now imagine yourself making the decision based on what matters most, and see yourself taking a step forward.

If an emotion arises, name it, and tell yourself, "It's okay to feel [blank] and still move forward."

AFFIRMATION: *"Every decision I make opens new possibilities. I am limitless."*

JULY 25

VISUALIZATION TURNS INTENTION INTO INSTRUCTION

Visualization is a powerful tool. But there's a dark side. Visualizing goals in a purely positive way can trap your brain into thinking the goal has already been reached, causing your motivation to vanish.

That's where WOOP comes in. Psychologist Gabriele Ottingen created the process to help people distinguish between fantasies and goals. It works like this:

State your *wish*. Picture your desired *outcome*. Name the likely *obstacle*. Then *plan* around it.

Visualizing potential obstacles is not about wanting to create them. It's about training your brain to stop fearing them when they show up. When your brain trusts that it can find a way past any obstacle, that's when it becomes truly limitless.

Visualization turns intention into instruction, guiding your brain toward the future you want to create—and have the power to create.

KWIK STEP: Pick a goal and use the WOOP process on it today.

AFFIRMATION: *"I turn my intentions into instructions. I am limitless."*

REASONS REAP RESULTS

Imagine today is the end of your life. What is your biggest regret?

Most people have something in their lives they're putting off. They know it's important, but they don't have the motivation to start, keep going, or finish.

But if you wait for motivation to come to you, it never will. Instead, you have to create it. One way to do that is to think *3H*: *Head > Heart > Hands.*

It's easy to visualize your goals, deep desires, and dreams in your head, but if you're not acting with your hands, you're likely procrastinating or self-sabotaging. Usually what's missing is the second *H*, the heart.

Your heart represents your feelings and emotions—the fuel to get you motivated. There is no more potent power than tapping into your purpose. Motivation isn't always about liking the task (usually not at first). It's about loving the result.

Maybe you don't like exercising every day, but you do it because there's a purpose you love, like feeling stronger in your body and being healthier.

It's the same with whatever deep desire, dream, or goal you have that requires sustained effort. Researchers have shown that when your goals align with your values—what psychologists call the *self-concordance model*—you will put in more sustained effort and make more progress over time.

To dig into this, ask the following questions:

1. Why does [insert goal/dream/desire] matter to me?
2. What will I gain from doing this?
3. What are the benefits or rewards?
4. How will I feel after accomplishing it?
5. How will it impact my career, relationships, health, and sense of well-being?

If you don't understand why you're doing something, then it's easy to procrastinate. But when you get clear on your purpose, you'll find that *reasons reap results.*

KWIK STEP: Identify one goal, dream, or desire you've procrastinated. Set a timer for five minutes, and spend one minute reflecting on each question above.

AFFIRMATION: *"Motivation doesn't come to me. I create my motivation by knowing my purpose. I am limitless."*

JULY 27

FALLING ISN'T FAILURE; STAYING DOWN IS

Sometimes, we fall hard onto the ground.

Loss, failure, or a mistake can leave us stunned, reeling, and unsure. Too often, we judge ourselves for these feelings. It's a lot easier to say, "I injured my knee" than to tell someone "I feel shattered inside."

These feelings are okay—we all experience them. We all fall. But we don't have to stay down. As the Japanese proverb says, "Fall seven times, stand up eight."

How? By mining for *GOLD*.

For each letter, pick one word that resonates—this will become your formula for rising again.

G: GRATITUDE OR GROWTH MINDSET. Transformation begins through gratitude, appreciating the adversity you experienced and how you've grown stronger because of it.

Or through a *growth mindset*, believing in your brain's ability to change, for the better, through neuroplasticity.

O: OPTIMISM OR OPEN-MINDEDNESS. Often, it's not the problem that needs changing; it's our attitudes and assumptions. Optimism believes that everything—even the difficult moments—will work in your favor. Staying open-minded lets you accept new experiences, knowledge, thoughts, emotions, and skills that will keep your brain flexible and adaptable.

L: LOVE OR LIFELONG LEARNING. Instead of trying to "fix" yourself, show yourself love. Studies show self-compassion results in more resilience, learning, and bouncing back from setbacks faster than self-criticism.

You can also allow yourself to embrace *lifelong learning*. You never stop learning because life never stops teaching.

D: DISCIPLINE OR DEDICATION. Healing takes time. Progress comes from small steps, taken again and again. Only through discipline or dedication will you remain consistent.

GOLD doesn't pretend the fall never happens or that it doesn't hurt. It reminds you that every fall is an opportunity to rise stronger and wiser.

Falling isn't failure; it's staying down that is.

KWIK STEP: Create your GOLD formula, picking one word for each letter, and consider how you can apply it to your life today.

AFFIRMATION: *"I fall, and then I rise stronger, quicker, and more limitless. I am limitless."*

JULY 28

TURN YOUR WOUNDS INTO WISDOM

Look up into the night sky, and you aren't seeing stars as they are in the moment. You're gazing at echoes of what they once were, of the light given off millions of years ago.

Like the past light of stars, we carry echoes of our pasts too. It's those invisible wounds and limiting labels formed by words, behaviors, and beliefs.

Maybe you're carrying a label that says you're broken, not smart enough, or talented enough. But your past doesn't have to define you. Growth begins the moment you decide to let the label go and rewrite your story.

To begin, try this four-part framework:

- **FIND THE LABEL.** What's a limiting label you've carried?
- **FIGURE OUT THE LIMITATION.** Where in your life does this label show up? How does it affect your behaviors, emotions, and habits?
- **FOLLOW THE THREAD.** Where did the label come from? Who labeled you? What might have happened that caused this?
- **FLIP THE STORY.** What have you learned because of your journey? How has it made you stronger? What's the opposite, limitless label you can adopt instead?

By changing your story from a negative to a positive, you're engaging in cognitive reappraisal and positive reframing—two techniques that support growth, learning, and meaning. It's not about ignoring your pain, pretending it didn't happen, or excusing what created it in the first place.

It's about freeing yourself—your heart and your brain—so you get to decide how your story finishes.

Like learning, improving memory, or building skills, releasing these emotional wounds can take time. You may also need to work with a skilled therapist. Remember, it's not about how long this journey takes; it's that you start.

The past can still hurt, but you have a choice to run from it or learn from it. Choose to turn your wounds into wisdom.

KWIK STEP: Think of one limiting label or story today. Use the four-part framework to flip it.

AFFIRMATION: *"I choose to turn my wounds into wisdom. I am limitless."*

DON'T HIDE FROM POTENTIAL SETBACKS. RUN THROUGH THEM.

Don't ask how to learn quickly.

Ask how to learn slowly.

Then avoid that.

When you have a problem to solve, first collect the facts. Make a list, create a file, and gather information. This helps your brain to focus. Then identify the potential gains. Optimism helps regulate your nervous system and lower stress.

After that, it's time to switch to the negative, to what you *don't* want to happen.

This is *inversion*, a thinking strategy that catches what positive planning often misses. This isn't brooding on the potential failure points. It's looking for weak spots and focusing your brain on what to avoid. This also gives you greater clarity about what skills or resources, habits or knowledge you might need to acquire.

So if you want a sharp brain, ask what makes it dull.

If you want to reach a goal, ask what stops you.

And if you want to win the day, ask what causes you to lose.

Then work on avoiding the risks.

Don't hide from potential setbacks. Run through them.

KWIK STEP: Pick something that matters to you and write down the ways it can fail. Pick at least one setback to run through today.

AFFIRMATION: *"I see potential setbacks and choose to face them. I am limitless."*

JULY 30

REMEMBER YOUR FUTURE

What if you could make tomorrow's dreams—your deepest desires and goals—feel as real as yesterday's memories?

How much more certainty and confidence would that give you? How much more gratitude would you feel knowing what you desire is already on its way? And how would it change how you show up today?

This is more than positive thinking—it's rooted in neuroscience. Your brain uses as many of the same networks to recall the past as it does to imagine the future. fMRI images from Harvard show significant overlap in these regions, so when you vividly imagine the future, your brain treats it almost like a lived experience. This skill of *episodic future thinking* strengthens decision-making, emotional regulation, and motivation, helping you delay short-term gratification to achieve long-term goals.

But it's not enough to imagine your future. I want you to *remember* the episodes of your life that you want to happen as if they already have. When you do, your brain engages the same circuits as real experience, preparing your body and mind to act accordingly, influencing your choices, your posture, your tone of voice, and your emotions.

Try this today. Imagine going to bed tonight, and someone asks, "How was your day?"

Visualize yourself smiling and responding, "I crushed it. Today was amazing."

Next, reverse-engineer it. Ask yourself, "What had to happen for me to feel this way?" then pick three personal things and three professional things that had to happen.

By remembering your future, you give your brain a blueprint to begin making connections and decisions, problem-solving, and motivating you toward this future.

The blueprint for your future and self already exists. Your task is to show up every day until you meet them. Remember your future, and you're one step closer to this reality.

KWIK STEP: Apply the "Remember Your Future" exercise for your day today and identify three personal and professional things that have to happen for you to have had the best day ever.

AFFIRMATION: *"My deepest desires and dreams have already happened. I am limitless."*

JULY 31

DON'T PANIC. GET PERSPECTIVE.

Five years ago to this day, what stressed you out?

How about two years ago? A year?

We can always find something to feel stressed about. The potentially stressful moments will never stop. But what *can* change is how we see, feel, and experience those moments.

Stressful moments are a lot like clouds, drifting across the sky, again and again. Some clouds are fluffy and white, others dark and stormy. Either way, the clouds come and go.

Whatever is stressing you now will pass too. It will go, and you might not even remember it five months from now, let alone in five years.

Harvard psychology professor and researcher Ellen Langer taught me a question to ask when you're feeling stressed about something: "Is it a tragedy or an inconvenience?"

Langer says that as soon as we ask ourselves "Is it a tragedy?" we tend to relax, because most things aren't. They're inconveniences that come and go like clouds passing in the sky.

This cognitive reframe can help reduce activity in the amygdala—our threat detector—which lowers our stress response, reduces cortisol and adrenaline, and helps engage our prefrontal cortex again. That's the region involved in rational, logical decision-making and emotional regulation. This allows us to think clearly about a situation and to go forward and fix things.

You've handled hard things before. Whatever you're handling now, you will get through it. Trust you can handle what's ahead. Don't panic. Get perspective.

KWIK STEP: Think of a stressful situation you're currently navigating and ask yourself, "Is it a tragedy or an inconvenience?" Notice how the answer makes you feel.

AFFIRMATION: *"I handle hard situations with ease. I am limitless."*

AUGUST 1

MISTAKES ARE MEANT TO GUIDE YOU, NOT DEFINE YOU

Blunders, screw-ups, errors . . . it's easy to forget they happen to us all, especially in the moment we've just messed up.

When it comes to mistakes, the real question isn't "How do I avoid making them?" it's "How do I stay positive and bounce forward even stronger after a mishap, big or small?"

What if it started with how you looked at mistakes?

Instead of seeing them as signs of failure, or something to fear, what if you saw them as opportunities to learn, adjust, and grow?

The brain has built-in signals that notice when you slip up. These signals can help support your brain to make adjustments so you're less likely to repeat the same mistake.

But there's a catch: Your brain learns best when you believe it can. Studies show people who believe intelligence can grow are more likely to treat mistakes as information, not inadequacy. That means mistakes can accelerate your learning if you're open to it.

They can also draw your attention to what matters, sharpen your focus, and help fuel motivation to do your absolute best.

Learning from mistakes will require self-reflection, awareness, and a willingness to try new approaches, develop new skills and capabilities, and replace old habit loops with new ones.

As useful as mistakes are, we often take them personally, believing they say something about us. They don't. They tell us nothing about who we are, what we're capable of, or what we're worth.

You make mistakes; mistakes don't make you.

Mistakes are meant to guide you, not define you.

KWIK STEP: Think of one recent mistake you made. What did you learn from it? And what adjustment will you make in the future?

AFFIRMATION: *"Mistakes guide me on my learning journey. I am limitless."*

GO FROM GOOD TO GREAT

"Good is the enemy of great," wrote Jim Collins in his best-selling book *Good to Great*.

This phrase has resonated so much, it's now commonly used in business, sports, and personal growth. Collins was clear his book wasn't about specific companies, but about the question: "Can a good company become great, and, if so, how?"

We can apply the same question to our brain. Can a good brain become a great one, and, if so, how?

Yes. It can. Anyone can take a good brain and make it great—make it limitless. Neuroplasticity is the brain's ability to rewire itself and to learn at any age.

To help your brain grow from good to great, what is one habit, behavior, or routine that's hurting you and pulling you away from your goals?

It might be smoking, or binge-watching videos that don't inspire you. Maybe it's eating foods that don't nourish you or looking at screens before going to sleep. Perhaps it's working seven days a week, keeping e-mail open all day long when you need to focus, or avoiding sending a difficult e-mail.

By bringing awareness to what you need to stop doing, you help yourself filter your day. It's a chance to pause and ask, "Is this helping or hurting me?" This question engages your prefrontal cortex, helping you override the impulse to act in ways that aren't serving you. This helps align your intention with the right action, so you keep moving in the direction of your goals and desires.

Stopping isn't about perfection. It's about a standard of excellence. Rather than settling for "good enough," you're declaring, "My brain is great, and I will nourish, train, and support it on the journey from good to great."

Go from good to great.

KWIK STEP: Identify something you want to stop doing and practice removing or cutting back on it today.

AFFIRMATION: *"I give my time, energy, and attention only to what empowers my brain, and I let go of the rest. I am limitless."*

AUGUST 3

REWRITE YOUR STORY. REWIRE YOUR BRAIN.

You are not your past.

You are not the labels other people placed on you.

You are not your limitations.

You are not the stories imposed on you by others.

Nor are you the stories you composed about yourself.

You can keep telling yourself all the reasons why you can't do something, or you can choose to write a new story.

One where you believe in yourself, where you train your brain to learn anything, and where you step into the version of you who's been patiently waiting for you all along.

You must be the one to change this. Your brain's job is to repeat what it's learned—to try predicting your future based on your past, even when it no longer serves you. And it's doing this because it thinks it's keeping you safe. What's familiar feels safe to the brain, even when it's not.

Your brain is capable of building new habits, even shaping a new identity for you. Through repetition of action, by telling yourself new stories, and by developing new skills, your brain will change. And with it, your life.

Your thoughts are often echoes of the past. So create new ones. Rewrite your story. Rewire your brain to one of limitless potential.

KWIK STEP: What is something you keep telling yourself that's limiting you? Rewrite it to be more encouraging and empowering. For example, "I'm terrible at learning" becomes "I am learning how to learn, and I'm improving every day."

AFFIRMATION: *"I control my story. I am limitless."*

AUGUST 4

DECISIONS MAKE A DIFFERENCE

Sometimes it feels like decisions get made for us instead of us making them.

I'm talking about the moment when you weren't planning on a job search until your organization downsized and eliminated your position. When you weren't planning on separating until your spouse said they wanted a divorce, or on caring for an aging parent before a devastating diagnosis hit. Sometimes it truly feels like life happens to you without you having wished, wanted, or visualized it.

Yet you have more agency than you may think.

Sometimes it's not about changing your life, but changing your responses to it. Your *internal locus of control* is the belief that you have the power or agency to influence events. This isn't about trying to control the uncontrollable, but accepting responsibility for what you can control—your actions, responses, and decisions. An internal locus of control can boost resilience, problem-solving, confidence, and better mental health.

This differs from an *external locus of control*, the belief that something outside of you has that power. If you repeatedly face setbacks that leave you feeling powerless, this can lead to learned helplessness, the belief that nothing you do matters. This mindset can cause depression, anxiety, procrastination, and stagnation.

If you're struggling with making decisions, especially in the face of challenging circumstances, then start with intention. Ask yourself: "Who do I want to become? What are my values?"

Questions like these help activate your prefrontal cortex, the "thinking" part of the brain, which helps balance the "emotional" part, the limbic system including the amygdala, the threat detector.

This won't stop the grief, confusion, or anger that comes with tough times, but it can help you navigate them with clearer thinking.

One decision has the power to change everything. Your decisions do make a difference.

KWIK STEP: What's one decision you already make that helps you align with who you want to become? What's one new decision you want to make?

AFFIRMATION: *"I choose my responses to life, and my decisions shape the person I choose to become. I am limitless."*

AUGUST 5

SOMETIMES YOU WIN. AND SOMETIMES YOU LEARN.

Superheroes eat mistakes for breakfast.

Not because they enjoy failing; they just don't fear it. It's how they grow, improve, and become stronger and wiser.

Mistakes are signs you're trying. They're important to your brain. Research using EEG (electroencephalography) shows that when you make a mistake, within a fraction of a second, your brain produces an electrical signal called error-related negativity (ERN). ERN acts as an internal alarm, telling your brain to adjust, refine, and strengthen new pathways, which is the core mechanism behind deep learning and skill-building.

This learning only happens if you can pause and sit with the discomfort long enough to learn from it.

Maybe the lesson is you need to develop new capabilities, improve focus, eliminate distractions, or say no more so you stop overcommitting. Maybe it's slowing down, taking a few deep breaths before responding in a meeting or to an e-mail. Or maybe it's using more memory aids to support attention, recall, and follow-through.

There are countless lessons that mistakes can teach you. When you learn from them, they can shape you into something even greater than before.

So if there's something you've longed to do, but have hesitated for fear of screwing up or looking foolish, consider this your sign.

Take the leap. Start the project. Apply for the job. Launch the offering. Learn a language. Travel. Whatever it is—begin. Start small. Figure you'll make a mistake or two. And trust you're strong enough to reflect, learn, and adapt.

You don't have to feel proud of the mistake. But you can feel proud you learned, grew, and kept going—just like superheroes do.

Sometimes you win. And sometimes you learn.

KWIK STEP: Sit in a comfortable seat, close your eyes, and take a few deep, slow breaths. Think of a recent mistake you made, then notice what comes up. How does your body feel? What emotions are present? Name whatever shows up, reminding yourself, "This is information. I am safe."

As the emotions recede, ask yourself, "What lesson am I to learn?" Pick one insight or small adjustment you can practice today or this week.

AFFIRMATION: *"I eat mistakes for breakfast. They help me grow stronger and wise. I am limitless."*

AUGUST 6

DEFAULT TO OPTIMISM

Most plants need rain and sunlight. But too much of either and there's no growth. With the right amount, they thrive.

When it comes to your brain, your thoughts are a lot like the weather, and stress is something like rain. Your brain needs a little stress to motivate and improve performance. "I'm afraid of looking bad and sounding foolish" can fuel you to practice, work harder, and study longer.

This is because stress triggers your brain's arousal networks, sharpening focus, strengthening memory, and releasing hormones that provide short energy bursts. The key is keeping this occasional, like a rain shower.

But when stress becomes chronic, or pessimistic thoughts like "this will never work" or "I knew that would happen" dominate, it's like a flood. Rational decision-making and emotional regulation become harder as activity in the prefrontal cortex decreases and amygdala activity increases. That's when you're more likely to avoid, procrastinate, or slip into perfectionism.

Optimism is the opposite. It acts like sunshine for your brain. It's the belief you have agency, and that good things are possible and likely in the future. Research finds that optimistic thinking improves well-being, buffers against stress, and boosts mental and physical health.

You can build optimism by reframing situations. Mistakes become lessons. Change becomes a beginning. Waiting becomes a pause. And rejection moves you closer to finding the right fit.

Optimism doesn't mean you ignore disappointment, grief, anger, or sadness. You counterbalance them. And it's not a constant state, just like the weather isn't always sunny. Some stress and even pessimism are natural. Be accepting and forgiving when they arise.

But default to optimism.

KWIK STEP: Identify one recurring pessimistic thought or recent stressful situation. How can you reframe it toward optimism?

AFFIRMATION: *"I make optimism my default setting. I am limitless."*

AUGUST 7

PROTECT YOUR PEAKS; HONOR YOUR VALLEYS

Nature moves in cycles. In the Northern Hemisphere, spring brings new growth, summer offers fullness, fall is for harvesting, and winter for stillness and rest before the cycle repeats.

Just as nature has rhythms, your energy does too. Every day, your brain cycles through peaks of focus and mental performance, followed by natural dips in energy and a need for recovery. This rise and fall is known as an *ultradian rhythm*, a naturally occurring cycle that influences energy, attention, and cognitive performance.

For most people, peak energy and alertness lasts about 90 minutes, sometimes up to 120, before the brain needs a 15-to-20-minute break to rest and recover. Then the pattern repeats. By aligning your day with this cycle, it can help you harness the full power of your brain, whether that's for studying, learning, or working.

The key is to block 90-minute deep focus sessions, followed by 15-to-20-minute breaks, throughout the day. For those 90 minutes, protect your focus by eliminating distractions. Put "do not disturb" on virtual communication channels, set your phone to airplane mode, leave it in another room, or use apps to block websites, e-mails, and social media.

During your breaks, stand, stretch, and do some light movement, drink water, breathe deeply, daydream out the window. The point is to give your brain a true break from the heavy cognitive work.

Pushing without pausing all day only makes a cognitive crash—fatigue, memory lapses, irritability, less focus, and declining performance—more likely. So protect your peaks, and honor your valleys.

KWIK STEP: Schedule one 90-minute focus session followed by a 15-to-20-minute brain break, and notice your productivity and how it feels.

AFFIRMATION: *"I protect my peaks and honor my valleys so I can rise to another peak. I am limitless."*

AUGUST 8

WITH CHALLENGE COMES CHANGE

To make a clay bowl by hand, a potter must mold the raw, wet clay, pinching and shaping the edges until they're satisfied. Then they must wait patiently until the clay has dried before sliding it into the kiln for firing at roughly 2000°F to 2400°F.

They cannot skip the final step. Without the fire, without the heat, no bowl would exist. It would crack and crumble, lose its shape, and never fulfill its purpose.

You are no different.

Whatever you're building toward—a relationship, career, business, healthier body, or quicker brain—you, too, must face the challenge of the forge. Research shows you don't develop the requisite skills, strengths, and resilience by avoiding challenges—by steering clear of the fire. But you also don't grow if you face so much stress that it overwhelms your ability to cope.

The sweet spot for growth lies in between. At just the right temperature, your brain will become more resilient, adapting and growing stronger through stressful experiences that challenge it.

Like a clay bowl, you—and your brain—are forged in the fire and heat. Stop avoiding it. Stop fearing it. Stop delaying it. Embrace it. Face it. And let it forge you.

With challenge comes change—*your* change.

KWIK STEP: What is one thing that you've avoided because it felt too hard? What action can you take today to start or face it?

AFFIRMATION: *"I embrace all challenges and face them with courage. I am limitless."*

AUGUST 9

REST, RESET, RESTORE IN NATURE

What do you do when you stare blankly at the screen, reread the same paragraph five times, or can barely stay awake during a meeting and nothing seems to help?

It's the moment when you feel so cognitively fatigued, overwhelmed, and stressed that five-minute mini-breaks to stretch, move, hydrate, or breathing practices all fail.

Instead of trying to push through, consider trying *shinrin-yoku,* the Japanese concept that loosely translates to "forest bathing." It was introduced in the early 1980s, when officials began worrying about rising stress, overwork, high-pressure office culture, urbanization, and growing separation from nature.

To counteract this, officials began encouraging people to step away from pavement and into the peace of the forest. This is more than walking in the woods. It's a multisensory experience, where you connect deeply to the natural world, tapping into what you see, hear, smell, and touch.

Science now confirms the Japanese were on to something. Studies on forest bathing show it can lower cortisol, reduce sympathetic nervous system activity (the fight, flight, and freeze stress response), slow pulse rate, improve mood, and even temporarily boost immune markers.

Who doesn't want or need more of that today?

While long stretches are ideal, even a brief 10-to-15-minute walk outside can boost attention and memory, and reduce stress. The key is to get out of an urban environment and into nature without listening to music, texting, or checking your phone. If you don't have access to an actual forest, don't worry; a park or any green space will do.

Your brain wasn't built for a 24/7 cubicle. It evolved with nature. So give it what it remembers and what it needs to stay sharp, present, and in emotional control. That's time in nature to rest, reset, and restore.

KWIK STEP: Take at least 10 minutes to walk and be in nature today, putting your phone on silent and immersing yourself and all your senses in your surroundings.

AFFIRMATION: *"I spend time in nature to rest, reset, and restore my brain. I am limitless."*

REPETITION IS THE MOTHER OF MASTERY

Top performers never get bored by the fundamentals.

True masters, whether in athletics, engineering, science or the arts, know that by mastering the foundational skills in their field, they will help their brain release resistance, overcome the fear and stress response, and open to more creativity, better problem-solving, and enhanced critical thinking.

And the way you master the fundamentals is through repetition and practice.

Famed cellist and 20-time Grammy Award winner Yo-Yo Ma says, "The goal of practicing is to achieve a freedom of the mind that enables you to physically do whatever you need to do."

He's talking about how with enough repetition, eventually the fundamentals become automatic. You don't have to consciously think about the act; your brain simply does it. It's like walking a well-worn path through the woods. Every action is a step your brain knows how to take because it's become ingrained.

Practice the fundamentals, and you can become a master. Repetition is the mother of mastery.

KWIK STEP: Pick one area of your life you're actively working on improving and write three core skills fundamental to mastering it. Then commit to spending time today on one of the core practices.

AFFIRMATION: *"I commit to mastering the basics through the art of repetition. I am limitless."*

AUGUST 11

WRITE TO BRING THE LIGHT

Walk into a dark room, and you'll feel around for a light switch. You cannot see what's in there until there's light.

Your mind is like a dark room.

Have you ever lain awake at night or felt distracted during the day replaying a past experience or imagining a future catastrophe? This is your mind in the dark.

But when you flip on the light, you see clearly. You can process and let go of the past. You can learn from it. Solve problems in the present. Generate new ideas to improve the future. You may even see how anger masked fear.

To flip the light switch in your mind, practice journaling.

Decades of research on expressive writing have shown that writing down our thoughts and emotions about difficult experiences can improve mood, reduce stress, and lead to greater well-being.

Studies also link journaling to reduced anxiety, especially in people who ruminate. It helps reduce activation of the brain's error-related negativity signal, which kicks in when we perceive we've made a mistake.

Putting words to your emotions and thoughts helps reduce amygdala activation, making the thoughts and feelings seem less dangerous. You're also activating the prefrontal cortex, which helps with problem-solving, emotional regulation, and critical thinking.

Practice journaling using expressive or free writing, which is pouring thoughts and emotions onto the page without structure or grammar.

You can also use prompts. Take something that's bothering you and ask, "What can I learn from this?"

Take a goal and ask, "Why do I care about this?" or "What are three things I feel grateful for?"

If you journal in the morning, you could ask, "What is one thing that must happen for me to win the day?"

If you journal at night ask, "What are three victories that made today excellent?"

Write to bring the light.

KWIK STEP: Journal for at least 10 minutes.

AFFIRMATION: *"I bring my thoughts and emotions into the light. I am limitless."*

AUGUST 12

CONTROL THE CONTROLLABLE

It's not your job to heal others, tolerate toxic behaviors, or change yourself in order to belong.

It's not your job to constantly sacrifice your needs for others' well-being, continuously compromise, or please everyone.

Our brains evolved to seek control of the environment. It's a biological imperative. When you believe your choices and actions influence your life, self-efficacy increases—and that's crucial for motivation, goal-setting, and resilience.

But you cannot control everything. Believing you can is an illusion that can increase decision-fatigue, anxiety, stress, and cognitive overload.

When you understand what you can and cannot control, you release the weight, pressure, and burdens that were never yours to carry.

It is your job to respect yourself, put your well-being first, and make yourself happy.

It is your job to leave toxic environments and people, to set boundaries, and decide what to say yes and no to.

And it's your job to continuously improve, grow, and learn.

Control the controllable and let the rest go.

KWIK STEP: What is one thing you're ready to release that isn't yours to control? And what is one thing you choose to prioritize that is within your control?

AFFIRMATION: *"I release what I cannot control, and I choose to prioritize what is. I am limitless."*

BECOME A MASTER OF CHANGE

What if what was holding you back from the life you want to live wasn't a lack of skills, capabilities, or confidence?

What if it was a story your brain learned and repeated so often that it feels like truth?

Buried deep inside us are stories we created about ourselves like:

I'm not smart enough.

No one listens to me.

I'm not lovable or talented enough.

I'm too old to change.

These are known as *cognitive distortions*—biased interpretations that get repeated so much they seem true.

Whether you want to build a skill, grow your business or career, or enjoy better relationships, there's likely a story that needs transcending. To transcend is to *end the trance,* to end the hypnosis you've lived under.

If you want something you've never had, then you've got to do something you've never done. One way to start rewriting those internal stories is to regularly challenge yourself to try something new. Take a new route to work. Visit a new park. Talk to a new person in line at the coffee shop. Research a new subject. Eat new food. Listen to new music. Read new genres. Play a new sport.

Exposing your brain to new things strengthens and creates new connections and neural pathways in different regions—that's neuroplasticity, the brain's ability to reorganize itself through experiences. You also get dopamine, the neurotransmitter linked to motivation and learning, that comes from novelty and anticipation. In this state, your brain becomes more alert and more focused.

The more "new" you introduce into your life, the more you train your nervous system to interpret change as safe instead of dangerous. And your brain begins to see possibilities instead of road blocks. This helps you follow through when you make intentional changes.

Life is boring when we stay within the limits of what we already know. Become a master of change, and change becomes who you are.

KWIK STEP: What is one new thing you can commit to trying today?

AFFIRMATION: *"I am someone who sets and achieves small goals. I am limitless."*

AUGUST 14

MOVE TO MOTIVATE

You wake up feeling motivated, right?

Wrong.

Even the most successful people rarely rise feeling motivated. They've simply trained their brain to act even when they don't feel like it. They don't wait for motivation; they do it.

The word *motivation* comes from the Latin *movere*, meaning "to move." That's the secret. If you want motivation, you start moving. Action creates dopamine, rewarding you for having acted and motivating you to do it again.

You can use the power of your mind and ability to imagine what's at stake to start that movement whether it's reading, studying, or practicing a skill. Vividly imagine the benefits and consequences of doing or not doing something. If you want to read every night, ask:

- What will I gain from reading?
- How will I feel after finishing?
- How will this affect my relationships? Well-being? Career? Health?
- What new possibilities might this unlock for me?

Then reverse it and ask:

- What's the pain that comes from not reading?
- What are the potential consequences from not following through?
- Who do I become if I don't read?
- How will this affect every area of my life?
- What will happen to my life if I don't act?

The truth is, you won't always feel like reading, working out, or practicing to build a new skill. That's okay. Just act anyway.

Move to motivate.

KWIK STEP: What is one action or habit you've been avoiding? Make a list of the benefits and consequences that come from taking and avoiding the action. What is one commitment you can make to yourself to act today?

AFFIRMATION: *"I don't wait for motivation. I create my motivation. I am limitless."*

AUGUST 15

BE A THERMOSTAT, NOT A THERMOMETER

When was the last time your mood changed instantly? Was it after reading an e-mail or news headline? Sitting in traffic? Something someone said?

You were fine one moment, then suddenly you weren't.

Most of us live like thermometers. When the temperature of a room rises, the thermometer rises. When the temperature falls, the thermometer falls. We lash out when someone says something we dislike; we feel stressed by unexpected problems, overwhelmed by doomscrolling, impatient with distractions, and anxious over delays. Eventually this leads to feeling unhappy, discontent, and disconnected from our own power.

Instead, try being a thermostat. You set the standard. You don't react to your environment. You gauge it, then intentionally set your inner temperature, and the environment responds to you. This begins by learning to regulate your inner emotional state.

Neuroscientist Jill Bolte Taylor suggests that strong emotions have a chemical surge that lasts about 90 seconds—unless we keep it alive with our stories.

When a strong emotion arises, pause and name it. "I notice I am feeling frustrated." Then reframe it. "This is a sign I care. I can use this energy to problem solve and grow."

This practice interrupts the amygdala from hijacking your behavior while increasing activity in your prefrontal cortex. That brings more emotional regulation, self-control, logic, and decision-making into the picture.

Every time you pause to name the emotion and reframe it, you create new neural pathways that strengthen emotional regulation and help your brain to stay calm and clear despite what's happening in the environment.

The goal isn't to change or stop an emotion. It's to stop them from controlling you and your actions.

Be a thermostat, not a thermometer.

KWIK STEP: What's a situation that's troubling you? Name a strong emotion you're experiencing around this situation, then reframe it.

AFFIRMATION: *"I am a thermostat. I am in control of my emotional temperature. I am limitless."*

MAKE SUCCESS FEEL SAFE

You can't stay in your comfort zone and unlock your potential. Life doesn't work that way.

Until you train your brain to feel safe in the unknown and the uncomfortable, it will always retreat to what is familiar. Your nervous system feels safe in what it knows even if that's limiting you. It's why "waiting to feel it's right" before taking action rarely works.

If you're not regularly stretching yourself, testing your skills, or trying what feels uncomfortable, it means you're not growing. You're stuck.

Here's how you know something is worth doing, continuing, and persevering through difficulties:

- If it's hard, it means you're growing.
- If it's unfamiliar, it means you're learning.
- If it stretches you, it means you're expanding your limits.

You'll never know how far you can go until you start pushing past what you think you're capable of.

Remember, success will usually feel uncomfortable when it's new. Take five minutes before you go to sleep; while you're lying in bed, visualize what success looks like, feels like, and means to you. You're training your nervous system to practice feeling safe in success.

Make success feel safe, and you'll make success that much easier and more meaningful.

KWIK STEP: Before falling asleep tonight, visualize yourself succeeding, and imagine it feeling safe and expected.

AFFIRMATION: *"I am comfortable with my growth and expansion. I am safe when I succeed. I am limitless."*

AUGUST 17

FOLLOW YOUR HEART, BUT BRING YOUR BRAIN TOO

Take one hand and touch your heart. Focus your attention on its beating, its pulsing, its strength.

You are here.

Your heart is beating. That means there's a purpose for you in this life. There's a reason you're alive right now. You don't need anything or anyone to dictate what you're worth or to determine your value—that's for you to discover.

But how? One way is through your superpowers. Just because you have them, doesn't make you a superhero—you have to use them to help others.

To become a superhero and fulfill your destiny, think: Purpose + Power.

Purpose is having something that lights you up.

Power is bringing that light to others through your talents, unique skills, knowledge, and learned abilities.

To find your purpose, follow your passions. Sometimes, you know immediately what those are. Maybe it's something you've loved since childhood. It could be an adversity you overcame, and in doing so, you developed skills that you now pass on to others struggling in a similar situation.

Maybe your passions lie undiscovered. The best way to uncover those is to go digging—to expose yourself to new experiences and see where your heart goes.

But then you need to use your brain to develop your power—to stay consistent, to keep learning, and to keep practicing so you keep growing. This is how you build competence and confidence.

So follow your heart, but bring your brain with you. That's how you merge your purpose with your power, and in the process become a superhero.

KWIK STEP: What is one thing that lights you up? What is one skill you have, or could build, that can support the passion? Finally, imagine sharing this with one person, helping, guiding, or serving them.

AFFIRMATION: *"My heart guides my purpose. My brain directs my power. I am limitless."*

DON'T FEEL BY ACCIDENT; FEEL BY DESIGN

We all go through times when we're overwhelmed by too many demands and not enough time. Every item on our to-do-list feels like it's in the number-one slot, and we're carrying the weight of it all.

Sometimes that pressure feels unbearable. All we want is to become more efficient—to work smarter, not harder—so life feels easier and more enjoyable.

Working smarter sometimes means saying no to more commitments, taking items off our to-do lists, eliminating distractions, and upgrading our capabilities.

But then there are times when we can't change anything on the outside. We have to change what's inside—our states and emotions.

While we never want to deny negative emotions, cultivating positive ones rewires the brain for better learning and creativity. Positive emotions increase dopamine and serotonin, which enhance neuroplasticity, focus, and problem-solving.

Just as you keep a "to-do list," create a "to-feel list." Next to your to-dos, write the state you want to cultivate, like feeling curious, bold, optimistic, or playful. Then ask yourself what would you need to do to create it.

That might mean a mindset shift, like asking new questions such as "What's important to me?" It could be actions like tidying your workspace to relax your nervous system or leaving your phone on silent to sink into deep work.

You get to decide how you feel. In doing so, you design your day, no matter what's on that to-do list. So decide right now how you will feel. "I feel loved." "I feel curious." "I feel connected." "I feel grateful."

Don't just feel by accident; feel by design.

KWIK STEP: Create your "to-feel list" for today, focusing on one to three emotions you want to cultivate, like curiosity, connection, or energy. Then add one action you can take to help create that state.

AFFIRMATION: *"I design how I feel so I can design my day. I am limitless."*

EXERCISE YOUR GRIT

The things that matter most in life usually require grit. They call for determination and dedication.

When you're starting out—a new workout, lesson one in a new class, reading the first chapter of a book—it's a lot like riding a bike down a hill. The excitement and nerves give you so much momentum that it requires very little effort to keep going.

Eventually, you reach a flat stretch or an uphill grade, and that's when the work really begins. That's when you have to dig deep, find your grit, and persevere.

The same thing happens when the novelty of the new wears off or life goes sideways. When your kid gets sick, you've slept very little, and the alarm goes off at 5 A.M., the last thing you want is to hit the gym. But it's your grit, determination, and dedication that helps move you anyway.

Don't wait until you need grit to build it. Start training for discomfort today.

At the end of your shower, turn it to cold. Sit in a sauna. Meditate or do deep breathing practices. Exercise. Learn a language, chess, a new dance, or a martial art. Push your mind and body slightly beyond your comfort zone each week.

These challenges are grounded in the process known as *hormesis*. When we expose our bodies and brains to moderate challenges for short durations followed by rest, it triggers beneficial adaptations in our cells and neurons, helping them rebuild themselves stronger.

You're also training your nervous system to stop interpreting the slightest discomfort as threatening. This helps reduce the stress response, and with it, the release of stress hormones, so you stay calm, clear, and confident during future stressful moments.

Get comfortable being uncomfortable. Exercise your grit.

KWIK STEP: What's one thing you can do to build your grit?

AFFIRMATION: *"I am building my grit. I am limitless."*

REST TO RISE, PAUSE TO DECIDE

It's estimated that your brain comes to roughly 35,000 crossroads every day.

That's the big and small decisions it must constantly make that will impact your energy, focus, and life. Sometimes these choices become too much. Suddenly, even simple decisions like what to wear or eat feel heavy and hard. This is decision fatigue.

As the day wears on, the more conscious decisions your prefrontal cortex makes, the more energy it burns, and the more exhausted it becomes, depleting your cognitive reserves. Studies show that decision fatigue can make us more impulsive, irrational, and more likely to procrastinate and avoid tasks.

So if you've ever found yourself reaching for a blueberry muffin instead of an apple, scrolling instead of sleeping, and saying yes when your heart longs for no, it might not be laziness or a lack of willpower.

It could be that you're mentally overwhelmed.

When you find yourself spinning and unable to make a decision, *stop.* Name what's happening, and recognize now isn't the time to make a choice.

Instead, walk away. Lean in to giving your brain the rest it needs and deserves. Let it daydream. Take a walk outside. Breathe in fresh air. Meditate. Eat a healthy meal. Talk with a loved one. Read. Listen to music. Journal. Do some deep breathing exercises, and get a good night's sleep.

Then in the morning, you can return to the crossroads, this time with more clarity. And from this space, now your brain has the energy it needs to see the best path forward.

The rest allows you to rise. The pause gives you space to decide.

KWIK STEP: List every decision you need to make, and pick one to prioritize now. Before deciding, first give your brain a mini-rest like deep breathing, stretching, or stepping outside, and then make the choice.

AFFIRMATION: *"I allow my brain to rest so I can make the best decisions. I am limitless."*

EVERY SETBACK IS FEEDBACK. EVERY MISTAKE, A MESSAGE.

Most people feel paralyzed by the fear of making a mistake—flubbing an important presentation, saying the wrong thing, underperforming.

Although the shame, fear, and self-doubt feel real in the moment, know this: You're not your mistakes, and they don't define your self-worth. No one is perfect, and we all have moments we wish we could redo.

It may feel like it, but mistakes aren't the end. They're the beginning of greater resilience, sharper problem-solving, and more confidence, if you allow them to be.

So how can you bounce forward stronger? By making an old mistake . . . OLD.

OWN. Take *accountability* for making things better. *Accept* your mistakes, forgiving yourself and others. *Acknowledge* you're human—you will make mistakes. *Apologize* swiftly and briefly if needed, saying, "I'm working on it, and I'm sorry." People will remember your integrity long after they've forgotten the mistake. Owning mistakes helps calm the emotional center of the brain—the limbic system—and engages the prefrontal cortex where decision-making, reason, and problem-solving exist.

LEARN. The best teacher is our last mistake. Situations often repeat until we've learned the lesson. Ask yourself, "What was I trying to do that went wrong?" Then, "Why did it go wrong?" Were you distracted, multitasking, exhausted, overcommitted, cognitively overloaded? If you're not sure, ask someone you trust.

DON'T REPEAT. Insanity isn't doing the same thing over and over expecting different results—it's a mark of a poor memory, of forgetting, or burying how the mistake made us feel. Instead, reflect on the experience and its lesson. Feel what comes up. Your amygdala signals the hippocampus to store emotionally charged memories more strongly, which is why reflecting on mistakes can help make the lesson stick.

Every setback is feedback. Every mistake, a message.

The question is . . . are you listening?

KWIK STEP: Think of a mistake still troubling you, then make it old using the OLD framework.

AFFIRMATION: *"Mistakes are lessons.*
I am listening to the lessons I need to learn. I am limitless."

AUGUST 22

WHO DO YOU NEED TO BE?

Would an angry person speak gently?

Would a courageous person avoid a calculated risk?

Would a loving person belittle or shame someone?

The answer is no. Our behaviors usually reflect who we think we are—our identity. Every identity carries predictable behaviors.

So when you need to perform, make a big decision, or face a dilemma, instead of focusing on what you need to *do*, focus on who you need to *be*. You can actually ask yourself, "Who do I need to *be* right now?"

If you're fighting with your significant other, instead of focusing on how you get them to hear you, choose to be compassionate. That one simple shift interrupts your brain's autopilot, forcing it to pause and choose differently.

Now it filters your options through a new question and perspective: "What would a compassionate person do?"

Instead of talking louder, you might listen more. Maybe you soften your voice or say, "I'm sorry." You might reach out with a gentle touch.

The person you become is shaped by what you repeatedly do. Choose a new identity, and your brain learns new behaviors to repeat.

So who do you need to be right now?

KWIK STEP: Think of a challenging situation you're facing. Then ask yourself, "Who do I need to be?" and write down the behaviors or actions this person would take.

AFFIRMATION: *"I choose my identity. I am limitless."*

AUGUST 23

SOMETIMES YOU DON'T NEED A NEW PLAN; YOU NEED TO TRUST THE ONE YOU STARTED

It takes an apple tree roughly 7 to 10 years before it can regularly bear fruit.

But from the moment the seed is planted, to its roots digging deep into the soil, to becoming the tiny sapling that fights its way to the surface, rising tall, and learning to survive—growth is happening, slowly and largely unseen.

If you knew your plan for transformation would take as long, would you still do it?

It can be tough to keep showing up, investing your time, energy, and effort, when it feels like you have nothing to show for it.

Yet that's how any new venture, and most of life, begins.

Your plan to learn and master a skill, whether that's the skill of business, writing, language, art, parenting, or teaching, requires repetition, consistency, and effort. Day after day. Week after week. Year after year.

Each repetition strengthens the neural pathways, reinforcing the connections you're using while letting the weaker ones fade through synaptic pruning. With consistency and sustained practice, the reinforced circuits fire faster and more efficiently. Over time, your brain reorganizes itself, making the new patterns easier to execute each time.

But you can't see this. You can't see what's happening beneath the surface, so it's easy to assume nothing is. Then you give up, trading the sustained effort for something new, swapping plan after plan.

Sometimes, that's the right call. Cut your losses and move on. Other times, your plan is like the apple seed that needs more time to grow into the tree. Your plan needs more time to fully mature. Stay consistent. Keep showing up. Do the work.

Sometimes, it's not that you need a new plan. It's that you need to trust the one you've started.

KWIK STEP: Take inventory of your long-term plans. What is one that needs more attention, effort, and time before you'll see results? Identify one small action you can take today to recommit and nurture it.

AFFIRMATION: *"I am willing to put in the time, energy, and effort to unlock my brain's potential. I am limitless."*

AUGUST 24

YOUR FUTURE SELF IS WATCHING . . . ACT ACCORDINGLY

Growth can be hard.

Usually that's for one of two reasons.

You might be leaving your comfort zone, stepping into the unknown, and trying something new—what mythologist Joseph Campbell called "crossing the threshold" in the Hero's Journey. It's when the hero leaves their known world to enter the unknown, where they will face countless obstacles, goblins, and challenges along the way (they'll also find allies and undergo transformation).

Or you might be staying *in* your comfort zone. Life can feel tough when we stay in a space where we're refusing to change and grow.

Whether you're living in the unknown or the known, a useful tool to help you progress on your journey is imagining that your future self is watching you right now.

UCLA professor Hal Hershfield calls this *future self-continuity*. His research shows that when we feel connected to our future selves, we treat them as extensions of us, not as strangers. This helps us make wiser decisions and delay immediate gratification to realize long-term goals.

So, if your future self was watching, what would they want to say to you at this moment? What mindset shift would they suggest? What small action would they recommend? And what would you most need to hear from them?

If you knew your future self was watching you, how would this change your life?

Live as though your future self is watching, and act accordingly.

KWIK STEP: Grab a pen and paper, then imagine your future self standing in front of you today. What would they tell you about life? What advice would they give you? Write it down.

AFFIRMATION: *"I show up today to meet my future self. I am limitless."*

AUGUST 25

WITH STRUGGLE COMES STRENGTH

Nelson Mandela spent 27 years in prison before helping South Africa end apartheid.

Oprah Winfrey grew up in poverty, experienced abuse, and didn't think she'd live to reach 60.

Albert Einstein didn't speak until he was three years old, and his teachers thought he was lazy and slow.

Countless people have found success—whatever that looks like for them—in spite of their struggles.

You're one of them.

We all have struggles, but strength doesn't come from ease or from following the path of least resistance. It comes from external pressure that forces internal change.

This is literally what's happening inside your body. Your cells adapt and become more resilient when exposed to moderate stress through the process of hormesis. Cells respond by activating repair and growth pathways that make them stronger, improving their survivability in the face of future challenges.

This concept is well understood in physical fitness, but it also applies to the brain. Cognitive challenges strengthen neural connections, protecting neurons from future stress.

You can probably remember a time when you thought, *I can't do this* or *I can't get through it.*

And yet you did.

Within you lies the potential to turn those struggles into strengths that then become your superpowers. Whether that happens depends on you, your choices, and your actions.

With struggle comes strength, if you choose.

KWIK STEP: Reflect on a time in your past when you struggled yet survived. What did you learn? What skills did it help you to develop? How is that time helping you now? Is there something happening in your life right now where you can apply this strength?

AFFIRMATION: *"From my struggles come my strengths. I am limitless."*

AUGUST 26

WHEN YOUR PURPOSE IS CLEAR, YOUR CHOICES ARE EASIER

Why did I say yes?

Every day, we're losing our finite time to tasks and commitments that don't move us toward the lives we're meant to build.

We're saying yes to baking cookies for another birthday party while only half-listening as our kids tell us about their day. We're stacking meetings back to back instead of blocking time for creativity, deep work, or studying. We're doing tasks that we could—and should—delegate.

Every "yes" misaligned with your goals and purpose is a "no" to you, to the person you're becoming, and to the life you're designing.

Getting clear on your purpose is only the first step. Real growth comes from aligning your actions with it. That takes boundaries.

When someone asks you to do something, instead of saying yes, tell them, "I'll think about" or "I'll get back to you." Then ask yourself, "Does this align with my purpose?" and "Will it move me closer to the life I want?"

Requests can trigger the brain's threat response, which is an ancient survival reflex connected to our fear of rejection. Pausing lets those signals fade so goal-directed networks can engage, helping you evaluate tradeoffs and make better decisions.

At first, saying no can feel uncomfortable. But repetition changes the brain's circuits. Every purpose-aligned action strengthens those neurological pathways. As the old habitual paths get used less, the brain prunes them away. This is how saying no without guilt eventually becomes a habit.

Get clear on your purpose, then say no to everything that doesn't lead you there. When your purpose is clear, your choices are easier.

KWIK STEP: What is something you need to say no to today?

AFFIRMATION: *"I act in alignment with my purpose. I am limitless."*

AUGUST 27

STOP SEEKING BALANCE; CREATE HARMONY INSTEAD

How do you create work-life balance?

What if you don't?

The word *balance* means "equal." Except very little in life is equal. Would you like to spend an equal amount of time at the gym as you do with your family?

Instead of striving for balance, what if you saw your work-life like an orchestra?

To create a symphony, every instrument plays its unique part. But they don't all contribute an equal amount. They don't play an equal amount of time, and not every instrument gets a solo. Yet, when they come together, they create something richer than any one instrument could make on its own.

This is a lot like your work-life. Every aspect, from time with your family to exercising, learning, working, socializing, playing, resting, and everything else, is like an instrument in an orchestra.

When played together with intention, they create *the symphony of your life.*

The key is integration. It's knowing what role each instrument must play and when, accepting this, making different decisions to support this, and then allowing it all to change as the needs and priorities of your work-life shift over time. In some periods, work will take the solo. Other times, it's your family, rest, or health. All the other parts are still making music, just not as loud or as often.

You feel stressed, tense, and frustrated when you start thinking, *My life should be different.* This is a *cognitive dissonance*—holding conflicting ideas, values, opinions that go against your actions.

By aiming for integration, you release cognitive dissonance and can enhance your *cognitive flexibility*—your brain's ability to change its focus and adapt easily and quickly. Cognitive flexibility is associated with more resilience to stress and negative events, more creativity, and a better quality of life.

Stop seeking balance in life and create harmony instead.

KWIK STEP: Make a list of the important "instruments" in your work-life today, such as your family, work, learning, playing, sleeping, or exercising. Note which instruments might be getting too much, or too little, time. What is one thing you can do today to create more harmony?

AFFIRMATION: *"I create harmony in my life. I am limitless."*

AUGUST 28

FAILURE FUELS GROWTH

Imagine this: You step to the front of the room to give an important presentation, and your mind goes blank. Or you're sitting across from a potential new client. You get so nervous you just ramble, forgetting to give them important details about why they should trust you, ending with them walking away.

"Failures" like these can leave you feeling defeated. That's why so many people fear failure as if it were one of the worst things that could happen.

Yet to your brain, it can be something else: an opportunity to upgrade.

Yes, success matters. It activates the brain's reward system, releasing dopamine to reinforce what worked.

But failure does something different. When paired with a growth mindset—the belief you can develop your intelligence and abilities through effort—then it activates other circuitry. Namely, the learning and problem-solving centers in the brain in order to help avoid that failure in the future.

Failure isn't the opposite of success. It's part of it—one of the most essential parts. When you reframe failure this way, then it actually reduces overreactivity in the amygdala—your brain's fear center—helping you stay calm when things don't go as planned.

If you keep telling yourself that failure is one way your brain learns, then before long, you'll even stop calling them failures. They simply become what they always were: fuel for your growth.

KWIK STEP: Recall a recent failure, and write one sentence about what you expected, then what happened, and one small change you'd make next time. Then take a deep breath and visualize yourself successfully applying the change.

AFFIRMATION: *"Failure fuels my brain's growth. I am limitless."*

AUGUST 29

LESS LEADS TO MORE

We've all heard the saying "less is more." But in a world constantly pushing us to do more, achieve more, and respond to endless demands on our time and attention, is this really true?

Yes. Cognitive load is the amount of information your working memory can process. In today's world, you're being bombarded by information—what I like to call *digital deluge*. It's all too easy for your brain to become cognitively overloaded, which can impact learning, decision-making, and focus.

This means you have to become protective and selective of what you allow into your life and what you give your precious time, energy, and attention to. Not everything matters.

Odds are, you're doing something right now that isn't yielding you the results you want, whether that's in your relationship, health, career, or even your brain's performance.

So what's the solution? Trim.

Maybe it's watching one less episode of your favorite show each night. Maybe it's spending five fewer minutes scrolling on your phone from bed after waking up. Or maybe it's eating one less sweet during the week.

Zero in on a single habit, routine, or behavior that isn't serving or supporting your next level of growth or learning.

This isn't about eliminating it completely. Just cutting back to free your time, energy, and attention so you can redirect it toward something greater.

Less leads to more.

KWIK STEP: Identify one habit, routine, or behavior you want to do less of, and do it today.

AFFIRMATION: *"My time, energy, and attention are valuable. I invest them only in what elevates me to the next level. I am limitless."*

AUGUST 30

FEAR IS A SIGNPOST, NOT A DESTINATION

"What if I fail?"

"What if I'm not enough?"

"How did I screw this up?"

Sometimes, we don't just experience moments of fear. It can feel like we're trapped inside them as they consume our every thought, emotion, and action.

Naturally, we want to make the fear stop.

But what if instead of seeing it as something to fight against or make disappear, you saw it as a signal, pointing you toward the skills and competencies you need to upgrade?

By leveling up, we tap into what psychologists call the *confidence-competence loop*. The more competent you are, the more success you're likely to have, which boosts your confidence, which increases your belief in yourself, which makes you more competent.

Consistent intelligent action, especially when you don't feel like doing it, cures most everything, including fear itself.

Creating the life you want can feel scary, but you know what's scarier? Regret. One day, you will take your final breath, and no one's opinion, no one's expectations, and no one mistake will matter.

Instead of fear limiting your abilities, use it to direct you toward the skills and competencies you need to invest more of your time, energy, and attention into building. The more you do this, the more you'll find fear no longer holds you back—it propels you forward.

Fear is a signpost, not a destination.

KWIK STEP: Identify one fear that you feel is holding you back, then break it into three small simple steps you can take to upgrade your skills and build more confidence.

AFFIRMATION: *"Fear is merely a signpost. I use fear to my advantage. I am limitless."*

THE BEAUTY IS IN THE CRACKS

If you dropped a ceramic bowl and it shattered, would you throw it away or fix what broke?

What if I told you you could repair it with lacquer dusted in gold, making it more beautiful mended than before it was broken?

This process is known as *Kintsugi*, the ancient Japanese art of repairing broken pottery with gold, silver, or bronze lacquer. The cracks don't disappear. Instead, the lacquer draws your gaze to them, making the object appear more striking because of its cracks.

Kintsugi is a metaphor for how we heal. When we fail, suffer loss, make a mistake, or experience a trauma, it often leaves us feeling broken. We're told to "bounce back" from these setbacks. But what if it was our inner cracks that made us—and our lives—more beautiful?

Psychologists Richard Tedeschi and Lawrence Calhoun call this *post-traumatic growth*. It's the idea that harmful experiences also have the power to positively transform us. Their research showed how many people can experience profound changes after trauma, including seeing new possibilities, having stronger relationships, finding personal strength, and having a deeper appreciation for life.

You will face setbacks, obstacles, and moments that leave you feeling broken. And you also have the power to mend your cracks with patience, knowledge, and self-compassion.

Just as Kintsugi uses what's broken in an object to make it more beautiful, you can use your "inner breaks" to make you and your life more beautiful than before.

The beauty is in the cracks.

KWIK STEP: Reflect on something that has made you feel broken inside, acknowledge it, then consider how it has helped you to grow.*

AFFIRMATION: *"I bounce back stronger when faced with adversity. I am limitless."*

*Depending on the trauma, this type of work may be best done with a trained professional, who can help guide you in a safe, therapeutic setting.

SEPTEMBER 1

THE LIFE YOU DESIRE HIDES IN THE WORK YOU'RE AVOIDING

Who doesn't want comfort?

How good does it feel to slip into warm clothes on a rainy day? To spend time with our favorite people over a delicious meal or reread our favorite book?

A part of us craves this comfort. It not only puts our nervous system into the parasympathetic state—rest and digest—it also signals safety to the brain. Safety requires less decision-making, meaning less energy.

But comfort doesn't grow our capabilities, confidence, or goals. For that, we need challenges—the ones found in the uncomfortable decisions, actions, and work we often put off.

Challenge brings change. Change brings adaptation. And adaptation brings growth. This is how your brain creates new neural pathways and connections.

When you feel caught in comfort, take these three steps:

1. **BREAK GOALS INTO CHUNKS.** Sometimes all you see is the mountain you must climb, forgetting you only get there one step at a time. Take your goal and break it into tiny actions that you can track. Just start somewhere, and you open a loop your brain will feel compelled to close. You're activating the Zeigarnik effect—the brain remembers incomplete tasks more than those completed—and using it for your benefit, to motivate you to continue until the task is finished.
2. **BE KIND TO YOURSELF.** Studies on self-compassion reveal that when you're hard on yourself, it leads to procrastination and more rumination. But being kind to yourself increases your motivation to take responsibility for your actions and improve yourself.
3. **TUNE IN TO YOUR WHY.** Success = H^3. Goals start in your *head*, move to your *heart*, then to your *hands*. If you know your goal, but you're procrastinating, you may not be tapping into your why—that's your heart, your emotions. Emotions fuels motion. *Why* do you want something? What are the rewards?

Do the work that feels uncomfortable. Run. Walk. Crawl if you must. Just keep going. The life you desire hides in the work you're avoiding.

KWIK STEP: What is one uncomfortable action or decision you've avoided? Use the three steps and notice how it feels.

AFFIRMATION: *"I make uncomfortable decisions and take uncomfortable actions. I am limitless."*

SEPTEMBER 2

RIDE YOUR ENERGY WAVE

Sit comfortably with your eyes closed. Take a few deep, slow breaths, letting your exhales be longer than your inhales.

When you feel calmer, then bring your awareness to the soles of your feet and notice how they feel. Then slowly move up through your body to the top of your head, pausing at different spots to focus on what you're feeling.

Is something painful? Sore? Stiff? If it is, imagine your breath pouring into that spot. With each exhale, imagine the stiffness releasing, the soreness calming down, the pain gently fading.

When you get to the top of your head, check your energy. Is it vibrant? Weak?

What you just completed is a body-scan meditation. It's a technique that can help increase your awareness of your body and its signals, or what's known as interoception—the ability to decipher internal signals. Studies suggest people with stronger interoception make better decisions and regulate stress more effectively.

That's partly because they've learned to manage their energy.

Energy operates on peak and flow cycles, governed by ultradian rhythms. Attention, alertness, and energy tends to peak then diminish after roughly 90 minutes and up to four hours for some people. Knowing this, you can begin scheduling your work and learning periods in 90-minute blocks.

But pair it with mindfulness techniques like a body scan so you're listening to your body. If you're in the zone and you're at 90 minutes, keep going. Likewise, if you're struggling rereading paragraphs, forgetting words and phrases, and find yourself dozing off, but it's only 40 minutes in, then take a short break, switch to working in shorter sprints, or stop for the day, if you can.

Discipline matters, but if you ignore your internal signals, you risk reaping diminishing returns instead of real results.

Energy peaks and flows. Learn to ride your energy wave.

KWIK STEP: While you're working or studying, do a body scan to check in with how you're feeling and your energy levels. Adjust accordingly.

AFFIRMATION: *"I am in tune with my body's energy levels. I am limitless."*

YOU DON'T HAVE EMOTIONS. YOU DO EMOTIONS.

We often say, "I'm angry," or "I'm frustrated," or "I'm happy."

We make these offhand statements without thinking, but our words shape the way our brain sees us. So when we say, "I am . . ." we are creating a belief system that becomes an identity our brain uses to determine who we are and what is possible—or impossible—for our lives.

But anger is not who we are. Frustration is not who we are. No emotion is.

Neuroscientist and psychologist Lisa Feldman Barrett describes emotions not as fixed reactions to the world, but as predictions our brain makes in the moment based on the sensory information we take in (through seeing, feeling, tasting, touching, hearing) and on our past experiences. This is known as the *constructionist theory of emotion.*

So feelings are really just actions your brain and body are doing.

You don't have anger. You *do* anger.

You don't have frustration. You *do* frustration.

You don't have happiness. You *do* happiness.

When you think of emotions as verbs, or actions, it means you can stop and do another. The power to change your actions lies with you. Whatever actions you take, you can choose to untake.

You don't have emotions. You do emotions.

KWIK STEP: Today, reframe one to three emotions, phrasing them as actions. "I did anger when that person cut me off on the road." "I did joy when I watched my kid's soccer game." "I did frustration when my co-worker interrupted me."

AFFIRMATION: *"I don't have emotions; I do emotions. I am limitless."*

SEPTEMBER 4

LITTLE BY LITTLE, A LITTLE BECOMES A LOT

Most people who know their why—their purpose—don't struggle because they lack motivation.

They struggle because the step to start feels too big. Or they believe everything has to be "just right" before they can hit Send on a proposal, take a sales call, or launch a new idea.

Deep down, it's the fear of failing or the shame of stumbling that overwhelms the brain.

This is your brain on perfection. It's your amygdala—the threat detector—firing and dampening activity in your prefrontal cortex, the center of decision-making, planning, and emotional regulation. Big steps feel high-risk, because your brain treats them that way, so you don't act.

But you know what your brain does like? Small, simple, and *achievable* steps it can repeat.

These tiny actions create a sense of relief, calming the nervous system and reducing cognitive overload. This is how you can begin disarming perfectionism while building sustainable momentum.

The key is consistency. No matter how small, keep showing up. As you do, you will start seeing results, which creates a sense of accomplishment. Tiny wins release dopamine—the molecule of motivation—signaling to your brain, "Do that again; it feels good."

This is also how you build self-trust, by proving to your brain that you're someone who acts, learns, adapts, and perseveres.

Perfection is an illusion. But progress gets your dreams made. Tiny steps taken over time create big changes. Little by little, a little becomes a lot.

KWIK STEP: What's a big goal you have that has been difficult to make progress on? What's one tiny, simple step you can take today?

AFFIRMATION: *"I take small, simple steps toward my future self, trusting that little by little, a little becomes a lot. I am limitless."*

PURPOSE IS YOUR POWER

The most meaningful pursuits in our lives often bring with them daunting, difficult, even seemingly dangerous tasks.

It's no wonder that we tend to procrastinate, convincing ourselves why now isn't the right time, or why we're not ready. But the rewards we seek are waiting for us on the other side, so we have to move forward.

When you're stuck and stagnant, try this. Identify a task or goal you've put off and ask four questions:

1. Why is it important that I start and finish this task?
2. What are the potential consequences—lost opportunities, friendships, results—from procrastinating or not following through?
3. Who will I become when I follow through?
4. Who will I become if I don't follow through?

When we direct our goals not only toward something we want, but also away from what we don't want, we tap into two motivational systems.

Approach goals, which move you toward purpose and growth, light up the brain's reward circuitry, boosting positive emotion and engagement. *Avoidance goals* (what you lose if you don't act) activate circuits connected to risk, loss, and urgency.

Understanding the purpose for *why* you want to grow your human intelligence and unlock your brain's potential will give you the power to push through anything.

Purpose is your power.

KWIK STEP: Think of a task you've put off or a goal you've stagnated on. Then take one minute to reflect on each of the four questions.

AFFIRMATION: *"My purpose is power, propelling me through procrastination. I am limitless."*

FROM BURNOUT TO BALANCE

We hear about burnout all the time.

Studies consistently report almost 50 percent of workers around the world feel stressed or burned out.

It's easy to think burnout comes from overworking. But what if burnout is actually about undernourishing our brains?

Sometimes we burn out not because we're doing too much, but because we're doing too little of the things that bring us alive and nourish our bodies and souls.

When you don't make time for the activities that light you up, your brain suffers. Your nervous system becomes stuck in the sympathetic state, making stress become the norm. This means your body doesn't get the signal to shift into the parasympathetic state, where it can rest and repair.

Plus, your reward system can get suppressed. Doing things that matter, that have meaning, and that bring you joy help release dopamine, aiding in motivation and pleasure.

When you're burned out, you're often numb. There's little joy, little meaning, and little motivation. By making time for activities you love, you help your nervous system shift into a relaxed state and reactivate your reward circuitry.

For you, maybe it's dancing or going to a comedy club. Maybe it's spending more time outdoors with loved ones, or simply relaxing by reading, engaging in a hobby, or binge-watching your favorite show. Yes, even binge-watching can be restorative. What matters is how you feel after. If you're left more hollow or numb, then that's not restorative—that's a distraction.

Rest means activities that make you laugh, leave you feeling happier, more engaged, more joyful, and more fulfilled.

Recovery isn't wasting time. It's the foundation for resilience, focus, and long-term performance.

Choose things that light you up, the ones that nourish you on a soul level. That's how you go from burnout to balance.

KWIK STEP: What is one restorative activity you can schedule today?

AFFIRMATION: *"I rest my brain to enhance my performance. I am limitless."*

SEPTEMBER 7

TRUST YOURSELF TO FIGURE IT OUT

Finish this sentence: "If I were more confident, I'd . . ."

". . . ask for a raise."

". . . make more money."

". . . wouldn't feel nervous going to events."

How many things do you long to experience if you only felt more confident?

Lacking self-confidence is heartbreaking. It stops you before you start. But when you have confidence in yourself, you trust in your abilities, knowledge, and capabilities. You'll launch that business, post a video online, ask someone out, put in for a promotion, and say yes to new opportunities despite the fear, anxiety, or worry that comes with stepping into the unknown.

Confidence doesn't eliminate those feelings; it simply says, "I see you, and still I act. I know that I am capable of doing this and handling anything that comes my way."

To start building more confidence, try tapping into the power of music. There are few practices that can instantly shift your emotional state more than music.

Studies show listening to music engages multiple networks in the brain involved with cognition, memory, attention, and emotional regulation. When you listen to music that moves you, it helps reduce stress, anxiety, depression, and other negative emotions while supporting focus, motivation, and performance—key to taking confident action—especially in high-pressure situations. Music has also been associated with structural changes in areas related to learning, emotional regulation, and social connection.

Pick a song that makes you feel confident, bold, and courageous, and play it before high-pressure moments or during times when you need a confidence boost.

Confidence isn't the absence of fear. It's trusting yourself enough to figure it out no matter what.

KWIK STEP: Pick your confidence song, play it, and notice how it makes you feel. Anytime you need a dose of confidence, listen to it.

AFFIRMATION: *"I trust myself. I am limitless."*

ACT YOUR WAY OUT OF BEING STUCK

You know what you need to do.

It's time to create and publish a social media post, restructure your team, talk to your boss about a raise, or finish the manuscript you're writing.

Yet you feel stuck.

Sometimes, you don't move forward because a part of you fears that you're taking the wrong step. You don't want to look foolish, make an incorrect choice, or create a situation you can't reverse. So you hesitate.

How do you *really* know when it's the right action? How do you know if now is the time?

You don't. You learn to feel the fear, and you still act.

In this instance, fear is a signal from your brain that it doesn't know what will happen. That's why stepping outside your comfort zone feels so uncomfortable. The brain prioritizes what feels familiar because that's more predictable, even if it keeps you stuck.

Action breaks that cycle. It forces the brain to stop overthinking and to focus on the goal you're going for and the task you've started.

But then you must keep acting to keep momentum. That's where measuring progress comes in. Chunk what you need to do into small, quantifiable steps that you can track.

If you need to write a speech, you could log the length and number of weekly work sessions, how much research you did, how many words you wrote out of how many remain, and for how long and often you practiced. Then shoot for doing 1 percent better the next time.

Action teaches the brain that uncertainty isn't always dangerous and acting isn't always threatening. Over time, that fear response becomes less intense and reactive.

There's no thinking your way out of being stuck. You have to act.

KWIK STEP: What is something you're stuck on? Take one small step toward it.

AFFIRMATION: *"I act to keep moving forward. I am limitless."*

DON'T AVOID MISTAKES; LEARN FROM THEM

We all know the saying, "If we don't learn from our mistakes, we're doomed to repeat them." Here's another, harder truth. We don't make a mistake twice. We hire the same people, market the same way, and get into the same arguments with our significant others. The second time is a choice.

The key is learning from your missteps so you can move forward. That's where the "Six Ps" come in.

1. **PREPARE.** Identify skills, resources, or tools that will prevent you from repeating the error. This activates your prefrontal cortex, which supports self-control, decision-making, and rational thought.
2. **PROGRESS.** You can't manage something unless you can measure it. Chart your progress and celebrate it. Small wins release dopamine, reinforcing learning and teaching your brain to stop fearing mistakes.
3. **PATTERNS.** Remember past mistakes and past solutions. Identify similarities to your current situation, and how you might solve it this time. Also look for recurring patterns and themes throughout your life, like needing better focus, fewer distractions, or more organization.
4. **PREVENTION.** Write what you think went wrong, a goal, or what you want to do in the future. If you missed a deadline, what can you do differently next time? Maybe you use memory aids like Post-It notes on your computer or reminders in your calendar.
5. **PURPOSE.** Create a list of reasons why you *don't* want to repeat a mistake. This taps into your purpose, making it less likely you'll fall into the same behavior again.
6. **PLAN.** Make a detailed plan for how you intend to avoid the mistake. Yet remain flexible, recognizing plans may change.

The people who achieve the most aren't the ones who avoid mistakes. They're the ones who learn the fastest from them.

KWIK STEP: What is one mistake you've been repeating? Choose one of the "Six Ps" (maybe the one that you resist the most?), and use it to intentionally break the pattern.

AFFIRMATION: *"I face my mistakes so I may learn from them. I am limitless."*

MAKE YOUR BIGGEST SETBACKS YOUR BIGGEST COMEBACKS

Some dreams are never meant to be.

For almost 10 years, the founders of Glitch spent millions of dollars building an online gaming company. And they did. They employed 40 people, and tens of thousands more played their game.

There was just one problem.

The founders were forced to admit the dream they built their lives around, the one they had invested hundreds of thousands of hours and millions of dollars into, wasn't working. They were months away from bankruptcy, shutting down the game, and laying everyone off.

Worse, there was no path to salvation.

Instead of forging forward, they pivoted to selling the internal communication tool they had built for themselves.

From the failed ashes of Glitch, Slack was born, a company Salesforce later acquired for *$27.7 billion.*

If Glitch's founders hadn't let go of their dream when they did, Slack might never have been.

Letting go can hurt. The brain registers pain more intensely than it does potential gains. This is known as loss aversion. It's why walking away from a relationship or job, or changing a habit, feels hard.

But you can change how your brain interprets loss.

Tell yourself, "I am willing to adapt my strategies and responses to changing circumstances." Remind yourself to open to new ideas, people, insights, approaches, and opportunities. Keep learning new skills and information. All of this helps strengthen cognitive flexibility. It helps you make better decisions, improves your creativity, and builds a more resilient brain.

Some dreams require grit. Others are vehicles to get you to the one that really matters. Don't cling to what no longer works. That's how you turn your biggest setbacks into your biggest comebacks.

KWIK STEP: What's one thing that isn't working? If you were allowed to let it go, what are three places where you could turn your energy instead? Write your answers.

AFFIRMATION: *"I am capable of easily and effortlessly changing my ideas, perspectives, and thinking. I am limitless."*

SEPTEMBER 11

USE YOUR PAST TO PROPEL YOU INTO YOUR FUTURE

A giant rock lay wedged at the bottom of a wide riverbed.

Its edges were once so sharp that it sliced anything that drifted too close. Years passed, and the river kept flowing. Sometimes rushing madly, other times flowing gently. Through it all, the rock could do nothing to change or stop the current, and nothing to keep its edges from becoming rounded and smooth.

All the rock could do was endure, allowing the water to shape and change it.

We're not so different from the rock.

Too often, we trap ourselves in thoughts of the past, in "I wish I could have . . ." or "if only. . . ."

When this happens, our brain reacts as though we're reliving the moment. The same emotional circuits in the amygdala and memory networks activate, bringing with it the old emotions and memories.

Before long, we can find that we're stuck in a kind of mental time-loop, reliving the same memory, the same shame, the same fear, the same regret. So instead of living in the present and moving forward, we're living in the past.

But the past is not a place for you to live. It's nothing more than water to a rock. It's meant to shape you, help you learn, grow, and move forward. Every mistake, every missed opportunity, every stumble smooths your edges.

Where the rock has no choice in its transformation; you do. You have the power to use your past to propel you into your future.

KWIK STEP: Write one to three regrets using the "If only I had . . ." or "I wish I could have . . ." statements. Then ask yourself, "What did that experience teach me that I use today?" Finally, identify one small step or mindset shift you can take today.

AFFIRMATION: *"I use my past to propel me into my future. I am limitless."*

SEPTEMBER 12

RECOVER TO RISE

Does this sound familiar? The alarm goes off, you roll out of bed, and you *still* feel exhausted even after sleeping seven hours.

If you're like many people, you reach for coffee hoping the caffeine will energize and clear the fog. Maybe it does for a bit, yet as the day drags on, you're still exhausted.

You're challenged not by a lack of time or motivation, but by a lack of energy. Your brain uses about 20 percent of your body's daily energy. When there's not enough fuel, or you've engaged in heavy cognitive work, your prefrontal cortex gets affected. That makes it difficult to think clearly, make decisions, focus, create, process information, or control emotions.

So what can you do when returning to bed isn't an option, yet pushing through fatigue doesn't work? Start by asking: "What's my recovery protocol?"

Recovery isn't a weekend practice. It's a daily habit just as important as exercise, nutrition, and sleep. When you allow your brain to recover, you shift into the parasympathetic state (rest and digest) and reduce neural inflammation.

So what is your recovery protocol?

Are you spending time in nature? Listening to relaxing music? Shutting off screens before bed? Meditating? Journaling? Surrounding yourself with "batteries included" people? Eating brain-enhancing foods like salmon, blueberries, and leafy greens? Exercising? Taking regular brain breaks?

Everyone's recovery practices will look slightly different. What matters most is giving yourself permission to have fun and experiment. See what works well. If something doesn't or you dislike it, let it go.

Recovering isn't slowing down or falling behind. It's fuel propelling you to greater progress. So recover to rise.

KWIK STEP: Assess your recovery protocol. What tools do you use daily that help your brain rest? And what's one new tool you want to try? Use it today.

AFFIRMATION: *"I recover to rise. I am limitless."*

SEPTEMBER 13

QUESTIONS LEAD TO POSSIBILITIES

The human brain can process about 11 million bits of information per second, yet the conscious mind can only handle 40 to 50.

That's a big difference, so to keep you sane, your brain acts like a deletion device, eliminating most of the information it absorbs and allowing through only what matters most.

This determines what you pay attention to and notice.

A key part of your attention system is the reticular activating system (RAS). It acts as a filter or gatekeeper between your unconscious brain and conscious mind. This is why you can sit in a coffee shop, deep in conversation, hear your name, and immediately turn your head toward the sound. You didn't recognize the voice, you recognized your name, because it's hardwired into your brain as important.

The RAS filters information based on its importance to your goals, thoughts, emotions, and beliefs.

If you ask, "What went wrong today?" your RAS will filter for information to answer the question. But ask, "What went well?" and your RAS allows that type of information through.

Priming your RAS with intentional questions works for every area in your life. If you don't want to work out, yet you know it's important, you could ask, "How can I move my body and enjoy it?"

Suddenly, an idea to take a dance class might pop into your mind. Later, you might see an ad for an intro to pickleball, or maybe a friend mentions how they're loving this new yoga studio, near your home.

It's not that these opportunities didn't exist before. Your brain just wasn't filtering them. They were irrelevant, but your question made them relevant.

So ask better questions, and your brain will find better answers and more possibilities.

KWIK STEP: Grab a pen and paper, and ask yourself, "What went well yesterday?" then write down all of your successes. Now, ask yourself, "How can I build upon my wins today?" Write what comes up and commit to taking at least one action.

AFFIRMATION: *"Questions direct my focus, so I ask ones that support my brain's peak performance. I am limitless."*

SEPTEMBER 14

TRAIN FOR CRISIS

"The bamboo that bends is stronger than the oak that resists," goes the ancient Japanese proverb.

When we face high-intensity, high-pressure situations like big projects, pivotal investor meetings, and exams, we want to bend like bamboo, not break like an oak. We want to stay calm, confident, and clear. But how?

What if you tried training for a crisis?

In business, many companies use data and analytics to create potential future scenarios. This allows them to plan ahead, stay proactive, and prepare for the worst.

You can use a similar method. When you're facing a stressful situation, imagine the worst way it could play out, then imagine the actions you'd take. Who would you speak to or recruit for help? What would you say to them? What skills would you draw on?

Creating a contingency plan reduces uncertainty for the brain, which dampens the amygdala-driven threat response, allowing the prefrontal cortex to remain engaged. This will help you act decisively and intentionally if the worst case arises (which it often doesn't).

This practice can help train your brain to become more cognitively flexible, better able to change perspectives and behaviors and to think quickly when situations shift. The faster your brain can do this, the less likely the stress response will kick in. That happens when the brain interprets the unknown and unpredictable as dangerous.

The brain can never actually predict the future—that's an illusion. So the more you train your brain to become comfortable in the uncomfortable, and to feel safe in the unknown, the less stressed you will feel.

Train your brain for crisis, and you'll become like the bamboo—bending without breaking.

KWIK STEP: Choose a stressful situation and think of the worst-case scenario that might arise. What actions would you take if it happened? Who would you speak to or recruit for help? What would you say to them? What skills would you draw on? And how might this outcome actually benefit you?

AFFIRMATION: *"I handle crises with unwavering confidence, clarity, and calmness. I am limitless."*

IT'S NOT ONE DAY; IT'S DAY ONE, TODAY

The perfect time to start a new habit, hobby, or skill is . . . never.

That day doesn't exist. You don't need a Monday. You don't need a new month. You don't even need a new year.

You only need one decision: to do it now.

The single act of beginning, even with a small action, surprises the brain. It breaks the pattern your brain expects. The result? You become more alert and focused as neurons fire in new patterns, strengthening fresh connections as your brain searches to adapt to the new experience.

By taking this one new small action, you're also changing how your brain sees you. Do something often enough, and it becomes part of your identity. Now, you're a person who follows through, who honors their commitments, who keeps showing up.

So when you take a step in a new direction, you're not just changing your behavior—you're literally changing your brain and becoming someone new.

All it takes is one step to bring you closer to your goals. One step to ignite momentum. One step to prove to yourself what's possible when you stop waiting and start moving.

One step in a different direction can completely change your destination, if not your destiny.

So it's not one day—it's day one, today.

KWIK STEP: Think of something you've been waiting to start "one day." What if you made today Day One? Identify one small step you can take today and do it.

AFFIRMATION: *"I do not wait for one day. I act today. I am limitless."*

SEPTEMBER 16

WITHIN EVERY DISADVANTAGE, THERE'S THE WORD *ADVANTAGE*

The ancient Japanese martial art aikido doesn't rely on overpowering or resisting an opponent. Instead, it uses timing to redirect the opponent's attacks back at them.

When it comes to failure, the brain learns in a similar way—by redirecting what doesn't work to change behaviors the next time. Except most people work so hard to avoid failing that they don't realize it's the very thing that accelerates their growth.

The brain doesn't grow from perfection—it grows from pressure. It adapts to build and strengthen new neural pathways when it's challenged, not when it's comfortable.

When used intentionally, failure becomes data. It tells you what works or needs adjusting. Just as the aikido master redirects attacks, you can redirect failure into progress.

When you miss a deadline, forget an important detail, or break your word, ask: "How can I turn this disadvantage into an advantage? What can I do differently next time? What might I have to release?"

Use this idea for any experience that doesn't go the way you expected. If someone says something hurtful to you, if you receive difficult health news, or you're struggling in a relationship, imagine how you can redirect the experience into a lesson.

This is how your brain adapts, becomes more cognitively flexible—and how you quietly calm a mind that fears failure.

Within every disadvantage, there's the word *advantage*. Find yours.

KWIK STEP: What's one disadvantage you've faced in life that has become an advantage? List every benefit you've reaped.

AFFIRMATION: *"I find an advantage in every disadvantage. I am limitless."*

SEPTEMBER 17

LEAVE COGNITIVE REPS IN RESERVE

The demands of life in our busy world often leave us feeling like we're drowning in tasks with no relief in sight. So relentless is this tide that it can seem like our only option is to keep treading water, trying to do more, faster, and more efficiently.

But if the pursuit of productivity leads to exhaustion, then it's not really efficient after all. When you're mentally fatigued, everything feels harder and slower—memory, processing information, making decisions, thinking clearly, even accessing positive emotions.

Instead of pushing your brain to break, what if you borrowed an idea from the gym—leaving some "reps in reserve"?

In strength training, this means stopping a set before you're exhausted, when you could still lift a few more reps without losing good form. Training this way helps athletes avoid injury, better manage fatigue, need less recovery time, and make consistent progress. This is different from training to failure, when you keep going until your muscles can't lift another rep.

This approach helps with learning and working too. When you leave a few cognitive "reps in reserve," it can reduce fatigue and support core functions like memory, problem-solving, decision-making, and emotional regulation.

When you study, try stopping before your attention wanders. If you're writing a report or creating a presentation, try pausing in the middle of a section. Look for opportunities to leave some reps in reserve, and notice how you feel the next day.

Not only will you help your brain conserve energy and reduce recovery time, but you'll also get a shot of motivation when you return to the task—that's because the brain likes closing loops, so it will want to get back to that task and finish it.

Burning out isn't a badge of honor. It's a signal your brain needs to recover. Rest before you reach exhaustion, and you'll have the reps in reserve ready to tackle the next day.

Leave cognitive reps in reserve.

KWIK STEP: What is one task you can pause in the middle of today?

AFFIRMATION: *"I rest my brain before reaching exhaustion, leaving some cognitive reps in reserve. I am limitless."*

DISCOMFORT DIRECTS YOUR DESTINY

At the slightest sign of discomfort, most people stop.

It's the moment conflict arises in an important conversation, you hit a snag building a website, or you get drawn into a disagreement volunteering for a cause you're passionate about.

This happens by design. Your brain is wired to protect you against feeling discomfort. Yet discomfort is what you need to grow and expand.

Think of it like going to the gym. You have movements you love and others you'd rather avoid. But the exercises you dislike are often the ones you need most to build the strength and mobility to stay active and healthy.

In the same way, challenges are the equipment your brain needs to expand beyond its limits. So instead of avoiding uncomfortable actions, seek them out.

Start easy. Try ending your next shower on cold, standing under the water for 10 to 30 seconds. Research suggests this can improve your mood and increase stress tolerance.

Practice focused silence—not talking or responding—for 30 minutes.

Try controlled breath work, holding your inhales for a few beats before slowly exhaling and holding your breath another few seconds.

Or simply decide you'll tackle the hardest task of your day first.

These practices are forms of stress inoculation. By exposing yourself to controlled discomfort, you teach your brain that it can survive stress, making it more resilient. Having that difficult conversation, showing up for that meeting, or taking a tough exam gets easier, because you've become a person capable of handling discomfort.

Your success in life is about more than mental intelligence; it's mental fitness too. Discomfort directs your destiny.

KWIK STEP: What is one slightly uncomfortable practice you can do today?

AFFIRMATION: *"I welcome difficult tasks, knowing they help strengthen my motivation muscle. I am limitless."*

WHAT WOULD . . . ?

When a door is locked, pushing harder won't open it. You have to find the right key.

When you're stuck having the same argument, procrastinating, or are frozen by fear, force doesn't work either.

That's what makes questions like "what would . . .?" so powerful.

You think of someone you respect or admire, and then you ask, "What would ________ do?" or "How would ________ think about this situation?" or "How would ________ solve this challenge?"

Asking questions like this helps unlock rigid thinking patterns. Your brain shifts out of its self-focused loop where it replays worries, fears, beliefs, and past stories. And it shifts into a new perspective, one with different beliefs and ideas.

When questions get posed to your brain, it seeks answers, directing your attention and focus to solving the problem. Now you're more likely to notice different patterns and possibilities in your environment.

New questions lead to new answers.

"What would ________ do?" also helps strengthen cognitive flexibility, your brain's ability to quickly shift perspectives and explore new ideas.

You can also ask, "What would the confident version of *me* do?" And pause to see, feel, and vividly imagine in detail what that version of you would do. Vivid imagination activates many of the same overlapping circuits that engage when you make a physical movement or take an action.

The answers you need are often inside you. You just need a way in. Let "What would . . . ?" help unlock the door.

KWIK STEP: What is one problem you've struggled solving? Think of someone you admire or respect who would confidently and competently solve it—or a version of yourself who could. Then ask yourself, "What would ________ do?" and do it.

AFFIRMATION: *"I am capable of solving every problem facing me. I am limitless."*

SEPTEMBER 20

TURN IMPULSIVENESS INTO INTENTION

Regret hits everyone.

Maybe you sent a quick text you wish you could erase, or you long to make a different decision or pull back a sharper comment than you had meant to deliver.

It's not that we want to act, or react, in these impulsive ways. They just sometimes happen. But every reaction we don't control becomes a chain pulling us away from our clarity, balance, and progress.

To break the pattern of impulsiveness, try practicing pausing first.

This doesn't mean suppressing emotions; it just means noticing them before they take control. It's acknowledging "I feel angry" instead of becoming the anger.

Pausing, even for one breath, helps your brain to step out of automatic patterns that drive behaviors. The pause gives you a moment to process, breathe, and see a situation as it is, not as your emotions color it.

When you react impulsively, your brain's emotional processing center, especially for fear, the amygdala, drives your response. When you pause and breathe, you activate the prefrontal cortex, the part responsible for logic, reason, and thoughtful decision-making.

By pausing, you're practicing what's called *response inhibition*—aligning actions with your goals.

That one breath also strengthens neural pathways between emotional and rational centers, training your brain to handle stress with less reactivity.

Between what happens and how you respond exists a tiny space. In it lives your power to *choose* your reaction, to *guide* your thoughts, and *protect* your peace.

Turn impulsiveness into intention.

KWIK STEP: Today, pause for at least one breath before making a decision, responding to a comment, or sending a message.

AFFIRMATION: *"I turn impulsiveness into intention. I am limitless."*

SEPTEMBER 21

SELF-TRUST IS BUILT, NOT BORN

There's a difference between self-confidence and self-worth.

Self-worth is knowing your value.

Self-confidence is believing in yourself. The word *confidence* comes from the Latin roots *con* (with, together) and *fidere* (trust) and can be understood as, "to have full trust." So self-confidence is really having full trust in yourself.

Lacking self-confidence means you spend more time doubting yourself, your abilities, your knowledge, even your worth. This can show up as being painfully shy, hesitating before speaking, or never sharing your ideas. It might mean turning down opportunities—a new position, project, or client—or avoiding risks like starting a business, asking someone on a date, or taking a class to improve your abilities.

This moment is about redrawing the borders and boundaries of what's possible in your learning and life by relearning to trust yourself.

Think of something personal or professional that you feel or felt deeply confident in, either now or in the past—a sport, baking, gardening, writing, organizing, time management, running meetings, or making sales pitches.

Did you start out feeling confident? No. You felt unsure, uncertain, maybe even a little afraid. But with repetition, consistency, and practice, you built confidence in yourself and abilities. That's how it works in any area of life.

Now:

- What's something you want but haven't done because you don't feel confident?
- What skills might you need to develop to increase your confidence?
- What support systems do you need to build?
- What would it look like to trust yourself in this situation, even without fully feeling confident?
- What's one small step you can take to move in this direction now?

Asking questions like these will help increase your self-trust. Remember, self-trust is built, not born.

KWIK STEP: First, think of a time when you felt fully confident. Next, answer the questions in today's entry.

AFFIRMATION: *"I am confident. I do confidence. I am limitless."*

A CLEAR MIND MAKES CLEAR DECISIONS

"Do you have the patience to wait till your mud settles and the water is clear?"

The ancient Chinese philosopher Lao Tzu wrote this in the Tao Te Ching some 2,500 years ago, yet its wisdom remains true today.

If you've ever lain awake at night wrestling with a big decision, you know how it can leave your mind feeling like you're trying to wade through muddy water. Every step requires enormous effort, while it's nearly impossible to make out the best way forward.

Which is why before making any decision, you need a way to clear your mind. That's where a *decision matrix* can help. It's a grid to help you see clearly the potential obstacles and opportunities, pros and cons, of each choice. This can help you avoid *analysis paralysis,* which is when the brain becomes overwhelmed by too many choices or fear of making the wrong one.

On the left side, you list the different decisions. Along the top, you write the factors that you're weighing.

For example, if you're considering letting go of someone on your team, you'd write the different decisions down the left side: keeping them in their current role, shifting their responsibilities, letting them go immediately, or letting them go three months from now.

Along the top, you'd write the important factors like performance quality, productivity, impact on the rest of the team. You can weigh each factor, too, on a scale of 1 to 5, so when you're finished, you can tally up the points to see which decision scores the highest.

You can use this matrix for any decision—your business, accepting a new position, a relationship, an opportunity—and you can make them as complex or as simple as needed. If a score doesn't turn out the way you wanted, you can reevaluate. Maybe some factors aren't as important as you thought.

Making big decisions with a muddy mind can lead to regret. But a clear mind makes clear decisions.

KWIK STEP: What is one decision that has weighed on you? Plot it using the decision matrix.

AFFIRMATION: *"I clear my mind, and the right decisions reveal themselves. I am limitless."*

SEPTEMBER 23

MAKE YOUR PURPOSE BIGGER THAN FEAR

"I'm so scared. I don't know what the future looks like."

"I'm terrified to take on this task because I don't have the skills to do it well."

"What if I fail?"

We all know, at least unconsciously, that fear limits us. That's by design. When the brain perceives something—real or imaginary—as threatening, the amygdala gets triggered. This small, almond-shaped group of neurons is responsible for activating our "fight, flight, freeze, or fawn" survival mode.

It's thanks to this ancient system that our ancestors survived in the wild against crocodiles, leopards, and bears. But the amygdala can't differentiate between being chased by a predator or facing a demanding deadline at work, an uncomfortable conversation, or doomscrolling.

With the amygdala constantly activated, we stay in a box. We don't take risks. We don't allow ourselves to be vulnerable. We don't go after what we want. We aren't as productive or prosperous as we desire and deserve.

Psychologists say we're born with only two natural fears: falling and loud noises. So those fears of public speaking, making a mistake, missing a deadline, or looking bad in front of someone are learned. Some experience in your past taught you to fear them. To your nervous system, they are real, but there is no actual risk threatening your survival. Since anything learned can be unlearned, that means you can unlearn fear too.

Take one irrational fear that cannot cause you harm, then write a purpose that's bigger. Make it so emotionally compelling that it gives you the courage to walk through the fear. Let's say you're afraid of going back to school later in life. Maybe your purpose is to provide your children with a sense of financial security and safety that you never had as a child.

Research suggests that a strong purpose can bolster us against repetitive negative thinking and reduce stress-related distress.

You're not your fears. You weren't even born with them. They were limitations thrust on you without your permission.

Make your purpose bigger than your fear, and fear will start to diminish.

KWIK STEP: Identify one irrational fear and write a purpose that's bigger than it.

AFFIRMATION: *"Fears are nothing more than limitations learned. Anything I learn, I can unlearn. Today, I choose to unlearn fear. I am limitless."*

FEED YOUR MISSION UNTIL IT FEEDS YOU BACK

When you choose to go to a seminar, take a weekly course, or commit to reading for 20 minutes nightly, you're sacrificing. You're deciding to give up one thing for something else.

Maybe that's extra sleep, working out, spending time with your family, relaxing, or working on your business. These things still matter.

Yet there are inflection points when choosing to stay at home—literally and figuratively—changes the direction of your life.

The truth is, these choices aren't always easy. No one sees beneath the iceberg. They don't see the money, time, balance, harmony, hobbies, comfort, sometimes even the health you're trading.

While these sacrifices are real, they're also investments.

You're trading short-term comfort and ease for long-term gains. Studies show delaying gratification engages and strengthens the prefrontal cortex. This region plays a vital role in self-control and long-term planning, making goal-directed behavior easier and more automatic.

But success doesn't happen overnight. It requires patience and persistence, often without immediate rewards. Sometimes, early results can be very discouraging. This is known as the *effort-reward disparity*. It's when your brain expects progress quickly, but there's little visible evidence to make the effort seem worthwhile. This can create doubt and worry, because the brain interprets the lack of progress as uncertainty and risk.

Your dreams and goals don't come without a price. The question is: Are you willing to pay it? Is your purpose for sacrificing—for investing—worth the cost?

If it's not, then stop. Because without purpose, without meaning, that's not investing; it's wasting your precious and finite resources.

But if it is, then keep going. Because whether it's time, energy, or comfort, those sacrifices are real—and so are the rewards, one day.

Feed your mission until it feeds you back.

KWIK STEP: Write one commitment you're making that feels costly. Name what you're giving up, then what it's buying you long-term. Then ask yourself, "Is this cost worth it?" If it's not, consider giving it up.

AFFIRMATION: *"I will feed my mission until it feeds me back. I am limitless."*

YOU DON'T HAVE ENERGY; YOU GENERATE ENERGY

Energy isn't like money in your bank account.

Energy is something your body and brain *generates* minute by minute.

That's more than a metaphor. It's a biological process. Inside your trillions of cells live tiny organelles called mitochondria. Known as the "powerhouses of the cell," one of their main jobs is to convert oxygen and nutrients into ATP—that's the energy your cells use to fuel all their functions, from moving your muscles to remembering facts and figures.

So while you do lose energy throughout the day, you can generate it too.

Equally interesting is your *perception* of energy. Research on "ego depletion" and "fatigue illusion" suggests that your perception of how much you have can deplete or increase it.

In a study published in the journal *Nature*, researchers found that when people felt they didn't have energy, it wasn't that their actual physical reserves were gone. It was that their brains had made assumptions about "fatigue milestones" during challenging tasks, points when the brain assumed the body should feel fatigued.

Sometimes, fatigue is real, and rest and recovery are your best solution. Other times, it's not that you're low on energy. It's that you need to consciously recharge it.

Try these simple steps to boost your energy reserves:

- **PAUSE AND BREATHE.** Close your eyes and inhale through your nose counting to four, then hold for a count of four, then slowly exhale to a count of six.
- **MOVE.** Do some jumping jacks, burpees, march in place, do some sit-ups. Get your energy moving.
- **CREATE EXCITEMENT.** Imagine something that makes you feel excited, that activates that feeling of being alive. Visualize this for 30 seconds.

You don't have energy; you generate energy.

KWIK STEP: When you feel your energy fall today, pick one thing from this list to practice.

AFFIRMATION: *"I have all the energy I need to get through my day. I am limitless."*

ALLOW HAPPINESS TO MOVE

Have you ever felt guilty for being irritable after a long day, or ashamed for feeling anxious or stressed when everything is supposed to be "good"?

You're not alone. There's this idea that we're meant to feel happy all the time. That we should stay positive and keep thinking "good" thoughts, focusing on what we want to achieve and how we want to be.

Yes, there's truth in these points. But there's a dark side to this mindset too. It's called toxic positivity. That's when we avoid, suppress, or ignore negative emotions. Emotions live on a spectrum. We can feel happy and sad. Proud and disappointed. Excited and anxious. Courageous and afraid.

Happiness is driven by external rewards. Joy comes from a deep internal place that has no connection to what's happening in your external environment.

When we feel sad, angry, or upset, it's often a sign our nervous system is responding to our environment. We evolved with a system that toggles between the parasympathetic state of rest, digest, and repair, and the sympathetic state of fight, flight, freeze, or fawn.

Problems arise when we stay stuck in negative emotions for prolonged periods. That's when working with a life coach or trained therapist can be helpful.

But for short durations, these negative emotions can help us, reflecting a healthy nervous system doing what it was designed for—helping us make sense of, adapt, and navigate our world.

Research has shown sadness can sometimes help us recover from failure, improve memory performance, reduce judgmental errors, improve motivation, and generate more effective interpersonal strategies. Then there's anger. Studies show it can help us achieve our goals more than remaining emotionally neutral, while boredom can encourage us to change.

The next time you feel sad, angry, or bored, instead of believing something's wrong with you, try observing the emotion just like a wave crashing against rocks or a cloud passing in the sky. Don't cling or resist.

Happiness isn't a 24/7 state. Allow happiness to move.

KWIK STEP: Place one hand on the top of your head and one on your heart. Now say out loud or to yourself one truthful sentence about what you're feeling and why. "I feel ______ because ______."

AFFIRMATION: *"I allow my emotions to move. I am limitless."*

FROM 9 TO 90, MAKE IT COUNT

Who are the two most important people you want to make proud?

Many of us will picture our parents or kids.

Instead of people outside yourself, what if it was your 9-year-old and 90-year-old selves?

Sometimes when I struggle with tough decisions, competing priorities, and feel stressed, overwhelmed, and exhausted, I'll visualize my nine-year-old self. I so vividly remember the boy everyone believed was "broken," who struggled to learn and read, who was always picked last in sports, and who got bullied.

And I think: *I want to make him proud. What do I need to do, think, or feel today to make this so?*

I want him to look at me with wonder, love, and pride, knowing every struggle he endured gave us this life. This helps guide my choices, actions, and priorities—I don't want to waste what he's gifted to me.

Then I use my imagination to travel into the future to meet my 90-year-old self. I feel the sense of peace radiating from my older self, as he says with pride, "What a beautiful life we created. We did good."

By imagining our past and future selves, it activates networks connected to memory and emotion, strengthening the connections to the different versions of ourselves through time. Psychologists call this *self-continuity*—the ability to experience ourselves across time and feel connected. Studies show this practice can increase emotional resilience, improve long-term planning and decision-making, and deepen meaning and authenticity.

It's so easy to get caught in daily stress that we can forget we're given a finite amount of time in this life. Our 9-year-old self lies in the rearview mirror, while our 90-year-old self waits just ahead.

Between them lies now. It's up to us to use this time well. From 9 to 90, let's make our time count.

KWIK STEP: Sit quietly for two minutes and imagine your nine-year-old self standing in front of you. How are they looking at you? What are they saying to you? Then for another two minutes, repeat this by imagining your 90-year-old self.

AFFIRMATION: *"Today, my actions, thoughts, and feelings make my 9-year-old self proud and my 90-year-old self proud too. I am limitless."*

MAKE ADVERSITIES YOUR ADVANTAGE

I've spoken about my immense struggles with reading and learning. How I was one of only two kids of Asian descent in my school. How I was bullied, picked last in sports, and speaking in front of the class terrified me.

Yet if you told me I could travel back in time and change it all, I wouldn't.

The universe has a funny sense of humor. I've built a career and a company teaching other people just like me how to accelerate their learning, read quicker, and uncage their brains, talents, and potential.

So if I went back to change my past, then I wouldn't have the life—the work, the purpose, the family, the skills, the knowledge—that I have now. I wouldn't *be* the person I am now.

The same is true for you, even if, some days, it doesn't feel like it, and you're exhausted, burned out, and frustrated by the adversities in your life.

While we may crave comfort, that's also not how our brain grows. It changes through challenge—by making mistakes, struggling, and persisting through tough experiences. When we push our brain by learning a new skill or facing difficult moments, it creates new neural connections that alter our brain's performance.

The adversities I faced in life became my greatest advantage. When you think about your life, how might it look, feel, and be different if you saw your adversities that way too?

Take one adversity and reframe it. What has it taught you? What skills did it help you develop? How has that adversity become an advantage? Who have you become because of it?

Adversities stop stealing your energy the moment you see them as your advantage.

Make adversities your advantage.

KWIK STEP: Reflect on an adversity you've faced. What has it taught you? What skills did it help you develop? How has that adversity become an advantage?

AFFIRMATION: *"Adversities are my advantage. I am limitless."*

HONOR YOUR FEELINGS

Put a little water into a saucepan, place the cover on top, put it on a burner turned to high, and wait a few minutes. As the water heats, the steam rises steadily building pressure until eventually . . . the lid pops off.

When we don't allow ourselves to feel all our emotions, eventually our lids pop off too—we snap when we don't mean to, feel overwhelmed by simple tasks, and feel frustrated and beaten down by events.

Our emotions aren't to blame. It's that we've suppressed them, but ignoring or pushing them down doesn't make them disappear.

Life is filled with difficult moments. We lose people we love. Jobs don't go the way we planned. We hit financial hardships. Our health takes a beating. Disappointment, regret, sadness, grief, loneliness, and fear are a part of life.

It doesn't help that we live in a comparison culture. We go online, and it seems like everyone's lives are easier than ours. We see their highlight reels—the beautiful vacations, fit bodies, well-behaved kids, immaculate homes—and we think, "What are we doing wrong?"

Nothing.

No one's life is without struggle. Everyone has challenges, setbacks, and obstacles. Instead of judging yourself during difficult times, instead of tamping down on what you're feeling, be accepting .

Allow yourself to experience and express your emotions without judgment. Studies show *affect labeling*—putting emotions into words—can help reduce the intensity of the feeling. It also helps increase feeling positive emotions sooner.

Resilience isn't found in denying parts of ourselves—it's in accepting it all. This is how you keep the lid of your life from blowing. Not by ignoring or suppressing emotions. But by honoring your feelings.

KWIK STEP: What's one difficult situation that has caused you some heartache? Gently acknowledge your feelings, labeling each one and giving yourself permission to feel.

AFFIRMATION: *"I accept all of my emotions as they are. I am limitless."*

SEPTEMBER 30

TRANSITION BECOMES TRANSFORMATION

Before the caterpillar becomes a butterfly, it spins a cocoon around itself. Inside, its body transitions into an almost liquid state before completing its transformation. There's no skipping that in-between space.

Like the caterpillar, your world is changing. Technology is shifting rapidly, requiring you to learn, grow, and evolve your human intelligence in ways you didn't expect, at the global and the personal level. You might have lost a job or relationship. You could be moving, starting a family, watching kids leave for college, or caring for aging parents. Transitions are happening—whether you asked for them or not.

Maybe you've felt this shifting. Perhaps you couldn't name it—this feeling where nothing makes sense, not even who you are.

In this space, your brain works overtime. It's wired for predictability and safety, so when the familiar disappears, the nervous system can signal "danger" even if none exists. This triggers the stress response, releasing hormones like adrenaline and cortisol, which disrupt sleep, memory, critical thinking, and creativity and weaken your immune system's ability to heal and repair.

Fortunately, your brain can change how it responds to transitions:

1. **BREATHE.** Deep, slow breathing is one of the quickest ways to shift your nervous system. Longer exhales activate the vagus nerve—the main pathway of the parasympathetic nervous system—bringing you into a more relaxed state.
2. **NAME.** Acknowledge what you're feeling without judgment. Studies show this helps reduce activity in the amygdala and increase activity in the prefrontal cortex.
3. **ASK.** Replace, "What's going to happen?" with "What am I learning? How am I growing?" This shifts the brain into a growth mindset, increasing resilience and adaptability.

You can't stop transitions. But you have the power to meet them differently. Stay present during the in-between, and transition becomes transformation.

KWIK STEP: Think of a transition you're going through today, then apply: Breathe. Name. Ask. Notice how you feel and what new ideas arise.

AFFIRMATION: *"I allow transitions to become positive transformations. I am limitless."*

RADIATE

The Season of Impact

(October 1–December 31)

Harvesting. Contribution. Legacy. These are the themes the season of autumn brings.

Like the fall, the next three months are a time for reaping what you planted, giving what you sowed, and looking ahead to your future.

The Season of Impact will help you:

- Strengthen your relationships and collaboration
- Tap into creativity, intuition, and flow
- Create impact in your community
- Teach what you've learned
- Become a lifelong learner
- Build longevity
- Live with more joy, gratitude, and generosity
- Embrace limitless reinvention

Welcome to the season where inner transformation meets external impact.

YOUR BRAIN LEARNS BY TEACHING

What if I told you that at 3 P.M. tomorrow, you'll be giving a TED Talk, teaching 1,200 people what you're about to learn right now?

How would this change your approach to absorbing the material? Do you think you might focus more? Take better notes? Would you simplify the idea, putting it into your own words?

Most people would. Teaching demands that we own—that we internalize—the knowledge and understanding. It must become a part of us in order for us to successfully teach it to someone else.

That's why I often say one of the quickest ways to learn anything is to teach it. Teaching accelerates learning, improves comprehension, and enhances memory, strengthening your brain's encoding and retrieval pathways.

When you do this, you're taking advantage of what's called *the explanation effect*. If you learn it with the intention of explaining it to someone else, you're going to learn it better. Because by teaching it, you get to learn it twice.

One of the best ways to learn by teaching is to use what's called the *Feynman Technique* (named after the Nobel Prize–winning physicist Richard Feynman). It's a four-step process to teach anything to anyone:

1. Identify the skill or concept you're teaching.
2. Write or explain it in your own words, preferably as if you were talking to a 12-year-old.
3. Notice if you stumble, stutter, or struggle explaining something. That's a signal you need to review the material again.
4. Now teach it for real, ideally to one person and see how you do.

This process works for anything, whether you want to learn a new language, master a musical instrument, or pick up a professional skill.

Your brain learns by teaching.

KWIK STEP: Pick one insight that you've already covered in this book and teach it to someone.

AFFIRMATION: *"I learn best when sharing what I know. I am limitless."*

OCTOBER 2

LIVE, LOVE, LEARN

"I wish I had the courage to live true to myself, not the life others expected of me."

This was the biggest regret that palliative care nurse and author Bronnie Ware wrote about in *The Top Five Regrets of the Dying.*

Picture this: You're at the end of your life. There's nothing left to do but look back. What do you say?

It's an uncomfortable thought, one your mind resists thinking about. *Mortality salience*—when you become aware of your death—triggers anxiety, and then the brain reaches for distractions and defenses to escape those thoughts.

Yet if you stay with the discomfort, it can catalyze breakthroughs.

Many people regret the dreams they never chased. The words they never spoke. The risks they never took.

If you think you could reach the end feeling the same, then why not do something about it now?

You get this one life. Why aren't you running toward your dreams like you're on fire?

If you're like many people, what's stopping you are people's opinions and expectations. You fear being laughed at, being judged, or failing, and so you hesitate. That's because your brain treats social judgment like danger. Studies show social rejection activates the dorsal anterior cingulate cortex, the same region involved in experiencing physical pain.

Your brain thinks it's protecting you. But in the end, it won't replay the criticisms. It will replay the choices you made or didn't. It will wonder, "What if I had?" and "Why didn't I?"

So forget about other people's opinions. If you train your brain to listen to the person in the mirror, you'll look back knowing you lived, loved, and learned with everything you had.

KWIK STEP: Imagine you're at the end of your life. What is a regret you have? Now, what is one small step you can take today to change it?

AFFIRMATION: *"I care about one person's opinion of me: mine. I am limitless."*

OCTOBER 3

GIVE AND YOU GROW. GROW SO YOU CAN GIVE.

What if the secret to your happiness and success wasn't found just in what you got—but in what you *gave*?

Look at nature, and you'll find the things that grow also give. It's the only way for a species, and the ecosystem, to survive. An apple tree doesn't keep its apples. They fall to the ground, feeding animals, insects, and the soil. A sunflower shares its seeds with birds, its nectar with bees.

You share this cycle too.

You weren't meant to grow alone. You were meant to grow for something. And that something helps bring meaning and fulfillment to your life—experiences that also matter for your brain. It constantly seeks meaning and searches for patterns in your experiences to decide what habits, behaviors, and thoughts you repeat.

When you give, it activates the brain's reward circuitry that's linked to pleasure and motivation. Acts of kindness increase oxytocin, the hormone of bonding, social connection, and trust. You also get a boost to dopamine and serotonin too, which improves your mood, focus, and sense of calm.

You can find opportunities to contribute every day—you just have to look.

Maybe there's a skill or knowledge you can teach. Maybe it's volunteering in your community at an organization you feel passionate about or donating to a cause you believe in. Maybe it's treating someone to a meal, mailing a thoughtful card to a friend or mentor, or running errands for an elderly neighbor.

Give and you grow. Grow so you can give.

KWIK STEP: What is one way you can contribute to something meaningful and worthwhile?

AFFIRMATION: *"I grow so I can give. I am limitless."*

OCTOBER 4

FEED YOUR BRAIN TO FUEL YOUR BRAIN

It's said that the best time to plant a tree was 20 years ago. The second-best time is today.

This idea holds true for what you eat too. Food fuels your brain—literally. If you didn't start eating for your brain health 20 years ago, then your best time to start is now.

Healthy brains rely on efficient neural connections, low inflammation, adequate blood flow, and well-maintained cellular membranes to function optimally. That's where food comes in.

Here are five top brain foods to include:

1. **AVOCADOS:** Avocados provide monounsaturated fats along with folate, vitamin E, and lutein, an antioxidant. Studies show eating avocados can improve memory and cognitive performance.
2. **WILD BLUEBERRIES:** Rich in flavonoids and anthocyanins, blueberries help reduce inflammation and oxidative stress. Studies suggest they may improve processing speed and memory, especially in people with mild cognitive decline.
3. **BROCCOLI:** Broccoli contains vitamin K, fiber, and sulforaphane, a compound that activates the body's antioxidant pathways.
4. **EXTRA-VIRGIN OLIVE OIL:** A large Harvard study found regular consumption of olive oil, high in polyphenols and healthy fats, was associated with a lower risk of dementia-related death.
5. **EGGS:** Eggs contain omega-3 fatty acids, lutein, and choline, which help produce neurotransmitters and form memories. Research has linked increased egg consumption with better cognitive outcomes, and suggested improvements in memory and cognitive performance.

Like exercise or sleep, eating these foods consistently is how you help support your learning, memory, and long-term cognitive health.

Feed your brain to fuel your brain, starting today.

KWIK STEP: What is one food you can incorporate into your diet this week?

AFFIRMATION: *"I choose foods that fuel my brain's performance. I am limitless."*

OCTOBER 5

TAKE TIME. MAKE TIME. CREATE MAGIC.

We live in an age of endless information. A time when we can gain more knowledge than our ancestors ever could. From podcasts to books, courses, and videos, we have so much to consume, yet so little time to be or become.

It's easy to get caught in the loop of learning, believing if we just consume one more piece of information, then we'll be ready to act.

But knowledge alone doesn't change your life—actions do. It's only by taking time and making time that you can create something truly magically.

Take Time. Your brain is not a machine that constantly runs on the setting "produce." It's a living network that needs care to perform its best. Practices like meditation strengthen the prefrontal cortex. Exercise releases BDNF, a protein that grows new brain cells. Sleep consolidates memories. Stillness and time in nature reset and relax your nervous system. This is how you prepare your brain for action and progress.

Make Time. Your brain enters flow—a state of deep work where time disappears—after roughly 15 minutes of sustained concentration and peaks around 45 minutes in. So, block 90 to 120 minutes as sacred time in your calendar for your best work. Use tools like the Pomodoro Technique to work in 25-minute chunks, then take a 5-minute brain break to move, hydrate, do deep breathing exercises, and get back to it.

Create Magic. When you take time and make time, you can create something extraordinary. Write the page. Record the video. Design the website. Put what you've learned into practice and start making magic.

Your life is important. And working on yourself is the *greatest* project you'll ever take on.

Take time.
Make time.
Create magic.

KWIK STEP: What is one thing you want to take time, make time, and create magic on today?

AFFIRMATION: *"I take time. I make time. I create magic. I am limitless."*

OCTOBER 6

A HAPPY BRAIN IS A HEALTHY BRAIN

What's the first thing that comes to mind when you hear the word *habit*?

For most of us, it's actions and behaviors like brushing and flossing our teeth, exercising, or talking to our kids or parents every Sunday.

The brain naturally seeks to create habits—shortcuts that require the brain to expend less energy.

But there's another type of shortcut the brain can create: emotional shortcuts. We can get into the *habit* of feeling discouraged, frustrated, or nervous when we start a new workout, go to a networking event, meet with a client, or join a class.

Just as you can teach your brain to create new habits, you can train it to default to a habit of happiness.

Neurologically, a state of well-being or contentment is supported by chemicals like dopamine, oxytocin, serotonin, and endorphins. Like cultivating a plant from seeds, you can cultivate happiness through daily acts such as:

1. **ENGAGING IN PHYSICAL ACTIVITIES.** Moving your body releases mood-enhancing neurochemicals including dopamine, serotonin, oxytocin, and endorphins.
2. **PRACTICING MINDFULNESS.** Being present has been associated with higher levels of happiness, and it lowers anxiety and depression symptoms.
3. **BEING GRATEFUL.** Acknowledging what you appreciate boosts well-being.
4. **BEING HELPFUL.** Whether it's volunteering or helping someone at work, this one act can boost your happiness and well-being.

Happiness isn't a 24/7 state, and that shouldn't be our goal. But it's possible to experience happiness more regularly.

And a happy brain is a healthy brain.

KWIK STEP: What is one thing you can do to boost happiness today?

AFFIRMATION: *"I cultivate happiness. I am limitless."*

OCTOBER 7

YOUR STATE SHAPES LEARNING

Think back to high school. What classes dragged? Now what do you remember learning in them? Probably very little.

Now recall the classes you loved—what do you remember from those? How did you feel sitting in class? Curious? Challenged? Inspired?

If every class felt boring and stressful, like it did for me, think about a hobby you love instead. What does it feel like when you're doing it or learning something new that improves your skill and knowledge?

I bet you can more easily recall the classes or hobbies you loved. And there's a reason why. All learning is state dependent—it depends on your emotional state.

When you're bored, you're less likely to pay attention, but if you're in an excited, curious, or playful state, then your amygdala gets involved. This almond-shaped group of neurons plays a big role in processing emotions and memory consolidation. When you're in a heightened emotional state, your amygdala interacts with your hippocampus, flagging the moment as something important to remember.

One of the best ways to ensure quick recall is connecting information with a strong emotion. Information combined with emotion create an unforgettable memory. Excitement, playfulness, a sense of awe, wonder, and joy, can help lock in learning.

When you need to remember or learn something, pause and ask:

1. What do I see in my mind's eye?
2. How does it make me feel?

Using different senses activates different learning styles, and adding visualization helps make the emotion stronger. This process works whether you're listening to a podcast, video, or audiobook, talking to someone, or in a meeting.

Your state shapes your learning.

KWIK STEP: Practice pausing and asking, "What do I see in my mind's eye? How does it make me feel?" when you're exposed to new information today.

AFFIRMATION: *"My learning is state dependent, and I choose my state. I am limitless."*

OCTOBER 8

YOUR EXTERNAL WORLD IS A REFLECTION OF YOUR INTERNAL WORLD

Walk into a spa and the first thing you feel is relaxed. That's by design. From the lighting to the soft music to the décor, someone made these intentional choices to create a calm and restorative environment.

Just as spas get designed to enhance relaxation, you can design your study and work space for optimal focus, engagement, and performance. Think: SPACE.

S — SELECT A DEDICATED SPACE. This could be a desk at home or the office, a table at the library, or a quiet coffee shop. Context-dependent learning means the brain remembers information better when you return to the same environment. Make it a place you enjoy, too. Anticipation can trigger the release of dopamine, which aids in attention, learning, and motivation.

P — PREPARE THE CONDITIONS. Use good lighting—not fluorescent, which can increase mental fatigue and eye strain. Aim for a comfortable temperature and good air flow, which bring more oxygen to your brain.

A — ARRANGE. Keep your space tidy. Visual clutter increases cognitive load.

C — COLLECT SUPPLIES. Have everything you need before you start—pens, notepads, a favorite drink, a calculator, music—so you don't break focus when you're in the zone.

E — ELIMINATE DISTRACTIONS. Tell your family and co-workers not to disturb you. Turn off notifications and alerts on your devices. Leave your phone on silent or airplane mode, or in another room. Research has found the mere presence of devices reduces cognitive capacity.

Your environment will never be perfect. But do your best to intentionally design a space that supports your brain. Your external world is a reflection of your internal world.

KWIK STEP: Find one thing you can do today to enhance your space so it supports your focus, engagement, and performance.

AFFIRMATION: *"I design my space. I am limitless."*

GRATITUDE IS MEDICINE FOR YOUR MIND

When someone asks, "How was your day?" do you default to what went right or what went wrong?

We're all guilty of putting energy into complaining, calling attention to what's missing and why we're unhappy. This is partly because of the brain's *negativity bias*: its tendency to focus, remember, and give greater weight to negative information and experiences.

While this is a crucial survival mechanism, it needs balancing. For every ounce of energy you spend complaining, what if you gave an equal amount to celebrating what you're grateful you do have and the problems you don't have?

Science shows that when you practice gratitude, it activates areas in your brain connected to learning, decision-making, and emotional regulation. It's also linked to releasing dopamine and serotonin, also known as "feel-good" neurotransmitters, which is why many psychologists consider gratitude a natural antidepressant.

Practicing gratitude has been linked to better sleep, better well-being, lower levels of depression, better moods and physical health, and improvements in self-esteem and feelings of worthiness.

Yes, there will always be aspects of life you want to change. And there is so much in life to feel grateful for.

Sometimes it's as simple as pausing to feel the awe that you're just alive. That you're awake, breathing, thinking, feeling, and experiencing life at this very moment in time.

Gratitude is medicine for your mind.

KWIK STEP: Tonight before going to bed, write three to five things you're grateful for, especially if they happened today.

AFFIRMATION: *"I am grateful for the blessings in my life. I am limitless."*

CHEER YOURSELF ON TO CHANGE

"You were amazing!"

"You crushed it!"

"I'm proud of you."

Who doesn't love to hear praise? But when was the last time *you* praised yourself? When did you celebrate *your* wins?

Not just the big milestones—promotions, anniversaries, test scores—but the small daily ones.

It's telling yourself, "Way to go!" after reading for 20 minutes.

It's "You did great!" after leading an important meeting.

It's saying, "Wow, I'm so proud of you for remembering," after recalling every item on your grocery list.

Even when something misses the mark—say, you get tough feedback at work—you can still praise yourself. Say, "Ouch, that hurt. Also, great effort! You're getting better, and you'll nail it next time."

Statements like these may seem small, but they're not. Praise helps the brain learn what behaviors to continue. Celebrating helps trigger the neurotransmitter dopamine. That's more than a "feel good" chemical; it acts as a learning signal, telling your brain, "Do that again." This is how you turn an action into a habit.

Research has found that when we reward ourselves for the effort—not just the outcome—we become more motivated to do cognitively tough tasks again, and to tackle even harder challenges.

Celebrating your wins also helps remove the power perfectionism can hold over you. You're rewiring your brain to stop expecting perfection and to see every effort as an opportunity to grow and learn.

Small wins stack. Cheer yourself on to change.

KWIK STEP: Praise yourself at least five times today.

AFFIRMATION: *"I cheer myself on. I am limitless."*

OCTOBER 11

IMAGINATION IS MORE POWERFUL THAN KNOWLEDGE

For 30 seconds, think about your home. Picture it in your mind.

What did you see? Your bedroom? Kitchen? Living room furniture? Pictures on the wall?

Did you notice what didn't appear in your mental picture? Words. When we play mental movies, there's no closed-caption text scrolling at the bottom. It's images—that's your imagination.

You use imagination constantly throughout the day, though usually without realizing it. It fuels creativity, problem-solving, focus, self-confidence, and empathy.

It turns out the brain doesn't differentiate between what happens in your mind and in real life. While you consciously know the difference, vivid imagination activates many of the same neural pathways as real experience.

This makes imagination more than a "childish fantasy." It's your brain rehearsing the future.

To help accelerate learning a skill or capability, or reach your goals faster, use the power of your imagination intentionally. Start by sitting quietly, taking a few deep breaths, then close your eyes. Imagine a goal or a challenge you want to overcome, and picture yourself experiencing the outcome.

Maybe that's you giving a clear, confident, and concise presentation.

It could be you closing a tough sale, staying calm during negotiations, or delivering your best work on a project.

Maybe you're playing the piano or table tennis. Or staying calm, firm, yet caring when your child has a tantrum.

Practice activating as many senses as you can. Feel the emotions. Hear the sounds. If there are scents or textures, imagine those too.

Knowledge is about "what is." But imagination is about "what can be." This makes your imagination more powerful than knowledge.

KWIK STEP: What's something you're struggling with or a goal you want to achieve? Spend five minutes with your eyes closed, visualizing your desired outcome. Use as many senses as you can to experience what it feels like in your body when you attain or overcome a goal or challenge.

AFFIRMATION: *"I use my imagination to achieve goals and accelerate learning. I am limitless."*

OCTOBER 12

PRACTICE DEMONSTRATIONS OF JOY

Have you ever received a compliment only to say, "It was no big deal?"

Most of us don't say thanks. We shrug it off and downplay it, or we point out what still needs fixing. We're so good at criticizing ourselves, even minimizing our successes, that we never think to celebrate our wins.

Except we should, because whatever we reinforce, we repeat. This is how we coach ourselves to change.

Celebrating your progress, no matter how small, releases dopamine in the brain's reward circuitry, signaling it to "do it again." As you're building new habits around constant learning, growing, or toward attaining a goal, the key is to celebrate during three pivotal moments:

1. **CUE**—when you remember to act.
2. **DO**—when you're in the process.
3. **DONE**—when you've completed it.

Giving yourself a little buzz can be as simple as saying, "Yes, victory!" when you open your laptop to work on your book, log into an online course, finish reading a chapter, or resist the urge to pick up your phone when it dings.

By celebrating yourself, you're pairing the behavior or habit that you want to reinforce with a positive emotional state. This helps strengthen neural pathways, making the habit easier to repeat next time.

Stanford behavioral scientist BJ Fogg says, "Emotions create habits," and one of the fastest ways to wire in a new habit is to celebrate—to make yourself feel good.

Practice demonstrations of joy, and you make learning into a lifelong habit.

KWIK STEP: Pick one habit you want to reinforce, and use Cue-Do-Done to celebrate yourself.

AFFIRMATION: *"I celebrate my progress, from the smallest wins to the largest victories. I am limitless."*

OCTOBER 13

ACT ON YOUR IDEAS

A few years ago, a friend of mine had a brilliant idea for an online course. A few months later, he texted me about an amazing new app. Several more months passed, and it was a book.

By this time, I stopped sending suggestions, asking how I could help, and offering to connect him with people.

Why? Because he was trapped in a loop of constant ideation, analysis paralysis, and overthinking.

To the brain, coming up with new ideas can feel rewarding, sometimes addicting. Whenever you imagine progress or success, your brain releases dopamine, a neurotransmitter associated with anticipation and motivation. So you feel good just thinking about taking action, even when nothing has happened.

Then reality hits. Your prefrontal cortex—which is responsible for decision-making and planning—starts considering all the possibilities and steps required. Simultaneously, your amygdala—the threat detector—activates, homing in on potential risks and uncertainty. Often, that initial excitement turns into fear, hesitation, self-doubt, and paralysis.

While it's great to come up with ideas, you know what's more important than the thinking and the knowing? The *doing*.

So, schedule your doing. For every minute you spend learning, spend an equal amount implementing. This is known as *implementation intention*, a technique where you link a behavior to a specific time—when, where, and how. Research shows this improves follow-through and can help you achieve your goals.

Remember, knowledge isn't power. It has the potential to be, but it can only become power when you apply it. Act on your ideas.

KWIK STEP: Choose something you've been learning about or have an idea for, and intentionally schedule time on your calendar today to implement it.

AFFIRMATION: *"I act on my ideas. I am limitless."*

OCTOBER 14

LISTEN FOR EXPOSURE; READ FOR MASTERY

Watch any travel show, and instantly pathways light up in your brain. The colors, sounds, and movement of cities like Tokyo, Paris, or Rome spark your brain's desire for discovery, novelty, imagination, and a desire to explore.

When you visit those same places, walking their cobblestone streets, taking in the dazzling lights, dining in their restaurants, and listening to snippets of conversations in languages you don't understand, the entire experience deepens for your brain. All your senses awaken and the emotional resonance grows stronger, meaning your brain will encode the memories in a way that makes recall stronger and quicker.

Just as there's a difference between watching a show about some far-off land and visiting it in person, there's a difference between listening to an audiobook and reading a physical copy.

Audiobooks only activate the auditory cortex, while reading triggers the visual cortex, which takes up more real estate in your brain and is one of the largest regions. Reading is also a complex cognitive process, employing multiple language networks, from sight to sound to meaning.

By holding a book, you're also experiencing what neuroscientists call *multisensory integration*. You're getting the sensation of touch as you flip the pages and feel the weight of the book. You might even engage smell if it's musty, and you hear the pages quietly swoosh as you turn to the next.

Multisensory integration helps enhance memory encoding, making it easier for your brain to recall key information later.

Does this mean you shouldn't listen to audiobooks? No! It's about using them strategically. Just as a travel show will give you a glimpse of a place, audiobooks offer you a great overview of material. But hard copies will give you a deeper and richer experience and longer-lasting learning.

So listen for exposure; read for mastery.

KWIK STEP: Prime your reading area with more sensory and emotional cues. Maybe that's enjoying warm tea in a special mug, sitting near a sunny window, or turning on relaxing, calming music.

AFFIRMATION: *"I read books for mastery. I am limitless."*

OCTOBER 15

FIND THE MIRACULOUS AND THE MAGICAL IN THE EVERYDAY

From sunsets and sunrises to a baby's birth and a child's laughter, some moments are more than poetic. They have a profound effect on the brain—if we allow it.

Awe is a state of feeling reverence and wonder for something outside ourselves. When we're in awe, the default mode network becomes less active, and with it, the inner chatter about ourselves, our pasts, and our future.

Awe also helps us feel more connected as our perspective shifts from our individual selves to something greater. Positive emotions rise and stress recedes. Time seems to slow and stretch.

You don't have to wait for awe to strike; you can cultivate this state by directing your intention and attention. Start by noticing your environment. Pause to listen closely to music that stirs you. Spend time in spiritual or religious contemplation. Gaze at the night sky. Let waves tickle your toes in wet sand. Look up at mountains. Notice petals on a flower. Be of service to someone in need. Seek out paintings and sculptures that amaze you.

It's easy to feel frustrated and frightened by the state of the world. But imagine how your life might feel, look, and be different if you also chose to see the world around you, the people in it, and your experiences through a lens of awe?

The more you notice these moments, the quicker awe becomes a habit. Your attention networks will be primed to seek out awe-inspiring moments everywhere.

Cultivate a state of awe, and you'll find the miraculous and the magical in the everyday.

KWIK STEP: Schedule five minutes in your calendar to seek out moments that inspire awe.

AFFIRMATION: *"I cultivate a state of awe, allowing it to elevate my mind and spirit. I am limitless."*

OCTOBER 16

TINY ACTS LEAD TO BIG IMPACTS

Imagine you're walking in a crowded parking lot when you come upon a person with their arms full, struggling to unlock and open their car door.

What do you do?

Many of us would walk right past, lost in our thoughts, replaying something that just happened or worrying about what's coming next. But if we realized how powerful a single act of kindness can be on the brain, maybe we'd act quicker.

Brain-imaging studies show that acts of kindness correlate with increased activity in regions linked with reward and bonding. So when you're kind, your brain releases various neurochemicals including dopamine, which reinforces positive behavior; serotonin, which makes you feel good; and oxytocin, which strengthens your sense of connection and bond with people. Combined, they elevate your mood, increase your overall sense of well-being, and activate your empathy.

And the more you practice these acts, the better for your brain it becomes. People who regularly engage in acts of kindness have reported more happiness and well-being, less stress and anxiety, more resilience, and greater self-esteem.

You're not the only one this helps, either. Research shows that just witnessing an act of kindness activates the same regions in the brain as it would if you had performed it. So others around you benefit too.

What if you committed to performing one random act of kindness per day?

This doesn't have to be a grand gesture. It can be something small that takes less than a minute, like holding open a door, writing a kind note, making eye contact and smiling with a stranger, buying someone a coffee, or giving someone you work with a genuine compliment.

You have the power to sprinkle positivity everywhere you go. So do it knowing that your tiny acts lead to big impacts.

KWIK STEP: What is one random act of kindness you can perform today?

AFFIRMATION: *"I act with kindness. I am limitless."*

REPETITION WITH MOTION REINFORCES RECALL

Watch an athlete, musician, or performer, and you aren't just seeing someone with technical mastery. You're watching someone who has blended motion and memory into one seamless skill.

That didn't happen overnight, but through repetition. And while repetition strengthens memory, repetition with motion ingrains it even deeper.

This is the idea behind the learning strategy known as dual coding. By combining verbal with nonverbal cues (a visual, image, or an action), the brain processes information along two different pathways.

By pairing words or concepts with movement, you engage a wider network of brain regions including motor, sensory, and memory systems. This overlap strengthens memory encoding, making recall faster and more reliable.

Let's say you're learning a new word, formula, or abstract idea. While learning, you could pair a specific hand gesture, act it out, or make a small movement, like raising your right leg an inch off the ground. In this way, your body becomes a mnemonic device—a memory aid. Every time you go to recall what you learned, your brain will remember the movement associated with it.

Numerous studies have shown that when learners use gestures or enact what they're studying, their memory improves and retention lasts longer.

By moving your body while you learn, your brain stops being a passive spectator and becomes an active participant. Now you're doing more than simply processing information—you're experiencing it.

Repetition with motion reinforces recall.

KWIK STEP: Pick a word you don't know and look up its definition, or use the one below. Now, as you repeat the word and definition out loud a few times, make a gesture or a small movement or act the word out. See if it stays with you.

Velodrome (noun): A sports arena equipped with a track for cycling.

AFFIRMATION: *"I move my body to reinforce my recall. I am limitless."*

OCTOBER 18

REMEMBERING CREATIVITY

Playing make-believe. Pretending to be something or someone else. Imagining fantastical worlds.

Can you remember moments like these as a child?

Without knowing it, you were wielding the power of your creativity and imagination to make sense of your world and your place in it. But somewhere along the way—at school or at home—you were told to stop. That imagining, playing, and pretending are only for little kids.

That's not true. Your brain continues to imagine throughout your life. When you think of a memory, you imagine it. When you set goals, you imagine possible futures. When you solve problems, you imagine the best solution.

What is imagination? It's creativity. You're constantly creating memories, goals, future scenarios, and solutions. So creativity doesn't end with childhood play. It's not something some of us have and others don't. It's simply that some people have learned how to consciously use their creativity.

You can do this too, and it starts in your dreams. The brain uses sleep cycles to help consolidate short- to long-term memories, solve problems, generate ideas, and process information and emotionally charged events.

The trick is remembering your dreams so you can use them to create connections, ideas, and solutions. To do this, try these three steps:

1. **SET YOUR INTENTION.** Before sleeping, set the intention for your brain to solve a specific problem or generate an idea. Then tell yourself, "I will remember my dreams." This helps increase memory encoding by priming your brain to focus its attention on the goal.
2. **MENTALLY REVIEW.** As soon as you wake, mentally review your dreams. This also helps solidify memory retention.
3. **JOURNAl.** Immediately record the dream, in vivid detail, in a dream journal. Handwriting involves more neural networks than typing, which improves memory retention and learning.

You didn't lose your creativity, so it's not about finding it. It's about remembering your creativity—about remembering the true you.

KWIK STEP: Tonight, practice remembering your dreams using the three steps.

AFFIRMATION: *"I remember my creativity. I am limitless."*

POWER YOUR BRAIN THROUGH PUZZLES

24 Across: World's largest peninsula (seven letters).

3 Down: Make known (six letters).

If you guessed "Arabian" and "reveal" from the crossword clues above, then you know the thrill (and slight dopamine hit) that comes from answering correctly. As rewarding as it is to fill out those black-and-white grids, it's also a way to help stave off cognitive decline.

In a study following older adults ages 62 to 80 with cognitive impairment, researchers from Columbia University found that people with mild cognitive impairment (thinking and memory challenges) who played crossword puzzles improved their cognitive test scores compared to those who played computer games.

Other studies have shown regularly playing crosswords may even delay the onset of memory decline, possibly from improving cognitive reserve. When we challenge our brain, it's forced to strengthen and build new efficient networks, while pruning away the less efficient ones. This is neuroplasticity, and with repetition, it's how the brain goes from tackling something challenging to making that same activity progressively easier.

Not only that, but crosswords act like a retrieval practice. That's a term used in learning to test our memory and knowledge. We tend to learn better, encoding the memory deeper, when we're confronted with *desirable difficulty*: something challenging enough to require effort, which strengthens future recall.

To your brain, solving crosswords is like pumping iron in the gym. It's strengthening its memory retrieval, language, pattern recognition, and sustained attention. All keys to supporting long-term brain health.

Power your brain through puzzles.

KWIK STEP: Challenge your brain by playing a crossword puzzle today. Find one that's slightly challenging, not debilitating.

AFFIRMATION: *"I choose activities that power my brain. I am limitless."*

ANCHOR YOUR FLOW

When you need to work on a tough project or study hard, which would you prefer:

A. Pushing and grinding your way to completion.

B. Feeling your best, performing your best, and having time slip away.

We'd all choose B. It's the flow state.

Psychologist Mihaly Csikszentmihalyi coined the term *flow* to describe the state of consciousness when people are so immersed in a task that it feels effortless and time vanishes. It's when skill and challenge collide, allowing us to reach peak performance.

We often think of flow as something only athletes or artists experience. But Csikszentmihalyi believed it was for everyone, and that everyone could learn to reach flow more often, whether in pursuit of athletics, deep work, or even daily life.

Flow doesn't happen when we're bored or when a challenge is so daunting that fear overwhelms us. Flow happens in a sweet spot when we have a clear goal, receive immediate feedback, and are challenged just enough to stretch our mind and body to achieve something we believe to be worthwhile.

It is, as Csikszentmihalyi described, the "optimal experience."

Rather than wait for flow to strike, you can help your brain shift into it by using environmental cues, or anchors, that signal "it's time for flow."

Some people only use their computer for work—no binge-watching shows or playing video games. So whenever the computer fires up, their brain knows it's time to work. Other people use objects, like a piece of jewelry or a hat; the physical act of putting them on acts as a cue. Others might listen to a specific song or say a prayer.

What you use is less important than creating the ritual, which helps improve performance and reduce anxiety.

Flow isn't an accident. It's a state you can cultivate. Anchor your flow, and you give creativity, performance, and well-being a place to land.

KWIK STEP: Today, pick one environmental anchor and use it before deep work to help enter flow.

AFFIRMATION: *"I create a flow state. I am limitless."*

OCTOBER 21

QUESTIONS ARE THE ANSWER

For a search engine to return results, you have to give it something to seek.

Your brain works the same way. Ask a question, and your brain will start seeking results. That's why questions are so powerful.

When you ask negative questions like "Why do my employees never do what I say?" "Why can't I lose weight?" "Why can't I remember things?" or "Why do I have to work so hard?" your brain responds with all the reasons why. But these search results don't lead to progress or growth—they keep you stuck in blame and shame.

Questions activate your salience network, which helps filter where your attention goes based on your goals and priorities. It's the reason you notice the seemingly random coincidence. It's not actually random. Your brain is simply paying closer attention.

This process works in the reverse too. If you prepare your mind with the right questions—the empowering, positive, and limitless ones—you'll start seeing solutions everywhere.

Instead of "Why?" questions, train your brain to default to questions that lead to new, more empowering actions:

- "How can I get my employees to work smarter, not harder?"
- "What's one thing I can do differently to lose weight?"
- "What's something simple I can do to improve my memory?"
- "How can I do this work more efficiently and enjoyably?"

Even if your brain doesn't generate an immediate answer, you've programmed your attention networks to start noticing possibilities.

Ask better questions. Because questions are the answer.

KWIK STEP: Think of an aspect of your life where you feel stuck or are struggling. What is one negative question you've been asking? How can you turn it into a positive question?

AFFIRMATION: *"I ask better questions that lead to better solutions. I am limitless."*

OCTOBER 22

FROM "ME" TO "WE"

We've all heard that children need praise. It's essential to their emotional, social, and cognitive development.

What you may not have heard is that even in adulthood, our brains need praise too. It's an ancient survival signal.

Humans evolved to survive in tribes. While our world is very different now, the brain still logs social rejection as a threat—even if it's not. Researchers have linked it to increased cortisol levels, indicating the brain can interpret rejection as dangerous. Neuroimaging studies also show the same region that lights up with physical pain—the anterior cingulate cortex—activates with social pain.

Deep down, we all still long to feel seen, heard, and accepted. Instead of waiting for someone to give us that, what if we went first?

Enter appreciation.

fMRI studies indicate that praise activates the brain's reward circuitry in much the same way receiving money does. When we genuinely praise and compliment people, it can stimulate their nervous system to relax, releasing hormones including dopamine, oxytocin, and serotonin that signal "You're safe. You're seen. You belong."

So start a "compliment campaign."

For everyone you interact with during the day, set the intention to praise them at least once.

You could say, "You did a great job clearly explaining your idea."

"I'm grateful to have you on our team."

"I appreciate how you handled that conflict calmly."

"I admire your courage to take on this new role with the company."

Focus your compliments less on outcomes and more on effort, traits, and actions. Be sincere. Be genuine. Speak from your heart.

This can also help you feel more connected in a disconnected world. Don't wait for someone to give you a compliment. Give them out freely. You never know what battles someone's fighting or how your words can make a difference.

This is how "me" becomes "we."

KWIK STEP: Challenge yourself to give one compliment to everyone you meet today.

AFFIRMATION: *"I freely compliment people and build my community. I am limitless."*

OCTOBER 23

IF KNOWLEDGE IS POWER, LEARNING IS YOUR SUPERPOWER

You might remember the classic tale "Rip Van Winkle," by American writer Washington Irving. It's a story about a man who falls asleep beneath a tree only to wake up 20 years later to discover an unrecognizable world. Gone are his friends and loved ones, the town he knew, and even his home.

Now, imagine the same thing happened to you. If you were to have fallen asleep under a tree 20 years ago, you'd awake to a world quite different too. Today, we live in an age of autonomous electric cars, spaceships that fly to Mars, and miniature supercomputers that live in our pockets.

Yet one aspect of life would seem strangely familiar: the classroom. When it comes to learning, our vehicle of choice is like a horse and buggy.

We might be living in the technological and digital 21st century, but our education system is still preparing us for a 20th-century world—one meant to train us to work on farms and in factories.

If I had a magic wand and could create today's ideal education system, I wouldn't base it on *what* kids should learn.

I'd teach them *how* to learn—understanding and optimizing their learning process so they can update and upgrade their knowledge and skills faster. I'd teach them to space their learning, spreading it out over shorter sessions, and I'd give them retrieval practices to test themselves instead of rereading.

You know the beauty of this? It doesn't matter that you weren't educated in this ideal school system. You can start your learning today.

You possess the keys to unlock it: curiosity, determination, effort. Once you unlock the meta skill of learning to learn, the world will open to you in remarkable ways.

If knowledge is power, then learning is your superpower.

KWIK STEP: Pick one subject or skill that you've always wanted to learn and start today. Maybe that's talking to an expert, reading a book, listening to a podcast, researching online, or signing up for a course.

AFFIRMATION: *"Learning is my superpower. I embrace it with enthusiasm and excitement. I am limitless."*

OCTOBER 24

TEST TO LEARN

Testing.

For many of us, this one word spikes fear. In school, we were tested after learning to measure what we knew. It wasn't to help us learn, but to decide if we "passed or failed," and if we were one of the "smart" kids.

It turns out, our schools had it backward. Tests are more than assessments—they're tools for learning.

This is the basis of what's called the *testing effect.* It's a form of active retrieval practice that helps strengthen memory. It's more effective than rereading or reviewing information.

As you learn, give yourself pop quizzes. Ask questions like, "What did I just learn?" or "How would I teach this to someone else?"

Questions like these force you to simplify topics in your own words, which improves comprehension and retention. When you teach someone, you also tap into the protégé effect. Research from Stanford found that when students studied believing they had to teach the material, they spent more time engaging with it and learned more than students who believed they were studying only for themselves.

This process also improves your metacognition—your self-awareness of what you know or don't know. When you recognize that you don't know something, this directs your attention to the gaps that need filling. It acts like a spotlight, so you pay closer attention to that information.

By starting with questions, you prime your brain to learn. That's the real power of testing. In school, we learned to be tested.

But in life, we test to learn.

KWIK STEP: Test yourself in one area today by asking questions like, "What did I just learn?" or "How can I teach this to someone?" You can even try testing yourself on the insight you've just learned on this page.

AFFIRMATION: *"I never fear tests. I welcome them. I am limitless."*

OCTOBER 25

WHO YOU SPEND TIME WITH IS WHO YOU BECOME

"Where did you hear that?"

Most of us have had that moment when a child says something so outrageous or shocking that we instantly want to know who they're mimicking. We know kids don't just blurt things out—they've heard it somewhere. That's how early learning works. Kids act like sponges, absorbing the language, habits, behaviors, attitudes, even beliefs of the people and the environment around them.

But this process never really stops. Our social networks continue influencing our neurological networks well into adulthood.

Your brain is wired to mirror the people around you. Specialized brain cells called *mirror neurons* help you to learn and empathize with people by observing their actions. When you watch someone perform an action, the same neurons in your brain fire as if you had done it. This can accelerate learning, making it easier for us to repeat the behavior in the future.

Then there's *emotional contagion*, which explains how we can unconsciously pick up and mirror someone's emotions. It's why you might find yourself physically mimicking their body language, smiling when they smile, resting your chin on your fist, or leaning forward while sitting at a table across from them. If you've ever noticed yourself adopting the attitudes, beliefs, words, or phrases, it's because your brain was built for this.

Of course, there's still free will. You can choose your thoughts, behaviors, attitudes, and beliefs.

But surrounding yourself with positive, supportive, inspiring influences—the kinds of people you are and want to be—makes those choices easier. Your brain will naturally pick up and mirror what it sees.

Who you spend time with is who you become.

KWIK STEP: Identify one positive influence in your life and reach out to them today. Invite them to connect—a phone call, meal, coffee—within the next week.

AFFIRMATION: *"I become who I spend time with, and I choose people who nourish my growth. I am limitless."*

OCTOBER 26

LOVE YOUR BRAIN, AND IT WILL LOVE YOU BACK

When we think about having a "lifelong partner," our thoughts usually turn toward the romantic.

Know who else is your lifelong partner? Your brain. It's been with you from the beginning, orchestrating every thought, movement, emotion, and even the experience of falling in love.

The concept of *neural romance* describes the role your brain plays in shaping relationships. Harvard researchers discovered that when we bond with someone, primitive networks in the brain, including the ventral tegmental area, light up and stay activated for a long time. These areas are associated with pleasure, focused attention, and motivation. Neurotransmitters, such as oxytocin, vasopressin, and dopamine, flood the system—making love feel good.

Just as successful romantic relationships thrive with care, your brain thrives when you treat it with love. Every thought you nurture, every habit you build, and every moment of rest is an act of self-love that rewires your brain for joy, confidence, and peak performance.

There are many ways to care for your brain. Here are a few:

1. **STIMULATE IT.** Puzzles, games, travel, and learning something new like dance, art, or an instrument challenge your brain to help build new synaptic connections.
2. **SWITCH ROUTINES.** Changing habits, like brushing your teeth with your opposite hand or taking a different route at a store, activates new neural circuits and improves cognitive flexibility.
3. **BE SOCIAL.** Meaningful relationships help reduce the risk of depression, anxiety, stress, and cognitive decline.
4. **MANAGE STRESS.** Meditation, spending time in nature, and taking a bath can reduce stress hormones like cortisol and strengthen the prefrontal cortex, which helps with emotional regulation.
5. **READ BOOKS.** Reading prevents cognitive and memory decline and reduces stress.

So love your brain, and it will love you back.

KWIK STEP: Show your brain love by choosing one activity from the list above to do today.

AFFIRMATION: *"I love my brain and it loves me back. I am limitless."*

EXPAND YOUR MIND TO FIT WHAT'S POSSIBLE

Most people limit themselves without realizing it.

It's frustrating when you work hard and put in the time, yet your goals still feel out of reach. It's easy to start thinking there's something wrong with you, to second-guess, doubt, and even feel discouraged about your capabilities.

But you're not failing because of what you're doing. You're failing because, like most people, you've probably shrunk your goals, desires, and dreams to fit the borders of your mind.

Most people never stretch far enough. It's in the stretch that your brain must find new ways of behaving, thinking, and adapting. It's the challenge—not the ease—that triggers the brain to form new connections and pathways. That's neuroplasticity.

That's why you want goals that slightly challenge you—not to destroy your confidence because they're utterly unattainable, but to push you beyond the comfort of your current thinking. This is known as the optimal challenge—it's the sweet spot where learning progresses most quickly.

When you're struggling to reach goals, pause and assess. Is your goal challenging, too easy, or too vague? Are you imagining and visualizing extraordinary possibilities or playing it safe?

What would you have to do to triple your earnings in one year?

What would have to change in your life for you to lose 20 pounds in one year?

What would you have to let go of—a mindset, belief, habit, emotion—to learn how to play an instrument in one year?

What you believe is possible drives your actions. In the end, becoming limitless is about advancing and progressing beyond what you currently *believe* is possible. It's about redrawing the borders and boundaries of possibility for your life with learning, education, training—and goals.

Don't shrink the possibilities for your life to fit your mind. Expand your mind to fit what's possible.

KWIK STEP: Pause and assess one goal you have. If it's not challenging enough, try visualizing something that would challenge you more. Then ask yourself, "What's one thing that has to change in my life today to make this real?"

AFFIRMATION: *"I expand my mind to fit what's possible. I am limitless."*

OCTOBER 28

WHAT YOU APPRECIATE APPRECIATES

There's a reason we tell young people to start saving money as early as possible. Compound interest grows over time. Almost all of an account's value comes from compound growth, not the money put in.

Tiny deposits pay big, and the same idea holds true with what we appreciate.

When we feel gratitude, it engages the ventromedial prefrontal cortex, the same part of the brain tied to experiencing learning, decision-making, and reward. Studies show when people recalled times that they felt grateful, it lit up that region just as it would have if they had received a reward.

Plus, the more we practice gratitude, the more it helps to reduce activity in the amygdala (the brain's alarm center). By regularly giving thanks, you can boost resilience to stressful situations, lower your fear response, and regularly feel calmer and more joyful. With repetition, you reinforce the neural pathways in your brain too, making it easier for your brain to notice and feel gratitude the next time.

Just as compound interest can grow your bank account, small daily deposits of gratitude can reshape your brain, yielding exponential returns in life.

What you appreciate appreciates.

KWIK STEP: Write three things you're grateful for today, then add one reason why. After each entry, pause for a moment to reflect on each, allowing the feeling of gratitude to well up.

AFFIRMATION: *"I am grateful for my life. I am grateful for who I was, for who I am, and for who I am becoming. I am limitless."*

OCTOBER 29

PROBLEMS ARE PUZZLES

I once had the privilege of interviewing the late producer and music legend Quincy Jones. "We all know about your amazing accomplishments and Grammys," I opened. "I want to know about your struggles. What are some problems you're currently facing?"

"I don't have problems," he said.

"We all have problems," I replied.

"No, Jim, I don't have problems. I have puzzles."

Until that moment, I'd never realized how much of my precious time and energy was spent living under the weight of my "problems." Suddenly, seeing them as "puzzles" flipped something inside. I felt a lightness, and I wanted to laugh.

Quincy didn't say this, but puzzles are games. They're challenges. They're goals. They invite curiosity, novelty, and anticipation—all things the brain is wired for. These states engage the brain's reward circuity, releasing little drips of dopamine—the molecule of motivation—urging us to find a solution.

Obligations, which are what we usually feel when we face problems, can narrow our thinking. They can trigger the threat and stress response, which, when chronic, can shrink areas in the brain like the hippocampus—the seat of learning and memory—and reduce creativity.

By reframing your problems as puzzles, you practice cognitive flexibility, which is shifting your perspective and thinking on a situation, and cognitive reappraisal, which changes how you feel about something by reframing the negative as positive.

So what if you never had problems to begin with? What if you saw "problems" as simply puzzles to creatively solve?

KWIK STEP: Think of one problem you're facing. How can you reframe this as a puzzle to solve? What different actions or decisions would you make with this shift?

AFFIRMATION: *"I see only puzzles in my life, never problems. I am limitless."*

OCTOBER 30

FUN FUELS FUNCTION

Children need to play.

It helps them process their feelings, make sense of the world, and develop problem-solving, critical thinking, and imagination.

What we forget is that even as adults, we need to play too.

Whether it's puzzles or board games, hiking, dancing, or making art, accessing a playful state has been associated with stress reduction and lower cortisol levels. It's been linked to increased release of dopamine and oxytocin, especially when play connects to social interactions too. Play helps increase creativity, supports cognitive flexibility, and improves memory and learning.

Learning is state dependent. When emotions like curiosity and excitement are present, the amygdala becomes more active. This helps signal to the hippocampus, "This moment matters." This invisible tag helps encode the memory deeper and make its retrieval in the future easier.

If you need a permission slip to slow down, rest, let go, and have fun, let this be it.

Go enjoy yourself.

Spend time doing activities where stress vanishes and time disappears. Find the moments that leave you feeling joyful, excited, and energized again.

And if you're unsure what those activities are, then go on a journey to discover them. Think back to what you loved to do as a kid. Try something that sounds fun, something you've always wanted to do, like a pottery or group fitness class. Join a club.

You choose what counts as play. All that matters is that you have fun. It's having fun that helps fuel your brain's function.

KWIK STEP: What is one fun activity you can do today?

AFFIRMATION: *"I use fun to fuel my brain's function. I am limitless."*

OCTOBER 31

SPRINKLE KINDNESS EVERYWHERE

Toss a pebble into a still pond, and the waves ripple in all directions.

That's what happens when we act with kindness in this world. One of the best antidotes for a mind racing with fear and anxiety is kindness. It's being of service.

This can be as simple as leaving an uplifting and supportive comment on someone's social media or texting someone with, "Thinking of you." It can be asking if someone needs help on a project at work or shoveling someone's steps after a snowstorm.

Our brain thrives off kindness. Being of service releases feel-good chemicals including oxytocin ("the love hormone"), dopamine ("the reward chemical"), and serotonin (connected to feeling calm, happy, and content).

Studies show that performing just one act per week for up to a month can reduce feelings of loneliness, social anxiety, and stress. And research suggests merely watching an act of kindness can increase feelings of happiness, calm, gratitude, inspiration, and boost resilience in stressful situations.

Everyone's fighting battles no one knows about. Be the person who brings hope, connection, and reassurance into someone's day. Be the person who sprinkles kindness everywhere.

You have no idea the ripple effect you'll make in someone's life.

KWIK STEP: Take 10 seconds and commit to reaching out to someone you haven't spoken to in a while just to say, "Hi, hope you're well!" Then look for other small acts of kindness you can sprinkle about today.

AFFIRMATION: *"Kindness is my superpower. I share it without hesitation. I am limitless."*

NOVEMBER 1

FLOW ISN'T MAGICAL; IT'S METHODICAL

Imagine starting a video game and the first battle you face is the final boss.

You'd die instantly.

You might try to win a few more times, but very quickly you'd quit, convinced the game was impossible, or you simply weren't good enough.

This is why most New Year's resolutions and big goals fail. Not because you're lazy or your brain is broken, but because the challenge is wrong.

Goals like "build a successful business" or "get in the best shape of my life" are too large and abstract for the brain to engage with. It needs challenges that hit a sweet spot—not so hard it gets crushed, but not so easy it gets bored.

When your brain is slightly challenged *and* your skills or capabilities are balanced, you can enter a flow state, where time collapses, focus sharpens, engagement peaks, and work feels effortless. Self-consciousness disappears, and you're immersed in the activity.

Flow doesn't find you—you find it. Here's how to start:

1. **PICK ONE QUEST.** Choose one area to improve: mind, body, relationships, or work. If you pick too many areas to focus on, attention fragments, and with it, progress.
2. **SET 90-DAY TARGETS.** What would progress look like in three months? You need enough time for change to materialize, but not so much that the goal feels unrealistically far away or it's easy to procrastinate.
3. **CREATE WEEKLY SUB-QUESTS.** Each week, have one clear objective that stretches your ability by roughly five percent. Something you're not certain you can do, but suspect you might.
4. **SCHEDULE FLOW WINDOWS.** The brain can sustain deep focus for about 90 to 120 minutes before it needs a break. Schedule a three- to four-hour distraction-free block to give your brain its best chance to reach flow.

Flow isn't magical; it's methodical.

KWIK STEP: Which step needs prioritizing? Focus on that today.

AFFIRMATION: *"I allow my brain to reach flow easily and effortlessly. I am limitless."*

NOVEMBER 2

PEOPLE DON'T CARE HOW MUCH YOU KNOW, UNTIL THEY KNOW HOW MUCH YOU CARE

Does it seem like no one listens to you?

You say something important in a work meeting, or to your partner or children, and you feel them shut down. They glance at their phones, possibly cutting you off mid-sentence.

It's frustrating and hurtful. We all want to be seen and heard, to know our ideas and perspectives matter.

What if you set an intention to listen to others more deeply first?

People feel intention. They know when we're distracted and when we're fully present.

Intention comes from the Latin word *intentio*, meaning purpose or aim. When you meet someone new, or listen to someone speak in a meeting, ask yourself: "What's my intention for remembering this person's name or what they're sharing?"

Intention acts like a signal, alerting your brain to what deserves its attention and energy. You're saying, "This information matters."

This engages the brain's salience network—the system that helps determine what's worth paying attention to. This network helps shift attention between the default mode network (daydreaming and self-focus) and the task-positive network (executive functioning, goal-driven behavior, and memory).

By directing attention, intention helps encode and store memories deeply, making retrieval quicker. This strengthens your ability to remember names, what someone said during a meeting, or information that matters to them.

Just as important, when someone feels truly heard, it creates connection and social safety. It helps their nervous system shift from fight or flight into rest and digest, increasing trust, openness, and cooperation. And this enhances their ability to listen to you in return.

In the end, people don't care how much you know, until they know how much you care.

KWIK STEP: Pick someone you're going to interact with today, and set your intention for remembering what happens. Test yourself later.

AFFIRMATION: *"I give my presence to everyone I meet. I am limitless."*

NOVEMBER 3

OWN YOUR LIFE

If you fuel yourself with the opinions of others—good or bad—eventually, you'll run out of gas.

Approval is an *extrinsic motivator,* coming from outside you. In the short term, it can fuel goal-driven behavior, but it fades quickly.

Intrinsic motivation is different. It comes from within. It's fueled by purpose, meaning, and a sense of satisfaction. It's linked to greater persistence, productivity, and performance. The brain sustains what feels meaningful. It's designed to make sense of experiences and link them to a story with you at the center.

Your brain creates meaning from your choices, not the approval you collected.

And there will come a day when you have reached the end of this journey, and you're faced with the questions:

Was I happy?

Was I fulfilled?

Did I laugh?

Did I love?

Did I learn?

Did I live the life I wanted?

Yes, learn from other people, and, yes, be open to their advice and feedback. But be the final decision maker. Own your dreams. Own your emotions. Own your actions. Own your life.

KWIK STEP: What is one decision or action that you can take that your future self would thank you for making today?

AFFIRMATION: *"I own my life. I am limitless."*

NOVEMBER 4

A PAGE A DAY KEEPS COGNITIVE DECLINE AT BAY

We're living in the Millennium of the Mind, a time when new information gets discovered faster than before. How do we keep pace? How do we stay relevant? How do we enjoy and get the most out of our time?

One way is reading. In today's world, it's not a nice skill to have; it's a must.

Neuroimaging research shows that stronger reading skills, especially over time, are associated with measurable changes in the brain's white-matter pathways. In a study out of Carnegie Mellon University, researchers found that after subjects completed a six-month reading program, white matter increased in the left brain region, critical for language skills.

White matter contains myelinated axons—nerve fibers that act like the brain's communication cables, which carry information to various regions in the brain.

It's believed that the more organized and well-myelinated these pathways, the faster and more efficiently information travels through the brain, helping you to improve most cognitive functions, from focus to learning to problem-solving.

Emerging studies also show that keeping white matter healthy plays an important role in improving cognitive reserve—that's the brain's ability to buffer against age-related cognitive decline.

So what should you read? Mix it up.

Just as a balanced diet is good for your health, reading a variety of genres, from fiction to nonfiction, is good for your mind. Different forms stimulate different neural networks. Fiction can activate regions connected to empathy and imagination, while nonfiction engages reasoning and memory.

Just start reading and keep going. A page a day helps keep cognitive decline at bay.

KWIK STEP: Block 15 minutes in your calendar for reading today.

AFFIRMATION: *"I read to strengthen my brain. I am limitless."*

NOVEMBER 5

YOUR BRAIN NEEDS TO BELONG

Your brain was built to belong.

Whether it's in a family, neighborhood, group, or team at the office, your brain needs social connection as much as it needs oxygen.

Yet in a world where connecting is easier than ever, we also feel more lonely, isolated, and disconnected than ever.

Studies show that loneliness activates our threat detector, the amygdala, raising stress hormones including cortisol. When cortisol remains elevated for prolonged periods, it weakens the immune system and increases inflammation. Chronic inflammation plays a role in many conditions, including arthritis, heart disease, diabetes, and some forms of cancer.

But relationships can act like defense mechanisms, signaling to the brain "we're safe."

In 1938, researchers at Harvard began tracking people's health, happiness, and longevity. Now, nearly 90 years later, that study has found that the strongest predictor of health and happiness isn't fame, fortune, exercise, or sleep—it is strong, healthy relationships with friends, family, and partners.

When we connect with people, even animals, the brain releases oxytocin, a chemical connected to bonding, trust, and feeling safe. Strong social connections are linked to lower stress levels, greater resilience, and better immune function.

Connecting comes from eye contact, meaningful conversation, listening, sharing, and laughing. While in-person gatherings matter, studies show meaningful online connections count too. Participating in peer support groups, not passively scrolling, can also reduce loneliness.

We all need someone to believe in us, encourage us, cheer for us, and challenge us.

If you haven't found that person yet, be that person for someone else. Join groups. Reconnect with an old friend. Ask someone to have coffee or join you on a walk. Start a collaborative learning group or support network at the office.

No one does life alone. Your brain needs to belong—and so do you.

KWIK STEP: What's one thing you can do today to connect with someone?

AFFIRMATION: *"I allow myself to connect with people who believe in me, and I in them. I am limitless."*

THINK LESS. KNOW MORE.

When you're stuck second-guessing, overthinking, or in analysis paralysis, where no decision feels like the right one, the best tool isn't more logic.

It's intuition.

We hear a lot about verbal, linguistic, and mathematical intelligence, but not much about intuition. Yet this wisdom is widely used by high performers and leaders. Studies suggest that many CEOs analyze the data but make the final call based on intuition.

Intuition is your nervous system and subconscious mind processing extraordinary amounts of sensory data, connecting it with memory, experience, and future goals faster than your conscious mind can handle.

But to work with intuition, you must first reclaim your attention. Intuition doesn't appear in constant noise, never-ending scrolling, or calendars chock full of back-to-back meetings.

It appears in quiet and stillness. When you're *being,* not doing.

One of the best "being" practices lies in journaling. Using pen and paper, set a timer for 5 to 10 minutes and free write. Let thoughts, feelings, sensations, memories, or ideas arise. There's no structure, no formatting, no need to use proper grammar. Simply allow your stream of consciousness to flow onto the page. Then, throughout the day, use the journal to record any gut feelings, senses, and ideas that come.

Journaling is great for your brain. Studies show expressive writing by hand increases connectivity in brain areas involved in memory and learning. It can also reduce depression and anxiety, improve life satisfaction, reduce cognitive load, and help process emotions.

With regular practice, you'll develop greater self-awareness and metacognition—that's thinking about your thinking. Over time, you'll learn to shift between your conscious and subconscious, between analysis and intuition, between thinking and knowing.

Think less. Know more.

KWIK STEP: Free write for at least five minutes. Then keep an intuition journal with you today, recording when you get a sense, hunch, or knowing.

AFFIRMATION: *"I trust my intuition. I am limitless."*

NOVEMBER 7

PROCESS LEADS TO PROGRESS

When you're sick, doctors have a process to get you well. They don't just guess. They ask questions and run tests. They listen to your heart, look into your eyes, and take your blood pressure. Before they treat, they diagnose.

In life, there are moments when you know exactly what you should do, but you don't. You procrastinate. You stall. You start strong but fall back. And sometimes you get stuck. None of this happens because there's something wrong with you.

There's something limiting you. And just like a good doctor, you need a process to diagnose it.

That's what the *Limitless Model* does. This three-part framework helps you identify where you're stuck and which limitations need treatment. If there's a gap between where you are and where you want to be, it's usually because there's a limit in one or more of these areas:

1. **MINDSET.** This is your attitude, assumptions—what you believe is possible, what you believe you deserve, and what you believe you're capable of achieving. If you learn how to remember names, but you don't believe you're someone who can, you won't. Your identity will override even the best techniques.
2. **MOTIVATION.** You could believe anything is possible, that you deserve it, and that you're capable. But without motivation, you won't achieve it. Motivation is your drive, your purpose, your energy, and your ability to take small simple steps toward your goal.
3. **METHODS.** You can have a limitless mindset and motivation, but if you're using outdated learning techniques like rote memory—repeating things in your head—instead of emotionally engaging with the material like creating images and associations, you'll fall behind.

Train yourself to ask, "Where's my limitation?" then focus on removing it. Process leads to progress.

KWIK STEP: What's one limit you can remove today to make progress toward your goals?

AFFIRMATION: *"I create the processes to make progress. I am limitless."*

NOVEMBER 8

GIVE THE GIFT OF GRATITUDE

Bills. Doctor's appointments. The news. That fight with your partner. Kids who forget to pick up their clothes off the bedroom floor. The aches and pains in your body. A life that doesn't feel like it's changing fast enough.

Before it's even lunchtime, it's easy to find at least 10 to 15 things that have gone wrong, that we don't like, or that we want to change.

This isn't bad, necessarily. Behavior and mindset change often comes when the "pain of staying the same" feels like too much. You need to notice what isn't working or doesn't feel right if you're to know what needs changing.

But what if instead of noticing *everything* you don't like today, you practiced gratitude too?

Gratitude isn't a "soft" habit. It's a powerful practice that supports your brain, heart, and immune system health.

Psychoneuroimmunology studies the intersection of our physiological and behavioral states with the brain and the immune system. Studies show that when we're stressed, it can cause inflammation, which can negatively affect our physical and mental health. It's also widely accepted that chronic stress can play a role increasing the risk of developing chronic diseases such as cardiovascular disease, Alzheimer's, and diabetes.

Feeling positive emotions like gratitude is one way to help protect your neuroimmune network. Research suggests that gratitude practices are linked with lower stress and inflammation, stronger social relationships, better sleep, and improvements in heart rate variability and certain immune markers.

There are aspects to your life that are amazing just as they are. Even the things you want to change can be seen through a lens of gratitude.

Give your brain the gift of gratitude, and gratitude will show you the gifts in your life.

KWIK STEP: What are three challenges you're currently facing? What are three gifts you can find in them?

AFFIRMATION: *"I am grateful for my brain. I am grateful for my body. I am grateful for my life. I am limitless."*

CURATE AND CULTIVATE THE CONDITIONS TO BE CREATIVE

Why do some of our best, most creative ideas strike as soon as we wake, or while we're showering or driving?

It's not coincidence or accident. It's because in these moments, your brain has shifted into the alpha/theta waves associated with creativity, intuition, and imagination.

There are four primary brain states. *Beta* occurs when we're wide awake, fully alert, and aware. *Delta*, when we're fast asleep.

In between the two are alpha and theta. *Alpha* is a relaxed awareness that helps form unique connections, identify patterns, consolidate memories, and is also ideal for accelerated learning.

Theta is a deeply relaxed state. In this state, it's as if the self-conscious, judgmental, and highly critical mind naps, allowing the unconscious brain to step forward, generating unexpected meaning, solutions, and ideas.

You can help your brain activate its alpha/theta states using simple practices like showering, driving, washing the dishes, gardening, even doing a puzzle.

Journaling within the first hour of waking also works. Take 10 to 20 minutes and write about your life. Let whatever thoughts, feelings, experiences flow onto the page. It can be as simple as "I'm writing and have nothing to say," or as specifc as "I feel stressed about having to pick up the kids after school while preparing for an important meeting with my team coming up."

Do this by hand. EEG studies suggest handwriting increases alpha- and theta-state activity. It might take some time before you notice the benefits, but do this a few times a week and see how it feels.

The question isn't whether you're creative. It's whether you're curating and cultivating the right conditions for your brain to be creative.

KWIK STEP: Journal for at least 10 minutes, ideally within the first hour of waking today or tomorrow.

AFFIRMATION: *"I cultivate my creativity. I am limitless."*

GIVE YOURSELF THE CARE YOU GIVE OTHERS

When so many people rely on you, it can feel hard to give yourself what you so freely give to others.

Yet when you're juggling kids, aging parents, demanding work, a significant other, friends, and community, you deserve care too. In fact, it's a nonnegotiable for your brain, health, and relationships.

By saying yes when you want to say no, you risk exhaustion, burnout, and resentment.

It's not that you've done anything wrong. It's that always saying yes activates your brain's threat detector—the amygdala—which can override your prefrontal cortex where reasoning, emotional regulation, and goal-oriented decision-making largely reside.

Your brain wants connection and a sense of belonging. Saying no, enforcing a boundary, and putting yourself first can trigger the fear of rejection and abandonment.

But research shows clear boundaries reduce resentment, improve trust, and lower chronic stress—all keys to stronger relationships.

How can you start putting yourself first?

Schedule at least 15 minutes of uninterrupted time in your calendar daily, just for you.

Try blocking off one hour a day in which you won't respond to e-mails, texts, or calls.

Practice saying no to taking on extra responsibility at work, when friends make a request, or to helping out at a school function or event.

If you've had soft boundaries, setting firmer ones will feel hard at first. Keep at it. Repetition retrains your nervous system to stop fearing saying no and to welcome it.

Boundaries actually give you more freedom. They create structure, clarity, and space so your brain can perform better.

Give yourself the care you give others.

KWIK STEP: What is one self-care practice that you've wanted to adopt? How can you take one step toward it today?

AFFIRMATION: *"I give myself the care I give others. I am limitless."*

BE JOY FILLED

"I'll be happy when . . .

"I get a raise.

"I lose weight.

"I get my degree.

"After I've finished my shift.

"When I've saved six months of expenses."

Many of us think we have to wait to feel happy—that it's tied to achieving and attaining. But real joy comes from within. It isn't the prize for reaching the top of the mountain. It's the energy that carries us forward. And it doesn't simply make us feel good. It makes us more productive.

Psychologists like Barbara Fredrickson believe that positive emotions broaden what's called your *cognitive scope*—that's how much information your brain can take in and process. Where emotions like anger can narrow your cognitive scope, joy widens it, helping your brain to see more solutions, make connections quicker, problem-solve faster, and remember more. By allowing joy to become an active state of being, you'll improve your creativity, critical thinking, problem-solving, and performance.

So instead of waiting for joy to arrive someday in the future, practice it in microdoses now. Listen to your favorite song. Spontaneously dance while making your coffee or tea. Laugh. Play. Be silly. Tap into gratitude. Visualize the activities and people who light you up.

Taking just 30 seconds to a few minutes to activate joy, you'll train your mind to stop seeing it as the result of productivity or an achievement, but as the fuel you're using to get there.

Don't wait for someday. Be joy filled today.

KWIK STEP: Pick one thing that sparks joy in your life—listening to your favorite song, petting an animal, savoring a cup of coffee or tea—and do it today. For a bonus, try doing this before something big, working on a project, meeting with your boss, or a conversation with your partner.

AFFIRMATION: *"I choose joy as my advantage. My joy powers my performance. I am limitless."*

NOVEMBER 12

YOUR BRAIN DOESN'T LEARN THROUGH CONSUMPTION; IT LEARNS THROUGH CREATION

Have you ever finished a book, and when someone asked you what it was about, you came up blank? Or maybe you left a conversation and forgot what the other person had asked you to do?

According to what's called the *forgetting curve*, we have a tendency to forget 60 to 80 percent of what we've heard or learned within 48 hours.

You can mitigate this memory erosion by taking notes by hand. Research consistently shows that handwriting notes versus taking them on a computer improves learning, memory, and cognitive performance. This is because using pen and paper activates more neural networks than typing, including sensory, motor, and visual systems.

But not all notetaking is created equal. There's an art and skill to it. The goal isn't to write verbatim. Instead, practice the Capture and Create Method.

It's simple. Draw a line down the middle of your page. On the left, write "Capture," and on the right, "Create."

Under Capture, you'll list all the relevant ideas, insights, and information. If you were taking notes on sleep, you'd write things like how to improve your sleep quality by using black-out curtains, keeping the room cool, or stopping caffeine after 12 P.M.

Under Create, you'd write about how to apply the information in your life. You could also use questions as prompts, asking and answering:

- "When will I use this?"
- "How can I use this?"
- "How does this compare to what I already know? Does it contradict it?"
- "Who would benefit from me teaching them about this?"

Use this practice for books, podcasts, and important meetings and conversations.

Your brain doesn't learn through consumption—it learns through creation.

KWIK STEP: Practice the Capture and Create Method during or after a meeting, conversation, or planning session today.

AFFIRMATION: *"I learn through creation. I am limitless."*

NOVEMBER 13

THE LANGUAGE YOU USE SHAPES WHO YOU ARE

"I am ________________."

Two of the shortest words in the English language are also the most powerful. Because whatever you put after them determines your destination.

It introduces your brain to the new version of yourself, the one patiently waiting for you on the other side of your transformation.

An easy tool to accelerate this change is to use your environment to help reinforce the new you. Write "I am __________" statements and leave them throughout your home and office where you'll regularly see them.

If it feels awkward at first, that's a great sign—it means you've hit a limitation. Chip away at it every day.

If saying "I am __________" feels like a lie, then add "willing" to the sentence. "I am *willing* to be __________." This tells your brain you're making a conscious decision, and it signals learning. You're learning to become this new version.

Be intentional with your words. The language you use shapes who you are.

KWIK STEP: Set a timer for three minutes. Now write "I am ________" and fill in the blank with as many "I am" statements as you can. For example, "I am a son." "I am a mother." "I am a leader." "I am a warrior." "I am unstoppable." Don't filter. Don't question. Just go.

AFFIRMATION: *"I am who I choose to be. I am limitless."*

NOVEMBER 14

WALK INTO WONDER

It's one of the most ancient activities known to us. We've used it to find food and shelter, as exercise, and even as a way to soothe our souls, generate new ideas, and imagine possibilities for the future.

I'm talking about walking.

The human body—and brain—evolved with walking. While we largely live in a sedentary culture now, our brain still craves those strides. They calm and quiet the nervous system, especially when in natural settings that signal safety and peace.

Not only is walking simply good for our health, but it's also one of the best, and quickest, ways to boost creativity, solve problems, and improve focus. Walking works by allowing your attention to drift and engaging your default mode network. That's the system associated with how you see yourself, think about your past, and imagine your future. It's most active when we daydream and imagine.

But how you walk matters.

Stanford researchers tested three groups of people on creativity. One group was tested while walking in rectangles, another while walking freely, and the last group while seated. In every test, the free-walking group outperformed the other two groups. In one, the free-walking group generated 60 percent more creative ideas.

So when you're stuck on a problem, you're unsure how to respond to something someone has said, or you just feel overwhelmed, stressed, or anxious, go for a short walk—on a treadmill or outside.

Let your brain be soothed and inspired by the ancient art of walking—and you may find yourself walking into wonder.

KWIK STEP: Walk for at least 10 to 15 minutes today. Don't use any devices, just let your body move. Notice how it feels as you walk and any thoughts, ideas, and images that spring up.

AFFIRMATION: *"I am creative when I walk. I am limitless."*

NOVEMBER 15

CHANGE THE CUE, CHANGE YOU

You know when you go to sleep vowing that tomorrow you'll wake up early to journal, meditate, or exercise?

Only when the alarm goes off, you hit Snooze. By the time you drag yourself from bed, you already feel exhausted, overwhelmed, and guilty for breaking a promise to yourself.

What if it could be different?

Imagine what life would feel like if your habits worked for you instead of against you. Imagine waking up with boundless energy. Feeling clear, focused, calm, and confident. Ready to sink into deep, creative work without fear that distractions will pull you away. Showing up as the version of yourself you desire and deserve—the one you know you're capable of being.

That version isn't some distant dream. It's within reach because your brain is built to adapt. Every thought and action weakens or strengthens neural pathways that turn behaviors into habits that also shape your identity. That's neuroplasticity.

You don't need to change everything overnight. You don't need to be perfect. You just need to start.

One way is by controlling your environment. When you control the external, you control the internal.

All habits run off a four-part loop: cue, craving, routine, reward. When you change your external environment, you change the visual cue, and a new loop follows.

Want to run in the morning? Put your sneakers next to your bed the night before, so they're one of the first things your brain sees when you get up. This will cue the thought "time for a run," encouraging the behavior.

Want to eat healthier? Put fruit on the counter instead of muffins.

Want to read more? Place a book by your favorite chair.

When your environment aligns with your goals, progress stops feeling like a struggle and starts feeling like momentum.

When you change the cue, you change you.

KWIK STEP: What is one thing you can change in your environment that aligns with your goals and who you know you can be? Make that change today.

AFFIRMATION: *"I create an environment that supports my goals. I am limitless."*

HONOR YOUR INTUITIVE INTELLIGENCE

Have you ever faced a fork-in-the-road moment, when the logical, rational choice was to choose one path, but something deep inside you urged you to take the other?

Whether it was in your career, a relationship, an unexpected opportunity, or even a red flag warning, it may have shown up as hunch, gut feeling, or small inner whisper. Did you go with it? And if you didn't, did you later think, *I should have listened?* regretting that you dismissed what you couldn't understand or explain?

That inner knowing, that sensing, was your intuition talking to you.

On the surface, intuition might appear separate from the brain. It's not. Intuition is another form of intelligence. It's the gut feeling that defies rational thought, logic, and facts, yet it's no less real.

Intuition, which everyone can access, is the subconscious mind recognizing patterns. It's drawing on memories and experience to pick up, sift through, and make meaning about the world in ways the conscious mind can't. Some research suggests the subconscious can process substantially more—upwards of billions—information per second. The conscious mind? Only 40 to 50 bits.

Instead of ignoring or downplaying your intuition, practice developing it, learning to listen and honor it as another source of deep wisdom to help you make better decisions.

Because when you repeatedly ignore your intuition, you don't just doubt that feeling, you start doubting yourself.

Like any skill, intuition strengthens the more you use it. When you face a decision, pause long enough to give your intuition space to speak. Listen, then act, then reflect on what happened.

Over time, your intuition becomes a valuable partner helping clarify your priorities and make progress toward your goals. Honor your intuitive intelligence.

KWIK STEP: Notice when a situation or small decision comes up today. Pause and pay attention to how your body feels, or if a quiet inner voice nudges you in a direction. Take that direction, then note the outcome.

AFFIRMATION: *"I honor my intuitive intelligence. I am limitless."*

NOVEMBER 17

WHAT YOU NOURISH WILL FLOURISH

The grass is greener where you water it.

This holds true for your brain too. If you want it to perform its best, you need to water it. One of the best ways to do this is what I call neurostacking: It's the art and science of stacking enjoyable and easy behaviors that will help unlock your brain's potential and power.

What does this look like?

- Listening to an audiobook while reading the physical copy simultaneously so you understand better and remember more
- Drinking a glass of water when you wake up to rehydrate your brain
- Making your bed to promote more ease, calm, and clarity
- Keeping a dream journal to improve your memory
- Practicing deep breathing exercises to increase oxygen flow to the brain and help improve cognitive function, alertness, and clarity
- Getting sunlight in the morning to reset your circadian rhythm and help improve sleep
- Moving your body to release BDNF, which acts like fertilizer for your brain; epinephrine, which helps with learning and memory; and norepinephrine, which improves your attention, focus, and emotional regulation

The best times to neurostack? Morning and evening before you go to bed. You have the most control over those two windows.

Neurostacking doesn't take a lot of time and often costs very little. If you're making coffee in the morning, then in the few minutes it takes to brew, you could do air squats, cross-crawls, or deep breathing, or write three things you're grateful for. You could go for a 15-minute walk in the morning, while visualizing what about the day will make it a "win."

Be intentional with your behaviors. They are like water to the fertile ground of your brain. Remember, what you nourish will flourish.

KWIK STEP: What three behaviors can you neurostack this morning or evening?

AFFIRMATION: *"What I nourish will flourish, so I choose what nourishes my brain. I am limitless."*

NOVEMBER 18

THE LITTLE THINGS *ARE* THE BIG THINGS

Life is so hectic, harried, and hurried that it can feel like we're trying to navigate Class V rapids. We're swept away by the never-ending to-dos, racing toward our goals, trying to balance work and family, and desperately paddling to keep from crashing head first into a boulder.

In this constant rush to do and achieve, it's easy to miss the quieter moments, the ones that ground us in the present and remind us of who we are and why what we do matters.

It's sipping our coffee before everyone in the house wakes. It's the unexpected text from a friend that makes us laugh. It's the sound of our kid's excitement as they tell us about their day. It's watching someone we've mentored nail a task.

So how can we train our minds to notice and capture these moments before they slip past?

We can develop a gratitude practice.

Studies show that regular gratitude practices engage brain regions involved in emotional regulation, meaning-making, and well-being, especially the anterior cingulate cortex and the medial prefrontal cortex. Gratitude also activates pathways linked to the brain's reward circuitry and systems that support feelings of pleasure and satisfaction. And studies even link gratitude to fewer symptoms of anxiety and depression, less stress, and better sleep patterns.

Try ending your day with a gratitude ritual. Start a dedicated journal and write down three positive highlights from your day before going to bed. Not only will you get the benefits from gratitude, but you'll also improve your memory, strengthen recall, and train your brain to focus more on the positive aspects of life. Over time, noticing and savoring the seemingly ordinary moments will become a habit.

In the end, the little things are the big things.

KWIK STEP: Before bed tonight, take 5 to 10 minutes and write down three positive things that happened during the day. Pause on each to recall all the details—what you heard, saw, felt.

AFFIRMATION: *"I notice the little things in life, which are the big things. I am limitless."*

NOVEMBER 19

PEOPLE PROGRAM YOU

Who are you?

How much of your habits, attitudes, beliefs, mannerisms, even your tone of voice came from within, and how much was absorbed from the people around you?

Social networks influence neural networks. The brain is wired to repeat the thoughts, emotions, and behaviors of your environment. Much of this happens unconsciously through the *chameleon effect*. We instinctively mimic the postures, mannerisms, facial expressions, and behaviors of the people we interact with.

Mirror neurons also help explain why. These cells fire when you perform an action and when you observe someone else doing it. And if you've ever felt stressed for no reason, it might be because of someone close to you. Emotional contagion primes us to notice and "catch" others' moods.

The challenge is that your brain doesn't pause to consider whether someone's thoughts, habits, or emotions are helping *you* become the person you want to be. It's just mirroring. This makes your choices about *who* you spend time with crucial.

To help bring more awareness about the people in your environment, think: WATCH.

W—WORDS. Listen to what people say.

A—ACTIONS. Notice people's behaviors, gestures, mannerisms, and activities.

T—THOUGHTS. Ask yourself, "Is this thought mine?" If it's not, then "Whose is it?"

C—CHARACTER. What are your standards? What will you allow in your life or not?

H—HABITS. What habits—eating, studying, relaxing—are truly yours?

Surround yourself with uplifting people and you give your brain a shortcut for learning, growing, and becoming. Remember: People program you. Choose intentionally.

KWIK STEP: Reach out to one person who always leaves you feeling better, thank them, and make a plan to get together within the week.

AFFIRMATION: *"I spend time with people who uplift me. I am limitless."*

NOVEMBER 20

FIND WHAT YOU LOVE, AND YOU'LL LOVE TO LEARN

Here's a thought experiment: Do you shrink your dreams to fit into your life, or do you expand your skills to meet your destiny?

Most people shrink unintentionally.

Maybe it's due to fear conditioning. If you tried something and were laughed at or got it wrong, your brain may have learned to avoid trying new things because that feels "dangerous."

Maybe it's a cognitive bias—a mental shortcut the brain uses to save energy. Negativity bias makes your brain cling to every risk and worst-case scenario.

Or maybe it's an identity limitation shaped early in life, like seeing yourself as shy or not smart, that keeps you from applying for a job, speaking up in a meeting, or trying a new hobby.

These aren't conscious choices, but patterns your brain created in its attempt to "keep you safe." Except it's only keeping you small and dimming your light—when you were born to play big and shine bright.

To reach any goal, you must break these patterns and embrace learning. That's how you develop and master the skills you need. While this can be tough, especially if school was negative or stressful, your brain can change.

What you once feared, you can learn to love, including learning itself.

If you learn to love learning, you become someone who expands their skills to meet their destiny. Someone who loves to learn is always growing. When you're curious and engaged, your brain releases dopamine, helping you absorb information faster and motivating you to keep going.

In this life, you're either growing or decaying. So keep your brain learning. Identify your goal and the skills you need, then learn. Practice. Make mistakes. Adjust. Keep growing.

And if you don't love learning yet, find something you do love. Then you'll love to learn.

KWIK STEP: What skill or subject lights you up? How can you find a way to weave learning about it into your day today?

AFFIRMATION: *"I love learning. I am limitless."*

NOVEMBER 21

STOP BEING YOUR WORST CRITIC AND START BEING YOUR BEST COACH

At the end of the day, when your head rests on the pillow, what do you think about? Does your mind fill with the day's wins, what you feel grateful for, and what you learned?

Or is it looping on that one thing you wish had gone differently, that you're kicking yourself for not doing or saying right?

Most people worry about what others are thinking about them. But the truth is, the person we spend the most amount of time thinking about is ourselves.

Left to its own devices, your brain will focus on self-criticism, self-judgment, and blame. That's because it has a built-in cognitive bias toward negativity. Brain imaging has linked self-criticism to increased activity in brain regions connected to error processing and resolution. The brain sees what went "wrong" as an error it must correct to avoid repeating it in the future.

Except this strategy backfires. Self-criticism activates the brain's defense mechanism, sending stress signals through the body, which can leave you feeling anxious and riddled with self-doubt—not primed to do better in future.

When you make a mistake or something doesn't go the way you planned, instead of doubling down on criticizing yourself, what if you lightened up? Could you remind yourself that it's not about perfection; it's about progress?

When that critical voice gets loud, you can also pause to replace criticism with curiosity. Practice observing the thoughts. Then say out loud or to yourself, "Isn't that interesting?" or "There goes that thought again."

Observing your thoughts creates space. And space helps reduce reactivity and a stress response.

This is how you reshape your mind. What you practice, you strengthen. Train your mind to stop reaching for self-criticism, and you start training it to see all experiences as opportunities for self-improvement.

Stop being your worst critic and start being your best coach.

KWIK STEP: Notice if there's a looping negative thought. If so, practice naming and observing it now. During the day, try to regularly check in on any negative thoughts, and gently notice as they arise.

AFFIRMATION: *"I am my best coach. I am limitless."*

LEARNING IS A LIFESTYLE

What if you could download decades of experience in a matter of days?

I'm not talking about AI. I'm talking about reading books. AI can give you quick information, but deep knowledge, understanding, and wisdom come from the people who've lived something, studied it, and become true experts in their domains.

Then to have them fill pages upon pages with their knowledge for you to learn from . . . I don't know a better life hack you could have.

There is a growing divide in this world, and it's not just between those who have and those who don't. It's between those who know things and those who don't.

The people who know things can make better decisions, better life choices, and position themselves to take advantage of new opportunities.

Your life is the sum total of the choices you make, and the only way to make good choices is to have a good foundation of knowledge, wisdom, skills, and abilities.

Constantly upgrading your mind makes you the ultimate adaptation machine. Learning is the vehicle. But it's not one trip; it's constant.

Learning is a daily practice: studying, reading, engaging in deep and meaningful conversations that stretch your mind beyond its current borders.

Learning isn't an event. It's a habit. Your brain grows when you use it consistently. New neurons fire. New synapses form. And as your inner world expands, so does your external world.

Stay a lifelong student. Make learning a lifestyle.

KWIK STEP: Learn something new today.

AFFIRMATION: *"I am a lifelong learner. I am limitless."*

YOUR MIND CRAVES CHALLENGES AS MUCH AS IT CRAVES FOOD

In the fairy tale "Goldilocks and the Three Bears," a young girl enters the bears' home. She tastes three bowls of porridge until she finds the one that's "just right." Then she repeats this with their chairs and beds. We tell this fable to our children as a cautionary tale, but also as a lesson in finding what's "just right" for them.

Like Goldilocks, your brain is sensitive to challenge, registering it as too little effort, too much, or just right.

The human brain evolved to solve problems. It hunted for food, built shelters, navigated danger, and learned to cooperate with its tribe. So when you strip away challenges, the brain doesn't relax. It becomes bored and turns on itself. The default mode network—the system responsible for self-awareness and thinking about the past and future—becomes overactive, leading to rumination and anxiety.

But challenge your brain too much, and without the skills to match, it registers danger, sending your nervous system into a panic or freeze state. This can lead to procrastination, perfectionism, and cognitive overload.

Instead, you want Goldilocks challenges—not too little and not too much, but just right. Hit this, and your brain is more likely to enter a flow state.

Psychologist Mihaly Csikszentmihalyi spent decades studying optimal human experience. He discovered the most focused, productive, deeply satisfied people reached flow—where time slows, distractions slip away, and complete immersion, engagement, and focus naturally happen.

Try increasing challenges by roughly five percent. When challenge exceeds skill by a small, manageable margin, you're not bored or overwhelmed. It's just enough to engage the brain, allowing it to function at its peak—in flow.

Your mind craves a challenge as much as it craves food. Find what's "just right" for you, and your mind works with you, not against you.

KWIK STEP: What is one area of your life where you're challenging your brain too much or too little? How can you adjust the level to "just right"?

AFFIRMATION: *"I feed my brain with the right challenges. I am limitless."*

HOW YOU DO ANYTHING IS HOW YOU DO EVERYTHING

Excellence isn't something you achieve; it's something your brain learns to become.

And it's not the big wins that train your brain to excellence. It starts in the small acts you take daily that demonstrate your values like making your bed in the morning.

Taking one or two minutes to tuck in the sheets and smooth them out does more than tidy your room. It helps improve your mood, reduces feelings of anxiety and stress, and improves your focus, attention, and productivity. That's because your brain likes order.

Like anything, the more you make your bed, the more it'll become a habit—something you do without consciously telling yourself to go do it. Over time, this ritual becomes more than simply a habit—it'll signal who you are. That's someone who shows up with care, intention, and excellence.

You can use this idea with anything, like tying your shoelaces instead of slipping them on, joining a conference call two minutes early, saying "I'm sorry" when you mess up, letting people finish what they're saying instead of interrupting, following through on commitments, sharing credit on a project or idea, or cleaning up after yourself in the kitchen.

When you set your standard to excellence, it ripples across everything you do. It shows up in how you relate to others, tackle projects, conduct yourself in a meeting, even care for yourself.

Remember, how you do anything is how you do everything.

KWIK STEP: What is one small daily behavior you can set your standard to excellence, like making your bed or tying your shoelaces? What needs to change in your life for you to make this consistent?

AFFIRMATION: *"I am excellence. Everything I do, I do with care, attention, and excellence. I am limitless."*

NOVEMBER 25

LIFE IS A LOTTERY YOU'VE ALREADY WON

The ultimate abundance is gratitude.

It's also one of the easiest ways to improve your brain's health and function. When you express gratitude, it influences your brain's neural pathways over time, strengthening circuits associated with positive emotion, emotional regulation, and social connection.

It also triggers your brain to release dopamine and serotonin, two neurotransmitters that play a role in your emotions, helping you to feel good and enhancing your mood. Dopamine helps drive motivation and pleasure, while serotonin supports well-being and mood stability.

Research suggests gratitude practices can help reduce anxiety, depression, worry, rumination, and stress, and predict better sleep quality.

So when was the last time you really paused to feel grateful?

Just as you likely put meetings, workouts, and learning on your calendar, consider scheduling time to reflect and practice gratitude daily. Take just five minutes in the morning and evening to pause, think, and genuinely feel what's going on in your life that you appreciate.

If you want to feel truly wealthy, count all the things you're grateful for that you have in your life that money can't buy.

While gratitude doesn't erase difficult moments or emotions, it can help prevent them from becoming the dominant story your mind creates.

Life is a lottery you've already won. Gratitude simply helps you remember this.

KWIK STEP: Take three to five minutes in the morning or evening—even better, both—for quiet contemplation and journaling on what happened in your life today that makes you feel grateful.

AFFIRMATION: *"I am grateful for my life. I am limitless."*

GRATITUDE MAKES WHAT YOU HAVE MORE VALUABLE

Do you want to be mentally sharper, more creative, and productive? Then ask yourself how often you practice gratitude.

Gratitude has been linked with less stress, reduced anxiety and depression, and more joy, resilience, and meaning. Part of this is biological. Feeling gratitude activates regions of the brain including the medial prefrontal cortex, involved with decision-making, emotional regulation, social connection, and memory. When you practice gratitude, the brain releases dopamine and serotonin, which help support positive moods, motivation, and emotional balance.

To activate this superpower daily, think THANKSGIVING.

TAKE A MOMENT. Every day, pause and reflect on what you're grateful for.

HEARTFELT. Don't just go think about gratitude; connect to the feeling. Combining emotion with thought improves your memory.

APPRECIATE THE SMALL JOYS. The smell of your morning coffee, a stranger's smile, an open parking spot: Training your brain to notice these moments gradually shifts your baseline toward positivity.

NOTICE. Catch your negative thoughts or stress spirals, then ask, "What can I be grateful for in this moment?"

KINDNESS. When you're grateful, you're more likely to act kindly toward others, which also boosts your brain's reward system.

START JOURNALING. Write three things you're grateful for daily.

GIVE THANKS DIRECTLY. Tell or text someone how much you appreciate them.

INTENTIONAL. Be specific, not general, with your gratitude, identifying the people, experiences, or moments in detail.

VISUALIZE. Connect gratitude to future success by visualizing your goal and feeling grateful you've already achieved it. This helps align your brain with goal setting and motivation.

INCREASE AWARENESS. Track how gratitude shifts your moods, stress levels, and brain power over time.

NURTURE RELATIONSHIPS. Express appreciation for people in your life to create deeper connection.

GRATITUDE isn't always about getting more. It's about taking what you have and making it more valuable.

KWIK STEP: Apply as many items from THANKSGIVING as you can today.

AFFIRMATION: *"I am grateful for this day. I am limitless."*

NOVEMBER 27

UNLEARN TO LEARN

Imagine running the same computer program for 20 years. No updates. No patches. No upgrades. Just the same program.

It's hard to imagine—impossible even—because your computer would crash.

In a way, that's what happens when we stop learning. Our thoughts, behaviors, habits, even how we solve problems, communicate, and find meaning in the world, stem from old programming that hasn't been updated in years.

People often say they have 20 years of experience, when it's more like they have one year, repeated 20 times. They rely on the same information, the same habits to solve problems, communicate, and collaborate, and it doesn't work.

As we age, it's understandable why learning gets downgraded on our priority list. We juggle aging loved ones, maybe children, responsibilities at home and work, our health. It's a lot.

Yet learning is the superpower that will help you navigate every challenge. The faster you learn, the quicker you'll have access to new knowledge that will update your software, enhancing your creativity, problem-solving, relationships, resiliency, and more.

In neuroscience, this is called *cognitive flexibility*—it's your brain's ability to adapt to new thinking and adopt new behaviors when confronted with new information and new environments.

Cognitive flexibility is key to learning. Cognitive flexibility makes it easier and quicker for your brain to absorb and integrate new information, change perspectives, and solve problems.

But first, you must unlearn what you know to be willing—at least temporarily—to let go of the belief that you already know something or have the skills.

Unlearning opens your mind to learning new information, new possibilities, new ways of doing something. And the more willing and able you are to let go of thinking you know something, the easier learning becomes.

Before long, learning becomes a skill, then a habit, and finally who you are. Unlearn to learn.

KWIK STEP: Identify one challenge you're facing and ask, "What is the exact opposite action, thought, or emotion of my typical approach?" Then take it.

AFFIRMATION: *"My superpower is learning. I suspect what I think I know allows new ideas, knowledge, and behaviors to flow into my mind. I am limitless."*

NOVEMBER 28

DISCIPLINE IS SELF-LOVE

When you make a mistake, skip a workout, or forget someone's name, do you beat yourself up with thoughts like *I should have done better, I should have done more, I should have tried harder*?

Or do you tell yourself, *It's okay, I'll do better tomorrow*?

If you're like most people, you probably go hard on yourself. This is a default setting of your brain, what's known as *negativity bias*. It's linked to increased amygdala activation, and it's the brain's tendency to hyperfocus on negative events and self-judgments, giving them more weight and recalling them faster than positive ones. It's why you can still vividly recall one time your boss gave you critical feedback a year ago, but have forgotten the 20 compliments you've received since.

There's also this belief—sometimes unconscious—that "tough love" makes us more disciplined. By criticizing our perceived failures, we think we'll motivate ourselves to do better next time.

But studies show a different picture. When we respond to mistakes we've made with self-compassion—treating ourselves with the same kindness we'd show to a good friend who made a mistake or was having a hard time—it actually increases motivation. Self-compassion is even linked to personal responsibility, self-confidence, and a growth mindset.

Research has also found that when using self-compassion instead of self-punishment, we tend to experience less anxiety and procrastination compared to self-critical people. And if that wasn't enough, self-compassion can even help us learn from our failures.

When you start seeing discipline as an act of self-compassion, then it reframes the hard things as acts of love toward yourself.

Extending compassion to yourself when you stumble ensures you will stand back up, step forward, and keep going.

Real discipline isn't self-criticism. Real discipline is self-love in disguise.

KWIK STEP: Think of a slip you made recently that you might be feeling guilty, ashamed, or discouraged about. Then reframe it. Tell yourself something supportive like "I know I intended to study for an hour yesterday, and I was just so exhausted it didn't. It's okay. Tomorrow I'll do better."

AFFIRMATION: *"I give myself the compassion and understanding that I deserve to grow. I am limitless."*

LEARN THROUGH MOVING

The human body has evolved a lot in the last 3,000 years. For one thing, we're shorter than our ancestors, and we have smaller brains.

But something that hasn't changed? Our brains were designed to learn through doing.

It's an ancient survival mechanism hardwired into us. Our ancestors didn't learn by sitting still. They learned by moving—tracking prey, foraging for food, crafting weapons and tools, and exploring the world.

The human brain evolved to remember *experiences*. It's a survival mechanism. What this means today is, when you move while learning, you're returning to a very natural and efficient way for your brain to absorb and retain information.

Any time you go to study, teach, brainstorm, or do any deep work, think of motion as your secret ally.

There are three key moments to pair learning with movement:

- **MOVE BEFORE LEARNING.** Light stretching, simple movements, or a gentle walk wakes up your nervous system, increasing blood and glucose flow to your brain, boosting alertness and focus for the task ahead.
- **MOVE DURING LEARNING.** Your brain will absorb information faster and comprehend it better when you pair it with movement. Try taking notes by hand, pacing, or using hand gestures.
- **MOVE AFTER LEARNING.** To reinforce memory, walk, pace, gesture while reviewing out loud what you've learned to help turn short-term memory into long-term.

When combined, these three stages make up the Motion Learning Loop—a repeatable learning cycle you can use to accelerate building new skills and gaining new knowledge. This creates a powerful cycle of energy and intelligence that will strengthen your body and mind together.

KWIK STEP: Pick something to learn today—it could be the insight you've found on this page—and practice using the Motion Learning Loop.

AFFIRMATION: *"I learn through moving. I am limitless."*

CREATIVITY IS IMAGINATION IN ACTION

Imagine a world where Nike shoes don't exist.

That was almost the case. In the late 1970s, aerospace engineer Frank Rudy pitched his revolutionary shoe concept to multiple shoe companies. They all responded the same way. They thought his design, which combined medical equipment and aerospace materials, was terrible.

But Nike eventually said yes, and it not only became one of the biggest brands in the world, but it also changed the industry.

Aerospace combined with medical equipment to make mass-market shoes? That's creative.

But creativity doesn't come from nowhere. It comes from taking information from different areas, connecting it, and recombining it in new ways. It isn't born—it's built. And like any skill, it's trainable and available to everyone.

Create space in your day solely for creativity. Schedule 15 minutes without devices or distractions. Take a walk, stare out a window, wash dishes, or clean the house—something that requires minimal focus, not intense concentration. This activates your default mode network, which fMRI studies link with creative thinking. Then consider a problem or area in your life where you feel stuck. Ask questions like:

- "What's a more creative solution to ________?"
- "What am I not paying attention to?"
- "How could I approach this more creatively?"

When questions get posed to your brain, it focuses attention on answering them. It's a natural reflex known as *instinctive elaboration*. New questions lead to new answers. So notice the answers that arise—images, memories, ideas. Daydream. Imagine. Don't filter; let it flow.

By allowing your mind to wander and asking different questions, you build your creativity. It's not magical or mystical. It's imagination in action.

KWIK STEP: Schedule 15 minutes for creativity training. What's one thing you can do that requires little focus? Then think of one area you want to improve or feel stuck, ask yourself at least one question, then let your mind wander and daydream.

AFFIRMATION: *"I am creative. I am limitless."*

DECEMBER 1

YOU'RE ONE ENVIRONMENTAL SHIFT AWAY FROM A BREAKTHROUGH

When an indoor plant wilts, it might need more or less water, or a different size pot.

Other times, what it really needs is a new spot. More shade, more sun, or to sit near other plants. And all it takes is this one small shift in location for the plant to thrive.

You might be doing everything right—using positive self-talk, building new habit loops, caring for your brain, and committing to your learning journey—yet something's not working.

Sometimes, it's not an internal issue—it's an external one. Just as a plant can't thrive in the wrong spot, you can't meet the future version of yourself in an environment that doesn't support your growth.

Shifting your environment doesn't have to mean something massive like quitting your job or moving to a new city. It can be changing who you spend an hour a week with. The people around you shape you in ways you can't always see. Science shows the brain naturally attunes to who you're around. *Mirror neurons* help you understand others' emotions and actions. That's why you can find yourself matching someone's energy and behaviors without realizing it.

Other times it's about creating a distraction-free space in your home, at your office, or another quiet place that signals to your brain "this is where I become who I'm meant to be."

And sometimes, it's as simple as tidying your environment. Behavioral psychology shows the physical environment is one of your strongest habit cues. Clutter, noise, and too many devices buzzing can increase cognitive load—making it harder to stay focused, regulate emotions, and remain relaxed.

What if you're just one environmental shift away from a breakthrough—from meeting the version of yourself you've been working so hard to become?

KWIK STEP: What is one environmental shift you can make today that aligns with who you're becoming?

AFFIRMATION: *"I create a physical environment that supports the life I desire and deserve. I am limitless."*

DECEMBER 2

EAT BETTER. THINK BETTER.

We've all heard: "You are what you eat." But what if you also *think* what you eat?

Your brain is an energy hog. It consumes approximately 20 percent of your body's energy, although it only makes up 2 percent of your body mass.

This power-hungry organ relies heavily on your diet to function its best. So a balanced diet isn't just good for your organs and muscles, it's good for your brain.

Some of the best foods you can feed your brain include:

1. **GREEN LEAFY VEGETABLES:** Vegetables like arugula, kale, and spinach contain lutein, vitamin K, dietary nitrates, and folate. Eating one serving per day of green leafy vegetables has been associated with slower cognitive decline.
2. **WILD SALMON OR OTHER FATTY FISH:** A good source of omega-3 fatty acids including DHA and EPA, which act like building blocks for brain cell structures. DHA and EPA have been linked to better learning, memory, and reduced neuroinflammation.
3. **TURMERIC:** This spice contains curcumin, a compound with anti-inflammatory and antioxidant effects. When combined with black pepper and a fat like coconut milk, curcumin is easier for the body to digest and absorb.
4. **WALNUTS:** Another rich source of vitamin E and omega-3 fatty acids, walnuts help reduce neuroinflammation and oxidative stress.
5. **DARK CHOCOLATE:** Cocoa flavanols have been found to support cognitive functioning and improve blood flow to the brain.

To support memory, learning, thinking, comprehension, and your brain's longevity, consider your diet. Do you regularly consume brain-supporting foods? If not, it's okay. Just try incorporating more into what you eat weekly.

Eat better. Think better.

KWIK STEP: Pay attention to everything you eat today. Are any of these brain foods on your plate? How can you incorporate one or more of these foods into your diet more regularly?

AFFIRMATION: *"I choose to eat brain-supporting foods. I am limitless."*

DECEMBER 3

DON'T PLAN THE FUTURE WITHOUT PROCESSING THE PAST

A new year is a chance for a new start.

But if you carry the noise from one year into the next, you'll start exhausted. This is where a year-end brain dump comes in.

In a journal or on a blank page, write everything still in your head from this year—every unfinished project, every unresolved situation, every experience still causing pain, and every worry, fear, or doubt that's still in play.

The simple act of dumping everything onto the page not only brings emotional release and relief, it also helps your brain to clarify what you're still clinging to. Then read back what you've written and notice if anything needs follow-up. If it does, commit to taking action now or in January.

The brain dump lifts you. The sort afterward decides your next year. Don't plan the future without processing the past.

KWIK STEP: Set a timer for five minutes and write everything you're thinking and feeling about this past year. Then review what you wrote and highlight anything that needs action. Finally, write the action and when you'll take it.

AFFIRMATION: *"I process my year first before moving to my next. I am limitless."*

DECEMBER 4

LEARNING IS NOT A SPECTATOR SPORT

The perfect chocolate chip cookie has a balanced ratio of dough to chocolate chips.

Reading to learn works the same way. You need the right ratio of plain text versus highlights. But most people aren't reading books; they're coloring in them.

Have you ever seen one—maybe one of yours?—where almost every sentence was highlighted?

It's easy to do, but it actually trains the brain to focus on the color, not on understanding the meaning.

To unlimit your brain and help it learn faster, practice avoiding the temptation to highlight everything to the point where the book glows in the dark. When everything becomes important, then nothing is. And the brain doesn't know what to throw away or keep.

Instead, highlight only the essentials—those sentences that trigger curiosity, strong emotions, an insight, or a breakthrough.

Then after each major section or chapter, pause and write down or record via a voice memo a few bullet points about what you remember. In your own words, explain what you learned. You can even link it to why it matters in your life or how you plan to apply it.

Finally, teach it to yourself in the mirror or to someone else. Teaching is one of the fastest ways to accelerate learning anything. By teaching, you also get feedback on what you understand versus what you don't.

These are active recall practices. Research consistently shows this improves retention and accelerates learning. The brain better solidifies memories and skills through activity—by retrieving and creating—than it does by rereading, highlighting, and repeating information.

Lifelong learning is not a spectator sport. It's active.

KWIK STEP: Take a book you're reading, and highlight only the essential material, then explain it in your own words, and teach it to yourself in the mirror.

AFFIRMATION: *"I am an active participant in my learning. I am limitless."*

DECEMBER 5

START FEELING GRATEFUL, AND YOU'LL HAVE A GREATER LIFE

I wish I had their life.

I wish my life were different.

We're all guilty of thoughts like these sometimes.

The Internet offers extraordinary opportunities for us to connect, yet these same connections can also lead us to compare our lives to everyone else. Without wanting it, we might find emotions like resentment, jealousy, envy, even self-judgment and lower self-esteem rising up.

Even when we know that many people only share the positive aspects of their lives, our brains still react. They're wired to track and respond to social hierarchies, paying more attention to the people we deem as having a higher status.

One way to interrupt the spiral is by expressing gratitude.

Studies show practicing it regularly can increase feelings of happiness while decreasing symptoms of anxiety and depression.

The practice can be as simple as a "gratitude jar." Every morning, on a scrap of paper, write down one thing you're grateful for, then stick it in the jar. When you feel low, reach in, grab one, read it, and remind yourself what you have to feel grateful for.

Or make a "gratitude notebook." Every morning or evening, write one to three things that made your day. While the "big" events are nice to note, the simple moments are even better. The driver who let you go, the stranger who held the door open, hearing your favorite song on the radio.

Your brain constantly filters information, but you can direct what gets through. When you focus on everything you don't have, that's what you notice all around you. But when you use gratitude to redirect your attention to the positive aspects of life, your brain will shift to notice more of those elements automatically.

You don't have to wait for a greater life to feel grateful. Start practicing gratitude, and you'll have a greater life.

KWIK STEP: Pick a gratitude practice and do it today, writing three things you feel grateful for.

AFFIRMATION: *"I am grateful. I am limitless."*

THE MORE YOU EARN, THE MORE YOU CAN RETURN

What's the fastest way to get an edge at work and in your life?

Become a quick learner.

If you can easily teach yourself to remember names, faces, and important client or product information, give speeches without notes, read three times faster, and generate more creative solutions, then you'll go far.

The faster you learn, the faster you earn.

Go gain more knowledge. Build your wealth. Free up more time in your calendar for what you want to do. Provide financial security for yourself and family. All of these are wonderful goals.

And there's something else waiting on this path: what you can give back.

When you give—your time, money, resources, and knowledge—you make a difference in the lives of people around you, and you train your brain, making a difference in your life too.

Studies suggest that acts of generosity may help reduce amygdala activation—lowering the fear and threat response and avoiding a flood of stress hormones throughout your body.

By sharing, you're also training your brain to embrace an *abundance mindset*—the belief that there's more than enough to go around, and whatever you give away, it's okay, because you'll receive more in the future. Research suggests abundance thinking can lead to better decision-making, more creativity, and long-term planning.

It differs from a *scarcity mindset*, which believes the opposite—resources, time, and money are limited. Studies show this mindset can reduce cognitive flexibility, make switching tasks harder, and sacrifice future wins for short-term gains.

It's not about how much you give—it's about the act.

Learn, earn, then return some of your time, talent, or treasure. The more you earn, the more you can return.

KWIK STEP: What is one way you can give back today?

AFFIRMATION: *"I live an abundant life. I learn so I can earn and then return. I am limitless."*

DECEMBER 7

STATE IS MORE IMPORTANT THAN STRATEGY

If you keep nodding off while rereading the same page, how well do you think you'll remember what you're learning?

You can know the best tactics—using a pointer, creating memory palaces, testing yourself—but learning is about more than tools. Learning happens in your body, including your emotions.

If you don't feel excited, engaged, or curious while learning, you won't prioritize it. If you feel bored, distracted, or exhausted while studying, then learning rarely sticks. These states cause your attention networks to disengage, and without attention, long-term memories can't form. Strong emotions, on the other hand, activate the amygdala, which signals the hippocampus that something matters. This helps consolidate the memory and makes retrieval later more efficient.

The same mechanism that turns moments into memories works with learning too. So before studying or working on anything important, *measure, then boost*. First determine your current state on a scale of 0 to 10. Zero is bored, exhausted, or distracted. Ten is energized, excited, and engaged. Next, ask, "What small mindset or physiological shift could I make to improve my score by *two*?"

For your mindset, would tapping into your purpose and your "why" help? Could you visualize the rewards you'll reap after? What if you "acted as if," like someone you admire or the version of yourself who already knows the material? Small shifts like these help regulate stress, prioritize values, and activate the brain's attention networks.

For your physiology, could you go for a 15-minute walk? Could you exercise to increase your heart rate? What about meditating or doing a deep-breathing exercise? Small physiological changes can release neurotransmitters like dopamine and norepinephrine, which support motivation, attention, and alertness—all critical to learning.

Don't try to learn with just your head. Using your body and heart to learn too. Create the right state first and learning follows. State is more important than strategy.

KWIK STEP: Practice measuring and boosting today.

AFFIRMATION: *"I create my state for learning. I am limitless."*

NATURE IS YOUR NEURAL RESET

Think of your brain like an electrical grid. During intense heat waves or cold snaps, demand for power surges. If grid operators are unprepared or lack reserve capacity, parts of the system can shut down or be forced offline, causing blackouts until supply and demand returns to balance.

Your brain works in a similar way. Cognitive overload occurs when the demands on the brain stretch it beyond capacity. That's one reason why everything can irritate you, why making a decision as small as what toothpaste to buy feels impossible, why you reread paragraphs five times, or why you stare blankly at a screen and can't find the right words to type.

Your brain has limited metabolic and attentional resources that can become depleted, and it needs refreshing. One of the simplest supports for recovery and avoiding these "cognitive blackouts" is something that costs you nothing and has no side-effects: immersing yourself in nature.

Research suggests that when you're in nature, it can help lower cortisol, blood pressure, and heart rate; reduce pain; improve concentration, focus, and working memory; and even temporarily improve the function of the immune system. Being in nature can also make you feel more alive—boosting your sense of vitality and energy.

If you want to help your brain better manage daily demands over the long run, carve out time to step outside every day. Go to a park or green space, put your phone on silent, resist the temptation to check messages, or even listen to music or a podcast.

This is how you keep your internal grid resilient. Nature is your neural reset.

KWIK STEP: Spend at least 10 minutes outdoors in nature without being on a device.

AFFIRMATION: *"I welcome time in nature, as nature is my neural reset. I am limitless."*

DECEMBER 9

IT'S HARD TO CREATE A POSITIVE LIFE FROM A NEGATIVE MIND

Imagine you're typing on your computer and you realize it only saves your mistakes.

The misspellings, errors in punctuation, and wrong word choices remain, but everything else you did right? Deleted.

You'd instantly know something was wrong, and you'd either buy a new computer or scan your old one for viruses.

Yet when our brain deletes our successes, leaving only our mistakes, we do the opposite. We criticize ourselves. We replay every mistake and second-guess what we "should" have done.

Our inner critic is so harsh and persistent that it overwhelms confidence.

This inner critic doesn't just appear. It's part of how our brain evolved to detect and correct mistakes. The anterior cingulate cortex is a part of the brain involved in evaluating and monitoring performance. Research shows that it becomes more active when we make mistakes or experience conflict.

This is so we can learn from what went wrong. While this helped keep our ancestors safe, it can harm us today.

That's why we need to consciously reprogram our brain by accepting, acknowledging, and applauding our micro-wins.

"Way to go, you read for 10 minutes."

"Awesome job, you opened a document and wrote 200 words."

"Nice work, you remembered to make that appointment."

Every time you celebrate the small wins, you rewire your brain to focus less on finding fault and more on finding success. Over time, this will strengthen your self-confidence and self-trust.

Your life is a reflection of your thinking. If you want a more positive life, you need to create a more positive mind.

It's hard to create a positive life from a negative mind.

KWIK STEP: Create a "Brag Board." Starting today, add one micro-win from the past 24 hours. If you want a bonus, add one win every day.

AFFIRMATION: *"I create a positive life from my positive mind. I am limitless."*

DECEMBER 10

DESIGN A FLOW-FRIENDLY ENVIRONMENT

***Flow** (verb)—to move in a stream; to proceed smoothly and readily.*

Artists and athletes talk about the flow state or being "in the zone." It's a state of consciousness where they lose their sense of self, their ego. It's like they merge into the task. It's where challenge meets skill, yet effort seems to dissolve as their performance flows from them, without second-guessing or questioning.

In flow, there's an incredible sense of reward and satisfaction as their performance peaks and time disappears. Five hours can seem like 15 minutes.

Flow may seem like a superhuman ability, something reserved for the very few, but it's not. Everyone can access it to enhance their performance, whether that's for studying, working, creative arts, athletics, or hobbies. But it does take practice and intention to cultivate your own flow state.

To help your brain reach flow more easily and reliably, begin with your environment. You want uninterrupted concentration, so eliminate all potential distractions.

Put your phones and devices on silent or airplane mode, leaving them in another room or turning them off.

Tidy your workspace, organize papers into piles, and remove clutter. Messy environments make it hard for the brain to fully focus. Visual mess diverts your attention.

And limit background noise. This might mean wearing noise-canceling headphones, listening to soothing music, using a white noise device, or telling people not to disturb you.

Design a flow-friendly environment, and you make it easier for your brain to move into flow.

KWIK STEP: What are specific steps you can take to design a more flow-friendly environment?

AFFIRMATION: *"I am capable of reaching the flow state. I am limitless."*

DECEMBER 11

FALL IN LOVE WITH LEARNING

The root of transformation is learning.

Because to grow you must learn new skills, new behaviors, and new ways of thinking.

But for a lot of us, learning feels hard and confusing, so we stop. When this happens, instead of giving up, think of it as an emergency—as an *SOS*.

S—STRATEGY. One reason we don't love learning is that we never learned how to learn. Nobody is born a great learner, but there's a method behind the magic. It's not how smart you are; it's how are you smart?

Learning is a strategy, so learn the skills of speed reading, focusing, testing yourself, spaced repetition, active recall, chunking, and more, and you can learn anything.

O—OPTIMIZE YOUR OPERATING SYSTEM. The control center for all learning is your brain. People upgrade their phones more than their minds. This doesn't have to be you. Through food choices, killing ANTS (automatic negative thoughts), movement, surrounding yourself with positive people, restorative sleep, and decluttering your environment, you can upgrade your brain, improving its productivity, thinking, memory, emotional regulation, and ability to learn.

S—STATE. All learning is state-dependent. Whether it's love, creativity, or motivation, those aren't things you have. They're things you do. Information is forgettable, but when it's combined with emotion, it becomes long-term memory. When you turn your internal state into a process you can own, then you can create those states on demand.

Whether you want to grow your business, career, relationships, health, hobbies, or human intelligence, it happens through learning.

Fall in love with learning, and you'll never stop growing or becoming.

KWIK STEP: Recall a moment when you learned something that amazed you. What is one thing you want to discover today?

AFFIRMATION: *"I love to learn. I am limitless."*

DECEMBER 12

BE → DO → HAVE → SHARE

A young man approached an aging samurai, asking to learn everything he could from the seasoned warrior. At first, the samurai, aching and tired, refused. But the young man's persistence changed his mind. For years, they trained side by side with the master sharing everything he knew—discipline, form, patience—until the student became a samurai himself and left to travel the world.

As the years passed, he had his own adventures, built his own reputation, earned riches, and found meaning.

One day, when the samurai was grizzled and gray himself, another young man approached him, eager to learn the sword. Seeing reflections of his past self, he agreed to share his knowledge, techniques, and teachings just as his master once did for him.

Be. Do. Have. Share. That's the cycle of mastery, and of life.

First, *be*. We tap into curiosity to discover who we are—our likes, passions, interests, unique skills, or the ones we want to build. We see the person we want to become, and so we start becoming them.

Then, *do*. We act, learn, and grow our skills, knowledge, and capabilities.

Next, *have*. As we apply what we've learned, we receive rewards and results that enrich our lives—our bank account, relationships, health, or career.

Finally, *share*. We pass along what we've gained so others may shine, expand, and rise too.

By embracing this cycle, we're tapping into powerful psychological principles like the protégé effect. Through teaching others, we deepen our understanding, activating neural pathways that strengthen memory and integration. We also tap into identity-based motivation. Research has shown that when our actions align with who we believe we are, we sustain our effort and growth longer than when we're motivated solely by external rewards.

Live this cycle, and you'll discover that growth and giving aren't separate—they're just different points on the same path that never ends.

Be. Do. Have. Share.

KWIK STEP: Think about an aspect of your life where you have applied, or can apply, the Be → Do → Have → Share cycle. Then consider if there's one step that needs more focus. What small step could you take today to support the cycle?

AFFIRMATION: *"I can be, so I can do, so I can have, so I can share. I am limitless."*

PUZZLES UNLOCK POWER

When was the last time you did something fun?

We often think play, fun, and joy are for kids. They're not. They're actually powerful states for the brain, enhancing our ability to learn, remember, and maintain cognitive health, especially as we age.

That's where the humble jigsaw puzzle comes in. Research suggests a potentially protective effect against age-related cognitive decline. Regularly solving jigsaw puzzles is associated with better cognitive function later in life, including memory, processing speeds, and reasoning.

Immersing yourself in a puzzle can also help the brain shift between focused attention and a more relaxed, creative mode via engaging the default mode network. This system is involved in self-reflection, memory, and meaning, and comes online when we're not hyperfocused on tasks. Working on a puzzle allows you to have a softer focus.

Completing a puzzle can also help improve your cognitive flexibility—your ability to switch between different concepts and tasks. As you shift pieces around the table, you use different cognitive strategies. You use your visual perception to scan for pieces, zooming into specific spots to see if a piece might fit. You even use perceptual reasoning to interpret and make sense of visual information—the colors, shapes, patterns—to find connections.

You also engage episodic memory, linking visual information to where and when you saw a piece.

So give yourself permission to step away from your devices. Slow down. Put on your favorite music. And train your brain with a jigsaw puzzle. It's more than fun. It's unlocking your brain power.

KWIK STEP: Try a puzzle today. You don't have to complete the entire thing. Take 10 minutes and notice how you feel while you're doing it.

AFFIRMATION: *"I choose activities that unlock my brain power. I am limitless."*

BE POWERFULLY PRESENT WITH PEOPLE

There's a parenting saying, often attributed to Jesse Jackson, that "Kids need your presence more than presents."

It's the simple truth that what children need most from parents and other adults isn't things, but undivided attention—eye contact, actively listening, asking questions, smiling, nodding.

We never grow out of this. We still want people's full attention. And when we don't have it, we notice.

Have you ever met someone at an event, started talking, and watched as they scanned the room? Or maybe they're talking, and the moment it's your turn, they check their phone. "I'm listening," they say, but you know they're not. It stings trying to talk to someone while they're distracted. It feels like you don't matter. Like they don't care.

If you want to connect with people for business, your career, or simply to grow your community, you need to remember not only their name, but *them*—their interests, hobbies, what matters most, and what they've said.

To do that, you need to be present. That means listening and hearing them. And how do you listen? Take the word *listen*, scramble it, and it spells *silent*.

Be silent.

Don't scan the room for other people you want to talk to. Don't plan what you're going to say next. Don't think about what happened earlier or may happen later. In a meeting, don't pick up your phone or check e-mail.

Keep your attention on the person you're speaking with. This allows your brain to focus, which is the first step to encoding information as memory. When you're distracted, toggling between people, screens, or your own thoughts, information never gets encoded deep enough for your brain to retrieve it later.

Presence also increases people's sense of social safety with you—the feeling of being accepted, respected, and not judged. When someone has your full attention, their nervous system signals to them, you're safe to be with.

Like kids, people don't want your gifts. They want your presence. Be powerfully present with people—and you'll leave a lasting impact.

KWIK STEP: How can you practice being powerfully present with someone?

AFFIRMATION: *"I am powerfully present with people. I am limitless."*

MOVE. MEDITATE. MULTIPLY.

We know mindfulness calms the brain, and exercise primes it for learning. So what happens when we combine them?

That was the idea behind the work of neuroscientist Dr. Tracey Shors, who created *MAP Training My Brain* as a way to break the brain's habit of getting stuck in ruminating thoughts, anxiety, and depression.

It starts with 20 minutes of focused meditation—placing your attention on your inhales and exhales. Next comes a 10-minute walking meditation where you again focus on breathing, counting each one. When a thought arises, you notice it without judgment and let it go, returning to counting your breath, starting at one. You close with 30 minutes of intense aerobic activity, increasing your heart rate to 60 to 80 percent of your max.

Participants in Dr. Shors's study did two sessions per week for at least six weeks. MAP Training participants significantly reduced post-traumatic and ruminating thoughts, symptoms of depression and anxiety, and significantly enhanced measures of self-worth compared to people who participated in only one intervention.

MAP Training is neurostacking. Each component works individually, but when combined, the benefits amplify. Mindfulness helps reduce stress, regulate emotions, and enhances insight, memory, and focus.

Movement gets your blood flowing, increases oxygen, releases endorphins and serotonin, which help improve memory and focus. Exercise also releases growth factors including BDNF, which supports neuroplasticity, and neurogenesis, the birth of new neurons in key regions including the hippocampus.

If an hour for MAP Training seems daunting, then work your way up.

Just remember, move. Meditate. Multiply.

KWIK STEP: Try MAP Training today, or at least once this week, and go at your pace.

AFFIRMATION: *"I move and meditate to help my brain perform its best. I am limitless."*

DECEMBER 16

MEMORY IS A MULTIPLIER

Forgetting what you just read, where you put your keys, or what your supervisor just said—these are not random memory lapses.

They're side effects of our device-driven world that has weakened our memory.

By relying on our devices to log phone numbers, solve math problems, and remind us of meetings, we've reduced how much we train our memory regularly. Like muscles, our memory operates under "use it or lose it."

Memory remains the foundation of learning, which underscores every goal you have, from career advancement to improved earnings and deeper relationships.

Because if you're not going to remember what you read, what's the point of reading at all? If you can't recall feedback your boss gave to you, how will you rise through the ranks? If you constantly lose your keys, how will you improve your self-confidence?

One powerful technique to improve memory is taking what you want to recall and connecting it to vivid images inside a familiar place like your office or home. This technique, known as a *memory palace* or the *method of loci*, is a practice the ancient Greeks and Romans used more than 2,000 years ago to boost recall.

Imagine preparing a presentation with five key points. In your mind, walk through your home, placing one point in each room. The first could sit on the doormat, then as you walk into the kitchen, the second is on your stove. The third is on the couch in the living room, the fourth is on the staircase, and the fifth is on your bed.

During the presentation, you'll mentally walk through your house, with each room reminding you what idea comes next. Decades of research show this technique improves short- and long-term memory.

Every skill, capability, and the knowledge you've gained strengthens when you improve your memory. Memory is a multiplier that cements your lifelong learning.

KWIK STEP: Practice creating a memory palace, taking information you want to remember and placing it in a familiar place. Then test yourself tonight.

AFFIRMATION: *"I have a strong memory. I am limitless."*

DECEMBER 17

SMALL ACTIONS. BIG IMPACT.

When a clam senses danger, it immediately snaps its shell shut.

Your brain does the same thing. When it senses danger, it snaps into survival mode, flooding your body and brain with stress hormones.

In this state, you're not making clear, rational decisions. You're emotionally reactive. You're closed off to creativity and flow. You're not seeing possibilities. And you're judging yourself and people around you.

When you feel caught in a survival situation, instead of focusing on your problem, do something for someone else first. This will help you shift your brain's state.

Neuroimaging studies show that helping someone is related to reduced stress-related activity in key areas of the brain connected to our stress and survival state. It's also related to increased activity in our reward circuitry and bonding networks that release chemicals like dopamine and oxytocin that counterbalance the stress hormones. Being of service actually makes us feel good.

When the threat response goes down, the brain areas responsible for rational thinking, creativity, emotional regulation, and planning come back online. Now you're ready to tackle your challenge.

There are so many ways you can help. You can check on neighbors. You can donate to worthy causes. You can be more intentional with the language you use. You can donate your time. You can share your expertise on social media. You can help a loved one.

Being of service doesn't have to be a grand gesture. It's simply looking for ways you can give back to the people in your life.

Classrooms aren't limited to four walls. You have talents. You have knowledge. You have gifts that have the power to positively impact someone's life. Help them, then help you.

Small actions. Big impact.

KWIK STEP: What is one way you can contribute at work, home, or in your community?

AFFIRMATION: *"I contribute my gifts and talents to those in need. I am limitless."*

GROW YOUR GRATITUDE

In the quiet moments during your day, when your mind drifts in the shower, on the drive home, or before falling asleep, do you think about what you have—or about what's missing from life?

Our brains are wired with a negativity bias, a survival mechanism that pulls our focus toward the negative—what's wrong, lacking, or missing—rather than the positive and what we do have.

But the reality is, you have more than you probably think.

Here's how to prove it to yourself: Make a list of everything in your life you *wouldn't* give away for any amount of money.

Maybe it's a relationship with a partner, parent, child, or friend. Maybe it's your grandmother's favorite cake pan from the 1940s, or your grandfather's battered toolbox. Maybe it's the drawing your child made when they were three, or your dog who curls against you even on your worst days. Maybe it's your health, eyesight, or ability to walk, talk, or hear.

This is the practice of gratitude. It activates brain regions linked to meaning, empathy, and connection, especially in the medial prefrontal cortex. It also helps calm the amygdala—the brain's threat detector. And gratitude engages the hypothalamus, which helps regulate your nervous system, lowering the stress response.

By committing to a regular gratitude practice—writing positive moments in a journal, meditating on what you're grateful for, or expressing appreciation to someone—you rewire your brain through neuroplasticity to experience abundance. You're training it to see what you have already, not what's missing or what you're working toward.

The more you practice gratitude, the more you'll start noticing an inner shift, feeling calmer, finding more meaning, and experiencing more joy.

You deserve to feel like you have more than you think you do. Grow your gratitude.

KWIK STEP: Make a list of everything that you have in your life that you would never give away for any amount of money. For each one, pause and feel in your body what each one means to you.

AFFIRMATION: *"My life is filled with abundance. I am limitless."*

KNOW WHAT MATTERS MOST

What matters most to you in your life?

It's such a simple question. Yet it's central to what the ancient Greek philosopher Socrates advised: "Know thyself."

Knowing thyself is knowing what you truly treasure.

This is like slipping a note to your brain, telling your attention networks what matters. It makes you more conscious—more aware—of what you're giving your time, attention, and energy to.

Otherwise, you're at the whim of everything else. You get distracted, feel overwhelmed, and have your goals eroded by the constant pull of other people's requests, the daily grind, and the unexpected challenges that arise.

By getting clear on what you cherish, you can make better decisions about what you say yes or no to. Knowing what matters becomes the filter for every decision you make.

Does spending an hour scrolling improve your relationship with your significant other? Does skipping a workout for the sixth day in a row help you build a stronger, healthier body? Does binge-watching your favorite show for five hours every night help you improve a skill?

When you know what's important, you can align your actions with your values. The more aligned actions you take, the more you'll experience real meaning, satisfaction, and a deep sense of fulfillment.

What's important to you today can also change tomorrow as you continue evolving. Let it.

Make a habit of asking what is most important to you in a relationship, career, health, learning, and life. Then ask if your actions align.

Know what matters most, and you'll make the most of your life.

KWIK STEP: Ask yourself, "What's most important to me in my relationships, career, health, and life?" Then ask, "What actions do I need to release or prioritize?" Finally, choose one action to focus on today.

AFFIRMATION: *"I know what matters most in my life. I am limitless."*

SAVOR THE SMALL

When we're caught in the swirls of stress, rushing from one meeting, deadline, and to-do to the next, the day feels endless.

But the truth is, life is terribly short. While training our brain to recall facts, figures, foreign languages, and formulas does matter, remembering the times we laughed, loved, and lived matters more in the end.

That's why one of the best things we can do to improve our memory and boost our well-being is to train our brain to savor the small. This isn't just a "feel good" saying. Science shows that when we pause to appreciate and notice a moment, the brain's reward and attention networks light up, strengthening the pathways that stabilize our mood, improve memory, and enhance resilience.

Studies show that savoring is associated with fewer depressive symptoms, less chronic pain, increased well-being, closer personal relationships, and greater happiness, resilience, and a sense of meaning in life.

So make savoring a daily practice. Find the small joys and victories happening every day that maybe you've felt too busy or stressed to notice. Maybe it's sipping that hot cup of tea on your way to the office, curling up with your favorite book while a pet sleeps against you, playing with your kids after work, crawling beneath soft, clean sheets, or talking with a loved one over a nice meal.

Your life is more than its big milestones. Keep reaching for them. Just remember to pause and notice the small moments that make up your days too. Savor the small.

KWIK STEP: Today, try to savor a particular moment, allowing yourself to notice all the sensations that come with it. Then tonight before you sleep, take five minutes to meditate on this moment, allowing your mind to recall everything that you saw, felt, and heard.

AFFIRMATION: *"I savor the small moments in my life, and I am grateful for them. I am limitless."*

DECEMBER 21

CREATIVITY IS THE ONLY INFINITE POTENTIAL YOU POSSESS

Everything humans have ever built, designed, or discovered can be traced to the same source. It's one most of us were taught wasn't meant for us.

From your favorite stories to rocket ships, from toaster ovens to technology, creativity has shaped our world time and again. Yet if you ask most people if they're creative, the answer is usually no.

But creativity isn't reserved for artists. It's not something you're either born with or not.It's a state your brain enters when imagination and analysis work together.

Research from Mass General Brigham suggests creativity doesn't occur in isolated brain regions, but through interconnected circuits—highways that information travels along between networks.

These circuits involve the default mode network, which activates when your mind wanders, like when you're on walks, while you're showering, or when you're daydreaming. The executive control network also lights up. That's involved with memory, attention, and decision-making. It's the interaction between these networks that's strongly associated with combining information in new ways, solving challenges, and generating innovative ideas.

Just as you can train your brain to focus, you can train it to be more creative.

Start with questions. Ask different questions, and you get different answers—also known as *divergent thinking*, which is the ability to generate new ideas. Asking questions you normally wouldn't stops the brain from defaulting to its standard solutions, opening it to explore new possibilities.

Take any problem or area you want to improve and ask questions like:

- "How can I solve this more creatively?"
- "How can I think about this differently?
- "What am I *not* seeing about ___________?"

There are no limits to what a creative mind can conjure. Start cultivating yours. Creativity is the only infinite potential you possess.

KWIK STEP: Think of one challenge or area you want to improve, and write a list of questions you haven't asked yourself before. Then sit quietly for a few minutes, letting your mind daydream about solutions.

AFFIRMATION: *"I am willing to unleash my creativity. I am limitless."*

USE YOUR SUCCESSES AND YOUR LESSONS LEARNED

Planning for the new year is loud.

IPeople are so focused on setting goals for what's ahead that they forget to pause and look behind them.

Before forging forward, practice an annual review. It's quieter and far more useful to do this before you start thinking about the new year. All you need is a pen and notebook and up to one hour for contemplation. During this time, ask yourself:

- What worked well this year? And why?
- What didn't work well? And why?
- What do I need to let go of? And why?
- What gets to keep traveling with me next year? And why?

The questions help bring clarity and focus to your brain, while answering the "why?" acts as both emotional processing and a motivation reset. It helps your brain to make meaning out of the year that's ending and to fuel your purpose and intention for next year's actions.

Your next year is not separate from this one. It's a continuation. Use your successes and the lessons learned to build a brighter brain and a more brilliant life in the year ahead.

KWIK STEP: Do an annual review using the four questions. Here's a tip: If you did the year-end "brain dump" at the beginning of this month, thinking back to that can give you a head start.

AFFIRMATION: *"I am building a brighter future upon my past successes and lessons. I am limitless."*

DECEMBER 23

IT'S BETTER WELL DONE THAN WELL SAID

You didn't learn to ride a bicycle by reading a book. Your brain needed to practice. You had to climb on, wobble, and fall, trying again and again until the cerebellum could fine-tune balance, coordination, and timing without thinking.

You learned to ride a bike by applying knowledge. And this is true for anything you want to learn. All the courses, speeches, and podcasts in the world won't change anything in your life unless you apply the knowledge you gain.

You can't be upset by the results you didn't get from the work you didn't do. But how do you take the first step?

You can start by asking the right questions while you're learning. Whenever you take in information, ask questions like:

- "How can I use this?"
- "Why must I use this?"
- "When will I use this?"
- "Who will I use this with?"
- "Who can I teach this to?"
- "Why would someone else need to know this?"

Questions like these put you in an action mindset. They function like implementation intentions—also known as "if-then planning," which helps to increase follow-through as you decide in advance how you'll act. If-then planning is often used to help build healthier habits. Here, it helps you to build the habit of applying what you learn.

These questions also orient your brain toward problem-solving, helping you combine information in ways you may never have considered.

Coming up with ideas and making plans is important, but don't get stuck in ideating and strategy. Don't just think or even talk about what you're learning. Get on the bike and apply it.

Remember, it's better well done than well said.

KWIK STEP: Try applying today's insight to today's insight. Ask yourself the questions above: how can you use, why must you use, when will you use, and to whom will you teach what you've just learned?

AFFIRMATION: *"I am a person of action. I am limitless."*

DECEMBER 24

MAKE SELF-LOVE THE STANDARD

We wait for others to respect us. We wait for others to love us. We wait for others to see us.

And in the end, that's all we're left with—waiting.

The truth is, we teach others how to treat us, and that starts with how we treat ourselves.

Instead of waiting until you have the time to show yourself love, what if you made it a daily lifelong mental habit like reading, gratitude journaling, or meditating?

Try using the *SELF-LOVE* framework:

SPEAK kindly to yourself.
EMBRACE imperfection.
LET GO of comparison.
FORGIVE your past.
LISTEN to your own needs.
OWN your worth.
VALUE your time and energy.
EVOLVE without pressure.

What you practice daily eventually becomes the habit you reinforce. Practice self-love, and your brain not only defaults to it, but expects it from others too.

Loving your mind and body is the greatest gift you can give to yourself and others. Make self-love the standard.

KWIK STEP: Choose a practice from today's list that resonates the most. Why does it resonate? How can you prioritize it today?

AFFIRMATION: *"Self-love is my standard. I am limitless."*

DECEMBER 25

THE LIFE YOU LIVE ARE THE LESSONS YOU TEACH

We've all experienced that moment when we watch someone make a decision that leads to a slow-motion car crash.

We think, *if only they'd change or let us help*, their lives would be different—better, safer, healthier, more successful.

But you can't change others no matter how hard you try. Think how hard it is to change yourself.

However, you can influence people. By being a positive, uplifting, energizing presence, you can influence someone else's life for the better. Just as you want to create a positive peer group surrounding you, you want to be that person for the lives you touch.

When we say we're "in sync" with someone, it's more than a phrase—it's happening in our brains. When people are emotionally engaged with each other—talking, telling stories, sharing experiences, collaborating toward a shared goal—their brain waves can synchronize. Even heart rates and breathing patterns can begin aligning.

Inside your brain are mirror neurons. When you observe someone's emotions or actions, those neurons activate in a way that allows your brain to simulate what the other person is feeling or doing. It works in reverse too, explaining why others may mimic your actions or feelings.

You don't change other people. You change yourself—your energy, attitude, mindset—and the world around you changes. You can become someone whose mere presence can bring a sense of peace, security, safety, and confidence to an environment.

By how you live, facing challenges, being open, resilient, kind, and focused, you teach others to do the same. And one day, your story of what you've overcome will become a part of someone else's survival guide.

The life you live is the lesson you teach.

KWIK STEP: Before interacting with someone today, take five slow, deep breaths. On each exhale, feel any tension leave your body. Silently ask, "What emotional state do I want to bring into the room?" Pick one, and allow yourself to feel it for a few breaths. As you're with the other person, try reminding yourself to stay in that state.

AFFIRMATION: *"I live the lessons I teach. I am limitless."*

LEARN FAST. LIVE BOLDLY.

Signing up for that course, reading that book, taking that weekend intensive—none of it matters if you can't remember what you learned two weeks later.

The six keys to making lifelong learning stick are in: *BE FAST.*

B — BELIEF. Everything starts with whether you think you can or think you can't. Belief tunes the brain's attention networks to notice opportunities, synchronicities, and solutions to support beliefs.

E — EXERCISE. Move your body. Regular exercise releases endorphins that enhance concentration, alertness, and focus. It also elevates BDNF, making it easier for neurons to form and strengthen new connections. In short, exercise prepares the brain for learning.

F — FORGET. Your mind is like a parachute. It only learns when it's open. So forget what you think you know.

A — ACTIVE. Learning is not a spectator sport. While absorbing information, ask yourself questions like "How can I use this in my life?" Even simple acts like taking notes by hand or sitting up tall to increase oxygen flow to your brain help make learning active.

S — STATE. Emotion plus information leads to long-term memory. Your brain doesn't treat all experiences equally when it comes to memory. Boredom signals to the brain, "This doesn't matter." Excitement or curiosity tell it, "This material matters. Pay attention, and save it." Change your state, and you change your ability to learn.

T — TEACH. When we know we'll have to teach someone else the material we're learning, we're likely to pay closer attention, engage more deeply, and study longer. When you learn, think about how you would teach the material to someone, then do it. When you teach it, you get to learn it twice.

Learning is nothing like what we were taught in school. With the right tools and tactics, learning can be fun, transformative, and empowering. Learn fast. Live boldly.

KWIK STEP: Which step in BE FAST can you improve? What's one way you can do that?

AFFIRMATION: *"I am capable of learning fast so I can live boldly. I am limitless."*

GRATITUDE IS CONTAGIOUS

When was the last time someone told you they genuinely appreciated you?

Do you remember how that moment made you feel—really feel? Maybe a warmth in your chest, a flush in your cheeks, a small energy spike. You may not have realized you needed to hear it, but you did, and it hit your heart harder than you expected.

That's the power of real gratitude expressed. It makes us feel seen, heard, and valued.

Our brain is primed to respond to gratitude. It activates reward circuitry and releases dopamine. Some research suggests it can increase serotonin, the neurotransmitter linked to calm and contentment. Gratitude also lights up regions connected to well-being, meaning, social connection, and empathy.

But too often, we keep those feelings of gratitude to ourselves. We think people know they've done a good job, they've made a difference, or they matter to us. But they don't always know, just as we don't always know the impact we're having on others.

What if you started expressing gratitude freely? Not only will you deepen your relationships and connections with others, but you'll also improve someone's life instantly.

Maybe you know someone who's facing adversity right now, or maybe you don't. Just as we don't easily share our gratitude, we don't always share our struggles. You could be standing or sitting next to someone fighting an invisible battle. Maybe they're caring for a dying parent or sick child. Maybe navigating a breakup or job loss, or waging an internal war with the dark recesses of their mind.

What if you could be the person who steps up, opens their heart, and says, "I'm so grateful for you" or "I appreciate what you've done"?

In seconds, you have the power to change the course of someone's day through your words.

Gratitude is contagious.

KWIK STEP: Pick someone in your life to write a "thank you" note to or express genuine gratitude to them.

AFFIRMATION: *"I easily express gratitude to the people in my life. I am limitless."*

DECEMBER 28

HEALTHY AGING STARTS IN YOUR BRAIN

There's a popular saying that goes, "In the end, it's not the years in your life that count; it's the life in your years."

But what if you could have both—more years *and* more life? More energy. More clarity. More joy. More moments you remember.

When it comes to longevity, that's really what we all want. But we get stuck on *how* to achieve it.

We're told that the key lies in biohacking, and in buying expensive gadgets and gizmos. While these can be nice to have, in the end, it always comes down to the fundamentals:

- **EXERCISE REGULARLY.** Studies consistently show that regular movement—walking, biking, and strength training—increases blood flow to the brain, stimulates growth factors like BDNF (brain-derived neurotrophic factor), reduces stress, and triggers the release of neurotransmitters central to enhancing learning, focus, and memory.
- **EAT MORE BRAIN-FRIENDLY FOOD.** Incorporating more foods like broccoli, leafy greens, blueberries, salmon, and olive oil helps reduce inflammation and oxidative stress in the brain.
- **KEEP CHALLENGING YOUR BRAIN.** Novel, effortful learning stimulates neuroplasticity—your brain's ability to rewire itself at any age. Do jigsaw puzzles and crosswords, play chess and ping-pong, read, and keep learning new skills.
- **CREATE CONNECTIONS.** Strong social bonds regulate stress hormones, reduce loneliness, and are associated with lower levels of inflammation.
- **PRIORITIZE SLEEP.** This is your brain's ultimate detox system. During deep sleep, the glymphatic system clears out metabolic waste, which has been linked to increased risk of neurodegenerative diseases.

Healthy aging doesn't start in your body—it starts in your brain. And no matter your age, it's never too late to start caring for it.

KWIK STEP: What area of your life needs prioritizing for longevity? What is one action you can take today?

AFFIRMATION: *"Longevity starts in my brain, so I prioritize its care. I am limitless."*

DECEMBER 29

WALK INTO THE FUTURE WITH A MIND THAT'S FREE AND CLEAR

The best poker players know when to hold their cards, when to cut their losses, and when to fold their hand and wait for a better one.

To thrive and succeed, your projects need the same discernment and discipline. You want to know when to keep playing your cards, when to kill what isn't working, and when to step back and redirect your energy.

Research has found that well-being depends on three capacities: Goal engagement (committing to what's working), goal disengagement (letting go of what isn't), and goal reengagement (redirecting toward something better).

December is an ideal time to reevaluate what to engage with, what to let go of, and what to redirect. So make a list of every project that's still open in your mind. For each one, mark: *Keep. Kill. Postpone.*

For what you "keep," write a clear next action you'll take to sustain your momentum.

For what you "kill," let it go. No judgment. No blame. No shame. No guilt.

Finally, for goals you "postpone," note when you want to revisit them—say, in a month, three months, six months, or longer. This doesn't mean you'll actually start them; only that you'll consider if they fit into your life then.

The people who thrive aren't the ones who keep doing the same things. They're the ones who've learned to make shifts intentionally. Don't drag the past year into the new. Walk into the future with a mind that's free and clear.

KWIK STEP: Make a list of your current projects and write next to them: *Keep. Kill. Postpone.*

For "Keep," write the next action you'll take.

For "Kill," say aloud, "I release this without resistance."

For "Postpone," note when you'll reconsider it.

AFFIRMATION: *"I walk into the new year with a mind that's free and clear. I am limitless."*

DECEMBER 30

MOVE FROM SURVIVAL TO SIGNIFICANCE

When we adults see a puddle, we usually hurry past, stepping around it or hopping over it. We do everything we can to not get wet or slow down.

Then there are children. They see a puddle, and they race toward it. Jumping in with both feet, they splash and play. They bend down to gaze at their reflection, laughing as they put their hands into the water.

They don't know it, but they're experiencing a state of awe—of wonder. Watch small children closely, and you'll see they regularly live in awe as they explore and interact with the world.

We once felt this too, but somewhere along the way, it stopped. Not because the world became less awe-inspiring, but because we stopped noticing.

You have the power to change this. You can train your brain to see wonder in the mundane again. Do this, and you will reap real cognitive rewards.

Awe is associated with increased activity in the vagus nerve, helping you feel calmer, more relaxed, and grounded. It reduces stress and increases oxytocin, which is connected to trust. Awe can also help reduce activity in the default mode network, leading to less rumination and noisy thoughts.

You feel awe when you allow people, places, things, and experiences outside of yourself to amaze you. Time in nature, listening to music, viewing art, having a deep spiritual practice, being of service, and witnessing moments like birth or death, can inspire awe. The more you pause to notice them, the easier it becomes for your brain to do it again.

Awe reminds you there's more to life than daily stresses and to-do lists. It reconnects you to reverence for life itself—for your life as it is today.

Let awe move you from survival to significance.

KWIK STEP: Find something that will help you cultivate a sense of awe. Spend time in nature, watch a child play, eat a piece of fruit, do something that helps remind you there is something bigger than the moment.

AFFIRMATION: *"I allow myself to enter a state of awe. I am limitless."*

DECEMBER 31

YOU ARE LIMITLESS

Growth isn't a climb straight up the mountain. It's a messy and beautiful cycle of resetting, rewiring, rising, and radiating.

As you close the year, may you look back at how far you've come. May you celebrate all your challenges and the changes that came, the struggles that led to finding strength, and the adversities that developed your advantages.

May you know that there is nothing you need to do, nowhere you need to be, and no one you need to become to be limitless.

You are already whole, yet still becoming.

So may you sleep easy knowing you can handle whatever tomorrow, next month, or next year has to bring.

May you wake up with your mind focused, your body energized, and your heart inspired for a new day.

May you move in the direction of your dreams.

May you discover new levels of awe, beauty, and gratitude.

May know your brain was built to adapt, learn, and change.

And, mostly, may you laugh, may you live, may you love, and may you learn, always.

You are limitless.

KWIK STEP: Write down everything you did this year that moved you forward—big and small. Then read the list slowly, placing one hand on your chest and silently acknowledging, "I did this." Finally, finish the following sentence: "In the year ahead, I am moving toward __________."

AFFIRMATION: *"I am the greatest project I will ever work on. I am limitless."*

LIMITLESS APPRECIATION

If you're reading this page, thank you. Of all the ways you could spend your mornings, you've chosen to spend a few minutes each day with me. Thank you for your trust, for your time, and for inviting me to be a small part of your big adventure.

To our global KwikLearning.com community, thank you for inspiring us to learn, grow, and serve with purpose every day.

To every podcast listener, every *Limitless* book reader, and everyone who has ever watched or shared our work, thank you for your curiosity and support. It's a joy to explore the limitless potential of human intelligence with you.

To my speaking and training clients, I am grateful to have shared this work with your audiences and teams. To my private coaching clients, thank you for your friendship and for teaching me so much in return.

To my longtime business partner, Alexis Banc. Almost two decades of dedication is only matched by your limitless vision. I am grateful for all your warmth and wisdom.

To our amazing Kwik Team past, present, and future who work hard every day serving our clients and community. Thank you for your caring and commitment.

Much appreciation to 4D—David Michail, Donna Stapleton, Richard Dolan, and JC Doornick. Deep gratitude for having my back (and business).

Rick, Flow, and Chuck, so much appreciation for your training, brotherhood, and making me and all around you better.

Dr. Halland and Dr. Garcia, deep thanks for taking such great care of my brain and body.

To my speaker agent, Chris Lee, thanks for helping me spread the mission on stages around the globe.

To my publicist, Allyssa Fortunato, thank you for broadcasting this message farther than I ever could on my own.

To Audrey, Lauren, Platinum Events, and Cat3 teams, it is a joy co-creating our LimitlessLive.com in-person experiences together.

To my many mentors past and present, so many to acknowledge, from my college friend's father (my one-hour mentor) to the teacher who stood up for this "boy with a broken brain." Thank you for the lessons.

To all my teachers—and teachers everywhere—thank you for choosing a profession that changes lives every single day. Having worked alongside so many educators, and growing up with a mother devoted to public education, I honor the heart, patience, and sacrifice your calling requires.

Reid Tracy, Patty Gift, Anne Barthel, and the entire publishing team. Honored to be part of the Hay House family.

Amanda Ibey, you helped me take my vision, voice, and life's work to make this book the best it can be. Thank you for being a true creative partner.

Clay Hebert, I am grateful for years of support and for quarterbacking this project. You put the clay in clarity.

Rory Vaden, thanks for your guidance in helping turn a mission into a movement.

Pete Garceau, thank you for designing an unforgettable book cover. I love the purple. Not only does it stand out on shelves and in minds—how fitting that color psychology suggests themes of wisdom, transformation, imagination, and purpose.

To my dear friends, too many to name here but you know who you are—thank you for giving me the time, space, and encouragement to do this work. Whether you checked in, lifted me up, or helped these ideas find their way into the world, I deeply appreciate and treasure our friendship.

To my beloved wife, thank you for reminding me every day that the most incredible intelligence is found in how we love, laugh, and live. You and our children are the greatest gift and blessing of my life. I'm endlessly grateful for the love of our entire family.

To my parents, my very first teachers and forever heroes. Thank you for believing in me before I believed in myself. Every good thing I've done or become is rooted in your love, encouragement, and example.

And finally, thank you again, dear reader. Thank you for choosing yourself and choosing this journey of becoming limitless daily. It's an honor to walk it with you as we unlock more of what's possible within ourselves and one another. The life we live are the lessons we teach. Always remember, there's a version of yourself patiently waiting. Keep showing up every day until you're introduced.

ABOUT THE AUTHOR

JIM KWIK (his real name) is a widely recognized world expert in memory improvement, brain optimization, and accelerated learning. After a childhood brain injury left him learning-challenged, Kwik created strategies to dramatically enhance his mental performance. He has since dedicated his life to helping others unleash their true genius and brainpower. For over 30 years, he has served as the brain coach to students, seniors, entrepreneurs, and educators. His work has touched a who's who of Hollywood elite, professional athletes, political leaders, and business magnates, with corporate clients that include Google, Virgin, Nike, Zappos, SpaceX, GE, the NBA, Twentieth Century Fox, Cleveland Clinic, Wordpress, and such institutions as the U.S. Air Force, United Nations, Caltech, Harvard University, and Singularity University.

Through keynote speeches, he reaches in-person audiences totaling more than 200,000 every year; his online videos have garnered hundreds of millions of views. Kwik is regularly featured in media, including *Forbes, Good Morning America, Entrepreneur Magazine, Entertainment Tonight, Dr. Oz,* HuffPost, *Fast Company, Inc., TODAY,* and CNBC. He is the host of the acclaimed *Kwik Brain* podcast, which is consistently the top educational training show on iTunes. KwikLearning.com's online courses are used by students in 195 countries.

Kwik, an advocate for brain health and global education, is also a philanthropist funding projects ranging from Alzheimer's research to the creation of schools from Guatemala to Kenya, providing health care, clean water, and learning for children in need. His mission: No brain left behind.

Connect with Jim Kwik at:

JimKwik.com (speaking, coaching, podcast)

KwikLearning.com (online programs)

X: @JimKwik

Facebook: @JimKwik

Instagram: @JimKwik

TikTok: @JimKwik

Text: 310-299-9362